BIBLE STUDY SOURCE· BOOK

BIBLE STUDY SOURCE· BOOK

Donald E Demaray

ZONDERVAN PUBLISHING HOUSE

OF THE ZONDERVAN CORPORATION
GRAND RAPIDS, MICHIGAN 49506

BIBLE STUDY SOURCEBOOK by Donald E. Demaray
A Zondervan publication

Formerly published as
Cowman Handbook of the Bible
Copyright © 1964 by Cowman Publishing Co., Inc.

Tenth printing 1981

ISBN 0-310-23621-5

Library of Congress Catalog Card Number 64-8717

Printed in the United States of America

I have worked at the Bible, prayed over the Bible, lived by
the Bible for more than sixty years, and I tell you there
is no book like the Bible.

It is a miracle of literature,
a perennial spring of wisdom,
A wonder-book of surprises,
a revelation of mystery,
An infallible guide of conduct,
and an unspeakable source of comfort.

Give no heed to people that discredit it, for they speak without
knowledge.
It is the Word of God in the inspired speech of humanity.

Read it through.
Study it according to its own directions.
Live by its principles.
Believe its message.
Follow its precepts.

No man is uneducated who knows the Bible, and no man is wise
who is ignorant of its teaching.
Every day is begun at its open page. It lies close at hand in
all my work.

I never go anywhere without it, and in it is my chief joy.

—SAMUEL CHADWICK

(Quoted in *Samuel Chadwick,* by Norman G. Dunning.
London: Hodder and Stoughton, 1933. p. 18).

FOREWORD

THE BIBLE was never intended to be a book for scholars and specialists only. From the beginning it was intended to be Everybody's book, and that is what it continues to be. The message which it contains is designed to meet a universal need; its central Figure is rightly called "the Savior of the *world.*" Although it was completed such a long time ago, the Bible never grows out of date, because the subjects with which it deals are those subjects which retain their relevance from one century to another, and concern us today as vitally as they concerned the people who first read the Bible.

Just because the Bible was completed a long time ago, however, we in our day need some help and advice if we are to understand it as fully as we should like to do. To meet this need my friend Dr. Demaray has written this book. This is not a student's text-book, but a handbook for the general reader who is interested in the Bible and its message and would like to have some background information on how it came into being and how it has come down to us in our language. Teachers in Sunday School and Bible Class will find it very helpful in enabling them to answer the questions which they are asked about the Bible from time to time; and other church workers will be glad to have it available for reference.

I am very happy to give it my warm commendation.

F. F. Bruce,

Rylands Professor of
Biblical Criticism and Exegesis in
the University of Manchester,
England

◄§ INTRODUCTION §►

T HE BIBLE is more than a mere book. It is *the* book. Werner Keller, a German historian (a secular historian at that) says that there is absolutely no book in human history which has had such a "revolutionary influence" or which "has so decisively affected the development of the western world." No book, declares Keller, has "had such a world-wide effect as the 'Book of Books,' the Bible."* There can be no doubt that the Bible stands out as the greatest book in all the history of literature and of mankind.

The Bible is *The* Book

Yes, the Bible is more than a mere book. The Bible is divine communication. It is God attempting to "get through" to man. In other words, it is God's "Word" to humanity.

Further, the Bible is *the* book because there is no other work in the world which has been read so long and so continuously. Both in antiquity and in the Medieval period it was copied incessantly. When the printing press came on the scene in the fifteenth century, it was the first book to be printed. From that day to this it has been the envy of publishers because of its fantastic power to sell; in point of fact, it inevitably outstrips the sales of most other literature by an astonishing margin. Over 25,000,000 Bibles or parts of it are sold yearly in every part of our world.

Beyond these facts, the transformed lives of people who come under its influence constitute eloquent testimony to its power and usefulness. Dr. Edward Blair of Garrett Biblical Institute tells the story of the soldier in World War II who, leaving for overseas,

The Bible and Transformed Lives

---

* Werner, Keller, *The Bible as History, A Confirmation of the Book of Books.* New York: William Morrow and Company, 1956, p. xxiv.

was handed a New Testament just as he boarded ship. His smart remark was, "Thanks, I may be short of cigarette papers over there." But weeks later, so impressed was the soldier by his new discovery, he sent money to assist in the distribution of this remarkable book.

Read behind the Iron Curtain

Today the most heavily banned book behind the iron curtain is the Bible. Yet people in Communist countries continue to read it. Prisoners discover it hidden in food packages; when it is discovered, it is, of course, confiscated, but not necessarily destroyed. There is documentary proof that some authorities read the Bible secretly, so curious are they about the faith it inspires.* That fact gives us a true insight into why the Bible is in such demand. It is receiving a vast attention around the world—even in Communist countries—not because it is a nice book, nor even because it is an entertaining book, but because it produces in persons a lively faith and a secure hope for now and for eternity.

Purpose of this handbook

The purpose of the *Bible Study Sourcebook* is to provide ready information about the Bible for the general reader. It is a source book that gives facts easily and quickly and succinctly. Simplicity and helpfulness have been kept in view from beginning to end, and facts are arranged in outline form with subjects listed in the margins. Church members and workers of all types—Sunday School teachers, youth sponsors, leaders, and pastors—will find this a useful reference tool.

Organization of the Book

This *Sourcebook* is divided into three parts each with three chapters. *PART ONE, OUR BIBLE: CHARTING ITS COURSE*, deals with Bible beginnings (chapter one), lists the history of ancient manuscripts and versions (chapter two), and finally traces the development of English Bible translations to its present versions (chapter three). *PART TWO, OUR BIBLE: BOOK BY BOOK*, analyzes the thirty-nine Old Testament books (chapter four), sketches the period between the Testaments (chapter five), and finally gives analyses of the twenty-seven New Testament books (chapter six). *PART THREE, OUR BIBLE: PERSONS, PLACES, THINGS*, handles first the major personalities arranged alphabetically (chapter seven) and deals with Bible places in terms of geography and archaeology (chapter eight). In the chapter called "Things" (chapter nine) the Tabernacle, Temple, synagogue, musical instruments, Jewish feasts and festivals, Jewish sects and parties, the Sanhedrin, plants and animals, time, measures, weights and money are all described in turn and in many cases pen sketches accompany definitions.

---

* See the fascinating incident in John Noble and Glenn D. Everett, *I Found God in Soviet Russia*. New York: St. Martin's Press, 1959, pp. 166–167.

Appendix I deals with church history because in a sense it is the extension of Bible history; major personalities are sketched in a manner similar to the descriptions in chapter seven. Appendix II offers bibliographical suggestions for the further study of the Bible.

I have the following people to thank for assistance in the writing of the *Bible Study Sourcebook*. Warm appreciation is extended to Professor F. F. Bruce, John Rylands Professor of Biblical Criticism and Exegesis, Manchester University, England, for reading a sizeable portion of the manuscript, making helpful suggestions, and giving personal encouragement.

Credits

To Gordon Rupp, Professor of Ecclesiastical History, Manchester University, goes hearty thanks for reading and making suggestions on Appendix I, "Thumbnail Sketches of Significant Personalities in Church History." His numerous kindnesses are much appreciated.

Dr. C. Elvan Olmstead, Bible Editor for David C. Cook and Company, has read chapter three, "Book by Book through the Old Testament" and chapter eight, "Places: Geography and Archaeology," and given helpful advice.

Dr. F. Taylor, Keeper of Manuscripts, John Rylands Library, Manchester, England, was most kind and helpful in providing photographs. Photographs were also supplied by the Matson Photo Service, Los Angeles, Frank J. Darmstaedter of the Jewish Museum, in New York, and Associated Newspapers, Ltd., London, England.

Donna Smith, who did most of the pen sketches, is to be commended for her skill and the willingness to share her talent with a wider public.

Marilyn Heiliger, my excellent secretary, has had a hand in the project from its earliest beginnings.

Dr. Ralph G. Turnbull, First Presbyterian Church, Seattle, has read a large part of the manuscript and made helpful suggestions.

Dr. George A. Turner, Professor of English Bible in Asbury Theological Seminary has read the typescript and made valuable notations.

Professor Ronald Phillips of the Botany Department, Seattle Pacific College, has read and made suggestions on the section entitled "Plants" in chapter nine. Dr. Harold T. Wiebe of the Zoology Department, Seattle Pacific College, has given advice on "Animals" (chapter nine).

My wife, faithful advisor, is my best critic.

The Seattle Pacific College students on the Holy Land study tour, summer, 1962, helped make picture-taking and the gathering of data a keen delight. Seattle Pacific College class-members in Acts and Church History (Fall 1961), and Old Testament Survey and Historical Theology (Winter 1962), assisted in collecting and recording data for chapter seven and Appendix I. Sources of information include *The New Bible Dictionary* (Inter-Varsity); Winifred Walker, *All the Plants of the Bible* (Harper); W. Corswant, *A Dictionary of Life in Bible Times* (Hodder and Stoughton); *The Oxford Annotated Bible* (Oxford); J. B. Phillips, *Letters to Young Churches,* and *The Gospels, Translated into Modern English* (Macmillan); G. Coleman Luck, *The Bible Book by Book* (Moody); Geddes MacGregor, *The Bible in the Making* (Lippincott).

Hodder and Stoughton has given permission to publish the quotation by Samuel Chadwick which appears at the front of the book. E. J. Brill, Ltd., of Leiden, The Netherlands, has given permission to quote *The Gospel According to Thomas,* Coptic text established and translated by A. Guillaumont, H.-Ch. Puech, G. Quispel, W. Til, and Yassah 'Abd Al Masih. Rand McNally & Company has permitted the use of their excellent and up-to-date color map series which add to the usefulness of this work. For information in chapter eight, I am especially indebted to the article in *The Oxford Annotated Bible* (1962) entitled, "Survey of the Geography, History, and Archaeology of the Bible Lands."

To Mr. Floyd Thatcher, past president of Cowman Publishing Company, and Mr. David E. Phillippe, president of Cowman Publishing Company, I wish to express hearty thanks for hours and days of hard work and complete cooperation in carrying this *Sourcebook* to its completion.

The Revised Standard Version is used throughout. The Copyright is held by the Division of Christian Education of the National Council of the Churches of Christ in the United States of America.

Donald E. Demaray

TABLE OF
CONTENTS

	page
Foreword	vii
Introduction	ix

PART ONE *OUR BIBLE: CHARTING ITS COURSE*

1. FIRST FACTS ABOUT THE BIBLE

The words "Bible," "Scripture," "Testament"	5
Arrangement of Old and New Testaments	6
Revelation and Inspiration	11
Interpretation	13
The Canon	18
Addendum: Chapters, Verses, and Words in the Bible	22

2. ANCIENT MANUSCRIPTS AND VERSIONS

Bible Languages	25
Papyrus and Parchment Manuscripts	26
The Scroll, the Book (Codex)	27
Original Manuscripts Lost; Changes, Accuracy of Text	28
Some Very Old Manuscripts of the Bible: Dead Sea Scrolls, Papyri, Codices	30
A Multitude of Witnesses	35
Ancient Translations (Versions)	36

3. ENGLISH TRANSLATIONS TO THE PRESENT

Wyclif: First Complete English Bible   45

Gutenberg Bible   46

Tyndale: First Printed English New Testament
from the Greek   47

Coverdale: First Complete English Bible Printed   47

Geneva Bible   48

Roman Catholic Bible (Douai)   49

King James Version (1611)   49

Modern Translations Into English: Revised Version,
American Standard Version, Revised Standard Version,
New English Bible, the Independent Versions (Moffatt,
J. B. Phillips, etc.)   51

PART TWO   *OUR BIBLE: BOOK BY BOOK*

4. BOOK BY BOOK THROUGH THE OLD TESTAMENT

Law: Genesis Through Deuteronomy   63

History: Joshua Through Esther   72

Poetry: Job Through Song of Solomon   92

Prophecy (the Four Major Prophets):
Isaiah Through Daniel   99

Prophecy (the Minor Prophets): Hosea Through Malachi   109

Miracles and Parables of the Old Testament   121

Chronological Table of the Old Testament Rulers   124

5. BETWEEN THE TESTAMENTS

Alexander the Great and Hellenism   127

The Seleucids   128

The Hasmoneans   128

Herod the Great   129

6. BOOK BY BOOK THROUGH THE NEW TESTAMENT

Gospels: Matthew Through John   131

Parables and Miracles in the Gospels   148

Acts and Paul's Letters Through Philemon 151

Chronological Chart of Paul's Journeys and Writings 152

The Other Letters Through Jude 174

The Revelation 181

Chronological Table of New Testament Rulers 183

PART THREE *OUR BIBLE:*
PERSONS, PLACES, THINGS

7. PERSONS: THUMBNAIL SKETCHES OF MAJOR
BIBLE PERSONALITIES 187
(Alphabetically Arranged)

8. PLACES: GEOGRAPHY AND ARCHAEOLOGY

A Bird's-Eye View of Palestine and Bible Lands 227

The People 233

The Canaanites and Archaeology 234

The Fathers of Israel 235

The Period of Moses 236

The Period of Conquest 237

The Monarchy, The Divided Monarchy 237

The Exilic and Post-Exilic Periods 241

The New Testament Era 242

9. THINGS

The Tabernacle, Temples, and Synagogue 247

Musical Instruments 253

Jewish Feasts and Festivals 257

Jewish Sects and Parties 260

The Sanhedrin 262

Plants, Animals, Birds 263

Time, Measures, Weights, Money 291

Appendix I Thumbnail Sketches of Significant
Personalities in Church History 299

APPENDIX II   Tools for the Bible Student (Bibliography):
             Study Bibles, Concordances, Bible
             Dictionaries and Encyclopedias, Atlases   329

MAPS   *following page 331*

INDEX TO PERSONS, PLACES, THINGS   351
INDEX TO SCRIPTURE REFERENCES   365

CHARTS AND TABLES

ARRANGEMENT OF THE HEBREW OLD TESTAMENT — 6

ARRANGEMENT OF THE GREEK OLD TESTAMENT — 7

ARRANGEMENT OF THE NEW TESTAMENT — 8

NUMBER OF CHAPTERS, VERSES, AND WORDS IN
  KING JAMES VERSION — 22

MIRACLES: OLD TESTAMENT — 121

PARABLES: OLD TESTAMENT — 123

CHRONOLOGICAL TABLE OF HEBREW RULERS — 124

PARABLES IN THE GOSPELS — 148

MIRACLES IN THE GOSPELS — 150

CHRONOLOGICAL CHART OF PAUL'S MISSIONARY JOURNEYS,
  EPISTLES, AND IMPRISONMENTS — 152

CHRONOLOGICAL TABLE OF NEW TESTAMENT RULERS
  WITH APPROXIMATE DATES — 183

CALENDAR OF JEWISH FEASTS AND FESTIVALS — 260

JEWISH MONTHS OF THE YEAR — 292

BIBLE
STUDY
SOURCE·
BOOK

PART ONE

OUR BIBLE: CHARTING ITS COURSE

*Ruins and large sarcophagus at ancient Byblos
on the Mediterranean coast about twenty-five miles north of Beirut.
The terms "Byblos" and "Bible" are both related
to the word "book."*

◆§1◆ FIRST FACTS ABOUT THE BIBLE

T HE WORD "BIBLE" COMES FROM THE GREEK The Word
"Biblia" (books). The singular form is "Biblion"; "Biblos" "Bible"
is a form of Biblion and means simply any kind of written
document. Originally Biblos meant a document done on papyrus,
a kind of paper made from an Egyptian plant (see "Plants" and
the chapter on "Ancient Manuscripts and Versions"). The Greeks
renamed Gebal, an ancient Phoenician port (near modern Jebeil,
twenty-five miles north of Beirut), Byblos (Byblus) because it was
a city famous for processing papyrus writing material. Moreover,
the inhabitants of Byblos were pioneers in the development of
writing and invented one of the first alphabets. Thus it was natural for the Greeks to name the place "Byblos," and centuries later
when the codex (a book with folded pages) was invented the term
persisted and came to be the word for "book." Our word "Bible"
means simply a "book."

"Scripture," "Scriptures" or "Holy Scriptures" are terms used "Scripture"
by the New Testament writers for the Old Testament or any part
of it. By the term "Scriptures" they meant the Divine Writings.
Paul speaks of "sacred writings" in II Timothy 3:15 and in verse
16 he uses the term "scripture." The expression "the Scriptures" is
used in Matthew 21:42; Luke 24:32; John 5:39; Acts 18:24. The
singular expression "the Scripture" usually refers to a particular
Old Testament passage rather than the entire Old Testament
(Mark 12:10; Luke 4:21; James 2:8). In II Peter 3:16 "writings"
is used to refer to Paul's Epistles and probably the Gospels; thus
we have substantial precedent for using both Old and New Testaments in our Christian Scriptures. Not all Christians, however,

have the same contents in their Scriptures. (See "Canon" elsewhere in this chapter.)

"Testament"   In our day the word "Testament" is used in making out a will; thus the expression, "last will and testament." But that is not the idea of the word as used in the Bible where it means "covenant." It would be better to speak of the Old Covenant and the New Covenant, but tradition (from Tertullian's time) has long since established the use of the word "Testament."

The Covenant idea goes back to Moses on Mt. Sinai (Exodus 24:3-8), and even before Moses to Abraham (there are even earlier hints of the Covenant, Genesis 6:18, e.g.) when God made a promise to His chosen people. In making that promise or covenant, God put Himself in a special relationship to His people, a saving or redeeming relationship. The Old Testament tells the story of how that special relationship was worked out in history. But a New Covenant was foreseen and hoped for by the Jews; indeed, Jeremiah (31:31-34) foretold that New Covenant (cp. Jesus' words in Matthew 26:28). That the New Covenant really came is proved by Jesus Himself when He said, "This cup is the new covenant in my blood" (I Corinthians 11:25). It is not surprising that Paul speaks of the Old Covenant (II Corinthians 3:14) and the New (II Corinthians 3:6), and the writer of Hebrews makes the difference between the Covenants one of his great themes (Hebrews 8:13, etc.).

The Old Testament: Its Arrangement   There are three divisions in the Hebrew Old Testament: the Law, the Prophets, and the Writings. This three-fold division is reflected in such New Testament passages as Matthew 5:17; Luke 16:29; Luke 24:44. Traditionally the Hebrew Bible contained just twenty-four books arranged in this pattern:

I.	II.	III.
LAW (TORAH)	PROPHETS (or NEBHIIM) (*pronounced* ne-vee-EEM)	WRITINGS (or KETHUBHIM) (*pronounced* ke-thoo-VEEM)
1. Genesis		
2. Exodus		
3. Leviticus		*Poetical*
4. Numbers	*Former*	14. Psalms
5. Deuteronomy	6. Joshua	15. Proverbs
	7. Judges	16. Job
	8. Samuel (I and II, one book)	*The Megilloth* (pronounced mi-GIL-oth)
	9. Kings (I and II, one book)	17. Song of Songs (Song of Solomon)

Latter	18. Ruth
	19. Lamentations
10. Isaiah	20. Ecclesiastes
11. Jeremiah	21. Esther
12. Ezekiel	
13. The Twelve	*Historical*
(Minor	22. Daniel
Prophets)	23. Ezra—Nehemiah
	24. Chronicles
	(I and II,
	one book)

These twenty-four books of the Hebrew Bible correspond with the thirty-nine of our Old Testament. The number is altered primarily by dividing the Minor Prophets into twelve separate books and by making two books each out of Samuel, Kings, and Chronicles. Ezra–Nehemiah is also made into two books.

In the Greek Bible (Septuagint), the Old Testament assumes a different arrangement, an arrangement determined by similarity of subject matter. It looks like this:

I. PENTATEUCH	II. HISTORY	III. POETRY AND WISDOM LITERATURE	IV PROPHECY
1. Genesis	6. Joshua		27. Hosea
2. Exodus	7. Judges	18. Psalms	28. Amos
3. Leviticus	8. Ruth	19. Proverbs	29. Micah
4. Numbers	9. I and II Kings	20. Ecclesiastes	30. Joel
5. Deuteronomy	(I and II Samuel)	21. Canticles (Song	31. Obadiah
	10. III and IV	of Solomon)	32. Jonah
	Kings (I and II	22. Job	33. Nahum
	Kings)	*23. Wisdom of	34. Habakkuk
	11. I and II	Solomon	35. Zephaniah
	Chronicles	*24. Ecclesiasticus (or	36. Haggai
	*12. I Esdras	Wisdom of Sirach)	37. Zechariah
	†13. II Esdras		
	(Ezra and		
	Nehemiah)		

---

* Not found in the Hebrew Bible.
  † I and II Esdras in the Vulgate and Douay Bible are Ezra and Nehemiah.
I Esdras is sometimes known as "Greek Esdras." II Esdras of the Septuagint is not the same as another book known as II Esdras (the Ezra Apocalypse). In the Vulgate III Esdras is "Greek Esdras" (Septuagint's I Esdras) and IV Esdras is the Ezra Apocalypse.

II.	III.	IV.
HISTORY *Continued*	**POETRY AND WISDOM LITERATURE** *Continued*	**PROPHECY** *Continued*
14. Esther (*with additions)	‡25. Prayer of Manasseh*	38. Malachi
*15. Judith	‡26. Psalms of Solomon*	39. Isaiah
*16. Tobit		40. Jeremiah
*17. I and II Maccabees		*41. Baruch
		42. Lamentations
		*43. Epistle of Jeremiah
		44. Ezekiel
		*45. History of Susannah (an addition to Daniel
		46. Daniel
		*47. Bel and the Dragon (an addition to Daniel
		*48. Song of the Three Holy Children (an addition to Daniel

This order is generally followed in the Latin Bible and in our own English Protestant Bibles. (See "Canon" elsewhere in this chapter.) Actually this arrangement is more chronological than that of the Hebrew Bible (for example, Ruth follows Judges because that story took place at the time of the Judges).

The New Testament: Its Arrangement

The New Testament is only about one-third the size of the Old. Its general arrangement is as follows:

GOSPELS   HISTORY   EPISTLES   APOCALYPSE

This outline was not determined by the order in which the books were written; had this been the case the Letters would appear first (either James or Galatians), and Mark would be the first Gospel. II Peter would be last, not the Revelation. The arrangement is built on a different principle, not order of writing. The Gospels are first because they introduce us to the Founder of our religion; He is the beginning of the whole story. Matthew is the first of the Gospels because it is the most Jewish and shows the fulfillment of the Old Testament in Jesus; thus, Matthew forms a bridge between the Old and the New. Acts follows the Gospels

---

* Not found in the Hebrew Bible.
‡ Not included in all the editions.

because it carries on the story for thirty years after Jesus' death and Resurrection. Paul's epistles are arranged generally in order of length, the longest being first, the shortest last. (For more on the arrangement of Paul's letters, see the chapter, "Book by Book through the New Testament.") Revelation concludes the New Covenant because it strikes the note of hope and consummation in the Last Day. Hebrews and the Catholic (General) Epistles elaborate and strengthen New Testament doctrine and were also added for their practical applications of doctrine. The whole put together takes this shape:

I.	II.	III.	IV.
GOSPELS	HISTORY	EPISTLES	APOCALYPSE
1. Matthew	5. Acts of the	6. Romans	27. The Revelation
2. Mark	Apostles	7. I Corinthians	
3. Luke		8. II Corinthians	
4. John		9. Galatians	
		10. Ephesians	
		11. Philippians	
		12. Colossians	
		13. I Thessalonians	
		14. II Thessalonians	
		15. I Timothy	
		16. II Timothy	
		17. Titus	
		18. Philemon	
		19. Hebrews	
		20. James	
		21. I Peter	
		22. II Peter	
		23. I John	
		24. II John	
		25. III John	
		26. Jude	

It is significant that very early in Christian history the twenty-seven books of the New Testament were bound up with the Hebrew scriptures. This provided a richer and fuller resource for both worship and defense of the Christian Gospel. Moreover, the Old Testament was recognized as preparatory to the New (Hebrews 1:1-2). This is why the Bible of the Apostles and their circle of Gospel preachers and workers was in fact the Old Testament, called "the Scriptures." The Old Testament offers a crystal clear witness to the coming Messiah, the Christ, Jesus of Nazareth (see

The Old and New Testaments Together

Jesus' own words in John 5:39). Further, the Old Testament contained the way of salvation through that coming Messiah (note Paul's words in Romans 3:21 and II Timothy 3:15). Most important of all, Christ Himself used the Old Testament, and by virtue of this authoritative example the Apostolic circle used it too.

Hear the words of Richard Hooker from his *Laws of Ecclesiastical Polity:*

> The general end both of the Old and the New (Testaments) is one, the difference between them consisting in this, that the Old did make wise by teaching salvation through Christ that should come, the New by teaching that Christ the Savior is come.

Thus the New is the fulfillment of the Old; the Old is what God did in the past, the New is what He dramatized in a Son.

> The New is in the Old contained,
> While the Old is by the New explained.
> The New is in the Old concealed,
> While the Old is by the New revealed.

The Language of the Testaments   The Old Testament was written originally in Hebrew, for it was the literary expression of the Hebrew people, the nation called Israel. It should be known, however, that Daniel 2:4b—7:28 and Ezra 4:8—6:18; 7:12-26 and Jeremiah 10:11 are in Aramaic, a language related to Hebrew and part of the Semitic family of languages (Arabic, Assyrian, Babylonian, Canaanite are also in that family). The New Testament was written in Greek, though some of it was first *spoken* in Aramaic, Jesus' daily language as well as the everyday tongue of His disciples.

The Span of Writing   The Hebrew scriptures were written over a period covering more than a thousand years, but the New Testament was written within the confines of the first century A.D., indeed in half a century. The history of the Old Testament covers even more than a thousand years, going back into the far-reaches of human and divine history. Archaeology has demonstrated a validity to the Old Testament history scarcely hoped for a generation or two ago; and ancient Hebrew and Near Eastern civilization can be studied together, the two having taken place at about the same time. As to the New Testament, the earlier Epistles of Paul, plus James perhaps, were written within the space of ten or twelve years (about 48 A.D. to 60 A.D.); the four Gospels and most of the other New Testament books were done between 60 and 100 A.D.

Variety   The Bible is the product of a remarkable variety. The social, economic, political, and religious aspects of life are all there. Its geography varies and so do its people. The rich and the poor, the free and the slave, the urbanite and the farmer, the educated and the ignorant—all walk in the pages of the Testaments. The deserts and the cities, the mountains and the valleys, the rivers and the seas—these too are part of the Biblical setting. Just as there is a variety of settings, so there is a variety of literary expressions in the Bible. Some parts are beautiful—one could say "polished"—as for example Acts 27 and 28. Other parts are rugged, and quite "off the cuff" (portions of Jeremiah). Apparently Bible writers were more interested in communicating truth than in flawless style; moreover, some wrote well by nature or under inspiration while others were plain in their writing habits. Most wrote in prose, but some in poetry, and some in both prose and poetry. Within these two divisions of prose and poetry there are such literary forms as drama, history, law, parable, riddle, fable, biography, sermon, proverb, and love story. The story of redemption is told in enough ways to appeal to the varied temperaments, backgrounds, and personalities of every generation in every part of the world.

Samuel Chadwick once said, "The Bible is a miracle of variety. In it there is every kind of literature, every type of humanity, every variety of temperament, every human need, every gift of wisdom and grace." "It meets," he said, "every man's circumstances, and need."

REVELATION AND INSPIRATION

Despite the variety of settings and literary forms, there is a strong unity of purpose in the Bible. Drama, history, law, are all used to make clear a central message. This no doubt is the reason the word Bible came to mean not many books, but *one* Book. (Greek "Biblia" is *plural* but became Latin "Biblia" which is *singular*.) **One Central Message**

What is this central message? It is contained in one word, SALVATION. God Himself provided this salvation, and in His very provision spelled out its meaning. He sent Himself in a Son, Jesus, who taught and lived salvation from sin. In the cross God provided the means of salvation, and the life and death of Jesus evoke a response in man either for or against God. God continues to show us salvation in His "Church"—a word used both in the New Testament (Matthew 16:18 "I will build my church") and in the Greek Old Testament. God spelled out salvation in His Written Word (the Bible), dramatized it in His Living Word (Jesus Christ), and demonstrates it today in His Continuing Word (the Holy Spirit in His Church).

The Bible is the revealed (unveiled, disclosed) Word of God about man's salvation. The central message of the Bible is the sum and substance of that revelation. That message or revelation was both acted out and spoken by God. It was acted out in the great events of Biblical history: the Exodus, the giving of the Law to Moses, deliverance from the Assyrians in the eighth century B.C., the Return from the Babylonian Exile, and especially in His Son Jesus Christ Who lived, died, arose, and ascended to the Father to be our Mediator.

Accompanying these saving acts were prophetic words. Moses was God's mouthpiece to the Israelites at the time of the Exodus, the recorder of the Ten Commandments and details of the Law; the prophets—notably Isaiah—spoke for God in terms of warning and encouragement during the Assyrian threat; other prophets declared God's Word during the return of the exiles. In the New Testament we have the record of Jesus Christ through Whom God Himself spoke. The Bible combines and interweaves the mighty acts of God (cf. Psalm 145) with the prophetic Word of God. It is in this interweaving of dramatic materials that *Revelation* is spelled out. History and prophecy were one in the sense that both were vehicles of communicating God's message. It is perhaps for this reason that in the Hebrew Bible the historical books are bound up with the books of the prophets.

Revelation and Response God revealed His will and purpose for man to evoke a response. The Bible, especially the Old Testament, records not only God's actions but man's reactions. It is possible to chart the up-and-down reactions or responses of the Hebrews: they were obedient but more often disobedient (the book of Judges is especially graphic on this point). Even as God's Revelation was expressed in both deeds and words, so man's response had a twofold expression. Both the words and acts of the Israelites are recorded in the Old Testament, and in the New Testament we have theology and its outworking in practice made astonishingly clear. The words "obedience" and "disobedience" sum up man's response to God's Revelation.

Revelation and Inspiration The English Word "inspiration" means "in-breathed." Since God in-breathed the Scriptural utterances, the Bible is a divine product; men were the vehicles God used to effect His message in writing. *How* this was effected (the process) is a mystery; *that* it was effected is a fact. Inspiration and revelation go hand in hand. Our inspired Bible is in fact the written revelation just as Jesus' words were spoken revelation. God's words and acts in real-life drama were revelation to the Israelites; the record of that drama is revelation to us centuries later. Redemptive history itself is revelation, so is the written story of that history. Inspiration and revelation are integral to each other, they are interwoven; both were and are necessary for the maintenance and growth of the Church. Revelation and inspiration took place when men were enabled to *see* and record God's mighty acts and prophetic words. So to see and record constituted miraculous gifts of God's Spirit to men and minds fired and illuminated.

The expression "Thus saith the Lord" occurs some 359 times in Scripture. God has spoken in His revealed Word and man must respond to it negatively or positively. To be exposed to the Bible is to be put in the position of deciding for or against it; it is that demanding. It is so because in history, human experience has demonstrated that the Bible holds the final word (is authoritative) in matters of (1) faith (doctrine) and (2) practice (moral behavior or ethics). The Bible is a book with a dual aim: to bring people to faith in God—that is, to God Himself—and to show people how to act. The Bible shows us how to establish right relationships with God, others, and ourselves. To recognize that fact is to recognize the authority of the Revealed Word; to respond to the authoritative Word is the key to harmonious individuals and a harmonious society.

The Revealed Word and Its Authority

In the Roman Catholic belief, authority is made up of two parts: the Bible and history or tradition. Protestants, in all honesty, must admit that its several traditions do play a part in general religious outlook; however, tradition plays no such important part as in Catholicism. The Protestant Reformers tended to operate on the principle that the Bible and the Bible alone is the real and sole authority in matters of doctrine and practice. Thus the Westminster Confession—as typical a Protestant creedal statement as can be cited—declares that the sixty-six Biblical books are "all . . . given by inspiration of God, to be the rule of faith and life."

This further fact must be established; namely, that the Bible is its own best authority, and one must read it for himself to discover its authority. The best Bible scholar cannot make this discovery for someone else, but the same Spirit that inspired the Bible will bear witness in the receptive person to its authority.

INTERPRETATION

The purpose of Bible interpretation is to make clear the meaning and message of God's Revelation. How do we interpret the Bible? The place to begin is in the recognition of what G. Campbell Morgan called the "contextual principle." The Bible must be viewed within its own context of language, time, place and situa-

Interpretation of God's Revealed Word

(1) Language

tion. Every part of it must be viewed in the light of every other part. Already it has been stated that the Bible was written in Hebrew, Aramaic, and Greek. Knowledgeable linguists are constantly attempting to pour into their translations of Holy Scriptures the real flavor and meaning of the original text. The peculiar word patterns or idioms are being unraveled for us in our own language with ever-increasing clarity as more and better translations are being published. But the layman too must become involved. He must take into account the difference between prose and poetry, prophecy and apocalypse, legend and fact. The Bible is ancient and oriental; that is, Near or Middle Eastern *not* European or American. Thus it is poor interpretation to read into God's revealed story of creation our own Western idea that it was all done in a six *day* period. Orientals think figuratively more than Westerners; they use poetry and imagination. Our literal and straightforward thought and word patterns cannot be forced upon this ancient, oriental Book where they do not apply.

(2) Time

Time, history, or what we might call the historical background needs to be understood to interpret the Bible aright. Of all ancient peoples, Hebrews had the keenest sense of history; that was because God revealed Himself in His acts and words through history. Not only the history of His saving acts must be known, but the environment in which those saving acts took place must be learned. The events of the Bible centered in the geographic area extending from Egypt, north through Palestine, Babylon and Assyria, on to Asia Minor and finally to Europe. Since the events of the Bible took place over several thousands of years, the historical movements of that great period must be carefully observed. If these movements and changes are not recognized, the interpreter finds himself in the awkward position of evaluating the behavior patterns of the Early Canaanite period by the high moral standards of Jesus. Along this same line it is absolutely essential that in our day we take from the Bible those teachings, exemplary or spoken, which apply to us in our own modern situation.

(3) Place

If the *time factor* has to do with historical background, the *place factor* has to do with geographical background. It is an accepted fact that weather and geographical position influence the whole culture of a people. In Egypt, where it is very warm and seldom rains, the people are slow-moving and require considerable sleep. Generally, however, in cooler climates people move faster and are more progressive in the removal of dirt and disease. Certain of the laws of the Pentateuch are definitely related to the warm weather conditions of the Near and Middle East. For example, the law against eating pork was good because pork spoiled

Clothing, customs, modes of transportation of Bible times persist until today.

quickly without refrigeration. In the light of this fact it would be very unfair to interpret the actions of the ancient Hebrews as ignorant simply because we are in a position to preserve and eat this meat today.

What was the actual living condition or situation of the ancient Hebrew, or of the more recent Jew in the New Testament period? To understand and empathize (stand in the shoes of another) with these ancient peoples in their everyday life, it is essential that we observe their customs and way of life with great care. Actually, we tend to do *picture thinking;* therefore, we get a more accurate picture of the Bible if we *visit,* as it were, the Bible peoples. Fortunately this is made possible through the wealth of material on Bible dress, manners and customs. In addition dictionaries of the Bible and similar reference works provide graphic pictures in art and written word. Today scholars are securing much of their information from the work of the archaeologists who are digging up civilizations of Bible times.

(4) Situation

G. Campbell Morgan, in enunciating the contextual principle of Bible interpretation, insisted it was absolutely necessary to view every book of the Bible, indeed every chapter and passage, in the light of the whole Bible. It is sometimes put this way: the best interpreter of the Bible is the Bible itself. An exaggerated example is this: The Bible says, "There is no God" (Psalm 14:1). Those are

(5) Seeing the Bible as a Whole

the actual words of the Scripture. But to broadcast that the Bible teaches atheism would be a highly dishonest and irresponsible act. One must read the statement, "There is no God," in its complete context, and as such it reads: "The *fool* says in his heart, 'There is no God.'" But in the interpretation of this text one must go even further than the immediate context; the remainder of the Bible must be viewed. The Bible begins with God (Genesis 1:1) and ends with God (Revelation 22:21), and in between nearly every line throbs and pulsates with the truth that there is a living God.

Bible Interpretation and the Holy Spirit

The great illuminator is the Holy Spirit. It is He—so Scripture (John 14:26), history and experience tell us—Who interprets the Bible for us. We must use the contextual principle in all its facets as outlined above—the Holy Spirit uses these "natural" media to make the Bible known to us; He makes it known in deeper dimension, too. The New Birth, for example, is not likely to be understood, much less experienced, by a knowledge of geography, history or archaeology. It takes the convicting and illuminating power of the Spirit of God to lay bare, to expose the fact of our sin and unworthiness, and show us the shattering fact of a loving God waiting to take even a sinner to Himself. The great spiritual truths of Scripture are revealed by the Spirit Himself.

Schools of Interpretation

If the interpreter is to see each part of Scripture in relation to the whole, there must be a guiding principle at work. This guiding rule has varied from age to age—from group to group and person to person. Some guiding principles and schools of interpretation are outlined below.

(1) The Allegorical School

The allegorical principle was used in ancient times and is employed by some in one form or another today. Alexandria, Egypt, was the center of this school of interpretation used by men such as Philo, Clement, and Origen. Allegory is the description of one subject under the guise of another. It was thought that this spiritualizing of Bible content got one into the very mind of the Holy Spirit; also, that it covered up the ethical problems of the Old Testament (e.g., God's command to kill the Midianites). In point of fact allegory did neither. In the Middle Ages and in some quarters today, doctrine was "obtained by" or "read into" simple narrative. Allegory is illegitimate precisely because it does not succeed in revealing self-authenticating truth, but through its subtle and "pious" mask casts suspicion on its user if not on Scripture itself.

(2) The Legalist School

This school really had its followers long before the present day. Paul struggled with the legalists (Acts 15, the book of Galatians) who insisted on keeping certain aspects of the Jewish Law in spite of the new Gentile climate and changed attitude in Christian living. In the Middle Ages a school of "moralists" arose; they tried to deduce from Bible passages the moral pattern that suited them. Today that same attitude persists in certain circles, the chief end of Bible interpretation being to "find another argument" for a particular point of view on behavior, but the doctrinal or theological aspect of Scripture is left almost entirely neglected. Conversely, the reverse may occur, in which case the Scriptures are interpreted to suit one's doctrinal position—the practical and ethical being left nearly unobserved. Frequently this legalist attitude of interpretation accompanies a kind of literalist handling of Scripture whereby a "proof text" is made to demonstrate a point on any given subject. This trick is used often by the cults.

The Protestant Reformers of the Sixteenth century brought together two approaches to Biblical interpretation: the straightforward or "obvious" meaning in Scripture, and grammatico-historical exegesis. It was argued that anything like allegorical interpretation was an attempt to hide the intended meaning of Scripture and as such was *illegitimate*. The Reformers cried out against this and any other method that prevented the Scriptures from "speaking for themselves." The term "grammatico" refers to grammar, the point being that simple grammatical analysis assists in getting plain meanings from plain sentences and even *not* so plain sentences. "Historical" has reference to the great line of comment on the Scriptures from the past: "What," they asked, "have the great minds of the past said about the Bible?" The reformers were especially interested in what the Church Fathers (Augustine, Jerome, etc.) said. "Exegesis" means getting out of Scripture what is actually there; its opposite is "eisegesis," reading into the text what one would *like* to see there. The Reformers did not always succeed in avoiding eisegesis, for everyone reads the Bible through the eyes and coloration of his own background; but it can safely be said that they did more than most up to their time to let the Bible speak for itself.

**(3)
The Reformed School**

This, too, is at once an old and current school of interpretation. The typologists, for example, see a "type" of Christ in Joseph of the Old Testament, in the would-be sacrifice of Isaac, in Moses and Joshua as deliverers. True, there is a point here; but Joseph, Isaac, Moses and others must be seen as *illustrations* and *suggestions,* and in no sense should they be taken literally as "types" of the Christ. The person of Christ is not the only object of the typologists, but the above examples illustrate their approach.

**(4)
The Typological School**

Some schools of interpretation have more than others to commend them. The allegorical school has a hint of truth; whereas,

**(5)
Christ Himself the Guiding Principle**

the Reformers were so successful in what they started that most scholars today, at least in the Protestant communion, are carrying forward and extending their work and method. The Legalist School has a point in holding fast the truth; the typologists have a point too, in that there are in fact foreshadowings of Christ and His work in the Old Testament. But when all is said and done, one must come to grips with the final Word, the Christ, through whom God spoke and continues to speak. This very Son of God, this Jesus of Nazareth, this Christ the Messiah must be the center of our interpretation of Scripture.

Just what does this mean? It means first that we must see how Christ Himself handled Scripture. How did He use the Old Testament? He saw it as foretelling His own coming for one thing. When it comes to doctrine, we must not forge ahead in the energy of the flesh to shape our own theology, we must ask what Jesus believed and let Him be the great determiner of our position. As to ethics, the life and example of Jesus constitute the perfect picture of human behavior. To be sure, it is not as simple as it sounds; there are conflicting pictures of Jesus in the minds of men. But at this point the Spirit of God is available to release us to truer and deeper meanings, and help untangle the real from the false for each individual. If this method of interpretation could be diagrammed, Christ would be put in the center of the circle. The spokes of the wheel converge in Him, the final court of appeal, and the circumference of the wheel would be the Holy Spirit Who holds the whole together in balance.

THE CANON

The word "Canon" is from the Greek *kanon* meaning a "level" or "ruler" as used by a cabinet maker or scribe. Figuratively, canon may refer to the standard or *rule* of conduct or belief, a list or catalog of what may and may not be done or embraced. Figuratively it also came to mean a list of books—of the Bible. Athanasius in the fourth century was the first to use the term in this sense.

Apocrypha   The Apocrypha are the fourteen or fifteen books or book additions which are not in the Hebrew canon but are in the Alexandrian Canon (i.e., the Septuagint). Most of these are accepted by the Roman Catholic Church as part of the Bible (see page 13 of this chapter). It should be underscored that these are not in the Hebrew Old Testament, but they were added to the Greek translation known as the Septuagint(LXX). The Alexandrian canon was always more or less variable with reference to books included, whereas the Hebrew canon is more fixed and stable. The Septuagint gives us our only source of the Alexandrian canon. The general order of the books in the Septuagint has been retained by Protestants through the Latin Bible (Vulgate) of Jerome. (The LXX and Vulgate also provide us with many of the titles for our Biblical books.) The Hebrew text and selection of books have been used, but neither the text nor the selection of books *per se* from the Septuagint has been retained. (On the "Septuagint," see chapter on "Ancient Manuscripts and Versions.") This does not imply that the Alexandrian canon is worthless, but it was less stable than the Hebrew. Thus Luther relegated the Apocrypha to its own section in his Bible; he called it "good and useful to read" but not as a basis for doctrine. Calvin excluded the Apocrypha entirely. The Church of England follows Luther; in article six of the Thirty-nine Articles, it is directed that the Aprocrypha be read "for example of life and instruction of manners, but yet doth it not apply them to establish any doctrine." The Bible Society of the British Isles cannot include the Apocrypha in their Bible editions; this is a by-law of the organization. But the Apocrypha is included in the American Version, the Revised Version, the Revised Standard Version, and is now in preparation in conjunction with the New English Bible project; the King James also included it. The publishers of these versions have frequently printed the Apocrypha in volumes separate from the sixty-six books, thus indicating the general view of Luther and Anglicanism. It is of further interest that evidence for the existence of some of the Apocryphal books in Hebrew has been discovered among the Dead Sea scrolls (e.g. portions of Ecclesiasticus).

The Reformation stood on the principle of the Bible and the Bible alone as the means of information on doctrine and ethics. The Reformers, as indicated above, rejected the Apocrypha as part of the Bible. Why? Because it contains false doctrines such as the justification of suicide, prayers for the dead, almsgiving as atonement for sin, the end justifies the means, superstition, and magic. Moreover, not a single New Testament writer quotes directly from the Apocrypha, a fact which constitutes a strong argument for the Protestant position.

When the Roman Church called the Council of Trent (1546) to combat the Reformation, one of its significant acts was to give formal recognition to the Apocrypha. Official recognition had never been given it, but as far back as Jerome in the fourth century, doubt was expressed. Jerome went to the Hebrew, Greek and Old Latin for texts from which to make a fresh Latin translation; and he, like Luther, relegated the Apocrypha to a place by itself. Further, the speed with which he translated the questionable books indicates the small significance he attached to them. Unfortunately, Jerome had little ecclesiastical authority. Though he was a great Biblical and linguistic scholar, the theologian, Augustine, in Africa had more churchly power, and in Augustine's part of the world the contents of the Greek Bible won universal credence. Thus the Alexandrian canon won the day and maintained it until the Reformation. The Roman Church continues to support the Apocrypha as part of the Word of God, although Catholic scholars today tend to describe the Apocryphal books as "deuterocanonical" (secondary).

The Pseudepigrapha and the so-called New Testament Apocrypha

The Pseudepigrapha (false writings) are ancient books dating in the late centuries B.C. and early centuries A.D. For the purpose of achieving status they were named for great Jewish personalities (Enoch, Moses, Isaiah), rather than for their real authors. This accounts for their collective title (*pseudo*: false). They have never been considered part of the Bible by Protestants or Roman Catholics. Most of the books were written before the time of Christ and are apocalyptic in character. They paint happy pictures of the future of the Jews. The pre-Christian pseudepigrapha include the following:

Book of Enoch (quoted in Jude)	Ascension of Isaiah
Secrets of Enoch (quoted in Jude)	Apocalypse of Zephaniah
	Apocalypse of Esdras
Apocalypse of Baruch	Testament of Adam
Assumption of Moses	Testament of the Twelve Patriarchs

Of the books after Christ, there were a number which circulated in religious circles. They purported to be of historical value, presuming to give data not in the Scripture itself on the disciples, Mary the mother of our Lord, Jesus' childhood, His resurrection, etc. The stories are legendary and imaginary for the most part, but there are bits of information here and there believed to be authentic. Some of the New Testament Apocrypha are as follows:

Gospel of James	Gospel of Nicodemus (or Acts of Pilate)
Acts of Paul	
Gospel of Peter	Acts of Peter
Acts of John	Acts of Andrew
Gospel According to the Hebrews	Acts of Thomas
	Apocalypse of Peter
History of Joseph	Apocalypse of Paul
Gospel of the Birth of Mary	Epistle of the Apostles

It is interesting to note that the books of the New Testament Apocrypha or Pseudepigrapha fall into the same categories as our authentic New Testament: Gospels, Acts, Epistles, Apocalypses. Fascinating bits of "information" are given in these books. Examples:

(1) Jesus was born in a cave (*Gospel of James*). (This is probably true. The traditional site of His birth is a cave over which is built the Church of the Nativity, Bethlehem, one of the oldest churches in the world.)

(2) Paul was "a man little of stature, slightly bald, crooked in the legs, well-preserved, with eyebrows joining and nose somewhat hooked" (*Acts of Paul*). (This too has a strong tradition behind it.)

(3) The man with the withered hand of Matthew 12:13 was a mason.

(4) The brothers of Jesus were sons of Joseph by another wife.

(5) Longinus was the name of the soldier at the cross.

(6) Veronica was the name of the woman with the issue of blood.

For further information on the Pseudepigrapha, see R. H. Charles' great edition, and M. R. James, *Apocryphal New Testament*.

Sacred books such as those discussed above circulated for a period of time with the Bible books, but eventually the best were selected under the guidance of the Holy Spirit. The Hebrew Canon, though not officially acted upon until the Council of Jamnia about 90 A.D., was for all practical purposes fixed before the time of Christ. That Old Testament was taken over by Christians as part of the Bible. The New Testament canon was fixed in the main by the late second century A.D. But even after that there was some uncertainty for a long time about the last five or six books of the New Testament. The first known listing of our twenty-seven books, as we now know them, was put together by Athanasius in 367 A.D. in his Easter letter.

This one word should be added—that not all Christian canons the world around are the same. The Roman Catholic canon (same as Greek Catholic) is cited above. The Ethiopic Church includes the books of Enoch (quoted in Jude) and Jubilees. Some Christians of the Syriac Church exclude II Peter, II and III John, Jude, and Revelation.

The Canon Fixed

Chapter Divisions (1250 A.D.)

It was not until 1250 A.D. that the Bible was divided into chapters. At that time Cardinal Hugo incorporated chapter divisions into the Latin Bible. His divisions, although for convenience, were not always accurate; however, essentially those same chapter divisions have persisted to this day.

Verse Divisions (1551)

Verse divisions were attempted by the ancient Hebrews, but those we now have were made just three hundred years after Cardinal Hugo's work on chapters. In 1551 Robert Stephens (Robert Etienne) introduced a Greek New Testament with the inclusion of verse divisions. He did not fix verses for the Old Testament. The first entire English Bible to have verse divisions was the Geneva Bible (1560). The King James verse and chapter divisions are not always accurate, as seen, for example, in Acts 7 where the story runs into chapter 8. A stricter division of subject matter would require that chapter 8 commence in another place, perhaps at the present verse 4.

Number of chapters, verses, and words (K.J.V.)

The following chart indicates the number of chapters, verses, and words in the books of the King James Version of the Bible, according to calculations made by the Gideons International.

BOOK	CHAPTERS	VERSES	WORDS
Genesis	50	1,533	32,267
Exodus	40	1,213	32,692
Leviticus	27	859	24,546
Numbers	36	1,288	32,902
Deuteronomy	34	958	28,461
Joshua	24	658	18,858
Judges	21	618	18,976
Ruth	4	85	2,578
I Samuel	31	810	25,061
II Samuel	24	695	20,612
I Kings	22	816	24,524
II Kings	25	719	23,532
I Chronicles	29	941	20,369
II Chronicles	36	822	26,074
Ezra	10	280	7,441
Nehemiah	13	406	10,483
Esther	10	167	5,637
Job	42	1,070	10,102
Psalms	150	2,461	43,743
Proverbs	31	915	15,043

Ecclesiastes	12	222	5,584
Song of Solomon	8	117	2,661
Isaiah	66	1,292	37,044
Jeremiah	52	1,364	42,659
Lamentations	5	154	3,415
Ezekiel	48	1,273	39,407
Daniel	12	357	11,606
Hosea	14	197	5,175
Joel	3	73	2,034
Amos	9	146	4,217
Obadiah	1	21	670
Jonah	4	48	1,321
Micah	7	105	3,153
Nahum	3	47	1,285
Habakkuk	3	56	1,476
Zephaniah	3	53	1,617
Haggai	2	38	1,131
Zechariah	14	211	6,444
Malachi	4	55	1,782
Matthew	28	1,071	23,684
Mark	16	678	15,171
Luke	24	1,151	25,944
John	21	879	19,099
Acts	28	1,007	24,250
Romans	16	433	9,447
I Corinthians	16	437	9,489
II Corinthians	13	257	6,092
Galatians	6	149	3,098
Ephesians	6	155	3,039
Philippians	4	104	2,002
Colossians	4	95	1,998
I Thessalonians	5	89	1,857
II Thessalonians	3	47	1,042
I Timothy	6	113	2,269
II Timothy	4	83	1,703
Titus	3	46	921
Philemon	1	25	445
Hebrews	13	303	6,913
James	5	108	2,309
I Peter	5	105	2,482
II Peter	3	61	1,559
I John	5	105	2,523
II John	1	13	303
III John	1	14	299
Jude	1	25	613
Revelation	22	404	12,000
Total	1,189	31,100	777,133

৯২৯ ANCIENT MANUSCRIPTS AND VERSIONS

T HE OLD TESTAMENT WAS WRITTEN ORIG-
inally in Hebrew and the New in Greek. Here and there
are smatterings of Aramaic, the language of Syria. Aramaic
gradually became the popular language of the Jews from the
Exile onward, and in New Testament times it was probably
spoken by Jesus and His disciples. Daniel 2:4b—7:28, Ezra 4:8—
6:18 and 7:12—26, and Jeremiah 10:11 were written in Aramaic.
See also II Kings 18:26. In the Gospels we hear Jesus speaking
in Aramaic: "Talitha cumi" (Mark 5:41); "ephphatha" (Mark
7:34); "Eloi, Eloi, lama sabachthani?" (Mark 15:34; cf. Matthew
27:46). Also, Jesus used the word "Abba" for "Father" in the
Garden of Gethsemane, and St. Paul used the same Aramaic word
in Romans 8:15 and Galatians 4:6. In I Corinthians 16:22 we
have the familiar word "Maranatha" ("Our Lord, come!"). In
Acts 1:19 there is "Akeldama" ("field of blood").

Aramaic, while related to Hebrew, is not a derivative of it.
The two languages are Semitic as are Arabic, Assyrian, Babylonian and Canaanite. These are very different from European
languages such as French, German and English. By comparison,
in our Western languages we write from left to right, Hebrew
is written from right to left. In Hebrew, vowels were spoken but
not written until they were added in the seventh century A.D.
by the Massoretes. Vowels are indicated by points and small marks
above or beneath the consonants. The oldest Biblical manuscripts
in both Greek and Hebrew contain no punctuation, words are
unseparated, and letters are in uncial form (block letters).

The Greek of the New Testament is in the common or every-

Hebrew
Aramaic
Greek

Koiné

25

day dialect of the time known as Koiné. But in the Gospels—there especially—it is Koiné under the influence of Aramaic. Behind the Koiné are Aramaic sayings, and here and there it shines through the Greek. Jesus spoke in Aramaic and His spoken words were put into written Greek. Gospel scholars frequently translate the Greek back into Aramaic, then into fresh Greek in the attempt to get the full flavor of the original spoken word. But the Aramaic influence—and Hebrew influence too, for that matter, since the Old Testament is the background out of which the New was born—must not be over stressed. In the last analysis, the Greek of the New Testament is authentic Koiné with the unmistakable characteristics of that ancient tongue.

How did the New Testament come to be written in this common tongue? In Jesus' day it was the international language. A man called Alexander of Macedon played a significant role in making it so. It was Alexander (fourth century B.C.) who conquered a great part of the ancient civilized world and wherever he went spread his own language. Thus from India to Rome, and all around the Mediterranean, common Greek came to be spoken. It was natural that the New Testament should be put down in this popular international language, rather than in the local Aramaic. That this was the case points to the fact that the Gospel is for the entire world, not just for a select and local people.

Papyrus and Parchment Manuscripts

Not until the invention of the printing press in the fifteenth century did the Bible appear in anything but hand written form. That means the New Testament, not to speak of the Old, was copied by hand for about fourteen hundred years, and there are some handwritten manuscripts as late as the sixteenth century. These handwritten copies are called manuscripts (*manu* is Latin for "by hand" and *scriptum* means "written").

The materials on which ancient manuscripts were produced were generally of two types, papyrus (II John 12) and parchment (II Timothy 4:13). Papyrus is a plant of the sedge family, a bulrush (see "Plants") which grows along the banks of the Nile River. The plant grows in thickness to about the size of one's wrist. The fibrous pith was removed and cut into very thin vertical sheets. The strips were laid along side one another and stuck together to make a larger sheet. Another sheet of similar size was laid cross-wise upon the first and the sheets thus obtained were hammered out to effect a thinner material. The final step was polishing with pumice stone. Finished sheets measured anywhere from three to eight inches by six to eighteen inches, and the color was light brown or sand. The finished papyrus piece looked like illustration above. On the front of the sheet (the writing side)

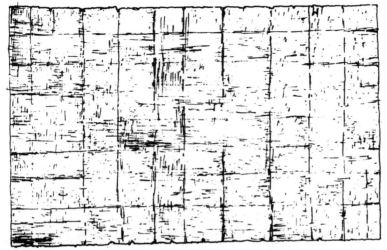

Pen sketch of papyrus writing material, showing the vertical and horizontal lines.

the lines run horizontally. This side is called the "recto." On the back side, the "verso," the lines run vertically. The actual writing was usually done with a reed ("calamus") cut into the shape of a writing instrument or pen (III John 13), and the ink (Jeremiah 36:18; II John 12) was made of soot, gum and water. Only the trained and skilled did the writing, and some, like St. Paul, who had access to a secretary (scribe), dictated and signed their names at the end of the documents to authenticate them. The cost of papyrus was very high, and, according to its quality and size, sold for the equivalent of five to seventeen cents per sheet! It was used for centuries and is a predecessor of paper (our word "paper" comes from "papyrus").

Parchment ("Pergamum," a city in Asia Minor which perfected parchment by the end of the second century and exported it) was more durable than papyrus. It was really treated animal skin. Skins of sheep and goats were dried and polished with pumice. Sometimes young animals were used because their skins produced a finer material; vellum, the extra thin, finest quality, was sometimes taken from animals yet unborn. Parchment was used from ancient times to the Middle Ages when it was replaced gradually by paper.

The Scroll

The use of papyrus and parchment by the Israelites and Christians made it possible to preserve long documents. Ancients wrote on whitewashed stones, metal, clay, wood and other materials on which not much could be written because of size limitations.

Scrolls were made by sewing or gluing sheets into long strips, the ends of which were attached to dowels made of bone or some other hard and durable substance. The length of the scrolls varied but was seldom more than thirty feet—just about the size required for the Gospel of Luke or Matthew. It appears from John 21:25 that the author of the Fourth Gospel ran out of space and was compelled to finish his book sooner than he anticipated because of lack of papyrus material. Since scrolls were heavy and awkward it was necessary to use assistants to help hold, roll and unroll them while the rabbis read in the synagogues. Writing was placed on the scrolls in vertical columns two or three inches wide. Comparatively few ancient Biblical scrolls survive; the Dead Sea Scrolls copy of Isaiah is a rare and magnificent example of the ancient scroll form. Even today in Jewish synagogues the Torah (i.e. the Law or Pentateuch) is done by hand on parchment and in the ancient scroll form. These scrolls are used in public worship as in ancient times.

The Book (Codex) The idea of a book, known technically as a "codex," was thought of and used only after the scroll had been employed for centuries. In fact, the book idea is thought to have originated about the first century A.D. Its predecessor was the diptych, wooden tablets which were joined by a leather thong, opening and closing like a book. Both scrolls and books were used from the first to the fourth centuries; after that the codex was used universally. The first books were made either of parchment or papyrus. Sheets were stacked, folded down the middle, then fastened together in the back to make a "quire." A number of quires were put together to form a "book." Frequently there were several columns to the page as in the Codex Sinaiticus.

The Codex form offered many advantages, two of which were convenience and economy. Convenience—it was easier to hold a book, though large, than a bulky and awkward scroll. Economy—both sides of the sheets could be used (not so with scrolls as a rule). Papyrus and vellum were scarce and thus expensive, but eventually paper reduced the cost of book making. Unfortunately, it did not appear in the Western world until the middle of the eighth century.

All Greek and Hebrew Originals Lost Not a single original manuscript of the Greek or Hebrew Bible exists today. The reason is not fully known, but perhaps the command of the Emperor Diocletian in 303 to destroy all Christian literature accounts for the fact. Another possible reason is that papyrus, probably the material on which most of the New Testament was written, does not last long except in very dry conditions. From one point of view, the loss of the originals ("autographs") is good, for mankind tends to worship things associated with the sacred. God is to be worshiped, not the Bible, much less the paper and ink used in its making. Though the autographs are lost, we are assured by scholarly research that the Bible we read is for all intents and purposes the one produced under divine inspiration. It is important, however, to remember that all Biblical manuscripts are copies.

Copy Errors

Scrolls and books were produced either by a person copying from another manuscript, or by a group copying from one giving dictation. It is easy to see how a copyist could, through weariness or inattentiveness, make errors. But the group method also produced mistakes; there were several reasons for this, but primarily mistakes resulted from what the scholar calls "errors of hearing." "Their" and "there" are pronounced the same in our language, but mean something quite different. Similar linguistic situations occur in Greek.

There were also "errors of seeing." Professor F. F. Bruce has illustrated this by the story of the atheist who had a plaque on his living room wall which read, GOD IS NOWHERE. He had a small daughter who was learning to read and write. One day the atheist took her into the living room and asked her to write what she saw on the plaque. She wrote, GOD IS NOW HERE. This will illustrate how errors of the eye probably occurred.

Yet Astonishing Accuracy

In the manuscripts that have come down to us there are in fact "errors of hearing," "errors of seeing," and other kinds of errors too. But the amazing thing is that the Bible has been as well preserved as it has. Copied thousands of times by hand, the great bulk of the manuscripts nonetheless demonstrates something very close to a consistent and authentic text. The classic statement on the accuracy of the New Testament is by the two great scholars of a past generation, Westcott and Hort: "The words in our opinion still subject to doubt can hardly amount to more than a thousandth part of the New Testament" (F. F. Westcott and F. J. A. Hort, editors, *New Testament in Original Greek* 1882, Vol. II, Introduction, p. 2).

One reason for the accuracy of the Old Testament was the Jewish belief in the sacredness of the Scriptures. Josephus said of the Scriptures: ". . . no one has ventured either to add, or to remove, or to alter a syllable . . ." (cp. Deuteronomy 4:2 and Jeremiah 26:2). In point of fact, the Jewish Scriptures were copied with scrupulous care. The scribes were the custodians of the sacred writings in Bible times and historically they were followed by the Massoretes (literally "transmitters"). The Massoretes flourished from about 500 to 1,000 A.D., and their efforts to preserve the Biblical text were both laborious and almost unbelievable. Such devices as these were employed: counting every letter in a book and locating the middle letter; counting every word and locating the middle word; listing the number of times a word or phrase is used in the Bible. Books with mistakes were discarded. So it is easy to see why the Scriptures have come down to us in almost perfect condition. Incidentally, the Massoretes, whose headquarters were in Babylonia and at Tiberias on Lake Galilee, provided notes, the "Massorah," to go along with the Old Testament text. One of the famous Massoretes of Tiberias was Aaron ben Asher. So well did the Massoretes preserve the Old Testament that their work has come down to us as the standard text and is called the "Massoretic Text," abbreviated by scholars MT.

Deliberate Changes

It should be noticed that on occasion some copyists deliberately made changes in the text. Sometimes they thought they were clarifying a doctrinal point; at other times they supposed they were clearing up a contradiction. But they would have done better to leave the text as it was. Some copyists put their changes in the margin, but others incorporated them right in the running text. Today textual critics must ferret out the true from the false.

Variations Essentially Inconsequential

Though there are variations in the Biblical texts (more in the New than in the Old Testament), most are quite inconsequential, and no great doctrinal truth is held in question because of textual errors. The many manuscripts witness together to provide us with a text both usable and essentially accurate. There is probably no passage in the New Testament for which the correct reading has not been preserved. The well-known scholar Sir Frederic Kenyon says that "no fundamental doctrine of the Christian faith rests on a disputed reading." He comments further, "It cannot be too strongly asserted that in substance the text of the Bible is certain." (*Our Bible and the Ancient Manuscripts,* revised by A. W. Adams. London: Eyre and Spottiswoode, 1958, p. 55)

SOME VERY OLD MANUSCRIPTS OF THE BIBLE

Raw Materials of the Textual Critic

Ancient manuscripts (texts) and translations (versions) constitute the raw materials with which the textual critic works. He also uses quotations from the Bible by the Church Fathers which hint at the character of their sources, but the quotations are not usually so important as actual texts and versions. The aim is to recover the original text. Generally, the older the manuscript the more important it is, but some late manuscripts contain very

Museum, Jerusalem, Jordan where some Dead Sea Scroll fragments are located. Other materials, including the complete Isaiah scroll, are in the Hebrew University across the border in Jerusalem, Israel.

early and authentic texts, in which case they are as important as the early copies. Bible manuscripts are not exactly alike and the textual critic must try to determine a correct text. The expert has manuscripts of the Old Testament from the third century B.C. to the twelfth century A.D., plus ancient translations in Aramaic, Greek, Syriac, Latin, and other languages. Of the New Testament, he has documents from the early second century A.D. to the sixteenth, plus ancient translations in a number of languages, particularly Latin, Syriac, and Coptic.

Below are recorded some of the major manuscripts from the second century B.C. through the fifth century A.D.

Up to 1947 our oldest Hebrew Old Testament manuscript, except for relatively unimportant scraps, dated in the latter part of the ninth century A.D. Our oldest New Testament manuscript was far older (by almost eight centuries) than our oldest Old Testament manuscripts. But now we have specimens of pre-Christian Hebrew texts. In 1947 the first of the Dead Sea Scrolls discoveries was made in a cave near the site of Qumran to the northwest of the Dead Sea. That first discovery included a complete Hebrew scroll of Isaiah, one of the oldest found and dating into the second century B.C. This, like many of the other Dead Sea Scrolls, is in remarkable agreement with the standard Old Testament text, the Massoretic Text. It was the first of the Qum-

Dead Sea Scrolls

ran materials to be published and is still the best known. After the first discoveries, other caves were systematically explored and materials from every book of the Old Testament except Esther were discovered. Bible commentaries and other kinds of religious works were also unearthed. Some of the Dead Sea materials are in the Jordanian museum at Jerusalem, and other materials, including the complete scoll of Isaiah, are in the Jerusalem, Israel. The great value of the Scrolls is that their Hebrew texts constitute a strong witness to the reliability of the Old Testament as we have known it for centuries. The Dead Sea Scrolls constitute the most dramatic example of Old Testament finds of the century.

Rylands Fragment of John (oldest N.T. fragment, second century)

C. H. Roberts found a 2½ by 3½ inch papyrus fragment in a collection at the John Rylands Library, Manchester, England. It contains thirty words in Greek from the eighteenth chapter of John (18:31-33, 37-38). This is the oldest manuscript portion of the New Testament known to exist and dates into the first half of the second century. It came from a codex, not a scroll. This we know because there is writing on both sides of the papyrus, a phenomenon rare in scrolls. The scholar knows the fragment by the symbol p^{52}.

Bodmer Papyri (about 200 A.D.)

In 1956, 1958 and 1962 Papyrus Bodmer II was published. It includes the first thirteen chapters of John in Greek in nearly perfect condition and fragments of the remaining chapters. It is dated at about 200 A.D. and is in the Bodmer Library near Geneva. In 1961 another Bodmer document, Luke 3:18 through John 15:8, was published. It may be as old as the last quarter of the second

The Rylands Greek Papyrus fragment from chapter 18 of John's Gospel, dating in the first half of the second century A.D.

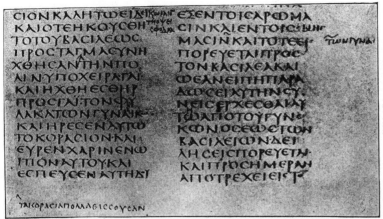

From the fourth century Codex Sinaiticus found by Tischendorf in St. Catherine's Monastery, Mt. Sinai. Uncials (block letters) are used, and there is no punctuation or separation of words. This photograph was taken from one of the scraps found in the waste basket, 1844.

century. Other Bodmer Papyri include Jude and II Peter in Greek (c. 200 A.D.), and Bible portions, from both Old and New Testaments, in Greek and Coptic.

Acquired in 1930 by Chester Beatty, the papyri were announced to the world by Sir Frederic Kenyon in the London *Times* for November 17, 1931. Materials from both Old and New Testaments in Greek are included, and dated in about the third century A.D. (some have dated them more generally from the second to the fourth centuries). There are eleven papyrus codices, seven from the Old Testament, three from the New, and one of part of I Enoch. The earliest copies of Paul's Epistles, with some gaps (notably the Pastorals: I and II Timothy and Titus), are in the group; also portions of the four Gospels and Acts which date just after 200 A.D. A part of the Revelation completes the papyri which are now at The Chester Beatty Library, Dublin, except for thirty leaves from the Pauline Epistles at the University of Michigan Library, Ann Arbor.

Chester Beatty Papyri (3rd century)

In 1844 twenty-nine year old Constantine von Tischendorf found forty-three parchment leaves of the now famous Codex Sinaiticus in the Monastery of St. Catherine on Mt. Sinai—hence the name of the manuscript. It appears that the monks were quite ignorant of its value because the forty-three leaves had been put in a wastebasket where Tischendorf found and rescued them. On a return trip in 1859 he was able, though with great difficulty, to persuade the monks to let him have what was left of the document (by now they apparently knew its value). Altogether this fourth century copy included the entire New Testament and most of the Old. Two non-Biblical documents (the

Codex Sinaiticus (fourth century)

Epistle of Barnabas and part of the Shepard Hermas) were included to make a total of 346½ leaves, 147½ of which made up the New Testament. Codex Sinaiticus, except for the original discovery of forty-three leaves which are at Leipzig, is now at the British Museum, London. Before its purchase from Russia on Christmas Day 1933 at the cost of 100,000 pounds, it had been in the Imperial Library of St. Petersburg (now Leningrad) for seventy-four years. The British public, including churches and Sunday Schools, contributed half the purchase price and the government the other half.

Codex Vaticanus (fourth century)

Another well-known document is the Codex Vaticanus, a fourth century copy. Discovered in the Vatican Library, and taken to Paris for a time by Napoleon, it is now housed in the Vatican Library, in Rome, and contains the Greek Old Testament (it is the oldest and best of the Septuagint manuscripts), and the New Testament through Hebrews 9:14 (all materials after that are lost). This and the Codex Sinaiticus are sister codices and are probably of Egyptian origin. They attest the best Greek text available.

Codex Bezae (fourth or fifth century)

Codex Bezae is a fourth or fifth century copy and contains incomplete texts of the four Gospels and Acts, plus a few verses of I John. The left hand pages show a Greek text and the right hand pages a Latin text. It is named for the Reformer, Beza, who presented it to Cambridge University in 1581. He acquired it from the monastery of St. Irenaeus at Lyons in 1562. It has 406 leaves but no doubt contained originally at least 100 more.

Codex Washingtonianus I (fourth or fifth century)

Codex Washingtonianus I is an important manuscript which is dated in the fourth or fifth century. Charles L. Freer bought it from a dealer in Cairo, Egypt, in 1906. The document, containing the Greek Gospels in the order of Matthew, John, Luke, Mark (as in Codex Bezae), resides at the Freer Art Museum which is in connection with the Smithsonian Institute, Washington, D.C.

Codex Alexandrinus (fifth century)

Codex Alexandrinus is a fifth century manuscript of the Old and New Testaments in Greek plus two non-Biblical books, the Epistles of Clement. It is thought to have been done by Thelka the Martyr. The book was presented as a gift to King Charles I in 1627 by Cyril Lucar, a Greek patriarch of Alexandria; hence its name. It is located in the British Museum, London, and was one of the Museum's foundation gifts.

Codex Ephraemi Rescriptus (a fifth century palimpsest)

An incomplete fifth century Codex of Old and New Testaments in Greek, Ephraemi is known as a palimpsest. The term "palimpsest" comes from two Greek words, *palin* meaning "again," and *psestos* meaning "scrubbed" or "rubbed"; thus, a palimpsest manuscript is one which has had the writing "rubbed" off so that the parchment could be used "again." In 1950 at St. Catherine's Monastery on Mt. Sinai a most extraordinary palimpsest was found, one which had been used five times and as such is known as the "quintuple palimpsest." In the case of the Ephraemi palimpsest, the Biblical text had been erased but chemicals were used with moderate success to restore the first writings. (Today, with ultra violet photography, chemicals are no longer used on palimpsests.) A treatise by St. Ephraem was written on top of the Biblical writing, thus the name of the codex. Included in it are sixty-four Old Testament pages and 145 New Testament pages out of an original 238.

A MULTITUDE OF WITNESSES

Old Testament manuscripts are commonly divided in papyri, uncials, and minuscules; New Testament documents into papyri, uncials, minuscules, and lectionaries. The last three types were done largely on parchment, relatively few on papyrus. Uncials are manuscripts copied in block letters while minuscules were done in cursive (running) letters as in handwriting. Of the New Testament manuscripts there are 247 uncials, and 2,623 minuscules. Because the uncials are older, relatively few remain in existence. There are seventy-eight papyri and 1,968 lectionaries, scripture lessons adapted for public worship. The lectionaries vary from the standard New Testament text but are close enough to be important textual witnesses.

Papyri, Uncials, Minuscules, Lectionaries

Altogether the papyri, uncials, minuscules, and lectionaries of the New Testament make up almost 5,000 documents, the number is growing yearly with added discoveries. Indeed, we have more manuscripts of the New Testament than of the Old, but in the case of the Old there is the compensating factor that the Jews copied their Scriptures with greater care than did the Christians (see section on "Accuracy").

The New Testament manuscripts are registered with a central authority in Germany. Caspar René Gregory was the "registrar" for a long time; today Professor Kurt Aland of Münster is the scholar responsible for cataloging the manuscripts. New Testament papyri are catalogued by the letter P, and the number of each manuscript is placed beside it to make P^1, P^2, etc. up to P^{78}. Uncials are usually catalogued with an o; thus, we have 01 to 0247. However in older systems uncials were classified alphabetically; thus, Codex Sinaiticus is known even yet sometimes by the first letter of the Hebrew alphabet, aleph; Codex Alexandrinus by A; Codex Vaticanus by B. (In the current scheme Sinaiticus is 01, Alexandrinus is 02, and Vaticanus 03.) The minuscules are codified simply by the numbers 1–2,623. Lectionaries are indicated by an "l." Le symbolizes the Gospels, la the Acts, lp Paul's Letters, lr the book of Revelation. Numbers 1 through 1,968 are added to indicate the particular lectionary. Old Testament manuscripts are catalogued by their own scheme, the uncials normally being given a letter and the minuscules a number. The names Holmes, Parsons and Rahlfs are connected with the history of Old Testament manuscript cataloguing.

Multitude of Manuscript Witnesses

It is truly amazing that there are so many manuscripts of the Bible. No other ancient literature can boast so many witnesses. In fact the writings of Greece and Rome exist in very few manuscripts, and these, for the most part, are later than the ninth century A.D.—only the manuscripts of the Latin poet Virgil (copies, of course) exist of an earlier date and these are three or four hundred years after his death. But Bible scholars have a superabundance of materials with which to work, and the materials are much nearer the time of their writing. This fact is another evidence of the wide appeal and providential preservation of God's Word.

ANCIENT TRANSLATIONS (VERSIONS)

The Septuagint (B.C. 250 following)

The scholar's term for translation is "version." There are ancient, medieval and modern versions. The Septuagint, a translation of the Hebrew Old Testament, is the oldest of the ancient versions in Greek. The Pentateuch (the first five Old Testament books) came out about 250 B.C. The remainder which followed, including the Apocryphal books, may not have been completed until the end of the first century B.C. Some parts are in good Koiné Greek, others in Semitized Greek. Some portions are faithfully translated (the Pentateuch), others abound in paraphrases and additions (Proverbs). This translation was a product of necessity since there were many Greek-speaking Jews in the ancient world. In fact, the international language in the Mediterranean area was Greek for several centuries. The Septuagint is abbreviated by the symbol LXX because of the tradition that about seventy translators produced it. It is interesting that the New Testament writers often quoted it instead of the Hebrew Scriptures. (Luke and the author of Hebrews used the LXX more than other New Testament writers, Matthew the least.) At least part of it was translated in or around Alexandria, Egypt. The titles we now use for the Old Testament books came in part from the Septuagint (in part from the Vulgate which is the Latin translation). Early Christians used the LXX, even adapted it, and eventually it was put along side the Greek New Testament to make up the whole Greek Bible. It went through Greek revisions, came out in varying Greek versions, and was translated into Coptic, Ethiopic, Gothic, Armenian, Arabic, Georgian, Slavonic and Old Latin. Today it is still the standard text of the Greek Orthodox Church.

Samaritan
Pentateuch
(pre-Christian)

The Hebrew Old Testament is the Bible of the Jews and the Hebrew Pentateuch is the Bible of the Samaritans. The Samaritans —so called because they inhabited Samaria (which took its name from the City of Samaria)—were part Jews. They were not allowed to help rebuild the Temple in the time of Ezra and Nehemiah, and they isolated themselves from their Jewish relatives, founding their own religious headquarters at Mt. Gerizim, near Shechem (modern Nablus). They made the Pentateuch their Bible and changed and adapted it to their own history and way of thinking (e.g. in Deuteronomy 27:4 "Ebal" has been replaced by "Gerizim"). The Abisha Scroll at Nablus, a copy of the Samaritan Pentateuch, is made up of two scrolls, neither dating before the Middle Ages. Another copy in existence dates into the thirteenth century—a scroll thought to have been discovered by the high priest Phinehas in 1355. Europe did not have a copy of the Samaritan Pentateuch until 1616. The Samaritan Pentateuch is simply a Hebrew edition in a slightly different script. It preserves to some extent a very old textual tradition, but there are so many changes due to lack of careful copying and other reasons, that this text is not always of help to the textual critic. A text of Exodus has been discovered at Qumran which has affinities with the Samaritan Pentateuch. The Samaritans exist in small numbers today and persist in using the Pentateuch as their Bible.

Targums
(Aramaic
Versions)

The targums are paraphrases or interpretative translations of most of the Old Testament (there are no targums of Daniel, Ezra, Nehemiah) in Aramaic. These gradually took the place of Hebrew as the common language after the Babylonian Captivity. In due course the Scriptures had to be put in the familiar Aramaic. Thus in the synagogues oral translations were made. The translator was known as the "methurgeman" and the translation as the "targum." In time these oral paraphrases were reduced to writing, some of them more literal translations than others. One of the recently discovered Dead Sea Scrolls is a targum of Job. Aside from this Dead Sea find, the earliest targum copies are from the fifth century A.D., though there is evidence for their existence in pre-Christian times. One famous targum is called Onkelos. In 1957 the Vatican Library announced the discovery in its archives of a fifteenth century copy of the targum known as "Jerusalem II."

In the second century A.D. when the international language changed from Greek to Latin, Latin translations began to appear. With the passage of a century or two the Latin versions grew in number as the use of Latin grew, but they became so varied and difficult that a great fourth and fifth century scholar, Jerome, was commissioned by Damasus, Bishop of Rome, to produce a stable Latin text. It was translated from the Hebrew, the Old Latin, and Greek. Jerome did part of his work in Bethlehem. The fact that he worked from the Hebrew text is significant since it was customary in his time to translate the Greek Septuagint. Unfortunately Jerome's work was adapted by others to the Septuagint, and it was not until the Renaissance and Reformation that serious attention was given the Massoretic (standard) Text. Fortunately our own English Bible, beginning with Tyndale, is from the stable Hebrew text, rather than from the less stable Greek Old Testament.

From a thirteenth century Latin manuscript, the opening initial of Deuteronomy is shown: above *Moses with tables addressing three Jews;* below *four Jews standing over a bed on which Moses lies dead. St. Jerome's name is associated with the standard (Vulgate) Latin text.*

Courtesy The John Rylands
Library, Manchester, England

From the Vulgate we get such familiar theological words as "election," "justification," "sanctification," "salvation," and "regeneration." The Vulgate includes both Old and New Testaments, and its name means "common" (from "vulgar"). It is still the official Bible of the Roman Catholic Church and was the Bible of the Middle Ages, though it was not given official recognition until the Council of Trent in 1546.

Syriac is a Semitic language akin to Aramaic and was used at Edessa and in Western Mesopotamia until Arabic superseded it in the thirteenth century A.D. Included in the Syriac versions are those listed below.

Converted in Rome and a disciple of Justin Martyr, Tatian prepared a harmony of the four Gospels interweaving the materials into one continuous story. He did this work about A.D. 180 and was the first to make a Gospel harmony. Whether he produced it originally in Syriac or Greek is unknown. But of the Syriac versions up through the fourth century, it was the Diatessaron which circulated most widely, even though it reflected his own heretical ideas.

In ancient times it was translated into Arabic and probably Latin, and it influenced the medieval Gospel harmonies of Europe and the East.

In 1892 Mrs. Lewis and Mrs. Gibson of Cambridge, twin sisters, discovered the so-called Sinaitic Syriac at the Monastery of St. Catherine on Mt. Sinai. It is a palimpsest (see "Codex Ephraemi" above) and contains the greater part of the four Gospels. The manuscript is still at Mt. Sinai but has been photographed, and in 1894 was published in an English translation by Mrs. Lewis.

(2) The Old Syriac (originated second century)

Also what is known as the Curetonian Syriac; named after William Cureton of the British Museum, was published in 1858. It contains the Gospels and is a fifth century copy of the Old Syriac. The original was brought to the British Museum of London in 1842 from Egypt.

The New Testament Peshitta ("simple"), a revision of the Old Syriac version made probably by Rabbula, became an "authorized version" of the Syrian Church. The total number of manuscripts preserving parts of the Peshitta is 243; almost half are in the British Museum, London. Two of these documents are from the fifth century (the oldest is dated 464 A.D.) and a dozen others from the sixth century. The Peshitta of the Old Testament, at least of the Pentateuch, is probably Jewish or Jewish-Christian in origin. The New Testament in this version lacks II Peter 2 and III John, Jude, and Revelation.

(3) The Peshitta Syriac (fourth century)

From the Four Gospels in the Peshitta form of the Syriac translation, this copy dating A.D. 550.

Courtesy The John Rylands Library, Manchester, England

Another of the Syriac versions, sometimes known as the Harclean because it is thought by some to have been re-issued by Thomas of Heraclea. The Harclean marginal notations of textual variances for the book of Acts are of help in ascertaining a correct text for that book. About fifty manuscripts from a Harclean revision are known to exist, most of them in England. The original Philoxenian now exists only in fragmentary form giving portions of the New Testament and Psalms. Some have suggested that originally there were the Philoxenian and Harclean, two quite separate translations.

(4) The Philoxenian Version (early sixth century)

This Syriac version of Old and New Testaments is known only in fragments and is in a dialect of its own (Syriac characters but

(5) The Palestinian Syriac (c. fourth to sixth centuries)

39

Palestinian Aramaic). It dates from the fourth to the sixth centuries and was used by the Melchite Church (Palestinian-Syriac Church). The fragments of this version made from the Septuagint exist in Rome, London, Leningrad and at Mt. Sinai.

Coptic Versions (third and fourth centuries)

Coptic was the language of early Egyptian Christians, the language which evolved from that of the Pharaohs. It was not written in hieroglyphics but in characters similar to Greek. In the third and fourth centuries the "Coptic" Christians came out with the Bible in their own language and dialects. Of the several dialects, two are of chief importance. One is the Sahidic for Christians in Upper (southern) Egypt, and the other is the Bohairic for Lower (northern) Egypt. The latter was a literary rather than a spoken language. The Old Testament appears in both dialects and was largely based on the Septuagint. There is in existence the entire New Testament in Bohairic and almost all of it in Sahidic. These New Testament translations are not to be dated before the third century A.D., and the Bohairic may be fourth century. The Bodmer Papyri (see above) include some Coptic materials.

Gospel of Thomas (c. 4th century)

A strange version, if it can be called a version, is the Gnostic *Gospel of Thomas* in Coptic. An accident revealed this and other documents. It all happened about 1945 or 1946 near the ancient site of Chenoboskion on the Nile River within thirty miles of Luxor, Egypt. A Christian tomb was exposed quite by accident when native Egyptians, not archaeologists, dug into it. In a clay jar

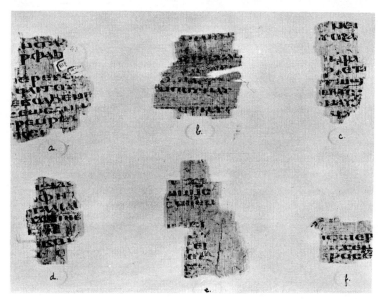

Perhaps the oldest surviving fragments of the New Testament in the Bohairic dialect of the ancient Coptic (Egyptian) language. From Matthew chapter 21.

were thirteen papyrus codices which contained about fifty individual documents including an *Apocryphon of John* and a *Gospel of Philip*. Twelve of the books are in the Coptic Museum, Cairo; the thirteenth, known as the Jung codex and containing the Gnostic *Gospel of Truth*, is at the Jung Institute, Zurich. (Gnosticism was an early cult which threatened the existence of Christianity. It believed in salvation through "Gnosis," special knowledge.) Sometimes known as the Nag Hammadi papyri (Nag Hammadi, not far from Chenoboskion, is the modern town where the discoverers sold their papyri for the equivalent of eight dollars fifty cents), the thirteen papyri are probably fourth century copies of second or third century Greek works, most of them Gnostic. *The Gospel According to Thomas,* published by Harper in English and Coptic in 1959, records some 114 supposed sayings of Jesus. The name of the disciple Thomas is appended to the work to give it authority, a common device in ancient times. The Coptic of the Thomas Gospel is Sahidic, dates about the fourth century, but is based on a Greek document of perhaps the middle of the second century. Beatitudes and parables are given, and familiar figures (St. Peter, John the Baptist, James brother of our Lord) are referred to. Some scholars have suggested a very few of the new sayings may be authentic, but little credence is given that view now. Most of the sayings are known to us in the Gospels, in papyri discovered towards the end of the last century at Oxyrhynchus, or in quotations by the early Christian writers. The basic suppositions of the Thomas Gospel are Gnostic, not Christian, and there is no real evidence of an eyewitness account here. None of the sayings are identical with the Gospel words of our Lord, though some are similar or parallel. Two of the sayings are as follows:

> "Blessed are the solitary and elect, for you shall find the Kingdom; because you come from it, and you shall go there again."
>
> "It is impossible for a man to mount two horses and to stretch two bows, and it is impossible for a servant to serve two masters, otherwise he will honor the one and offend the other."

"Agrapha" is a term used by scholars in reference to the "sayings" of Jesus not recorded in the Gospels. The 114 sayings in the *Gospel of Thomas* are the largest collection of agrapha; others are found in the writings of early Christian authors. The sayings have been collected and printed in English in R. M. Grant and D. N. Freedman, *The Secret Sayings of Jesus,* English translation by

A note on the "Agrapha"

W. R. Schoedel (New York: Doubleday, 1960). The term agrapha means literally "unwritten," which refers to the fact that the sayings are not written in the Gospels; they are written elsewhere, of course. There is one agraphon in the New Testament, "It is more blessed to give than to receive" (Acts 20:35); it is an agraphon because it is not written in the Gospels.

The other Ancient Versions

(1) Gothic (fourth century)

The Gothic version was done by Ulfilas ("Little Wolf"), a fourth century figure. He invented an alphabet and reduced Gothic, a Germanic dialect, to writing. The celebrated Silver Codex—done on purple vellum with silver ink—is at the University of Uppsala, dates in the fifth or sixth century and contains portions of all four Gospels. The Gothic translation is a faithful one, though the six available manuscripts are incomplete.

(2) Armenian (fourth century)

The Armenian, done for Armenian Christians in the fourth century, has been called the "Queen of the Versions" because of its beauty and accuracy. Mesrop, a soldier turned missionary, and Sahak did the work of translation. Like Ulfilas, Mesrop invented an alphabet. (How many alphabets have been invented, how many languages reduced to writing in the process of translating the Bible!) The Armenian version was revised sometime after the fifth century.

(3) Georgian (c. fifth century)

The Georgian version was the Bible of the ancient peoples of Georgia, located in the mountainous region between the Black and Caspian Seas. They first heard the Gospel in the fourth century, but their translation probably did not emerge until the fifth century.

(4) Ethiopic (c. fourth or fifth century)

Little is known about the origins of Christianity in Ethiopia (cf. Acts 8:26-39). Just when they had a Bible is unknown too, but perhaps it was in the fourth or fifth century. The earliest copy of this version is thirteenth century and most copies are sixteenth and seventeenth century.

(5) Nubian (date unknown)

Nubia was located between Egypt and Ethiopia—its version is known as the Nubian. From about the sixth to the fourteenth centuries these people embraced Christianity, after that Islam became their religion. Only tenth or eleventh century fragments of the Nubian version remain; when the original was done is unknown.

(6) Sogdian (date unknown)

The Sogdian version (central Asia) is very incomplete and little is known about it.

(7) Old Arabic (date unknown)

Old Arabic translations were made in the eighth century by John, Bishop of Seville, in the tenth century by Isaak Velasquez of Cordoba, and in the thirteenth century in Egypt. It is not known whether there were translations before the eighth century.

(8) Old Slavic (c. ninth century)

In the ninth century, according to tradition, the Greek brothers Cyril and Methodius, missionaries to the Slavs, began a translation of the Gospels. There are about twelve manuscripts of the Old Slavic version of the Gospels dating from the eleventh to fourteenth centuries.

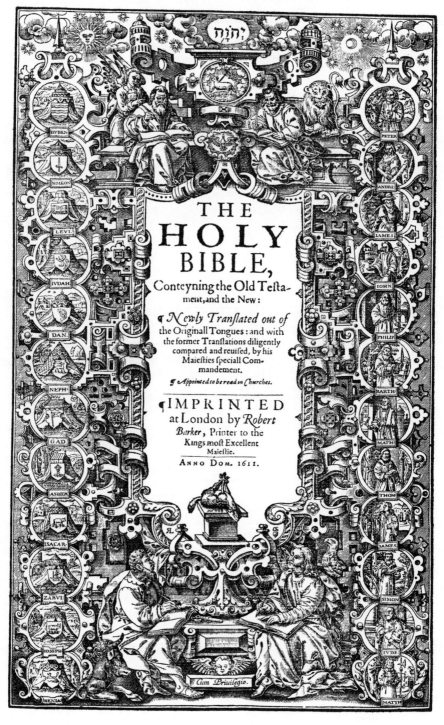

יהוה

THE HOLY BIBLE,

Conteyning the Old Testa-
ment, and the New:

❡ *Newly Translated out of*
the Originall Tongues: and with
the former Translations diligently
compared and reuised, by his
Maiesties speciall Com-
mandement.

❡ *Appointed to be read in Churches.*

❡IMPRINTED
at London by *Robert*
Barker, Printer to the
Kings most Excellent
Maiestie.

ANNO DOM. 1611.

Cum Priuilegio.

*The title page of the first edition of
the King James Bible (Authorized Version), 1611.*

⤳3⤳ ENGLISH
TRANSLATIONS
TO THE PRESENT

LONG BEFORE THE INVENTION OF PRINTING ENG-
land possessed the Scriptures, in Latin at first, and then parts
in Anglo-Saxon. Teutonic invaders introduced the Anglo-
Saxon language into England; only fragments of their writing
remain. The fragments are from Scripture. Paraphrases, free translations and renderings were done by Aelfric, King Alfred, Caedmon, and others.

In the eighth century Bede translated the Psalms and Gospels **Bede (eighth**
into Anglo-Saxon, but he died before completing the rest of the **century)**
Bible. It was not until the fourteenth century that the first English
version of the entire Bible was completed; prior to that only fragments had been translated. About 1330 some fifty-two English
translations of the Psalms appeared with accompanying Latin text.

John Wyclif* (born 1320), probably with the help of Nicholas **Wyclif: first**
of Hereford who we think did a good share of the Old Testament, **complete English**
produced the first complete English Bible. For his part in the **Bible (1380-1384)**
translation, Hereford was put out of the Roman Catholic Church
and imprisoned. The translation was done from the Vulgate of
Jerome, which was considered the standard text of the time. It was,
of course, copied by hand since printing was not invented until the
next century. But enough copies were made so that circulation on
a limited scale was possible. It took some ten months to make a
single copy, and each copy cost forty English pounds—a tremendous sum of money for a book in that or any day. John Purvey

---

* His name has been spelled twenty-seven different ways! Examples: Wycliff,
Wycliffe. See Charles Gulston, *Our English Bible: No Greater Heritage* (Grand
Rapids: Wm. B. Eerdmans, 1961), p. 89.

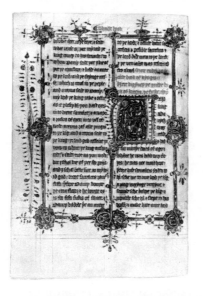

A page from the Bible of John Wyclif, the first complete Bible in the English language.

Courtesy The John Rylands Library, Manchester, England

revised Wyclif's translation between 1395 and 1408. People who could not afford a Wyclif Bible rented it at considerable cost just to get a single hour of reading—a load of hay was sometimes given for a few pages. Some were imprisoned, others burned for reading or owning it; indeed, in 1519 six men and women died at the stake for teaching their children the Lord's Prayer and the Ten Commandments in English. Interestingly enough the Wyclif Bible was not printed as such until 1850 when it came out in four volumes. On May 4, 1415, thirty-one years after his death, the Council of Constance excommunicated Wyclif, ordered his bones dug up and burned. The ashes were thrown into a river, but from there they went eventually to sea and have gone around the world even as the Bible itself has.

Invention of Printing (Gutenberg Bible before 1456)

At this point, we should note the invention of printing and its influence on the translation and publication of the Word of God. The very first complete book done on the movable type printing press was produced by Johann Gutenberg in Mainz, Germany, before the year 1456. The actual date of the invention of the printing press is unknown. Gutenberg, it is thought, carried out experiments prior to 1439. At any rate, the first book printed was the Bible in Latin. It is sometimes called the Mazarin Bible because a famous copy of it belonged to the library of the seventeenth century French statesman, Cardinal Jules Mazarin. In 1488 the first Hebrew Old Testament was done by the Soncino press of Lombardy.

A page from the famous Gutenberg Bible, done before 1456 on the first printing press in Mainz, Germany.

Courtesy The John Rylands Library, Manchester, England

The First Greek Testaments came out in the sixteenth century; they were done by Erasmus (1516) and Ximenes (1520). Incidentally, Erasmus' Greek text, though not too accurate, wielded a strong influence until the last part of the nineteenth century when newer and better texts were available.

The first printed English New Testament from the Greek was that of Tyndale. It was printed at Worms, Germany, by Peter Schoeffer (sometimes known as Peter Quentel) who did 3,000 copies, only two of which still exist, one in the Baptist College, Bristol, England, the other—minus seventy-one leaves—in St. Paul's Cathedral Library, London. All the rest were probably burned. Published in 1525, Tyndale's Bible was done on the Continent of Europe (at Cologne and Worms) while he was in exile, because it was unpopular—even unlawful!—to translate the Bible in England. Latin was thought to be the "sacred" language; therefore, it was argued, the Bible must be kept in that tongue. But Tyndale, often called the father of the English Bible, cried out for a Bible every English ploughboy could understand. He persisted until he completed his translation, and copies were issued and secretly imported into England in bales of cloth, flour sacks, and the like. He did portions of the Old Testament from the original Hebrew—he published only the Pentateuch (1530), and Jonah (1531)—but was martyred before he could finish it. His imports into England were burned by the hundreds at St. Paul's Cross, London. Even clergy gathered the Bibles for burning! The persecuted translator suffered imprisonment and wrote this now famous and pathetic letter from his cold cell: Send me "a warmer cap, for I suffer extremely from cold in the head, being afflicted with a perpetual catarrh, which is considerably increased in the cell. A warmer coat also, for that which I have is very thin; also a piece of cloth to patch my leggings; my shirts are also worn out." He also asked for his Hebrew Bible and dictionary. He was martyred perhaps without his requests being answered. On October 6, 1536 in the town of Vilvorde, near Brussels, Tyndale was strangled and burned. His last words were, "Lord, open the King of England's eyes." God was to answer that prayer.

The first complete English Bible done on the printing press was translated by Myles Coverdale. Printed in 1535, it was published outside England for Coverdale's own safety, in Zurich(?), Switzerland. Two years later it was printed in England. Actually, the New Testament—and some of the Old—was essentially the work of Tyndale. (Tyndale's translation also influenced the King James Version). This was the first edition to provide chapter summaries. A curious (if delightful) printer's error in the Coverdale

Tyndale: First Printed English New Testament from the Greek (1525)

Coverdale: first complete English Bible printed (1535)

version is seen in Psalm 119:161, "*Printers* have persecuted me without cause." Psalm 91:5 is interesting too, "Thou shalt not nede to be afrayed for eny bugges by night." ("Bugge" is the old English word for any imaginary source of fear such as a hobgoblin.) But "the valley of the shadow of death," and "I will fear no evil for thou art with me" are magnificent expressions which were carried over into the King James Versions.

Matthew's Bible (1537)

Matthew's Bible was the first version authorized by the King of England, and thus holds an important position in the history of the English Bible. It was done by John Rogers (he used the pseudonym Thomas Matthew for protection) and published in 1537. Out of a study of this version the first English concordance was done by Marbeck, a church organist.

Any freedom to read the Bible was to be lost shortly, though temporarily, and in 1543 an act of Parliament forbade women—"except noble or gentle women"—from reading it, even privately, under pain of death. Rogers relied heavily on Tyndale and Coverdale; in fact about two-thirds was Tyndale's and one-third Coverdale's. So the work was more an edition than a new translation. A revision, commissioned by Thomas Cromwell, was edited by Coverdale himself in 1539 and was called the "Great Bible"—its size was approximately 15 by 9 inches. Sometimes it is known as the "Chained Bible" because it was chained to reading desks in the churches, one being given to each church. Rogers was burned February 4, 1555, while "thousands of thrilled spectators" looked on. But his own children, it is said, "so comforted him that it seemed as if he had been led to a wedding." Another revision of Matthew's Bible was that issued by Richard Taverner in 1539. It was dedicated to King Henry VIII and influenced both the Douai and King James Versions.

"Great Bible" (1539)

Taverner's Bible (1539)

Geneva ("Breeches") Bible (1560)

The complete Geneva Bible (printed in Geneva, Switzerland) appeared first in 1560 (the last edition in 1644). Dedicated to Queen Elizabeth, it was for over seventy years *the* Bible of England. It is sometimes known as the "Breeches" Bible because of the translation of Genesis 3:7, "They sewed figg tree leaves together and made themselves breeches." The scholarship of the Geneva version was superior for its day, an evidence of which is the fact that Paul was not made the author of Hebrews (most modern scholars are convinced that Paul did not write that particular Epistle). The best English translation to that date, the Geneva Bible was done mainly by three men, Whittingham, Sampson, and Gilbey. It was highly valued by the Scottish people too, because it was the first Bible ever printed in Scotland (1576–79). The Geneva Bible was unique for several reasons:

1. It called sharp attention to the dubious character of the Apocrypha.

2. It was the first to use italics for words added to make up full idiomatic English.

3. It was the first whole English Bible with verse numberings.

4. It was the first to use Roman type rather than Old English type.

The Geneva Edition was smaller than Coverdale's, Rogers', or the Great Bible, and thus more portable. It is easy to see why it was the most popular up to this time. The King James Version preserved the Geneva rendering, "The Lord is my Shepard, I shall not want."

In 1568 (revised 1572) Archbishop Matthew Parker and several bishops and Bible scholars produced a Bible. This was interesting because some of the translators initialed their particular passages. But the renderings were of varying quality and the whole work did not succeed in supplanting the Geneva Bible as some supposed it would.

Bishop's Bible (1568)

The Roman Catholic version of the Bible usually goes by the name Douai (sometimes spelled Douay) from the town in France where the Old Testament was translated by English exiles who had escaped at the time of the Protestant Queen Elizabeth. The New Testament had been done earlier (1582) in Rheims and was the very first Roman Catholic New Testament in English. The Old Testament came out in 1609–1610 in two volumes. This translation into English was made from the Latin Vulgate.

Roman Catholic Bible: Douai Version (1582 & 1609-1610)

The King James Version is, of course, the great classic of English Bibles. But it was not so much a new translation as a careful revision of existing translations, and "in many of the changes which they (the translators) introduced," said one, "their ear for rhythm and their fine knowledge of English completed in noble fashion the long toil of eighty-six years from 1525 (Tyndale) to 1611." Indeed, its beautiful cadences and magnificent language, coupled with the fact that many of its word patterns are a very part of modern speech, make it integral to the culture of our English-speaking world. It is no wonder it continues to outsell all other versions. Time tested, it carries a tremendous authority. It was five years in preparation and forty-seven men did the work. The final manuscript is now lost, but originally it was purchased by Robert Barker, the King's printer, for 3,500 English pounds, which included the copyright. The most famous printer's error in the English language may be "strain at a gnat" (Matt. 23:24); it

King James Version (1611)

should read "strain *out* a gnat," but the mistake has been preserved since 1611. (Incidentally, at least one scholar has suggested that "at" rather than "out" was the intended reading and no mistake at all; but this view is not given wide credence.)

Doing the version was the suggestion of John Reynolds, Puritan preacher and educator. King James, who was possessed of a curious fascination for Bible lore and theology, agreed to the idea at the Hampton Court Conference of 1604, although work was not begun till 1607. The King was too poor to help finance the translation. Six groups, including Anglicans and Puritans, were assigned to do the translation. The Old Testament was done by three groups, the New by two, and the Apocrypha by one. Two groups met at Oxford, two at Cambridge, and two at Westminister. The rules for translating included the following:

> 1. The Bishops' Bible was to be consulted first, only then the others. (Actually there were also other versions which influenced the Authorized. John Eadie said it has the "graceful vigor of the Genevan, the quiet grandeur of the Great Bible, the clearness of the Tyndale, the harmonies of Coverdale, and the stately theological vocabulary of the Rheims."*)
>
> 2. The chapter divisions already fixed must be retained whenever possible.
>
> 3. Marginal notes were to be omitted. (The notes in the Geneva Bible had caused controversy.)
>
> 4. The companies were to meet to compare translations.
>
> 5. It was permissible, even suggested, to advise with Biblical linguists not on the official committee.
>
> 6. Words added to clarify were to be put in italics.

John Wesley's New Testament (1755)

There were a number of private Bible translations in the seventeenth and eighteenth centuries. One was done by the founder of Methodism, John Wesley. The *Explanatory Notes on the New Testament* (1755) included a rather conservative revision of the King James Version. In the first instance, Wesley did his revision "for plain, unlettered men who understand only their Mother Tongue." A good language scholar, Wesley did a meticulous study of the Greek Testament and in his translation made some 12,000 alterations. "I have never so much as in one place, altered it, for altering sake: But there, and only, where, first, the Sense was made better, stronger, clearer, or more consistent with the Context:

---

* *The English Bible* (London: Macmillan and Co., 1876), Vol. II, p. 226.

Secondly, Where the Sense being equally good, the Phrase was better or nearer the Original. . . ." He divided his text into paragraphs because he believed this made the Scriptures more intelligible to the reader. Wesley was ahead of his time in this, and in a number of his alterations he anticipated the Revised Standard Version.

Modern Translations Into English

The first four translations listed below are "official" in the sense that they were approved by inter-church groups. These translations follow in the succession of scholarly renderings in the line of the King James Version.

On June 22, 1870, work was begun in England on *The Revised Version,* a revision of the King James. It was not the aim of the translators to make the language conform to modern usage; they even left the King James archaisms where "no misunderstanding" of the text would result. It was, moreover, a quite literal translation. The New Testament was published May 17, 1881. May 19, 1885 saw both Testaments published together. Unlike the King James, the Revised Version included paragraph divisions. American scholars had been invited to make suggestions. However, their ideas were not taken too seriously, though some were either incorporated or put in an appendix.

Revised Version (1881 & 1885)

The American scholars promised not to publish a new revision of the Bible for fourteen years (from the time of the Revised Version). Thus, in 1901 *The American Standard Version* was published. The term "Jehovah" was used in place of "Lord" and "God," paragraph divisions were indicated, general content headings were put at the top of pages, and marginal notes were improved. The Lochman Foundation has brought out a new edition of the *American Standard Version* called *The New American Standard Bible*. The Foundation scholars have gone to enormous effort to improve this version, with the aims of preserving its essential character for a new generation and making available an accurate translation from the original.

American Standard Version (1901)

In February of 1946 the New Testament Revised Standard Version was published. It made an impact on the Christian world from the first. Some disliked it, but most American Christians, together with English-speaking people in other parts of the world, found it readable and easy to understand. The Old Testament was published in 1952. The aim was to allow the best Greek text to say what it really meant, and to say it in plain, up-to-date English. Most scholars agree that this aim was accomplished. But

Revised Standard Version (1946 & 1952)

this was a *revision* of the 1611, 1881, and 1901 versions. Men competent in Biblical scholarship, English language, and public worship, from twenty seminaries and universities were headed by Luther A. Weigle, chairman of this committee of translators. James Moffatt, until his death in 1944, was executive secretary of the committee. Some of the characteristics of this translation are as follows: quotation marks are used to indicate direct speech; poetical passages are put in a format to indicate them as such; and important variant readings are indicated in footnotes at the bottom of the pages.

New English Bible (1961)   Produced by an interdenominational team of British scholars, with C. H. Dodd as director of the translation committee, the New Testament portion of the *New English Bible* appeared in 1961, appropriately enough at the three hundred fiftieth anniversary of the King James Version (1611). It had been eighty years since a new official New Testament had been done in England. The aim was somewhat different from that of the Revised Standard Version; namely, to make a *new* translation (not a *revision*) from the original Greek text. The translation is not intended to be literal or slavish. (Greek cannot really be put into a word-for-word translation anyway.) This is definitely a thought-for-thought translation. Consequently, it is a much freer rendering than any official British or American translation to date. It has the added advantage of having had experts in English style work over the translation of the theological scholars to insure the best English usage possible at this time.

Young's Translation (1862)   Robert Young, in the year 1862, published the *Literal Translation of the Bible*. Young was better known for his *Analytical Concordance to the Bible*. He was something of a master of Eastern languages, though he made his living as a book seller in Edinburgh. Young attempted a word-for-word rendering of the original Greek and Hebrew and it has been called, "probably the most literal translation ever made." The Old Testament translation reflects his own highly individualistic views of Hebrew tenses.

Bible Union Version (1864, Improved Edition 1913)   The American Baptist Publication Society, in 1913, produced an "Improved Edition" of an 1864 translation, the *Bible Union Version*. This is a unique translation because wherever the word "baptize" occurs the term "immerse" follows in parentheses.

Rotherham's "Emphasized" Version (1872 and 1897-1902)   Joseph Bryant Rotherham, a man acquainted with the Greek and the Hebrew, produced what he called *The Emphasized Bible*. The New Testament first appeared in 1872 and the Old Testament between the years of 1897 and 1902. He furnished his text with signs to communicate shades of emphasis in the original. In addition, Rotherham devised an elaborate system of underlining, including double and triple underlining, pausing, etc., to indicate appropriate vocal inflections for reading aloud. Thus the title, *The Emphasized Bible*. Recently Zondervan Publishing Company (Grand Rapids, Michigan) reissued it.

Twentieth Century New Testament (1898-1901, 1904)

The Twentieth Century New Testament is still enjoying rather wide circulation. A "Tentative Edition" was published in three parts between 1898 and 1901 in London. Thirty-five anonymous translators, mostly non-professional, did the work. Recently some of the names were revealed by Dr. Kenneth Clark of Duke University; it was a most remarkable group. Two women were included, Mrs. Mary Kingsland Higgs, wife of a Congregational minister, and Mrs. Sarah Butterworth Mee, also a minister's wife and the mother of six. The latter knew no Greek (one other of the group knew no Greek). W. T. Stead, editor of *Review of Reviews,* and Ernest Malan, an engineer, were very active in the project. Both ministers and laymen made up the rest of the thirty-five, but did not do their work in connection with a University or an official Church body—they undertook the project purely on their own initiative and out of a sense of desperate need to make the Bible intelligible to ordinary men and women. As such, their work proved of immense importance and a forerunner in the movement of twentieth century "modern-language" translations. It took fourteen years to complete the project. It was revised in 1904. Time, space, money, and official titles were all given in nearest English equivalents; modern paragraphing and quotation marks were used. There was an attempt in this work to put the New Testament books in chronological order of writing (e.g., Mark precedes Matthew); however, in the most recent edition (1961) by Moody Press, the books are put back in traditional order and there are slight modifications in the text.

Way (1901 and 1906)

Arthur S. Way, well-known translator of the classics (Virgil, Homer, etc.), produced in 1901, *The Letters of St. Paul to Seven Churches and Three Friends* (London). In the second edition (1906) the book of Hebrews was included. He also translated the Psalms. His aim was clarity through careful expansion and translation, and the idiom is plain and modern.

Weymouth Translation (1903)

Richard F. Weymouth was a layman who, in 1903, produced *The New Testament in Modern Speech*. Ernest Hampden-Cook assisted in editing the work which is well known for its literary quality and carefully shaded translations of Greek verbs. Up-to-date paragraphing, the notes and section titles also help account for its wide usefulness. The first American edition was a revision by J. A. Robertson and it was published by The Pilgrim Press (now by Harper and Row).

Moffatt's Translation (1913 and 1924)	In 1901 James Moffatt published at Edinburgh *The Historical New Testament*. But his really famous translation is the quite different, *The New Testament: A New Translation* (Edinburgh, 1913). The Old Testament came out in 1924. A one volume edition under the title, *A New Translation of the Bible* was issued in 1926. Both Testaments underwent final revision in the year 1935 (Harper). Moffatt rendered such terms as "Lord" and "Jehovah" by the expression "the eternal," except the title "Lord of hosts." This is a modern-speech translation, vigorous and fresh, and as one has said, Dr. Moffatt "often caught the deeper significance of a passage where the more literal translations failed."
Holy Scriptures according to the Massoretic Text (1917, 1963)	The Jewish Publication Society of America published in 1917, *The Holy Scriptures According to the Massoretic Text, A New Translation*. The Massoretic Text is the ancient and standard Hebrew text of the Old Testament. It was done by a committee of scholars headed by Max L. Margolis. Done by Jews for Jews, some older Bible words were retained, yet it has proved helpful to many modern-minded Jews. Currently a revision is being produced. The first of three volumes, the Pentateuch, was published in 1963; two volumes—the Prophets and the Writings— will be completed by 1975. Dr. Harry M. Orlinsky of Hebrew Union College—Jewish Institute of Religion, New York, was editor-in-chief of the new Pentateuch. The fresh translation is being brought out to bring the language and scholarship up to date.
The Shorter Bible (1918)	In *The Shorter Bible* a modern English translation of Bible history was given as a continuous, chronological whole. Section headings were supplied independent of Bible chapters. It was brought out in 1918 by Charles Foster Kent, assisted by C. C. Torrey, H. A. Sherman, F. Harris, and Ethel Cutler.
Riverside New Testament (1923)	*The Riverside New Testament* was issued in 1923 and revised in 1934. William G. Ballantine's goal was to provide a translation in contemporary English in an attractive form. Interesting features include the abandoning of verse divisions and an index of persons and subjects.
Goodspeed's New Testament (1923)	In 1923, Edgar J. Goodspeed, a University of Chicago professor of Greek, published *The New Testament, An American Translation*. His aim was a translation in the "American" idiom in contrast to Moffatt's "modern colloquial British English." Goodspeed avoided "thee," "thou," "hast," "makest," etc., even when Deity was addressed.
Centenary (Montgomery's) Translation (1924)	Helen B. Montgomery of Rochester, New York, published *The Centenary Translation of the New Testament* in 1924 (2 vols., Philadelphia). The translation marked the one hundredth

54

anniversary of the American Baptist Publication Society in distributing, translating and publishing Bibles. Mrs. Montgomery's aim was "a translation in the language of everyday life" so long as it did not "depart too much from translations already familiar and beloved." She added catchy captions (as J. B. Phillips did later), such as "Paul's Swan Song" and "A 'close-up' of Sin."

The Bible: An American Translation is a combination of Goodspeed's *New Testament* and Smith's *Old Testament*. John Merlin Powis Smith (died 1932) was a Baptist born in London and a professor of Bible in America. A year before his death, Smith's *Old Testament* (published first in 1927 with the help of three other men, T. J. Meek, Leroy Waterman, and A. R. Gordon) was put together with Goodspeed's. Smith's aim was to make a truly American translation "in the sense that the writings of Lincoln, Roosevelt and Wilson are American." Subject titles were included and terms like "thee" and "thou" were retained only in address to God. Though not slavishly literal, Smith's translation was not a paraphrase like Moffatt's.

T. J. Meek made a later revision of the Smith translation included in the University of Chicago Press Smith-Goodspeed volume, *The Complete Bible, An American Translation* (1939). In 1933, *The Short Bible, An American Translation*, was issued; nine books were omitted; for the other books brief introductions were provided.

In 1934, G. W. Wade produced *The Documents of the New Testament*. This was an independent translation of the New Testament arranged in what Wade believed to be their proper chronological order. He has expanded the translation (explanatory phrases are in italics), hoping to increase the clarity of the text.

The American, Charles B. Williams (not the Englishman Charles Kingsley Williams), did *The New Testament in the Language of the People* in 1937. He worked especially on the translation of Greek tenses, attempting to give just the right shade of meaning. Dr. Williams was a teacher of Greek in America, and his work has had fairly wide use in this country.

Jesus spoke in the Aramaic language, a dialect of Hebrew. Though we possess practically none of Jesus' words in the actual Aramaic, George Lamsa has attempted to reconstruct an Aramaic text not only of the Gospels, but the entire Bible. He translated the Syriac into Aramaic and in turn into English. *The New Testament According to the Eastern Text* came out in 1940, based on Lamsa's Aramaic text. The Gospels had previously been released in 1933. In 1957 he produced his version of the entire Bible, including both Old and New Testaments.

An American Translation (Smith-Goodspeed) (1931)

Wade's Translation (1934)

Charles B. Williams' New Testament (1937)

Lamsa's Translation (1940 and 1957)

Confraternity Edition (New Testament, 1941) (Old Testament, 1948)	The Confraternity Edition of the New Testament is a revision of the Douai (Roman Catholic) version in the light of the original Greek, and the New Testament appeared in 1941 (Paterson, New Jersey). Its twenty-seven translators, taking five years to complete their work, aimed at doing a work in current English. Paragraph divisions are included and poetry put in an appropriate format. Parts of the Old Testament, translated from the Hebrew, have now been published.
The Bible in Basic English (1941 and 1949)	*The New Testament in Basic English* was issued in 1941 (Cambridge). The Old Testament counterpart came out in 1949. The aim was to do a translation using only the basic English vocabulary. Samuel Henry Hooke, a British Old Testament scholar (University of London), headed a committee of translators and worked with a psychologist, Charles Kay Ogden. They found 850 words in the basic English vocabulary to which were added fifty special Bible words and one hundred other words helpful in understanding poetry. The attempt was to limit the translation to these basic words. Occasionally shades of meaning were lost because of the limited vocabulary.
Wand's New Testament Letters (1943)	*The New Testament Letters,* which first appeared in Australia (1943), later in England with a few corrections (1946), is "a free translation or close paraphrase" by J. W. C. Wand. The aim was to expand the epistles for purposes of increased clarity, especially the more complex passages. The colloquial language is well chosen, and he has produced what has been called "an argument that is astonishingly faithful to the original." He deliberately cast his translation in the style a modern bishop would use in writing a letter to his people.
Knox's Translation (1944 and 1948-1950)	The late Monsignor Ronald A. Knox, a Roman Catholic scholar in England, did *The New Testament of our Lord and Savior Jesus Christ* in 1944 (London), basically a translation from the Latin Vulgate. It has been widely used by both Protestants and Catholics. His Old Testament, including the Apocrypha, was issued in two volumes in 1948–50. He used modern paragraphing but retained traditional "thee" and "thou" forms. He hoped to do a translation in "a sort of timeless English" and yet "have something of an old-fashioned flavour about it."
Berkeley Version (1945 & 1959)	In 1959 the Berkeley Old Testament came off the press (bound up with it was the New Testament). The Old Testament was the work of some twenty scholars and was stimulated by Dr. Garrit Verkuyl, Editor-in-chief, an immigrant (as a youth) to this country from Holland. He published the New Testament in 1945 (Berkeley, California). Included are footnotes, explanation of weights, measures, and monetary values in American terms. His

56

aim was an accurate translation in the language in which modern man works and thinks.

In the year 1950 the Jehovah's Witnesses publication society, known as the Watchtower Bible and Tract Society, published the *New World Translation of the Christian Greek Scriptures*. In 1953 the Old Testament counterpart came out under the title, *New World Translation of the Hebrew Scriptures*. As would be expected, this translation reflects the theological bias of the Jehovah's Witnesses group. A famous example is John 1:1, "the word was a god." The word "Jehovah" is employed in some 237 passages in the New Testament. More than one authority has criticized the too familiar phraseology of the expression "Excuse me, Jehovah." **New World (1950 & 1953)**

Based upon a basic vocabulary of about 1,500 common words, Charles Kingsley Williams (not to be confused with Charles B. Williams) produced *The New Testament, A New Translation in Plain English* (London, 1952). Williams did not limit himself entirely to the 1,500 words. He used upwards of 200 additional words. This work is obviously similar in purpose to the "basic English" Bible. **Charles Kingsley Williams' New Testament in Plain English (1952)**

In 1952, E. V. Rieu's *The Four Gospels* was published in the Penguin Series (paperbacks). Previously Rieu had translated several of the classics (a good qualification, according to F. F. Bruce, for translating Biblical Greek), but now he attempted a portion of the New Testament. The simplicity of the work, together with his extensive introduction and notes, help provide a valuable translation. Dr. Rieu's son, C. H. Rieu, brought out a translation of *The Acts of the Apostles* in 1957. **Rieu's Gospels (1952)**

Kenneth Wuest has brought out an expanded version of the New Testament in three volumes: *The Gospels* (1956), *Acts through Ephesians* (1958), and *Philippians through Revelation* (1960). This expanded translation, with the aim of revealing the various shades of meaning in the Greek text, could be compared with the Amplified version, and both are designed to aid the student who does not know Greek. **Kenneth S. Wuest (1956, 1958, 1960)**

The Authentic New Testament was published in 1956 and is a translation by the Jew, Hugh J. Schonfield. He omitted chapter and verse divisions and attempted to create for modern minds the Jewish atmosphere of the first century. His introduction, notes, section titles and index contribute to its usefulness. In England a paperback edition has been released by Panther (1962). **Authentic New Testament (1956)**

Twelve thousand hours of research were invested in the production of this work. The Lockman Foundation of California **Amplified (1958 & 1962)** helped finance the project. The research secretary was Frances E. Siewert. Piling up alternate renderings, including synonyms, was the method followed with the intended purpose of giving the full meaning of the Greek, since Greek words frequently cannot be translated by a single English word. It may be categorized as an *expanded* translation (compare Wuest above). The New Testament came out in 1958. Part II of the Old Testament (Job through Malachi) was released in 1962.

**Phillips'
Translation
(1958)**

J. B. Phillips has, perhaps more than most translators, pierced the sonic wall into the mind of modern man. *Letters to Young Churches* appeared first (1947). Originally, he had done this paraphrase of Paul's letters for the young people in his church who, he confessed, became very sleepy when he read the King James Version. C. S. Lewis said of Phillips' expanded paraphrase that it made the Word of God like a familiar picture just cleaned. In 1952 *The Gospels in Modern English* came out. Then followed his translation of Acts in 1955 called, *The Young Church in Action*. Finally in 1957 *The Book of Revelation* was published. These four volumes were bound together making the complete *New Testament in Modern English*, published by the Macmillan Company in 1958. Included in the one volume edition are a good index and maps.

**Norlie's Simplified
New Testament
(1961)**

Olaf M. Norlie has done the *Simplified New Testament* (Zondervan, 1961); included is a translation of Psalms by R. K. Harrison of Wycliffe College, Toronto. This translation represents an attempt to shorten sentences, use simpler words and remove the solemn style. Subject or paragraph headings are included. The title for one printing of this volume reads, *Children's Simplified New Testament;* actually it is for everyone.

**The Living New
Testament (1967)
and The Living
Bible (1971)**

Kenneth N. Taylor has done *The Living New Testament* (1967) and *The Living Bible* (1971). Published by Tyndale House, this version has sold in the millions in its various editions. Billy Graham comments that the style is in newspaper English and thus easy to be understood by contemporary man.

**Good News
for
Modern Man**

Today's English Version ("Good News for Modern Man"; New Testament only; published by American Bible Society, 1966). Inexpensively published for mass circulation, this version has attained considerable popularity. In attempting to present the New Testament in very simple form, the richness of Biblical thought has sometimes been lost, e.g., the use of "put right" instead of "justify." This version may help many to become Bible readers, but they should not depend exclusively on it, nor stop with it, but go on to other versions of the Bible.

Summary

The great number of translations of the Bible into English shows us the long pilgrimage of man in his endeavor to translate the eternal truth revealed centuries ago. They attempt to bring it into the vernacular of the man who has to read and think in today's world so far removed from the world of Eastern shepherds. Our individual preference and choice of translation or translations will be reflected in our homes and our teaching of youth. But, of course, the process of translation will continue. The reason is at least twofold: (1) Words change in meaning and new words are added to the vocabularies; (2) Discoveries from papyri and archaeology are giving us a better understanding of the meaning of Holy Scripture.

PART TWO

OUR BIBLE: BOOK BY BOOK

Abraham's Well at Beersheba.
Note the grooves caused by the ropes used for drawing water.

◄§ 4 ◊► BOOK BY BOOK THROUGH THE OLD TESTA- MENT ◊►

LAW: GENESIS THROUGH DEUTERONOMY

THE TERM "PENTATEUCH" (*PENTE* MEANS "five," *Pentateuch* "five scrolls") refers to the first five books of the Old Testament. These are also known as the "Torah" or "Law" because from ancient times the Jews have respected this five-volume work as their Law. Sometimes called the "Five Books of Moses," Moses himself is the dominant character and was the great legislator of the children of Israel over a forty-year period.

These books come to grips with the main lines of revelation to the Hebrews: In Genesis there is the revelation to Abraham, Isaac, Jacob, and Joseph (the Patriarchs or "fathers") against the backdrop of God's creativity and man's sin. In Exodus there is the double revelation of deliverance out of Egyptian slavery and the giving of the Law on Mt. Sinai. Leviticus makes clear the truth and necessity of holy living. In Numbers God guides His people in their onward march to the Promised Land. In Deuteronomy Moses summarized God's message in Law and history to that point, and the Ten Commandments are repeated (chapter 5). Throughout all of this God revealed Himself in actual historical acts; consequently it is no wonder that the Jews, more than any other ancient people, took history seriously. To repeat, in the historic event God revealed Himself to His people.

Until modern times all Christians and Jews believed that Moses was the author of most or all of the Pentateuch. Exodus 24:4; Deuteronomy 31:9, 24-26, for example, indicate his authorship of parts of the Pentateuch. Some later passages (e.g. Joshua 1:7, 8; I Kings 2:3; II Chronicles 34:14) seem to acknowledge Moses as author of the Law. Also, the New Testament appears to assume his authorship (e.g. Luke 24:27, 44; John 1:45; Acts 28:23). Nowhere does the Bible say Moses wrote *all* the Pentateuch. He did not, for example, write the account of his death at the end of Deuteronomy. But today some hold to the view that several or even many participated in the authorship and editing of the first five books of the Old Testament. This view has been challenged, especially in conservative circles. But what is clear is that there were written sources for the Pentateuch (e.g. "The Book of the Wars of the Lord," Numbers 21:14). Moses, an educated man who would appreciate the value of records, could have taken the genealogical and other records and coupled them with the materials revealed by God (e.g. the Creation) and woven them into a continuous story. Copyists and editors added materials and made revisions here and there and the books of the Law took their present shape about the time of Saul and David or a little later. That in brief is the current position on Mosaic authorship.

GENESIS

Authorship and Date

See above under "Pentateuch."

Destination

The people of Israel.

Key Verses

Genesis 12:1-3. "Now the Lord said to Abram, 'Go from your country and your kindred and your father's house to the land that I will show you. And I will make of you a great nation, and I will bless you and make your name great, so that you will be a blessing. I will bless those who bless you, and him who curses you I will curse; and by you all the families of the earth will bless themselves.'"

Purpose and Theme

Genesis is a Greek word meaning "origin" or "beginning." This is an appropriate title for the book that tells in religious language the origin of heaven and earth, man, sin, death, and the Jews.

The title of the book indicates the purpose of the book—to relate beginnings. The first eleven chapters present the beginning of universal history from Adam to Noah. Chapters twelve through fifty give the history of the Hebrew Patriarchs (fathers) from Abraham to Joseph.

The one God is the Creator of all (chapter 1). Man was His crowning act in creation; sin was man's great act of disobedience (chapters 2, 3). The characteristic of man's sin is that where there is pride there is resistance to authority–rebellion. That rebellion is basically against God and as such (for God is just) comes under divine judgment; thus, the flood event of chapters 6–9. But once punished, man persisted in his sin (chapter 11); this is the predicament of man, that though he is punished and though he knows better he nonetheless sins. But if man's character is to sin in spite of knowledge, God's character is to have mercy in spite of man's persistent disobedience. In theological language God's mercy is known as "grace," which is in one sense the real message of the Bible from Genesis to Revelation. Though Adam and Eve had sinned, though Cain had killed his brother Abel, though mankind had disobeyed God, He saved a remnant through Noah. In Abraham that remnant became the elect, the Israel of God, and is continued today in those truly identified with the Church. Through Abraham and the elect of Bible times, God was to provide the great deliverer Moses and the greater Deliverer Jesus. Joseph too is a type of deliverer: though treated cruelly by his brothers, he saved them from certain death due to famine when a ruler in Egypt.

Man sinned; God judged, redeemed and gave new life. These mighty acts are revealed in the creation, the flood, the lives of Abraham and the Jewish Fathers. The saving acts of God are the theme of Genesis as of the Bible as a whole.

Outline

ADAM TO NOAH: THE BEGINNING OF HISTORY (chapters 1–11)
Universal Creation (chapter 1)
Adam and Eve, the Fall (chapters 2–3)
Cain and Abel, the First Murder, Adam's Descendents
(chapters 4–5)
Noah, the Flood, the Covenant of the Rainbow
(chapters 6–9)
Nations Begun (chapter 10)
Languages Begun, Shem to Abraham (chapter 11)

ABRAHAM TO JOSEPH: THE HEBREW FATHERS (chapters 12–50)
Abraham (chapters 12–25)
Isaac and His Twin Sons Jacob and Esau (chapters 26–36)
Joseph (chapters 37–50)

EXODUS

Authorship and Date

See above under, "Pentateuch."

Destination

The people of Israel.

Key Verse

Exodus 3:8. "And I have come down to deliver them out of

65

Purpose and Theme

The Children of Israel were led out of Egypt by Moses.

the hand of the Egyptians, and to bring them up out of that land to a good and broad land, a land flowing with milk and honey . . ."

Our title "Exodus" comes from the Greek translation of the Old Testament (known as the Septuagint), and means "outgoing" or "departure." This is a fitting name for the book which tells the story of the departure of the Jews from Egypt through the Sinai desert as they make their way to the Promised Land, a story which is continued in the next two books of the Pentateuch.

Moses is the great figure around which the events of Exodus take place. He is seen at the outset of the book as a baby, grows up to be the leader of the Israelites as they take their exit from Egypt and wander in the wilderness, and it is to Moses that the Law is given. Of his greatness in history there can be no doubt. Nor can there be doubt about the greatness of the two central events of the book: (1) the deliverance from Egypt and (2) the giving of the Law. These two events have proved significant for

The Matson Photo Service, Los Angeles

Mt. Sinai (Horeb).

the entire Judeo-Christian history. In them God has revealed Himself; they constitute further examples of His saving acts. The Exodus meant deliverance and is celebrated to this day by the Jews in the Passover (see "Feasts and Festivals"); likewise the Law, focalized in the Ten Commandments, is the sum and substance of morality for the Jews. For Christians, too, the Exodus and the Law are essential: Christ on the Cross is the Passover Lamb, celebrated at the Lord's Supper and experienced in the deliverance from sin as the children of Israel were delivered from Egypt. The Ten Commandments form the basis of Western Christian law and when kept illustrate holiness.

The Nile River of Egypt.

Outline

It is a curiosity that there are forty chapters in the book of Exodus, the same number of chapters as there were years of wanderings. The forty chapters are divided into three parts—History, Law, Worship—as follows:

HISTORY: DELIVERANCE FROM EGYPT (chapters 1-18)
  Israel in Slavery in Egypt (chapter 1)
  Moses called as the Deliverer (chapter 2-4)
  Pharaoh, Moses, the Ten Plagues (Blood, frogs, lice, fleas, murrain, boils, hail, locusts, darkness, death), the Passover (chapters 5-12)
  The Journey Begins, the Crossing of the Red Sea (chapters 13-14)
  God's Provisions: Song, Sweet Water, Quail, Manna, Victory (over Amalek), Advice (from Moses' father-in-law, Jethro) (chapters 15-18)

LAW: GIVEN ON MT. SINAI (chapters 19-34)
  The Law Given to Moses, the Ten Commandments (chapters 19-31)

The Law Broken by the People, the Golden Calf, the
Broken Tablets (chapter 32)
The Law Restored, the Second Tablets (chapters 33–34)

WORSHIP: CENTERED IN THE TABERNACLE (chapters 35–40)
Offerings and Workmen for the Construction of the Taber-
nacle (chapter 35)
Construction and Furnishings of the Tabernacle
(chapters 36–39)
Dedication of the Tabernacle (chapter 40)

LEVITICUS

Authorship and Date

See above under "Pentateuch."

Destination

The children of Israel, Aaron and his descendants.

Key Verse

Leviticus 20:26. "You shall be holy to me; for I the Lord am
holy, and have separated you from the peoples, that you should
be mine."

Purpose and Theme

This book was written primarily to make clear to the Jewish
people what it means to live a holy life. Laws designed for
righteous living coupled with instructions to the priesthood are
outlined. The tribe of Levi was dedicated to the priesthood, thus
the term "Levitical priesthood." (The title "Leviticus" means "the
levitical [book].") The priests were responsible for public worship, and worship is obviously related to the holy life. The priesthood of the Old Testament looks forward to the Great High
Priest (Jesus Christ) in the New.

Because the aim of the book was to challenge the people to
holy living and holy worship in the presence of a holy God, such
words as "holy," "sanctify," "sanctuary," "hallow," are used well
over 100 times. The word "sanctify" means quite literally "to set
apart" for the purpose of God.

The sacrificial system with its offerings and oblations is referred to dozens of times. Atonement is emphasized, as is spiritual
cleanliness; indeed, *Atonement* and *Holiness* are key ideas for
understanding this book. Leviticus makes clear that the proper
way to come to God is through sacrifice (chapters 1–7), and this
emphasis looks forward to the shed blood of Jesus Christ on
Calvary. The holiness of God's people is underscored in chapters 11–27.

Outline

WAYS OF APPROACH TO GOD (chapters 1–10)
By Sacrifice: Offerings of Meal and Animals (chapters 1–7)

By Agents: the Priests (chapters 8–10)

WAYS OF HOLY LIVING BEFORE GOD (chapters 11–24)
   With Regard to Food (chapter 11)
   With Regard to Motherhood (chapter 12)
   With Regard to Leprosy (chapters 13–14)
   With Regard to Private Living (chapter 15)
   With Regard to Worship and the Day of Atonement
      (chapters 16–17)
   With Regard to Human Relationships, Lay and Priestly
      (chapters 18–22)
   With Regard to Seven Holy "Days" (or periods): Passover,
      Unleavened Bread, First Fruits, Wave Loaves, Trumpets,
      Day of Atonement, Tabernacles (see "Feasts and Festi-
      vals") (chapter 23)
   With Regard to Oil and Showbread (chapter 24)

WAYS OF ETHICAL EXPRESSION: LAWS AND VOWS
      (chapters 25–27)
   Sabbatical (seventh) and Jubilee Years, the Poor, Promises
      and Warnings (chapters 25–26)
   Vows to the Holy God (chapter 27)

NUMBERS

See above under "Pentateuch." **Authorship and Date**

The people and priesthood of Israel. **Destination**

Numbers 1:2–3; 14:19. "Take a census of all the congregation **Key Verses**
of the people of Israel, by families, by fathers' houses, according
to the number of names, every male, head by head; from twenty
years old and upward, all in Israel who are able to go forth to
war, you and Aaron shall number them, company by company."
   Numbers 14:19. "Pardon the iniquity of this people, I pray
thee, according to the greatness of thy steadfast love, and according
as thou hast forgiven this people from Egypt even until now."
   The purpose of this book is historical. The forty years of wan- **Purpose and**
derings in the desert are related. The census of some two genera- **Theme**
tions is indicated (the title "Numbers"—Greek *Arithmoi*—is
used because the generations of Jews during the wilderness wanderings are *numbered*). The term "wilderness" is used some forty-
five times in the book. God disciplined His people in the forty
years wilderness experience because they sinned by their unbelief
and disobedience. But the care and guidance of God is powerfully

69

revealed. Even though Israel revolted, God never broke His covenant; He guided them faithfully to Canaan, the land promised to Israel's fathers. Israel is unfaithful, God is faithful. But in all this His holiness is not obscured. The rulings for becoming clean before coming into God's presence, dramatize His holiness. His punishment of idolatrous Jews (chapter 25) further denotes His justice and holiness. The holy God is the faithful guiding God of the covenant.

Outline

THE CENSUS AT SINAI: PREPARATION FOR THE JOURNEY (chapters 1–9)

Organization: Counting of the People, Tribes Readied and Arranged (chapters 1–2)

Levites Instructed, Rituals, Offerings (chapters 3-8)

The Celebration of the First Anniversary of the Passover (chapter 9)

THE JOURNEY FROM SINAI TO KADESH-BARNEA (chapters 10-12)

The Outset of the Journey (chapter 10)

Complaints and God's Punishments (chapters 11-12)

THE WANDERINGS (chapters 13-20)

Spies Give Bad Report on "Promised Land" (chapter 13)

Israel Refuses to Enter Promised Land; God's Punishment; Forty Years Wilderness Experience (chapter 14)

Directives for Entering the "Promised Land" (chapter 15)

Key Events to Aaron's Death: Korah's Rebellion, Aaron's Rod Buds, Instructions to Levites, Return to Kadesh-Barnea, Moses' Sin, Aaron's Death (chapters 16-20)

THE JOURNEY FROM KADESH-BARNEA TO THE JORDAN (chapters 21-36)

Complaints, Sins but Ultimate Victory; Serpent of Brass, Balaam, Immorality (chapters 21-25)

New Census, Joshua Selected to Succeed Moses (chapters 26-27)

Offerings and Vows (chapters 28-30)

Israel's Victory Over the Midianites (chapter 31)

Tribal Organization and Geographical Location, Journeys Reviewed, Cities of Refuge (chapters 32-36)

DEUTERONOMY

Authorship and Date

See above under "Pentateuch."

Destination

The children of Israel.

Evening light on the Dead Sea and the Mountains of Moab, from the Shrine of Moses in the Wilderness of Judea.

Key Verses

Deuteronomy 10:12-13. "And now, Israel, what does the Lord your God require of you but to fear the Lord your God, to walk in all his ways, to love Him, to serve the Lord your God with all your heart and with all your soul, and to keep the commandments and statutes of the Lord, which I command you this day for your good?"

Purpose and Theme

The title "Deuteronomy" is Greek for "repetition of the Law." The Law, with interpretation and amplification, is given to the new generation about to cross over into Canaan. The admonition to keep the Law and to follow God is given repeatedly. Such words as "do" and "keep" are found literally dozens of times in the book of Deuteronomy. Moses underscores what happens to people when they disobey the Law (tragedy), and what happens when they keep the Law (the blessings of righteousness).

This is a very touching book because it is here we have the final messages of Moses to the children of Israel just before they crossed the river Jordan into the Promised Land. The final events of Moses' life and ministry are recorded. Deuteronomy falls naturally into two great parts: chapters 1-30, the final messages of Moses; and chapters 31–34, the closing events of Moses' life and ministry.

Outline

MOSES' FINAL MESSAGES (chapters 1-30)

Message No. I: From Horeb to the Plains of Moab, the Journeys in Retrospect (chapters 1-4)

Message No. II: The Ten Commandments Restated and Explained with the Additional, "You shall love the Lord your God with all your heart, and with all your soul, and with all your might" (6:5) (chapters 5-26)

Message No. III: A Message (in terms of blessings and curses, obedience and disobedience) to be dramatized, Half the People Standing on Mt. Ebal and Half on Mt. Gerizim Calling Back and Forth to Each Other (chapters 27-30)

MOSES' LIFE ENDS: FINAL EVENTS (chapters 31-34)

At 120 Years of Age, Moses is Ready to Die, and Admonishes Israel to "Be strong and of good courage" (vss. 6, 7, 23) (chapter 31)

A Farewell Song of Moses (chapter 32)

Moses' Blessing on Israel (chapter 33)

The Last Events of Moses' Life and His Death (chapter 34)

HISTORY: JOSHUA THROUGH ESTHER

THE PENTATEUCH is the first major division of the Old Testament. It contains history and Law but was named for the latter element by the Hebrews. The Jews looked upon the rest of the Old Testament as commentary on the Torah. The second major division is called the "Historical" section and is composed of the twelve books from Joshua through Esther. These books give us the history of Israel in Canaan under Joshua, the judges, and the kings, and tell of the return from captivity.

JOSHUA

Authorship and Date

Much of the material in Joshua suggests eyewitness accounts, and Joshua himself seems to have been one of the sources for the book (24:1-26). The "Book of Jasher" (10:13) is mentioned. There are hints of other sources (18:6, 9 and the lists of towns). The book as we now have it was not written by Joshua, for it records events which took place after his death (the conquests of Debir and Laish), and it records Joshua's death. The book itself is anonymous, and the date of its completion is unknown.

Destination

The children of Israel and posterity.

Moses looked out over the Promised Land, Joshua led Israel into it.

Joshua 1:2-3. "Moses my servant is dead; now therefore arise, go over this Jordan, you and all this people, into the land which I am giving to them, to the people of Israel. Every place that the sole of your foot will tread upon I have given to you, as I promised to Moses."

Key Verse

The purpose is an historical one, namely to record the conquest and division of the land of Canaan. It is thus no wonder that such words as "possess" and "possession" along with "inheritance" occur a number of times. The book shows very clearly how God's promises for the Promised Land were fulfilled. Warnings are also

Purpose and Theme

The Matson Photo Service, Los Angeles

Air view of the River Jordan's serpentine course. A general view looking northward.

given in terms of what happens when God's people fail to keep their part of a bargain. There is here clear witness to the Israelite God Who has the power to succeed in the fight for the building of His Kingdom, and to the fact that He invites men to share in that Kingdom by participating in the Covenant. Though the children of Israel sin, God is faithful to His covenant as He has been in the past; though they fail in complete obedience (17:13; 18:3), God does not fail them. Moreover, it was imperative that God show His chosen people the dangers of rubbing shoulders daily with the pagan Canaanites: this could jeopardize their faith in the one true and powerful God, and lower their moral standard. The book looks forward to the New Testament in the Rahab account (Hebrews 11:31), for example, and in the conquest of Canaan, symbol of the building of Christ's Kingdom.

Outline

THE ENTRANCE INTO THE PROMISED LAND (chapters 1-5)
>Preparation to Cross the Border into the Promised Land, Rahab Protects the Spies (chapters 1-2)
>The Jordan prepared for the Crossing, the Entrance into Canaan (chapters 3-5)

THE CONQUEST OF THE PROMISED LAND (chapters 6-12)
>The Central Area Campaign (chapters 6-8)
>>The Fall of Jericho (chapter 6)
>>Defeat at Ai because of Achan's Sin, followed by Victory and the Capture of Ai (chapters 7-8)
>The Southern Area Campaign (chapters 9-10)
>>The Crafty Strategy of Gideon (chapter 9)
>>The Defeat of the Amorites (chapter 10)
>The Northern Area Campaign, the Victory at Merom (chapter 11)
>Summary of Kings Defeated (chapter 12)

THE DIVIDING OF THE PROMISED LAND (chapters 13-22)
>Reuben, Gad, the Half-Tribe of Manasseh: East of the Jordan (chapter 13)
>Judah (in association with Caleb): South (chapters 14-15)
>Ephraim and the Other Half-Tribe of Manasseh: West of the Jordan (chapters 16-17)
>The Other Tribes (seven in number) Placed (chapters 18-20)
>Cities of the Levites Appointed (chapter 21)
>Return of Eastern Tribes, Building an Altar to Jehovah, (chapter 22)

JOSHUA'S FINAL MESSAGES AND DEATH (chapters 23-24)

Jewish tradition says that Samuel was the author of this book, but Christian scholars are agreed that no one knows for certain who wrote it. Perhaps Samuel or one of his associate prophets compiled it. There are sources for the book (written records left by the judges themselves, e.g.), but it was probably compiled near the beginning of the monarchy, perhaps during Saul's reign (1050/45?–1011/10).

Authorship and Date

Apparently for the Jewish people, also posterity.

Destination

Judges 2:16-17. "Then the Lord raised up judges, who saved them out of the power of those who plundered them. And yet they did not listen to their judges, for they played the harlot after other gods and bowed down to them; they soon turned aside from the way in which their fathers had walked, who had obeyed the commandments of the Lord and they did not do so."

Key Verses

The purpose is to handle the historical material from the death of Joshua to the time of Samuel. The people were now evil, now repentant, and this recurring cycle is impressively communicated. The book shows the confusion that exists when people follow their own whims instead of submitting themselves to responsible leadership. A keynote of the book is, "Every man did that which was right in his own eyes" (Judges 17:6, 21:25). The judges themselves were saviours or deliverers (3:9) of their people, as well as leaders who exercised justice. There were six major judges in the book of Judges, five minor ones, and one called Shamgar ben Anath is given but one verse (3:31). Empowered by God's Spirit (6:34), they were God's instruments. Note the tragic inevitability of man's sin when left to his own devices: "But whenever the judge died, they turned back and behaved worse than their fathers . . ." (2:19a).

Purpose and Theme

ISRAEL'S FAILURE AND THE CONSEQUENT INSTITUTION OF JUDGES (chapters 1-2)

Outline

ISRAEL'S TWELVE JUDGES (chapters 3-16)
 Othniel, Ehud, and Shamgar (chapter 3)
 Deborah, Her Song of Victory (chapters 4-5)
 Gideon (chapters 6-8)
 Wicked Abimelech (not a judge) Makes Himself a King (chapter 9)
 Tola and Jair (chapter 10)

Jephthah (chapter 11)
Ibzan, Elon, Abdon (chapter 12)
Samson (chapters 13-16)

APPENDIX: ISRAEL'S EVILS AND RESULTING CONFUSION
    (chapters 17-21)
Micah's Idolatry (chapters 17-18)
Crime at Gibeah, Punishment (chapters 19-21)

RUTH

Authorship and Date

Unknown. Ancient Jews believed Samuel to be the author, a view not held probable today. There is no clue in the book itself. The story, but not the writing, took place in "the days when the judges ruled" (1:1) and the references to David (4:17, 22) show the writing was after he had ascended the throne. Just when, and whether sooner or later, is unknown.

Destination

Israel and posterity.

Key Verses

Ruth 1:16-17; 4:5-6, 17. "But Ruth said, 'Entreat me not to leave you or to return from following you; for where you go I will go, and where you lodge, I will lodge; your people shall be my people, and your God my God. Where you die I will die, and there will I be buried. May the Lord do so to me and more also if even death parts me from you.'"

4:5-6 "Then Boaz said, 'The day you buy the field from the hand of Naomi, you are also buying Ruth the Moabitess, the widow of the dead in order to restore the name of the dead to his inheritance.' Then the next of kin said, 'I cannot redeem it for myself, lest I impair my own inheritance. Take my right of redemption yourself, for I cannot redeem it.'"

4:17 "And the women of the neighborhood gave him a name saying, 'A son has been born to Naomi.' They named him Obed; he was the father of Jesse, the father of David."

Purpose and Theme

A pastoral, Ruth traces the ancestry of King David to Ruth the Moabitess, thus indicating an historical purpose. But it is more; it seeks to show that genuine religion is not confined to people of any one race or nation. Moreover, the content of filial devotion is significant: "But Ruth said, 'Entreat me not to leave you or to return from following you; for where you go I will go, and where you lodge I will lodge; your people shall be my people, and your God my God; where you die I will die, and there will I be buried. May the Lord do so to me and more also if even death parts me from you.'" The Hebrew *rut* (Ruth) may be a contraction from *reut* meaning "female companion," which Ruth surely was to Naomi. This meaningful story about Ruth reveals that divine blessing is upon the one who serves God. This is one of two Bible books named for women, the other being Esther. It should be noted that Ruth was a Gentile and a forebear of David and Jesus, a fact which demonstrates the inclusion of Gentiles as well as Jews in the Messianic promise (Matthew 8:11). Boaz also looks forward to Christ in that he played the part of a kinsman redeemer (Leviticus 25:25, 47-49), and Jesus is our Kinsman-Redeemer. The Ruth story looks forward to Pentecost too: it was customary for Jews to read this harvest story at the Weeks or Wheat Harvest Feast, later known as the Feast of Pentecost (Acts 2).

RUTH'S DETERMINATION TO STAY WITH NAOMI, RUTH'S ARRIVAL
    IN BETHLEHEM (chapter 1)

RUTH'S FIELD LABOR AND BOAZ' KINDNESS (chapter 2)

NAOMI'S GUIDANCE AND RUTH'S APPEAL TO BOAZ (chapter 3)

RUTH AND BOAZ MARRY, RUTH'S SON, DAVID'S ANCESTRY
    (chapter 4)

I SAMUEL

Authorship and Date

Unknown. Oldest Jewish tradition accredited the book to Samuel, but his death is recorded in 25:1. On the basis of I Chronicles 29:29, it has been suggested that Samuel, Nathan, and Gad did the work. We do know that Samuel produced records in writing (I Samuel 10:25). I and II Samuel cover the period from about 1050–960 or 965 B.C. Just when the books of Samuel were completed is unknown.

Destination

Presumably the Jewish people and posterity.

Key Verses

I Samuel 8:19-20. "But the people refused to listen to the voice of Samuel; and they said, 'No! we will have a king over us, that we also may be like all the nations, and that our king may govern us and go out before us and fight our battles.'"

Purpose and Theme

I Samuel records Jewish history following the period of the Judges; in fact, it gives us information from the birth of Samuel to the death of Saul. Samuel was both a judge and a prophet, and he connects the period of the judges with the period of the monarchy.

I Samuel shows the origin of the monarchy (Kingdom); it

makes clear the criteria of a good king, and it cries out for righteous leadership.

Samuel was a man of deep piety, completely dedicated to God. In a sense he looked forward to Christ, for he was prophet (the first and the head of a school of prophets), priest (he followed Eli), and a kind of king (actually a judge, the last of the judges). Ancient Jews may have considered Samuel the greatest figure since Moses, and his distinguished position in history was secured by his national leadership and the fact that he anointed the first king of Israel (Saul), and the greatest king (David). Samuel's righteous leadership should be underscored: the people recognized him as God's prophet (3:20), he was a good priest at a time when priests were evil (2:12ff), and his death was nationally lamented (28:3). No doubt his mother Hannah had a great deal to do with his godly life, for she herself was a pious woman and dedicated him to the Lord. But when Samuel grew old, though he himself did not waver in righteous living, his two sons whom he appointed as judges in the district of Beersheba, were so dishonest that the elders of Israel protested and there followed a demand for a king. Samuel warned the people of what was involved in having a king, and he made clear that merely keeping pace with surrounding pagan nations was only a proud and sinful reason for having a king (8:9ff). Saul was made that first king, however, and what a pathetic, mentally disturbed figure he really was. He could not distinguish between the material and the spiritual, he was fickle and did not obey God. At the end of his life he confessed, "I have played the fool" and he committed suicide. (Contrast that with what another Saul—Saul of Tarsus—said: "I have fought a good fight.") Out of Saul's career should be brought to light his disobedience of God's command to exterminate the Amalekites (15:3), and Samuel's great words of censure that "obedience is better than sacrifice," that "right ritual is no substitute for a right heart."

(On David, see II Samuel.)

Outline

SAMUEL THE PROPHET AND JUDGE (chapters 1-7)
    Samuel's Birth (chapter 1)
    Hannah's Prayer Song, Eli's Sinful Sons (chapter 2)
    The Boy Samuel Receives a Call from God (chapter 3)
    Eli's Sons Punished, Eli's Death (chapter 4)
    The Ark of the Covenant in Philistine Hands, then Returned to Israel, Etc. (chapter 5-7)

SAUL THE KING (chapters 8-15)
    Israel's Desire for a King (chapter 8)

Saul Anointed King (chapters 9-10)
Saul Defeats Ammon (chapter 11)
Samuel's Retirement Address: ". . . Serve the Lord with all your heart" (chapter 12)
Saul's Disobedience Against God (chapters 13-15)

DAVID ENTERS THE PICTURE (chapters 16-31)
David Anointed to be Future King (chapter 16)
David and Goliath (chapter 17)
David and Jonathan (chapter 18)
David's Life Sought by Saul, Etc. (chapters 19-23)
David Spares Saul's Life (chapter 24)
Samuel's Death, Nabal (chapter 25)
David Spares Saul Again, Saul's Confession "I have played the fool" (chapter 26)
David Flees Saul (chapter 27)
Saul and the Witch of Endor (chapter 28)
David's Battles, Saul Defeated and Killed (chapters 29-31)

II SAMUEL

Authorship

Unknown. In the Hebrew Bible the books of I and II Samuel are one; thus the information about the authorship of I Samuel applies to II Samuel.

Date

See information above under I Samuel.

Destination

The Jewish people and posterity.

Key Verse

II Samuel 5:5. "At Hebron he reigned over Judah seven years and six months, and at Jerusalem he reigned over all Israel and Judah thirty-three years."

Purpose and Theme

The book covers nearly the entire period of David's reign (forty years according to I Kings 2:11). Thus the purpose is to record the history of the Jews from Saul's death to the beginning of Solomon's reign, and to demonstrate the power of the monarchy during this greatest period in Israel's history.

David did not always obey God, but he was a far more consistent leader of men than Saul. His youthful days as a shepherd built a strong body and taught him the wisdom learned in the out-of-doors from nature. He amazed everyone by killing Goliath (his sling probably carried a one pound stone and it is estimated that skilled marksmen could hurl such a stone at a speed of 100–150 miles per hour). In the protection of his sheep, he had learned methods of defense which gave him confidence against a giant.

His trust in the Lord gave him a victory. And he was to know greater victories later, military victories. His capture of Jerusalem was a high point in Jewish history, for that city was to be the great religious center of Israel. His keen religious sense is illustrated in his bringing the Ark to Jerusalem (6:1-23) and his desire to build a house for God (7:1-29). His artistic temperment, which expressed itself in music and poetry, endears him to aesthetic souls. The related capacity to feel deeply is expressed in his pathos over the deaths of Saul, Jonathan, and Absalom. But his sin with Bathsheba illustrates the tragic truth that even a very good and gifted man can yield to temptation. One must admire the courage of Nathan the prophet for exposing the sin to the sinner himself (11:1—12:14). Note, too, the tragic results and by-products of David's sin.

Outline

DAVID'S REIGN AT HEBRON OVER JUDAH FOR SEVEN AND ONE-HALF YEARS (chapters 1-4)

David's Song of Lament over Saul and Jonathan (chapter 1)

David Made King over Judah; Ishbosheth (ish-BO-sheth), Saul's Son, King over Israel (chapter 2)

David is Sought out by Abner to become King over all Israel, but Abner is Murdered (chapter 3)

Ishbosheth is Killed (chapter 4)

DAVID'S REIGN AT JERUSALEM OVER ALL ISRAEL FOR THIRTY-THREE YEARS (chapters 5-24)

David Captures Jerusalem (chapter 5)

The Ark is Brought to Jerusalem (chapter 6)

God's Promise to David (chapter 7)

David Extends the Borders of His Kingdom (chapter 8)

David is Kind to Mephibosheth (me-FIB-o-sheth), Jonathan's Son (chapter 9)

David Defeats the Ammonites and the Syrians (chapter 10)

David Sins Against Uriah, Nathan's Sharp Words "You are the man" (chapters 11-12)

The Absalom Events, Absalom's Temporary Defeat of David, Absalom's Death, David Mourns, "O my son Absalom, my son, my son Absalom!" (chapters 13-18)

David Mourns Absalom, Joab Kills Amasa (chapter 19)

Sheba's Rebellion Defeated (chapter 20)

Saul and Jonathan Re-buried (chapter 21)

David's Song of Thanksgiving and Deliverance (chapter 22)

David's Last Words, David's Mighty Men (chapter 23)

David Numbers Israel and Judah (chapter 24)

The Jerusalem Temple area as it looks today. The Large building with the dome is called the Dome of the Rock or sometimes the Mosque of Omar. Solomon built the first of Israel's Temples.

I KINGS

Unknown. Jewish tradition says Jeremiah wrote both I and II Kings. In modern times some scholars have held to this view, and it is interesting that II Kings 24:18—25:30 resembles closely Jeremiah 52. But there are enough problems in this view of authorship to make it improbable. Sources were used—examples: the "Book of the Deeds of Solomon" (I Kings 11:41), the "Book of the Chronicles of the Kings of Judah" (I Kings 14:29 and elsewhere), the "Book of the Chronicles of the Kings of Israel" (I Kings 14:19 and elsewhere). It is thought these were official documents, and other sources may have been employed too. There has emerged the view that a contemporary or near-contemporary of Jeremiah did the books of Kings in the first half of the sixth century B.C. (I and II Kings are one book in the Hebrew Bible; in the Septuagint Samuel and Kings are I, II, III, IV Books of the Kingdoms, and I, II, III, IV Books of the Kings in the Vulgate.)

Authorship and Date

The People of Israel and posterity.

Destination

I Kings 8:25. "Now therefore, O Lord, God of Israel, keep with thy servant David my father what thou hast promised him, saying, 'There shall never fail you a man before me to sit upon the throne of Israel, if only your sons take heed to their way, to walk before me, as you have walked before me.'"

Key Verse

The purpose of I Kings is to trace Israel's history from David's death to Ahab's death, and to show that most of the kings turned their backs upon God in spite of the Covenant. God's promise to David (II Samuel 7:12-16) is the basis for judging Judah's kings; indeed the kings in I and II Kings are compared with David himself who kept, for the most part, the Covenant, and King Jeroboam who did not keep the Covenant is also used for comparative purposes. Most kings were evil, like Jeroboam; a few were good, like David: Asa (I Kings 15), Jehoshaphat (I Kings 22), Hezekiah (II Kings 18-20), Josiah (II Kings 22-23). But even these good kings had, like David, their defects. David's parting words to Solomon make clear the way of a righteous rule (I Kings 2:1ff). Solomon's greatness and kingly reign, the division of the kingdoms into North ("Israel") and South ("Judah") through the reigns of Ahab in the North and Jehoshaphat in the South—all are told in I Kings. Elijah enters the picture (as Elisha does in II Kings) as a kind of bridge between the earlier era and the period of the prophets.

Outline

SOLOMON'S REIGN (chapters 1-11)
    King David's Last Days (1:1—2:11)
    Solomon's Reign Begun (2:12—46)
    Solomon's Prayer for Understanding (chapter 3)
    Solomon's Wise Judgment and Administration (chapter 4)
    The Building of the Temple (chapters 5-7)
        (The Temple was arranged like the Tabernacle.)
    The Dedication of the Temple, Solomon's Sermon and
        Prayer (chapter 8)
    God's Promise to Solomon (chapter 9)
    Solomon Visited by the Queen of Sheba (chapter 10)
    Solomon's Sins, His Punishment, and His Death (chapter 11)

HOSTILITY AND THE DIVIDED KINGDOM: REHOBOAM AND JEROBOAM
        TO AHAD (chapters 12-16:28)
    The Ten Tribes Revolt, the Kingdom Divided North and
        South, Rehoboam Reigns in the South, Jeroboam in the
        North (chapters 12-14)
    Abijah and Asa Reign Over Judah (15:1-24)
    Nadab Reigns Over Israel (15:25-32)
    Baasha Reigns Over Israel (15:33—16:7)
    Elah Reigns Over Israel (16:8-14)
    Zimri Reigns Over Israel (16:15-22)
    Omri Reigns Over Israel, Omri Establishes Capital
        at Samaria (16:23-28)

THE REIGN OF AHAB, ELIJAH THE PROPHET (16:29—22:53)
    Elijah Foretells Three Years' Drought but He is Fed at the
        Brook Cherith; He Raises the Widow's Son from the
        Dead (16:29—17:24)
    Contest: Elijah vs. Prophets of Baal and the Ensuing Rain
        (chapter 18)
    Elijah Encouraged, "a still small voice" (chapter 19)
    Ahab's Victory Over Ben-hadad, but Ahab's Sin (chapter 20)
    Ahab and Jezebel kill Naboth to Get His Vineyard (chapter
        21)
    Ahab Killed in Battle (chapter 22)

*The Brook Cherith
in the Wilderness of
Judea area.
St. George's Convent
in the side of
the cliff. Elijah
was fed at the
Brook Cherith
(1 Kings 17:2-6).*

The Matson Photo Service, Los Angeles

II KINGS

See above under I Kings.

Authorship
and Date

The Jews and posterity.

Destination

II Kings 17:19-20. "Judah also did not keep the commandments
of the Lord their God, but walked in the customs which Israel
had introduced. And the Lord rejected all the descendants of Israel,

Key Verses

83

Sunset over Mt. Carmel, on which there was a contest between Elijah and the prophets of Baal (I Kings 18).

The Matson Photo Service, Los Angeles

and afflicted them, and gave them into the hand of spoilers, until he had cast them out of his sight."

Purpose and Theme

The aim of II Kings is to record the history of the Jewish people from the deaths of Ahab and Jehoshaphat to the Babylonian Captivity and a few years beyond the Captivity. The story at the outset of II Kings commences about the ninth century B.C. and it carries on through and beyond the Captivity of 586 B.C. The great cry of the Old Testament—that those who obey God and His Covenant (Exodus 19:5; 24:3-8) have His blessing and those who disobey have His wrath—is clearly seen in II Kings, especially in chapters 17-23. This principle is dramatically and historically illustrated in the fall of Israel at the hands of Assyria (II Kings 17) and of Judah at the hands of Babylon (II Kings 25). Thus I and II Kings convey the same message, that man's rebellious act results in God's punishing act.

Outline

ELISHA THE PROPHET SUCCEEDS ELIJAH (chapters 1-12)
    Elijah's Last Days, His Translation to Heaven (chapters 1-2)
    Elisha Predicts Victory Over Moab (chapter 3)
    Elisha Performs Miracles: Widow's Oil, Son of the Shunammite Raised from the Dead, Naaman's Leprosy Cured, etc. (chapters 4-5)
    Ben-hadad Besieges Samaria (chapter 6)
    Syrian Army Flees (chapter 7)
    Hazael Becomes King of Syria (chapter 8)
    Jehu Made King of Israel, Kills Jezebel and Others (chapter 9)

84

Jehu Executes the Sons of Ahab and Wipes Out the Worship of Baal (chapter 10)

Athaliah Captures Judah's Throne for Six Years, then Joash Becomes King (chapter 11)

Joash Repairs the Temple (chapter 12)

FROM THE DEATH OF ELISHA TO THE CAPTIVITY OF THE NORTHERN KINGDOM (chapters 13-17)

Elisha's Death (chapter 13)

The Reign of Amaziah Over Judah, Joash and Jeroboam II Over Israel (chapter 14)

Uzziah (Azariah) Reigns Over Judah (52 years) Followed by Jotham; Zachariah, Shallum, Menahem, Pekahiah, Pekah Over Israel (chapter 15)

Ahaz Reigns Over Judah (chapter 16)

Assyria Carries Away Ten Northern Tribes into Captivity (chapter 17)

JUDAH'S HISTORY FROM HEZEKIAH TO THE CAPTIVITY OF THE SOUTHERN KINGDOM (chapters 18-25)

Hezekiah King of Judah, Hezekiah vs. Sennacherib, Sennacherib's Army Slain by Hand of the Lord (chapters 18-19)

Hezekiah's Sickness, Miraculous Cure, Hezekiah's Death (chapter 20)

Manasseh's Evil Reign (21:1-18)

Amon's Evil Reign (21:19-26)

Good King Josiah and His Reforms (22:1—23:30)

Jehoahaz' (Shallum) Reign (23:31-35)

Jehoiakim's (Eliakim) Reign (23:36—24:7)

Jehoiachin's (Jechoniah, Coniah) Reign, His Exile to Babylon (24:8-17)

King Zedekiah Carried Away Captive by Nebuchadnezzar, Final Destruction of Jerusalem (24:18—25:30)

I CHRONICLES

An old Jewish tradition said that Ezra was the author of I and II Chronicles. Ezra may have been the compiler of Chronicles which was done earlier than the books Ezra and Nehemiah. Samuel, Kings, registers, and records were used as sources. **Authorship**

About Ezra's time, possibly between 430 and 400 B.C. **Date**

To the Jews who had returned from the Captivity. **Destination**

85

| Key Verses | I Chronicles 28:9-10. "And you, Solomon my son, know the God of your father and serve him with a whole heart and with a willing mind; for the Lord searches all hearts, and understands every plan and thought. If you seek him, he will be found by you; but if you forsake him, he will cast you off forever. Take heed now, for the Lord has chosen you to build a house for the sanctuary; be strong and do it." |

| Purpose and Theme | In the Hebrew Bible, I and II Chronicles, like I and II Kings, are one book. The suitable title "Chronicles" comes from Jerome's Vulgate. Interestingly enough, Chronicles covers the same general period of history as Samuel and Kings (from the earliest Hebrew Kings through the Babylonian Captivity), but from a very different point of view. Kings sounds as if it were written by a prophet —note the long references to Elijah and Elisha—and Chronicles sounds as if it were written by a priest—thus the numerous references to the Temple. Priests, Levites—anything at all to do with worship—are mentioned in Chronicles. It is therefore normal that the writer of Chronicles should refer more to the Southern Kingdom, in which Jerusalem and the Temple were located, than to the Northern Kingdom. Chronicles therefore is a history of the Davidic line with special reference to Temple, priests, and worship. These Jews who returned from the Captivity, being under the influence of the pagan Persian monarchy, must be reminded of their real unity in the real God. There was now no other basis for national unity; Jews no longer had their own monarchy. The aim, then, is not merely historical, but deeply spiritual. The blessings of true religion are underscored, and the oneness of the people of the Covenant is said to be centered in God. |

Outline

IMPORTANT JEWISH GENEALOGIES (chapters 1-9)

Patriarchs: Adam to Jacob to Esau, also the Family of Esau (chapter 1)

Sons of Israel (Jacob), the Descendants of Judah and David to Zerubbabel and the Return from Captivity (chapters 2-3)

Further Genealogical Information on the Family of Judah, the Descendants of Simeon (chapter 4)

The Descendants of Reuben, Gad, and Manasseh (5:1-26)

The Descendants of the Families of Levi (5:27—6:81)

Descendants of Issachar, Benjamin, Naphtali, Half-Tribe of Manasseh, Ephraim, Asher (chapter 7)

More Genealogical Information about Benjamin's Descendants to the Time of Saul (chapter 8)

Citizens in Jerusalem after Return from Captivity (chapter 9)

SAUL'S LAST DAYS AND THE REIGN OF KING DAVID
(chapters 10-21)
David's Mighty Men (chapter 12)
    Saul's Last Days and His Death (chapter 10)
    David Crowned King (chapter 11)
    David's Mighty Men (chapter 12)
    David Brings the Ark from Kirjath-jearim to Jerusalem,
    Victory of the Philistines, Psalm of Thanksgiving
    (chapters 13-16)
    David Forbidden to Build the Temple (chapter 17)
    The Record of David's Authority and Victories (chapters
    18-21)

THE PREPARATIONS FOR THE BUILDING OF THE TEMPLE TO DAVID'S
DEATH AND SOLOMON'S ENTHRONEMENT (chapters 22-29)
    David's Preparation of the Materials for the Building of the
    Temple (chapter 22)
    David's Organization of the Levites, Priests, Temple Mu-
    sicians, and Temple Workers (chapters 23-26)
    David's Organization of Civil and Military Authorities
    (chapter 27)
    David's Final Words, Solomon Enthroned (chapters 28-29)

II CHRONICLES

See above under I Chronicles.

Authorship
and Date

Jewish people returned from Captivity.

Destination

II Chronicles 5:1; "Thus all the work that Solomon did for the
house of the Lord was finished and Solomon brought in the things
which David his father had dedicated and stored the silver, the
gold and all the vessels in the treasuries of the house of God."

Key Verses

36:14: "All the leading priests and the people likewise were
exceedingly unfaithful, following all the abominations of the nations; and they polluted the house of the Lord which he had
hallowed in Jerusalem."

I Chronicles tells of David's reign and his fond hope to build
the Temple; II Chronicles tells of Solomon's building of the
Temple, but also of the apostasy of the Jewish people and their
neglect of Temple worship.
(See also the discussion above under I Chronicles.)

Purpose and
Theme

SOLOMON'S REIGN (chapters 1-9)
    Solomon's Vision from God, His Wealth and Wisdom
    (chapter 1)

Outline

Solomon's Final Preparations for the Building of the Temple (chapter 2)

The Erection of the Temple (chapters 3-4)

The Dedication of the Temple (chapters 5-7)

Solomon's Activities; a Visit from the Queen of Sheba, Solomon's Death after a Forty-year Reign (chapters 8-9)

JUDAH'S HISTORY TO ITS FALL (chapters 10-36)

The Nation Divided Just after Rehoboam Begins His Reign, He Strengthens His Kingdom, He Dies after a Seventeen-year Reign (chapters 10-12)

King Abijah's Reign, His War Against Jeroboam (chapter 13)

Asa Begins His Reign Well, Reformation, His Failure and Death (chapters 14-16)

Jehoshaphat's Bad Alliance with Ahab, Jehoshaphat Rebuked, Judah Invaded under Jehoshaphat but Delivered (chapters 17-20)

The Wicked King Jehoram Reigns (chapter 21)

The Wicked King Ahaziah Reigns, Athaliah, Joash Becomes King, Temple Repaired, Josah Murdered (chapters 22-24)

King Amaziah's Reign and Wars with Edom and Israel (chapter 25)

The Reign of Uzziah (Azariah), His Transgression (chapter 26)

King Jotham's Good Reign, the People's Apostasy (chapter 27)

King Ahaz' Wicked Reign (chapter 28)

King Hezekiah's Good Reign, His Great Passover Observance, Reformation, Hezekiah Miraculously Delivered from the Assyrians (chapters 29-32)

King Manasseh's Wicked Reign, His Reformation, His Son Amon's Reign, Amon's Murder (chapter 33)

King Josiah's Good Reign, Reformation, Killed in Battle with Egypt's King (chapters 34-35)

Kings Jehoahaz, Jehoiakim, Jehoiachin, and Zedekiah are Wicked Rulers; the Babylonian Captivity of Judah (chapter 36)

EZRA

Authorship and Date

Unknown, but perhaps Ezra ("helper"), a priest and a scribe, was author or compiler. He used sources for events he did not witness himself. Ezra lived in the fifth century B.C.

Destination

The Jewish exiles returned and returning from Captivity.

Key Verse

Ezra 2:1. "Now these were the people of the province who came up out of the captivity of those exiles whom Nebuchadnezzar the king of Babylon had carried captive to Babylonia; they returned to Jerusalem and Judah, each to his own town."

Purpose and Theme

The story is told of the Jewish restoration from the Babylonian Captivity, including re-establishment in Jerusalem and Judah. In fact, Ezra gives us almost all the information we possess on the Jews from the Captivity of Babylon under Cyrus (539 B.C.) to Ezra's entrance into Jerusalem in 457 B.C. Note, too, the relationship of the last of II Chronicles and Ezra 1:1-4. The book is written from the religious point of view, the Jews being viewed as a kingdom of priests and as a holy nation to walk in the bright light of the Law. There are two quite distinct returns from the Babylonian Captivity: the one under Zerubbabel (chapters 1-6), the other years later under Ezra (chapters 7-10). God's overruling providence is seen in Cyrus letting the Jews rebuild their Temple (chapter 1); yet, they prefer the comforts of their homes in Babylon to the unsettled conditions of Judah (chapter 2). Though they started well (chapter 3), they allowed opposition to stop the rebuilding project (chapter 4). But once again, after some years, the project was taken up due to the revival that came because of the preaching of Haggai and Zechariah, and the Temple was finished in 516 B.C. (chapters 5-6). Ezra comes to Jerusalem, at the command of King Cyrus, to inspire and discipline the people according to Jewish Law (chapter 7). He brought with him more exiles (chapter 8), and struggled with the problems of relocation, especially mixed marriages between Jews and pagans (chapters 9-10).

Outline

THE FIRST RETURN FROM EXILE AND THE REBUILDING OF THE TEMPLE UNDER ZERUBBABEL (chapters 1-6)

Cyrus Releases Exiles to Rebuild the Temple, Yet Jews Prefer the Comforts of Babylon (chapters 1-2)

The Rebuilding of the Temple (chapters 3-6)

Altar Built, Temple Foundations Laid (chapter 3)

Samaritan Opposition: Delay of some years (chapter 4)
Haggai and Zechariah Inspire Return to Work (chapter 5)
The Temple Completed (chapter 6)

THE SECOND RETURN FROM EXILE UNDER EZRA (chapters 7-10)
Preparation and Return to Jerusalem Under Ezra (chapters 7-8)
Ezra Mourns and Prays Over the People Who are Living Unseparated from the World (mixed marriages), Ezra's Reforms (chapters 9-10)

NEHEMIAH

Authorship and Date

Perhaps Nehemiah ("Jehovah comforts"), a layman and the governor of Judah for about twelve years was author, though Ezra and Nehemiah were originally one book. This much can be said, that memoirs of Nehemiah, as well as other sources, were used by the compilers who completed his work perhaps in the fifth century B.C.

Destination

The Jews returned to Jerusalem from the Captivity.

Key Verse

Nehemiah 4:6. "So we built the wall; and all the wall was joined together to half its height. For the people had a mind to work."

Purpose and Theme

The book tells the beautiful story of Nehemiah's deep concern for the people of Jerusalem and for the city itself. This concern expressed itself in prayer for the rebuilding of the city walls—in spite of great opposition. Nehemiah as governor of Jerusalem, and Ezra as a priest in Jerusalem, instituted reforms among the people, also inspired revival. The message of the book is seen in the execution of a goal through prayer and tenacity (even firmness) in the face of frustration.

Outline

RESTORATION OF THE CITY WALLS OF JERUSALEM UNDER NEHEMIAH (chapters 1-7)
Nehemiah Hears of the Problems of His People in Jerusalem, Grieves, is Sent to Jerusalem (chapters 1-2)
The Walls Rebuilt, Despite Opposition and Greed (chapters 3-6)
Nehemiah Provides for Rule over Jerusalem (chapter 7)

REFORMATION AND REVIVAL UNDER EZRA AND NEHEMIAH (chapters 8-13)
Ezra Serves as Teacher of the Law (chapter 8)
Reformation and Revival (chapters 9-10)

Problems of Repopulation of Jerusalem Handled
   (chapter 11)
Dedication of the City Walls (chapter 12)
Nehemiah's Return to Jerusalem (apparently he left Jerusalem after chapter 12) (chapter 13)

ESTHER

Author

Unknown. Mordecai has been suggested. The author appears to have been a Persian (though quite Jewish in point of view), since the book reflects firsthand acquaintance with Persian life and habits.

Date

After the death of Ahasuerus (Xerxes I) (10:2) who died 465 B.C. The last half of the fifth century B.C. is the general date.

Destination

To the Jews dispersed in parts of Persia (cf. 9:20).

Key Verse

Esther 4:14. "For if you keep silence at such a time as this, relief and deliverance will rise for the Jews from another quarter, but you and your father's house will perish. And who knows whether you have not come to the kingdom for such a time as this?"

Purpose and Theme

The book tells the story of Divine deliverance of dispersed Jews at the time of the Persian King Ahasuerus (485–465 B.C.). They were destined to die because of the wicked prime minister Haman, but through Esther and Mordecai, they were spared. Mordecai became prime minister in Haman's place. Esther had risked her life to save her people.

The book serves the further purpose of making clear the origin of the Feast of Purim. It is interesting that though this is the only book in the Bible in which the name of God does not appear, the book shows very clearly the *hand* of God at work in the life of His people the Jews. This is the only Old Testament book not represented in the Dead Sea Scrolls finds.

Remains of the third city wall (Agrippa's wall) north of the present Jerusalem City Wall. The book of Nehemiah tells about the restoration of Jerusalem's walls.

The Matson Photo Service, Los Angeles

Outline   Esther Made Queen of Persia (chapters 1-2)

      The Queen Vashti is Dethroned by King Ahasuerus (chapter 1)

      The New Queen Esther is Seated on the Throne (chapter 2)

      Haman Attempts to Kill the Jews but Fails, Mordecai's Help (chapters 3-10)

      Haman seeks to Destroy the Jews (chapter 3)

      Mordecai Communicates to Esther, Esther Intercedes, A Banquet with the King (chapters 4-5)

      Mordecai Honored by the King, Haman Dishonored and Hanged (chapters 6-7)

      Mordecai Promoted to Haman's Position (chapter 8)

      Jews Delivered and Victorious Over Their Enemies, The Feast of Purim (chapter 9)

      Mordecai's Greatness (chapter 10)

POETRY: JOB THROUGH SONG OF SOLOMON

We come now to what are sometimes known as the Poetical Books; namely, Job, Psalms, Proverbs, Ecclesiastes, and Song of Solomon. These books are largely poetry, thus their collective title. Poetry is found in other books of the Bible (Lamentations, the prophets, etc.), but tradition assigns the five listed above to this category.

JOB

Authorship and Date

The book gives no very definite clues. Suggestions on date vary from Post-Exilic times (as late as third century B.C.) to Patriarchal times (sixteenth century B.C.). Some have placed it in the age of Solomon (tenth century B.C.).

Destination

Unstated, but certainly a magnificent story for posterity.

Key Verses

Job 1:21-22. "And he said, 'Naked I came from my mother's womb, and naked shall I return; the Lord gave and the Lord has taken away, blessed be the name of the Lord.'"

"In all this Job did not sin or charge God with wrong."

Purpose and Theme

The book of Job, largely a poem, grapples with the age-old problem of why the righteous suffer. Job himself is a righteous person, but suffers almost the gamut of misfortune, losing his health, family, and material possessions. His so-called "friends"— four of them—counsel him on the reasons for his suffering. Sin, hypocrisy, lying, pride, and general wickedness are suggested as causes. Jehovah Himself does not accuse Job of any wrongdoing as the cause of his suffering; rather He states that finite man cannot know or understand the ways of infinite God. The book concludes by observing that Job, even through his terrible affliction, enters into a new, richer, and deeper experience of God. The trial has been a testing, not a punishment.

THE PROLOGUE (chapters 1-2) **Outline**

> Job, a Godly Man, Suffers the Destruction of His Material Possessions and Family—All with Jehovah's Permission (chapter 1)

> Job's Health is Now Destroyed (probably by elephantiasis), Job Refuses to Curse God, His Three Friends Observe a Seven-Day Silence out of Respect for His Great Suffering (chapter 2)

JOB AND HIS THREE FRIENDS DISCUSS AND GRAPPLE WITH THE PROBLEM OF HIS SUFFERING (chapters 3-41)

First Discussion Cycle (chapters 3-14)

> Job Complains, Wishes He Had Never Been Born and that he Would Now Die (chapter 3)

> Eliphaz' First Speech: Job Suffers Because He Has Sinned and God is Punishing Him (chapters 4-5)

> Job's Reply to Eliphaz: Just Where is the Sin in My Life? (chapters 6-7)

> Bildad's First Speech: Job Suffers Because He is a Hypocrite (chapter 8)

> Job's Reply to Bildad: Job is Bewildered—How Can He Approach God with Effectiveness and Declare His Innocence? (chapters 9-10)

> Zophar's First Speech: Job's Pretence of Innocence Only Heaps Sin upon Sin and He Should be Suffering Even More than He is (chapter 11)

> Job's Reply to Zophar: Job's Friends are Really Giving Him No Comfort, He Cannot Understand His Suffering, Nonetheless He Places His Trust in God (chapters 12-14)

Second Discussion Cycle (chapters 15-21)

> Eliphaz' Second Speech: Reiterates that Job Suffers Because He is Unrighteous, he ought to Confess (chapter 15)

> Job's Reply to Eliphaz: His so-called Friends are no Comfort, They are "Miserable," He has the Feeling

that Both Man and God Have Deserted Him (chapters 16-17)

Bildad's Second Speech: Not only God but Nature Itself is Opposed to Wrongdoing, thus Job's Suffering—It is Inherent in the Nature of Things that the Wicked Suffer (chapter 18)

Job's Reply to Bildad: Though All Criticize—Even Make Sport of—Job, His Faith Rises to Cry "I know that my Redeemer liveth . . ." (chapter 19)

Zophar's Second Speech: Are You Accusing *God* of Wrongdoing You? The Wicked Come to a Terrible End (chapter 20)

Job's Reply to Zophar: Your "reasoning" is not Borne Out in Experience because Frequently the Wicked *Prosper* (chapter 21)

Third Discussion Cycle (chapters 22-41)

Eliphaz' Third Speech: Suffering Cannot be Due to Piety, then It Must be Due to Sin; Recommends Repentance (chapter 22)

Job's Reply to Eliphaz: Oh! Where Can I Find God? The Wicked Sometimes Escape Suffering! (chapters 23-24)

Bildad's Third Speech: No Matter What Experience Seems to Reveal, Job is Arrogant, He Must Have Sinned! (chapter 25)

Job's Reply to Bildad: He Holds Unyieldingly to His Original Statement that He Has not in fact Sinned (chapters 26-31)

Elihu, not Zophar, Speaks this Time (really a series of speeches): Suffering is Not Always the Result of Sin, God Chastens the Righteous Sometimes, God Does Not Always Explain His Ways (chapters 32-37)

Jehovah, Not Job, Replies this Time: Man is Finite and therefore Cannot Explain the Mysteries of the Infinite God and His Providence (chapters 38-41)

EPILOGUE: NEW RELIGIOUS EXPERIENCE AND RESULTANT BLESSING THROUGH SUFFERING (chapter 42)

Lessons from the Book of Job:

1. The purposes and causes of suffering are not always clear.
2. Suffering may be beneficial, it can strengthen character and enrich personality.
3. Finite man cannot understand fully the justice of God; justice will be completed and perfected in eternity.

4. The righteous who suffer may suffer misunderstanding, but not God's misunderstanding.
5. God provides sustaining grace for trying times—that quite literally.

PSALMS

Authorship and Date

Headings suggest the traditional view of authorship as follows:

> 73 Psalms accredited to David
> 12 Psalms to Asaph, a musician
> 11 Psalms to the Sons of Korah, Levites doing Temple service during David's time
> 2 Psalms to King Solomon
> 1 Psalm to Ethan, perhaps a musician under David
> 1 Psalm to Moses
> 1 Psalm to Heman
> 49 so-called Orphan Psalms (Psalms without indication of authorship)

The Greek (Septuagint) Version indicates Haggai and Zechariah as authors of five Psalms. The Psalms were written over a long period of time, from Moses to the Exile, but most were done about 1000 B.C. though time should be allowed for additions and revisions.

Destination

Written for Jewish worship experiences, they now serve, and have served, as the basis of private and public worship of Christians and Jews.

Key Verses

Psalm 1:1-2. "Blessed is the man who walks not in the counsel of the wicked, nor stands in the way of sinners, nor sits in the seat of scoffers; but his delight is in the law of the Lord, and on his law he meditates day and night."

Purpose and Theme

The Psalms was the hymnbook of the Temple. As such, it is a guide to prayer and praise (the Hebrew title, *Tehillim,* means "Songs of Praise"). The Psalms contain the moods, doubts, joys, and hopes universal to the human heart. There are Psalms of faith in adversity (e.g. 90, 91), of praise (Psalm 8, 113-118), godliness (1), penitence (51), and nature (19). There are also royal Psalms to be used at a coronation or royal affair (110, 21). The Messianic ones (e.g. 2, 8, 16, 22, 31, 40, 41, 45, 68, 102, 110, 118) are especially meaningful to Christians. Historical Psalms (78, 81, 105, 106) are especially meaningful to Hebrews, for they tell of God's faithfulness to His Covenant. National Psalms (129, 137) also have great meaning for Jews.

Some titles (superscriptions) refer to musical directions (Psalm 4); others have no known meaning (e.g. the term "maskil," Psalm 69). "Songs of ascents" (Psalms 120-134) may be pilgrim hymns sung on the "ascent" to Jerusalem and the Tem-

"Like the chaff which the wind drives away" (Psalm 1:4). Grain is still winowed today as in Bible times.

ple. The strange and repeated word "Selah" perhaps indicates the appropriate point for a musical interlude.

Outline

The Book of Psalms is much too long and of too great variety to attempt an outline as such. But it should be noted that the book is divided into five smaller books (perhaps to remind the reader of the five books of the Pentateuch) as follows:

BOOK   I: Psalms 1-41   BOOK IV: Psalms 90-106
BOOK   II: Psalms 42-72   BOOK   V: Psalms 107-150
BOOK III: Psalms 73-89

Psalm I is an introduction to the entire book of Psalms; each of the five sections concludes with a doxology, and Psalm 150 is the doxology to the whole book as well as to section five.

PROVERBS

Authorship

Ancient tradition says not one but several people wrote the Proverbs. In the text titles of Proverbs we read that Solomon (1:1, 10:1; 25:1), Agur (30:1), and Lemuel (31:1) wrote sections of the book. The titles also indicate that certain "wise-men" wrote other sections (22:17; 24:23). Probably some of these Proverbs emerged through oral tradition and were eventually copied down.

Date

Impossible to say. Solomon lived in the tenth century B.C.; some of the Proverbs were copied down or written in Hezekiah's time (25:1), and he lived in the eighth century B.C. The Proverbs grew up over a long period of Jewish history and its final form was fixed at an unknown date.

Destination

Apparently Solomon's son (Rehoboam presumably) (1:8; 2:1; etc.); to all Jewish children (4:1); to all Jewish people; indeed the Proverbs are most apropos to the whole human race.

Key Verses

Proverbs 3:5-6. "Trust in the Lord with all your heart, and do not rely on your own insight. In all your ways acknowledge him and he will make straight your paths."

The Proverbs is an intensely practical book. The nearest thing to it in the New Testament is the book of James. The proverbial form cuts deep into the thinking of man and elicits responses. Every area of human life is treated, and moral and ethical implications are drawn. Evil associates, immorality, intemperance, bickering, falsifying, shady business ethics, sloth, selfishness—all are handled with an incisiveness unmatched in the world's literature. Generosity, reverence for God, careful child rearing, the power of influence (both of men and of women), young manhood— these are the areas of positive instruction. All in all, the Book of Proverbs constitutes a genuinely helpful manual of everyday living. *Wisdom* (knowledge plus the ability to use it meaningfully) is exalted throughout and is a key word of the book. Note that in Proverbs wisdom begins with, and centers in, God.

Like the Book of Psalms, Proverbs is too big and heterogenous to permit a detailed outline. The following division of material is general only:

WISDOM VERSUS FOLLY (chapters 1-9)

MISCELLANEOUS PROVERBS OF SOLOMON (10:1—22:16)

MISCELLANEOUS PROVERBS DEALING WITH HUMAN RESPONSIBILITY, AND RULES FOR RIGHTEOUS LIVING (22:17—24:34)

MISCELLANEOUS PROVERBS OF SOLOMON (Copied by Hezekiah's Scribes—25:1) (chapters 25-29)

PROVERBS OF AGUR (chapter 30)

PROVERBS OF LEMUEL (31:1-9)

THE VIRTUOUS WOMAN: AN ACROSTIC (31:10-31)

ECCLESIASTES

Unknown. An old tradition says Solomon, but this is not well-grounded (the writer, e.g., uses past tense in 1:12).

Not clear from the text; possibly to young Jewish men (11:9; 12:12).

Ecclesiastes 2:11, 13; 12:13-14. "Then I considered all that my hands had done and the toil I had spent in doing it, and behold, all was vanity and a striving after wind, and there was nothing to be gained under the sun. Then I saw that wisdom excels folly as light excels darkness."

"The end of the matter; all has been heard. Fear God and keep his commandments; for this is the whole duty of man. For God will bring every deed into judgment, with every secret thing, whether good or evil."

The word "Ecclesiastes" means "preacher" or "assemblyman" (Hebrew *Qoheleth*) and is the title of his office. It is the preacher's aim to make clear that the things of this world are mere vanity, they are unrewarding in the depth dimension. Satisfaction of the human heart is achieved in terms of wisdom, not folly. The conclusion to the book indicates its Gospel thrust: ". . . Fear God, and keep his commandments; for this is the whole duty of man. For God will bring every deed into judgment, with every secret thing, whether good or evil" (12:13-14). There is no meaning in life and creation apart from God. In Him is meaning and satisfaction, apart from Him is meaninglessness and intense dissatisfaction. This is the considered conclusion of a man who has tried now this, now that—indeed everything—in an attempt to come to a sound philosophy of life and living.

Outline

THE PROLOGUE (1:1-11)

The Heading (1:1)

The Theme of the Book Introduced: the Vanity of all Worldly Things (1:2-11)

THE VANITY OF ALL WORLDLY THINGS (1:12—6:12)

The Vanity of Searching after Purely Human Wisdom (1:12-18)

The Vanity of Pleasures (2:1-11)

The Vanity of Human Wisdom and Riches (2:12-23)

The Vanity of Human Effort (2:24—3:15)

The Vanity of the Wicked and the Oppressors (3:16—4:6)

The Vanity of One Attempting a Task by Himself, Work is more easily done by Two People (4:7-12)

The Vanity of Folly and Riches as over Against Wisdom and Poverty (4:13-16)

The Vanity of Empty Words (5:1-7)

The Vanity of Riches (5:8—6:12)

OBSERVATIONS ON WISDOM AND FOLLY (7:1—12:8)

The Well-Ordered Life as over Against the Mass of Mankind Which is Sinful (chapter 7)

In Actuality the Wicked do not Fare Better than the Righteous—It Only Looks that Way (chapters 8-9)

The Excellence of Wisdom (chapters 10-11)

Remember God in Youth (12:1-8)

EPILOGUE: RESPECT GOD, KEEP HIS COMMANDMENTS (12:9-14)

There is an old tradition supporting the view that Solomon wrote this book (cf. 1:1) in the tenth century B.C.

Song of Solomon 8:6-7. "Set me as a seal upon your heart, as a seal upon your arm; for love is strong as death, jealousy is cruel as the grave. Its flashes are flashes of fire, a most vehement flame. Many waters cannot quench love, neither can floods drown it. If a man offered for love all the wealth of his house, it would be utterly scorned."

This ancient oriental song or poem communicates the sacredness and purity of human love. As such, the book describes the love and marriage of King Solomon ("the beloved") and a peasant girl ("the Shulamite"). Genuine love is true and noble, and this is expressed in a series of talks or speeches primarily by Solomon and the country girl. While the poem celebrates the beauties of human love, it also suggests the intensity of the love of God for His children. It is a parable of divine love which is the source of human love. The book may also be viewed as symbolic of the love of Christ for His Bride, the Church.

THE MEETING OF THE BRIDE AND BRIDEGROOM, THEIR DELIGHT IN ONE ANOTHER (1:1—3:5)

THE ESPOUSAL (3:6—4:16)

TEMPORARY SEPARATION, THE BRIDE LONGS FOR HER BRIDEGROOM (5:1—6:3)

LOVE TO ONE ANOTHER EXPRESSED (6:4—8:14)

PROPHECY (THE FOUR MAJOR PROPHETS): ISAIAH THROUGH DANIEL

THERE ARE four major prophets: Isaiah, Jeremiah, Ezekiel, and Daniel. Originally they were called "major" simply because of the size of their books. Traditionally the book of Lamentations has been coupled with the book of Jeremiah—it is thought Jeremiah wrote both—and thus there are five books to consider in this section, though only four prophets. The function of the prophet was twofold: (1) forthtelling and (2) foretelling. Forthtelling is crying out against the evils of the day, an act demanding courage and conviction. Foretelling, a rarer function of the prophet, is looking ahead into the future. Old Testament prophets did both forthtelling and foretelling.

ISAIAH

Authorship and Date

Isaiah, son of Amoz and resident of Jerusalem, was an eighth century prophet of remarkable insight, a religious genius, and a man who lived close to God. He made his home in Jerusalem and was in contact with civil rulers and authorities, to whom he preached as well as to the commoner. The Mishna says Isaiah was killed by Manasseh and the Apocryphal *Ascension of Isaiah* says he was "sawn asunder." Some commentators have suggested that Hebrews 11:37 is a reference to Isaiah's death. He lived in the eighth century B.C., and his ministry extended approximately from 740, when he was called and anointed for his work (chapter 6), to 700.

Destination

Especially to Jerusalem and Judah, though there are warnings to the Northern Kingdom and to surrounding Gentile nations (e.g., Babylon, Moab, Damascus).

Key Verses

Isaiah 7:14. "Therefore the Lord himself will give you a sign. Behold a young woman shall conceive and bear a son and shall call his name Immanuel."

61:1-3. "The Spirit of the Lord God is upon me, because the Lord has anointed me to bring good tidings to the afflicted; he has sent me to bind up the brokenhearted, to proclaim liberty to the captives, and the opening of the prison to those who are bound; to proclaim the year of the Lord's favor, and the day of vengeance of our God; to comfort all who mourn; to grant to those who mourn in Zion—to give them a garland instead of ashes, the oil of gladness instead of mourning, the mantle of praise instead of a faint spirit; that they may be called oaks of righteousness, the planting of the Lord, that he may be glorified."

Purpose and Theme

Isaiah writes with a passion of the righteousness of God and the necessity of faith (some have compared this book with Romans), the coming Messiah and the deliverance He will bring, the need for moral and religious reformation in Judah. As to the latter, Isaiah cries out against mere form in worship, morals, and politics; he declares that it is not enough to act as if one believed in holy behavior, rather one must *be* holy. Isaiah prophesied during the reigns of Kings Uzziah, Jotham, Hezekiah, Ahaz, and he speaks out fearlessly against evil and commends heartily righteous acts. Isaiah the "Evangelical Prophet," more than any other Old Testament writer, looks ahead to the coming Messiah (note especially 7:14 and chapter 53).

PROPHECIES ABOUT JUDAH AND JERUSALEM (chapters 1-12)
  The Moral Condition of Jerusalem and Judah (chapters 1-5)
    Sham and Sin, God's Indictment Against Judah (chapter 1)
    God's Judgments Against Sham and Sin, and Subsequent Blessing (chapters 2-4)
    The Parable of the Vineyard with Application (chapter 5)
  Hope for a Divine Deliverer (chapters 6-12)
    Isaiah's Vision and Commission: Deliverance Available (chapter 6)
    Isaiah's Message to Ahaz, but Rejection of Deliverer (7:1—8:8)
    Isaiah Encouraged: A Righteous Remnant Accepts Deliverer (8:9—9:7)
    Isaiah's Nation Near Disaster: The Deliverer Rescues Nation (9:8—10:34)
    Isaiah's Future Hope for Israel: The Reign of the Deliverer (chapters 11-12)

GOD'S VIEW OF INTERNATIONAL AFFAIRS (chapters 13-27)
  Babylon and Assyria Attempt to Conquer by War and Torture: The Righteous God will not Tolerate Such (13:1—14:27)
  Philistia Puts Faith in Weapons and Military Alliances, but in point of Fact GOD Controls History (14:28-32)
  Moab is Proud, but Pride Fosters Prejudice (chapters 15-16)
  Samaria (North Israel) Has Neglected Her Historic Spiritual Foundations (chapter 17)
  Ethiopia Needs to Learn that Confidence is to be had by an Adequate View of God (chapter 18)
  Egypt has a False Trust in Human Wisdom, but Egypt with Her "Wisdom" and Assyria with Her Might will One Day Worship with Israel at the Altar of Jehovah (thus the missionary thrust of this chapter) (chapter 19)
  Egypt and Ethiopia will Suffer Military Humiliation Which is a Lesson to Judah (chapter 20)
  Babylon's Imperialism (21:1-10)
  Short Oracles Concerning Dumah (perhaps a name for Edom), and Arabia (21:11-17)
  Judah not Grateful for Help (chapter 22)
  Tyre Suffers from Materialism (chapter 23)
  The Universe, its Judgment and Redemption (chapters 24-27)

GOD IS MAN'S ONLY HOPE (chapters 28-35)
  It is Folly for Judah to Put Her Trust in an Alliance with Egypt (chapters 28-29)

It is Folly to Rely on Egypt (chapters 30-31)

The Age of Justice, Jerusalem Women Warned, the Outpouring of the Spirit (chapter 32)

The Destruction of Assyria Told (chapter 33)

The Final Judgment and Redemption (chapters 34-35)

HISTORICAL INTERLUDE ON EVENTS IN HEZEKIAH'S REIGN (chapters 36-39)

The Assyrian Threat to Jerusalem (chapters 36-37)

Hezekiah's Illness, Healing, and Song of Gratitude (chapter 38)

Hezekiah's Foolish Pride (chapter 39)

ISRAEL'S FUTURE GLORY (chapters 40-66)

Comfort and Deliverance for the Captives (the Birth of Christ Announced) (chapters 40-48)

Comfort and Assurance for Israel (chapters 40-41)

The Lord's Servant (chapter 42)

The Lord Redeemer, Israel's Final Restoration (chapter 43)

God Versus Idolatry (chapter 44)

The Commission to Cyrus (chapter 45)

Babylon's Idols Versus God, the Destruction of Babylon (chapters 46-47)

The Folly of Israel's Unfaithfulness (chapter 48)

The Suffering and Ministering Servant (Christ Portrayed) (chapters 49-57)

"I am the Lord your Savior, and your Redeemer, the Mighty One of Jacob" (chapter 49)

Israel's Rejection of the Messiah, Yet His Faithfulness in spite of Suffering (chapter 50)

God Will Redeem and Restore Israel (chapters 51-52)

"With his stripes we are healed" (chapter 53)

The Joy of Redeemed Israel (chapter 54)

Free Offer of Mercy to Everyone (chapter 55)

A Call to Righteousness Versus Idolatry and Wickedness (chapters 56-57)

Final Conflict but Future Glory for God's People (chapters 58-66)

Mere Formalities Versus Genuine Repentance (chapter 58)

Confession of National Wickedness, Zion's Redeemer (chapter 59)

The Future Glory of Zion (chapter 60)

The Messiah Brings Good Tidings to the Afflicted
(chapter 61)
The Future Glory of Jerusalem (chapter 62)
God's Wrath against the Nations (chapter 63)
Prayer for Forgiveness (chapter 64)
"New heavens and a new earth" (chapter 65)
The Lord's Judgments and Zion's Future Hope
(chapter 66)

JEREMIAH

Jeremiah. He dictated the book to his secretary Baruch (36:1-8, **Authorship**
32). He prophesied from about 626–580 B.C. There is evidence of **and Date**
editing in the book of Jeremiah.

Judah and Jerusalem especially, but also to the nations round **Destination**
and about Judah (1:5).

Jeremiah 1:5. "Before I formed you in the womb I knew you, **Key Verse**
and before you were born, I consecrated you; I appointed you a
prophet to the nations."

Jeremiah's purpose, under God, was to warn Judah that her **Purpose and**
sins would result in chastisement from the North (the Babylo- **Theme**
nians), and that in the near future. His prophecy did in fact
come true and took expression in the Babylonian Captivity (Jerusalem fell in 586 B.C.). Jeremiah also cries out against the sins

of the surrounding nations. But
there is a brighter side to his
message: for example, his
prophecies of the coming Messiah (e.g., chapters 23, 31, 33).
Jeremiah 33:16 is a great Messianic promise: "In those days
Judah will be saved and Jerusalem will dwell securely. And
this is the name by which it
will be called: 'The Lord is our
righteousness.'"

Near the outset of Jeremiah's
ministry, the good King Josiah
instituted his famed reforms
(begun 621 B.C.), the Temple
being repaired and idol worship
outlawed. This cheered the peo-

*Jeremiah wrote
about the potter
and the clay
(Jeremiah 18,19).*

The Matson Photo Service,
Los Angeles

ple of earnest intent such as Jeremiah, but he knew that surface reform was not sufficient, that the very heart of the people must be altered. Repentance thus became one of his great cries. Idolatry must be replaced by revealed religion, God must be recognized as the Covenant God, God will judge Judah and Israel for sexual sins. This straightforward preaching fell on deaf ears; Judah was inflexible in her sinful ways. Exile and punishment came. But a day will come, said Jeremiah, when truth will prevail and the Covenant will be respected once more—this was to be the Messianic age.

Outline

JEREMIAH CALLED AND EMPOWERED (chapter 1)

JEREMIAH CONDEMNS JUDAH AND FORETELLS BABYLONIAN CAPTIVITY (chapters 2-29)
Judah's Apostasy (chapter 2)
Judah Worse than Israel (chapter 3)
Judah Threatened with Military Invasion (chapter 4)
Warning: "You have eyes to see but see not" (chapter 5)
Impending Punishment (chapters 6-9)
Idols shall be Done Away (chapter 10)
The Tragedy of the Broken Covenant (chapter 11)
Jeremiah's Complaint and God's Answer (chapter 12)
The Linen Girdle (chapter 13)
Judgment on Judah Inevitable (chapters 14-15)
Jeremiah to Remain Single (chapter 16)
Those are Blessed Who Trust in God, Sin of Breaking the Sabbath (chapter 17)
The Potter and the Clay, and the Potter's Earthen Flask (chapters 18-19)
Jeremiah Persecuted for His Prophecies (chapter 20)
Warnings to King Zedekiah, King Jehoiakim, and the Leaders of Israel (chapters 21-23)
The Two Baskets of Figs (chapter 24)
The Captivity Foretold and Jeremiah's Life Threatened (chapters 25-27)
The False Prophet Hananiah Rebuked (chapter 28)
Jeremiah's Letter to the Exiles (chapter 29)

JEREMIAH FORETELLS RESTORATION (chapters 30-33)
Return from Exile Promised (chapter 30)
Mourning to be Turned to Joy (chapter 31)
The New Covenant (chapter 32)
Restoration under the Messiah (chapter 33)

JEREMIAH FORETELLS JUDGMENT (chapters 34-44)

Zedekiah, the Rechabites, and Jehoiakim (chapters 34-36)
Jeremiah Suffers Imprisonment, Relieved, Delivered
  (chapters 37-39)
The Remnant Seeks Guidance, Refuses God's Guidance
  and Goes to Egypt Taking Jeremiah, Jeremiah Rebukes
  Idolatrous Jews in Egypt (chapters 40-44)

JEREMIAH'S PROPHECIES AGAINST THE NATIONS (chapters 45-51)
A Parenthetical Passage: Jeremiah and His Secretary Ba-
  ruch (chapter 45)
Against Egypt (chapter 46)
Against Philistia (chapter 47)
Against Moab (chapter 48)
Against Ammon, Edom, Damascus, Kedar, Elam (Persia)
  (chapter 49)
Against Babylon . . . Also the Restoration of the Jews
  (chapters 50-51)

JEREMIAH'S SUMMARY OF THE CAPTIVITY OF JUDAH (chapter 52)

LAMENTATIONS

From ancient times Jews and Christians ascribed the work to | **Authorship**
Jeremiah, who prophesied from about 625 to 580 B.C. | **and Date**

Judah and any nations or people who would profit from | **Destination**
Judah's mistake.

Lamentations 1:1. "How lonely sits the city that was full of | **Key Verse**
people. How like a widow has she become, she that was great
among the nations. She that was a princess among the cities,
has become a vassal."

A supplement to the book of Jeremiah, Lamentations is quite | **Purpose and**
literally a *lamenting* over Judah's sins and the subsequent destruc- | **Theme**
tion she suffered. Here is at once a sad cry for what has happened to God's people (their capture and the capture of Jerusalem
under Nebuchadrezzar, 586 B.C.) and an earnest appeal for repentance. In this setting, suffering is judgment upon sin. The
vanity of human effort is underscored in chapter four.

AFFLICTION, MISERY, SORROW OVER CAPTIVE ZION (chapter 1) | **Outline**
DESTRUCTION A JUDGMENT FROM GOD (chapter 2)
HOPE FOR DIVINE MERCY (chapter 3)
PRESENT DESTRUCTION CONTRASTED WITH PAST HAPPY STATE
  OF BEING (chapter 4)
PRAYER FOR MERCY (chapter 5)

EZEKIEL

Authorship and Date

Ezekiel the priest (1:3), a contemporary of Jeremiah, lived in the sixth century B.C. and appears to have prophesied from about 593–571 B.C.

Destination

To his fellow Jews in the Captivity and those still in Palestine, also to foreign nations.

Key Verses

Ezekiel 36:24-28. "For I will take you from the nations, and gather you from all the countries, and bring you into your own land. I will sprinkle clean water upon you, and you shall be clean from all your uncleannesses, and from all your idols I will cleanse you. A new heart I will give you, and a new spirit I will put within you, and I will take out of your flesh the heart of stone and give you a heart of flesh. And I will put my spirit within you, and cause you to walk in my statutes and be careful to observe my ordinances; You shall dwell in the land which I gave to your fathers, and you shall be my people, and I will be your God."

Purpose and Theme

Ezekiel's home was Jerusalem and he was of a priestly line. He was the son of one Buzi, and with the deportation of Jehoiachin Ezekiel himself was taken into exile to Babylon (1:1). Ezekiel had a wife and a home according to 24:16-18, and 24:1, 15-18 informs us that his wife died on the day the siege of Jerusalem began. Much of his prophecy is recorded in the first person. His call to prophesy, having come in the fourth month of the fifth year of the captivity (1:1-2), and the last date recorded in the book of Ezekiel being the first month of the twenty-seventh year (29:17), his ministry lasted at least twenty-two years. It is evident from 14:14, 20 and 28:3 that he knew the prophet Daniel.

Against this backdrop of acquaintance with people, events, and conditions, Ezekiel writes his strange prophecy. In figurative language he reveals to the Jewish people that their predicament is the product of their own sin; past and present rebellion is underscored. Man is indeed responsible for his acts. But God is ever faithful in spite of man's carelessness and thus He offers deliverance to the repentant. Ezekiel foretells the day when Israel will be reunited with her own king, and will worship the one true God in the reconstructed Temple. Judgments are pronounced upon foreign nations as well as Judah; these judgments have a twofold message: (1) doom on the wicked countries, (2) they will not prevent the redemption and restoration of God's chosen people. Such statements as "The soul that sinneth, it shall die," "Turn ye, turn ye, for why will ye die?" and the longer one in 36:25-27, are classic.

IMPENDING JUDGMENT UPON JUDAH AND JERUSALEM: PROPHECIES GIVEN BEFORE THE FALL OF JERUSALEM (chapters 1-24)

Introduction: Ezekiel's Initial Vision of God's Glory, His Call (1:1—3:21)

A Second Vision of God's Glory (3:22-27)

Symbolic Activities Dramatize the Destruction of Jerusalem (chapters 4-7)

Vision and Punishment of Jerusalem (chapters 8-11)

God "Gives Up" Jerusalem to False Teaching and False Prophets (chapters 12-14)

Punishment Inevitable and Necessary (chapters 15-17)

God's Just Dealings with the Individual (chapter 18)

Lamentation over the Princes of Israel (chapter 19)

Final Warnings before the Fall of Jerusalem (chapters 20-24)

JUDGMENT UPON FOREIGN NATIONS (chapters 25-32)

Against Ammon (25:1-7)

Against Moab (25:8-11)

Against Edom (25:12-14)

Against Philistia (25:15-17)

Against Tyre (26:1—28:19)

Against Sidon (28:20-26)

Against Egypt (29:1—32:32)

RESTORATION FORETOLD: PROPHECIES AFTER THE FALL OF JERUSALEM (chapters 33-48)

A New Covenant, God's Love for the Sinner (chapter 33)

God's Care of His Flock (chapter 34)

Devastation of Edom (chapter 35)

A Clean Heart and New Spirit for Israel (chapter 36)

Restoration of Israel Symbolized in the Vision of the Dry Bones (chapter 37)

The Prophecy Against Gog of the Land of Magog (chapters 38-39)

A Vision of Restored Israel Symbolized by Describing the New Temple to be Built (chapters 40-48)

DANIEL

Daniel, a contemporary of Nebuchadrezzar, Belshazzar, Darius, and Cyrus. According to both Jewish and Christian traditions, Daniel wrote the book in the sixth century B.C.

The Jews, but also partly for Babylonians.

| Key Verses | Daniel 7:13-14. "I saw in the night visions, and behold, with the clouds of heaven there came one like a son of man, and he came to the Ancient of Days and was presented before him. And to him was given dominion and glory and kingdom, that all peoples, nations and languages should serve him; his dominion is an everlasting dominion which shall not pass away, and his kingdom one that shall not be destroyed." |

| Purpose and Theme | God's sovereignty over the kingdoms of this world is the great overarching purpose or theme of Daniel. To be sure, pagan Babylon lords it over Israel momentarily, but only because God permits her to be the instrument of His punishment of the Jews. But pagan nations will lose their power someday, for God is the real and ultimate ruler of the world. Indeed secular power is limited now as evidenced in the supernatural power of God to free Daniel from the lions and the three Hebrew children from the fiery furnace. Even Nebuchadrezzar is forced to recognize the superiority of God's power to his own monarchical power. In the last days God will in fact bring about the Kingdom which will never be destroyed. (In this connection note 7:13 on the second coming of the "son of man" with "the clouds of heaven.") How relevant Daniel's message is for us in the twentieth century who fear the "kingdoms" of materialism, Communism, and general paganism! |

| Outline | THE GREAT STORIES OF DANIEL (chapters 1-6) |

THE GREAT STORIES OF DANIEL (chapters 1-6)

The King's Food and Drink Refused by Faithful Hebrew Young Men (chapter 1)

The Great Image in Nebuchadrezzar's Dream (chapter 2)

Shadrach, Meshach, Abednego Delivered from the Fiery Furnace (chapter 3)

Nebuchadrezzar's Dream about the Tree, Daniel's Interpretation of the Dream (chapter 4)

Belshazzar and the Handwriting on the Wall (chapter 5)

Daniel in the Den of the Lions (chapter 6)

THE GREAT PROPHECIES OF DANIEL (chapters 7-12)

Daniel's Dream about the Four Beasts (chapter 7)

Daniel's Dream about the Ram, He-goat, and Horn (chapter 8)

Daniel's Prayer and Its Answer (chapter 9)

Daniel has Another Dream (chapter 10)

Conflicts between Persia and Greece, and between the South and the North (chapter 11)

The End Time: Tribulation but Resurrection (chapter 12)

PROPHECY (THE MINOR PROPHETS): HOSEA THROUGH MALACHI

THERE ARE twelve Minor Prophets: Hosea, Joel, Amos, Obadiah, Jonah, Micah, Nahum, Habakkuk, Zephaniah, Haggai, Zechariah, Malachi. They are known as "minor," not because their message is any less important than that of the Major Prophets, but because their books are smaller in size. There is the same strong social and religious thrust in their writings as in the Major Prophets. In the Hebrew Bible they are put together into one book called "The Twelve."

HOSEA

Hosea ("salvation"), son of Beeri (1:1). An eighth century B.C. prophet, he was a contemporary of the great Isaiah, and of King Jeroboam II of Israel and Kings Uzziah, Jotham, Ahaz, and Hezekiah of Judah (1:1). He was also a contemporary of the prophets Amos and Micah (he was younger than Amos and older than Micah). Like Hosea, Amos prophesied in the North (Israel). Hosea prophesied between c. 786 and c. 725 and before the Assyrian captivity of the North (c. 722 or 721 B.C.). — **Authorship and Date**

The Northern Jewish Kingdom known as Israel, and sometimes called Ephraim. There are occasional warnings to Judah, the Southern Jewish Kingdom. — **Destination**

Hosea 3:1. "And the Lord said to me, 'Go again, love a woman who is beloved of a paramour and is an adulteress; even as the Lord loves the people of Israel though they turn to other gods and love cakes of raisins.'" — **Key Verse**

The story of Hosea's unfaithful wife Gomer is analogous to Israel's unfaithfulness to Jehovah. Idolatry is an expression of Israel's sin. One can see the awful tragedy of sin in this prophecy. But God will win Israel back to Himself, for though she is unfaithful, He is faithful. Sin, punishment, renewal through forgiveness and grace are the three great messages of the book of Hosea. The book constitutes a story and analogy of great power. — **Purpose and Theme**

HOSEA'S UNFAITHFUL WIFE LIKE ISRAEL'S UNFAITHFULNESS (chapters 1-3) — **Outline**
    The Unfaithful Wife (chapter 1)
    The Unfaithful Nation (chapter 2)
    The Analogy Summarized: Wife Returns, Israel Will Return (chapter 3)

ISRAEL'S UNFAITHFULNESS SPELLED OUT (chapters 4-13)
> God's Controversy with Israel (chapters 4-5)
> Steadfast Love is Better than Burnt Offerings (chapter 6)
> Woe to Israel! (chapter 7)
> "Sow the Wind and Reap the Whirlwind" (chapter 8)
> Punishment for Unfaithfulness (chapters 9-10)
> God's Heartfelt Cry of Love for Wayward Israel (chapter 11)
> The Guilt of Israel in the Light of Her Superior Opportunities (chapters 12-13)

THE FINAL PLEA: RETURN, O ISRAEL, RENEWAL IS IN GOD (chapter 14)

JOEL

Authorship and Date

Joel ("the Lord is God"), the son of one Pethuel (1:1). He is referred to only once in the whole Bible outside the book of Joel, namely in Acts 2:16 where his prophecy of the outpouring of the Holy Spirit is quoted. Little is known of the man himself, but it is thought he lived in Jerusalem. He lived perhaps in the ninth century, but there is no definite information on when he lived or when the book was written.

Destination

Judah (the Southern Kingdom).

Key Verses

Joel 2:28-29. "And it shall come to pass afterward, that I will pour out my spirit on all flesh; your sons and your daughters shall prophesy, your old men shall dream dreams, and your young men shall see visions. Even upon the menservants and maidservants in those days, I will pour out my spirit."

Purpose and Theme

The theme of the book of Joel is "The Day of the Lord." There will come a day of God when the enemies of Israel will be cast down and she will be blessed. People will turn to God, indeed the Spirit of God will be poured out upon "all flesh" (2:28). The plague of locusts (chapters 1 and 2) is analogous to coming judgment, but God will deliver Israel.'

Outline

THE LOCUST PLAGUE (1:1—2:27)
> Superscription (1:1)
> The Plague (1:2-20)
> The Day of the Lord is Coming, Deliverance (2:1-27)

THE OUTPOURING OF THE SPIRIT OF GOD (2:28-32)

JUDGMENT ON NATIONS, JUDAH DELIVERED (chapter 3)

Amos

Amos ("burden")—not to be confused with Isaiah's father Amoz (or Amotz)—lived in the town of Tekoa which was located five miles southeast of Bethlehem and about twelve miles south of Jerusalem. Amos was a sheepherder (1:1) and dresser of sycamore fruit trees (7:14). Sycamore fruit was something like figs (see "Plants") and is said to have been eaten only by poor people. Out of this ordinary and everyday work, God called him to be a prophet: ". . . The Lord took me from following the flock, and the Lord said to me, 'Go, prophesy to my people Israel' " (7:15). He prophesied in the North (Israel) for a short time during the reign of Jeroboam II (785-740 B.C.), and during the time of Uzziah (780-740 B.C.). Authorship and Date

To North Israel, also to Judah in which territory he lived. Destination

Amos 4:11-12. " 'I overthrew some of you, as when God overthrew Sodom and Gomorrah, and you were as a brand plucked out of the burning; yet you did not return to me,' " says the Lord. 'Therefore thus I will do to you, O, Israel; because I will do this to you, prepare to meet your God, O Israel!' " Key Verses

9:14. " 'I will restore the fortunes of my people Israel, and they shall rebuild the ruined cities and inhabit them; they shall plant vineyards and drink their wine, and they shall make gardens and eat their fruit.' "

God chose Amos to speak a forthright word to Israel. Israel was enjoying a period of prosperity, had forgotten her Covenant relationship with God—indeed had broken her Covenant in awful sinning—and was generally irreligious (5:12). To be sure, there was a lip service kind of worship, but the pattern of daily living made it perfectly clear that worship was quite unconnected with practice (5:21-24). Selfishness, greed, immorality, idolatry, oppression of the poor through extortion, bribery, and injustice (2:6-8)— all these sins and more were committed. Amos cried out for repentance (5:14-15) in the light of the coming doom, and though Assyria is not mentioned specifically, it is clear that the Exile is predicted. But Israel is not grieved, not ready to repent (6:6) and disaster is the inevitable consequence (9:1-8). Purpose and Theme

Thus one of Amos' purposes is to warn the people. But there is a second purpose, that is to tell of God's readiness to deliver. Chapter nine speaks of deliverance and in reality includes a promise of Messianic blessing. Ever the theme of the Old Testament prophets, they declare that though people are unfaithful to the Covenant, God remains faithful. Note the emphasis on justice throughout the book.

Outline   PROCLAMATION OF JUDGMENT AGAINST THE NATIONS (chapters 1-2)
Superscription (1:1)
Against Foreign Nations: Damascus, Philistia, Phoenicia (Tyre), Edom, Ammon, Moab (1:2—2:3)
Against the Chosen People: Judah and Israel (2:4-16)

JUDGMENT AGAINST ISRAEL (chapters 3-6)
Israel to be Punished (chapter 3)
Israel has not Profited from Past Punishments (chapter 4)
God Laments over Israel, Life Comes from seeking the Lord (chapter 5)
Woe to the Unjust (chapter 6)

FIVE VISIONS OF COMING JUDGMENT (7:1—9:10)
Vision of the Plague of Locusts (7:1-3)
Vision of Fire (7:4-6)
Vision of the Plumbline, Historical Materials (7:7-17)
Vision of the Basket of Summer Fruit (chapter 8)
Vision of the Destruction of the Temple (9:1-10)

PROMISE OF MESSIANIC BLESSING (9:11-15)

OBADIAH

Authorship and Date   Of Obadiah ("worshiper of Jehovah") nothing is known except that he was a prophet and the writer of the book which bears his name. Obadiah is the shortest book in the Old Testament. The period of writing is not known with certainty. Verses 11-14 sound like the destruction under Nebuchadrezzar at which time the Edomites were involved in the destruction (Psalm 137:7). It appears from verses 5-7 that the prophet described tragedy which befell Edom after the fall of Jerusalem. The book would then date at the time of the Exile or just after; that is, 586 and following.

Destination   Edom, a small nation located south of the Dead Sea. This is the nation descended from Esau. The entire prophecy is directed to this little country. However it should not be assumed that the book was actually sent there by the prophet. It was for the benefit of the Israelites (verses 17-21), especially the people of Jerusalem, even though in captivity.

Key Verse   Obadiah 15. "For the day of the Lord is near upon all the nations. As you have done, it shall be done to you, your deeds shall return on your own head."

Edom has cruelly treated Israel and this prophecy is to under-score the fact of punishment and the coming of the Day of the Lord. Other prophets who prophesied against Edom were Amos, Isaiah, Jeremiah, Ezekiel, Malachi. Pride was often pointed out as the root of her sin. But Edom is humbled. Edom suffers her just reward; Judah is delivered. Edom and the other nations will be destroyed, Judah established and enlarged by the power of the sovereign God. The relation of Israel (Jacob) and Edom (Esau) in salvation history as it relates to the Kingdom of God is made clear in this little prophecy.

Purpose and Theme

HEADING (1a)

Outline

EDOM'S PRIDE, UNBROTHERLINESS, AND MIGHT IS BROUGHT LOW (1b-15)
—The Sin of Esau against Jacob (10-14)

THE COMING DAY OF THE LORD: EDOM PUNISHED, ZION DE-LIVERED (15-21)

JONAH

Jonah ("a dove"), son of Amittai (1:1), from Gath-hepher in Galilee. The only Old Testament reference to Jonah, outside the book of Jonah itself, is in II Kings 14:25, which connects him with the time of King Jeroboam II (reigned 785-740 B.C.).

Authorship and Date

Not specifically indicated, but the missionary objective is the city of Nineveh, capital of Assyria.

Destination

Jonah 1:12. "He said to them, "Take me up and throw me into the sea; then the sea will quiet down for you; for I know it is because of me that this great tempest has come upon you."
3:5. "And the people of Nineveh believed God; they proclaimed a fast, and put on sackcloth, from the greatest of them to the least of them."

Key Verses

Jonah is the outstanding missionary book of the Old Testament. It demonstrates God's love for the Gentiles (4:11), a message always difficult for Jews to comprehend, and especially so these hundreds of years before Paul the missionary to the Gentiles. The character of this prophecy is entirely different from the other books of the Prophets; this gives a personal life story with emphasis upon God's dealings with the man Jonah. The lessons of the book are manifold: when God speaks, answer and follow Him in faith; God wants to show His mercy upon *all* peoples, Gentiles as well

Purpose and Theme

as Jews; that people—indeed a great city—can repent when God's appointed servants obey Him. It is of further significance that Jonah's stubbornness characterized the stubbornness of the Israelitish nation as a whole. . . . Also note that Jesus referred to the story of Jonah as a figure of his own death and resurrection (Matthew 12:40-41).

Outline

Jonah's Disobedience and its Results (chapter 1)

Jonah's Prayer in the Fish's Belly (chapter 2)

Jonah's Obedience and its Results in Deliverance of Thousands from Destruction (chapter 3)

Jonah's Further Chastisement for His Lack of Love for Souls (chapter 4)

MICAH

Authorship and Date

Micah. The name (but not the same person) appears in Judges 17:1, 4. His name means "who is like unto the Lord." He was from the town of Moresheth (near Gath), twenty miles southwest of Jerusalem. Micah is mentioned in Jeremiah 26:17-19 as prophesying during the time of Hezekiah, and Micah 1:1 indicates more specifically the period of his ministry during the reigns of Jotham, Ahaz, and Hezekiah (c. 738–698 B.C.). Micah may have been a younger contemporary of Isaiah who lived in the eighth century B.C.

Destination

Both the Southern and Northern Kingdoms, i.e., Israel and Judah.

Key Verses

Micah 4:3. "He shall judge between many peoples, and shall decide for strong nations afar off; and they shall beat their swords into plowshares, and their spears into pruning hooks; nation shall not lift up sword against nation, neither shall they learn war any more."

6:8. "He has showed you, O man, what is good; and what does the Lord require of you but to do justice, and to love kindness, and to walk humbly with your God?"

Purpose and Theme

To underscore the sins of the Jews in both Kingdoms, North and South, and the impending judgment which is the inevitable result of sin, but also to show the eventual restoration.

Chapters six and seven use the interesting analogy of a lawsuit, Jehovah being the plaintiff, Israel the defendant. Jehovah is angry with His people, who have forgotten their deliverance out of Egypt and the meaning of worship, but have remembered all too well sinful ways. At this word, Israel breaks down and prays for forgiveness and pleads for the return of the Lord in their midst.

Bethlehem, showing the older section. "But you, O Bethlehem Ephrathah, who are little to be among the clans of Judah, from you shall come forth for me one who is to be ruler in Israel, whose origin is from of old, from ancient days." (Micah 5:2, R.S.V.)

Micah concludes his prophecy with marked effect: he plays upon the meaning of his own name ("who is like unto the Lord?" 7:18). . . . He alone forgives and loves again. In a word, the theme of Micah is judgment because of sin, but future salvation because of God's grace.

Outline

AGAINST ISRAEL AND JUDAH (chapters 1-2)
> The Superscription (1:1)
> Samaria and Judah Objects of God's Wrath (1:2-16)
> Reasons for God's Wrath (chapter 2)

JUDGMENT BUT RESTORATION THROUGH GOD'S GRACE (chapters 3-5)
> Judgment, Jerusalem's Destruction (chapter 3)
> Restoration, the Establishment of God's Kingdom (4:1—5:1) (note: 4:1-3 is seen with some variation in Isaiah 2:2-4)
> Birth of the Messianic King and His Kingdom (5:2-15)

PUNISHMENT BUT GOD'S MERCY ASSURED (chapters 6-7)
> God's Complaint, Obedience is Required (chapter 6)
> Moral Corruption but God's Compassion (chapter 7)

NAHUM

**Authorship
and Date**

Nahum ("consolation," "full of comfort"), contemporary of Jeremiah, lived in Judah, probably in the town of Elkosh. It appears from 3:8 that the capture of No-amon (Thebes) in Egypt had already taken place; that capture by the Assyrians is dated at 661 B.C. Nahum was composed before the fall of Nineveh (612 B.C.) which he predicts; therefore, the book was done somewhere between 661 and 612 B.C., perhaps about 620.

Destination

Nineveh, capital of Assyria (1:1), but also to Judah (1:15) who needs to see the justice of God at this time in history when she suffers under the oppression of Assyria.

Key Verses

Nahum 1:1. "An oracle concerning Nineveh. The book of the vision of Nahum of Elkosh."

3:7. "And all who look on you will shrink from you and say, Wasted is Nineveh; who will bemoan her? whence shall I seek comforters for her?"

**Purpose and
Theme**

The downfall of Nineveh and the vindication of Judah is the prophet's subject. It is interesting that Jonah also was a prophet to Nineveh. Utter destruction is prophesied, reasons for God's judgment are given, and ultimate victory for His people by means of His sovereign saving acts is guaranteed. Assyria's oppression will not be permitted to hide God's justice. Judah had attempted to protect herself by alliances with other nations, thus having forgotten God's promises, but God Himself will deliver her on the political level . . . and the spiritual level too. God had not forgotten His promises. Nahum's twofold prophecy bore this out: Nineveh would fall, Judah be vindicated. The prophet used both poetic (chapter 1) and prophetic (chapters 2 and 3) forms to communicate his message. Assyria has ignored God, Judah has made alliances; Assyria will be destroyed, Judah will do well to see Assyria's fate as a warning.

Outline

GOD'S MAJESTY AND HIS JUDGMENT UPON SIN (chapter 1)

THE SIEGE OF NINEVEH (chapter 2)

THE REASONS FOR NINEVEH'S DOWNFALL: HER SIN UNDERSCORED
(chapter 3)

HABAKKUK

**Authorship
and Date**

Habakkuk, of whom nothing is known outside of what is indicated in the book itself. When he prophesied is uncertain; perhaps in the late seventh and/or early sixth century—that is, around 600 B.C.

Judah.

Habakkuk 2:4. "Behold he whose soul is not upright in him shall fail, but the righteous shall live by his faith." **Key Verse**

This is an interesting kind of prophecy, for it is not direct address at all but the relating of an experience of the prophet. He appears to have complained to God for His lack of concern about Judah's sin (1:2-4). The Lord's answer: He is in fact concerned and will punish Judah by the Chaldeans (1:5, 6). Habakkuk continues to complain, this time over what appears to be God's lack of concern over the Chaldeans' cruelty (1:13). The prophet retires to a quiet place to seek God's answer (2:1). God's answer this time: Babylon will be punished too. The righteousness of God is underscored, and the great declaration—"the just shall live by faith" (2:4)—is to show that the enemy cannot "live" but ultimately will be punished for his tyranny and idolatry (2:6-19), and that God's people ("the just") will be preserved in the time of trouble. Habakkuk now knows that righteousness will triumph and he lifts up a prayer for God to show Himself once more in a saving act comparable to what He did long ago. Habakkuk concludes his prophecy with a great statement of confidence in God (3:17-19). **Purpose and Theme**

HABUKKUK'S COMPLAINT: IT APPEARS THAT SIN GOES UN-PUNISHED (1:1-4) **Outline**

HABAKKUK RECEIVES AN ANSWER FROM GOD: JUDAH WILL BE PUNISHED BY THE CHALDEANS (1:5-11)

HABAKKUK'S FURTHER PROBLEM OR COMPLAINT: WILL THE WICKED CHALDEANS GO UNPUNISHED? (1:12—2:1)

HABAKKUK RECEIVES ANOTHER ANSWER: THE CHALDEANS WILL NOT ESCAPE PUNISHMENT (2:2-20)

HABAKKUK'S PRAYER (chapter 3)

ZEPHANIAH

Zephaniah ("he whom Jehovah has hidden"), who traces his ancestry back to Hezekiah (1:1) (probably the king of Judah). **Authorship and Date**

1:1 says "in the days of Josiah . . . king of Judah." Josiah reigned from about 640–609 B.C. It has been sugegsted that the prophetic messages were preached prior to Josiah's reforms, because Zephaniah pictures a totally transformed people.

Judah and Jerusalem (1:4), also to some pagan nations. **Destination**

Zephaniah 1:14. "The great day of the Lord is near, near and hastening fast; the sound of the day of the Lord is bitter, the mighty man cries aloud there."

Purpose and Theme

To warn Judah of the coming "day of the Lord," the day of reckoning or doom. Doom is inevitable if corruption and unrighteousness continue. Not even the fact that they are the chosen people will stay God's punishment for He is just. Assyria will be used as the instrument of God's punishment. This day of judgment will be "the Day of the Lord," for He will prove His justice. It is no wonder Zephaniah attempts to inspire fear and repentance, but he also assures that the righteous will be delivered. The righteous are the remnant, pure and good, who will praise God in song. Coming deliverance, as in the other prophets, is not left out.

Outline

"THE DAY OF THE LORD" (*Dies Irae*) OF GOD'S JUDGMENT UPON JUDAH (1:1—2:3)

AGAINST THE HEATHEN NATIONS (2:4-15)

JERUSALEM'S SIN BUT HER FUTURE SALVATION (chapter 3)

HAGGAI

Authorship and Date

Haggai ("my feast"). An old tradition says Haggai was a Levite and that he returned to Jerusalem from the Babylonian Captivity with Zerubbabel.

During the second year of the reign of King Darius of Persia (520 B.C.), two prophets preached and recorded the essence of their messages; namely, Haggai (Haggai 1:1) and Zechariah (Zechariah 1:1). The two prophets are mentioned together in Ezra 5:1 and 6:14.

Destination

The people of Jerusalem, Zerubbabel the governor of Judah, and Joshua the High Priest (1:1, 13-14; 2:2, 21).

Key Verse

Haggai 1:14. "And the Lord stirred up the spirit of Zerubbabel the son of Shealtiel, governor of Judah, and the spirit of Joshua the son of Jehozadak, the high priest, and the spirit of all the remnant of the people; and they came and worked on the house of the Lord of hosts their God."

Purpose and Theme

The completion of the Temple is the theme of Haggai. The year after the people had returned from the Exile, work on the Temple had begun; but now the people were discouraged. The prophet cries out against the prevalent idea that God's work is of secondary importance and must await economic solution. The economic problems are in fact God's judgment; when the people put

God's work back in its rightful place, *then* problems will find solution. Haggai is raised up to challenge the people to finish the great building project. Messianic inspiration is included and comfort, too. Zerubbabel is said to be God's choice of a governor of Jerusalem and a type of the Messiah (2:23).

Outline

First Message: Negligence in Completion of the Temple (chapter 1)

Second Message: Courage, Messianic Promise (2:1-9)

Third Message: Disobedience means Absence of God's Blessing (2:10-19)

Fourth Message: Comfort—God will Fulfill His Promises (2:20-23)

ZECHARIAH

Zechariah ("Jehovah remembers"), son of Berechiah and grandson of one Iddo (probably same as in Nehemiah 12:16). If the Zechariah of Nehemiah 12:16 is the same as this Zechariah, he was a priest. Zechariah began his prophetic ministry two months after Haggai in the year 520 B.C. Chapters 9-14 may have been written later than 520.

Authorship and Date

Jews who had returned from the Exile (1:2, 3; 7:5), Joshua the High Priest (3:8), and Zerubbabel the governor (4:6).

Destination

Zechariah 9:9-10. "Rejoice greatly, O daughter of Zion! Shout aloud, O daughter of Jerusalem! Lo, your king comes to you; triumphant and victorious is he, humble and riding on an ass, on a colt the foal of an ass. I will cut off the chariot from Ephraim and the war horse from Jerusalem; and the battle bow shall be cut off, and he shall command peace to the nations; his dominion shall be from sea to sea, and from the River to the ends of the earth."

Key Verses

Like Haggai, Zechariah's aim was to challenge the people to finish the building of the Temple. Zechariah was greatly concerned with the spiritual implications of the challenge. He also makes some of the most revealing and inspiring Messianic declarations in prophetic literature.

Purpose and Theme

Introduction (1:1-6)

Outline

Zechariah's Visions (1:7—6:15)

Vision of the Horses: God's Judgment on the Nations and Jerusalem, and the Temple to be Rebuilt (1:7-17)

Vision of the Four Horns (Assyria, Egypt, Babylon, Medo-Persia): These Enemies will be Punished (1:18-21)

Vision of a Man Measuring Future Dimensions of Jerusalem: God's Salvation will mean Enlargement (chapter 2)

Vision of High Priest in Dirty Clothes: He Pleads for Mercy and Receives it (chapter 3)

Vision of the Candlestick and Two Olive Trees; Obstacles to Building Kingdom to be Removed by God's Spirit (chapter 4)

Vision of the Flying Roll: Divine Judgments (5:1-4)

Vision of the Ephah and Weight of Lead: Iniquity, God's Restraining of Sin (5:5-11)

Vision of the Winds: God's Judgments (6:1-8)

Vision of Restoration: Messiah's Deliverance (6:9-15)

QUESTION OF FASTING: GOD WOULD RATHER HAVE OBEDIENCE (chapters 7-8)

DESTRUCTION OF THE NATIONS AND DELIVERANCE OF THE KINGDOM (ISRAEL) (chapters 9-14)

The Messiah will Rule, other Nations Perish (chapters 9-10)

The True Shepherd (Messiah) and the False Shepherd (chapter 11)

Israel's Future Repentance and Turn to God (12:1—13:6)

Purification of Israel, Future Glory of Jerusalem (13:7—14:21)

MALACHI

Authorship and Date
Malachi ("messenger of Jehovah"), of whom nothing is known, wrote his book apparently after the Temple had been reconstructed, perhaps in the fourth century B.C.

Destination
To the Jews who have returned from Captivity, also to priests (1:6, 2:1).

Key Verse
Malachi 3:9. "You are cursed with a curse, for you are robbing me; the whole nation of you."

Purpose and Theme
The aim is to make clear the sin and apostasy of Israel and to underscore the judgment of God (1:3, 4, e.g.) that comes to the sinner but the blessing that awaits the repentant. That the people have not always honored God, that priests have become lax in doing their liturgical assignments, that priests have also caused the people to err because of false instruction, that mixed marriages (with heathen people) have taken place—all these sins are decried.

That God is sovereign is also spelled out and Malachi's teaching about God is important. The grace of God, past and present, is unfolded (1:2; 2:4, 5; 3:6, etc.). The Messiah will come to fulfill His purposes and cleanse His people. The people must obey the Law of Moses and thus prepare for the Great Day of the Lord. Note the reference to tithes and offerings in 3:8-10.

Malachi is the link between the Old and New Testaments, and is the last voice until John the Baptist. About 400 years lapsed between Malachi and John.

Outline

Israel's Sin and Apostasy (chapters 1:1—3:15)
    The Priests' Sins (1:1—2:9)
    The People's Sins (2:10—3:15)

Blessing for those who Repent (3:16—4:6)

MIRACLES

Old Testament

Sodom and Gomorrah destroyed	Genesis 19:24
Lot's wife turned to salt	Genesis 19:26
Isaac's birth	Genesis 21:1-3
Burning bush not burned up	Exodus 3:2
Aaron's rod changed into a serpent	Exodus 7:10-12
Plagues of Egypt	
1. Water turned to blood	Exodus 7:20-25
2. Frogs	Exodus 8:5-14
3. Lice	Exodus 8:16-18
4. Flies	Exodus 8:20-24
5. Murrain	Exodus 9:3-6
6. Boils	Exodus 9:8-11
7. Thunder, hail, etc.	Exodus 9:22-26
8. Locusts	Exodus 10:12-19
9. Darkness	Exodus 10:21-23
10. Death of the firstborn	Exodus 12:29-30
Red Sea divided; Israel passes through on dry land	Exodus 14:21-31
Marah waters sweetened	Exodus 15:23-25
Manna sent daily	Exodus 16:14-35
Water from the rock at Rephidim	Exodus 17:5-7
Nadab and Abihu destroyed for offering "strange fire"	Leviticus 10:1-2
Fire in Israelites' camp for discontent	Numbers 11:1-3

Korah swallowed into the earth, then fire and plague	Numbers 16:32ff
Aaron's budding rod	Numbers 17:1ff
Meribah rock smitten twice for water	Numbers 20:7-11
Brazen serpent; Israel healed	Numbers 21:8-9
Jordan river stopped; Israel crossed on dry land	Joshua 3:14-17
Walls of Jericho destroyed	Joshua 6:6-20
Sun stands still, then hail	Joshua 10:11-14
Samson's strength	Judges 14-16
Water flows from hollow place at Lehi	Judges 15:19
Dagon falls before the ark; tumors on Philistines	I Samuel 5:1-12
Beth-shemesh men slain for looking into the ark	I Samuel 6:19
Thunderstorm produces panic in the Philistines' army	I Samuel 7:10-12
Thunder and rain in harvest	I Samuel 12:17-18
Sound in the mulberry trees	II Samuel 5:23-25
Uzzah struck dead for touching the ark	II Samuel 6:7
Jeroboam's hand withered	I Kings 13:4-6
Widow's meal and oil increased by Elijah	I Kings 17:14-16
Widow's son raised from the dead	I Kings 17:17-24
Elijah fed by Brook Cherith after predicting drought. Also fire and rain after Elijah prayed.	I Kings 17-19
Aphek wall falls on the Syrians	I Kings 20:30
Ahaziah's captains and men burned	II Kings 1:10-12, 14
River Jordan divided by Elijah and Elisha	II Kings 2:7-8
Elijah taken to heaven in chariot of fire	II Kings 2:11
Jericho waters remedied with salt	II Kings 2:21-22
Bears destroy forty-two mocking "young men"	II Kings 2:24
Jehoshaphat gets water, so does the allied army	II Kings 3:16-20
Widow's oil multiplied	II Kings 4:2-7
Shunammite's gift of a son and his raising afterwards from the dead	II Kings 4:14-37
Deadly pottage cured with meal	II Kings 4:38-41
Hundred men fed with twenty loaves	II Kings 4:42-44
Naaman cured of leprosy, and the disease transferred to Gehazi	II Kings 5:10-27
Ax-head made to swim	II Kings 6:5-7
Syrian army blinded and cured	II Kings 6:18-20

Elisha's bones revive the dead	II Kings 13:21
Sennacherib's army destroyed	II Kings 19:35
Shadow of the sun goes back ten degrees on the sun-dial of Ahaz	II Kings 20:9-11
Uzziah struck with leprosy	II Chronicles 26:16-21
Shadrach, Meshach, and Abednego delivered from the furnace	Daniel 3:19-27
Daniel saved in the den of lions	Daniel 6:16-23
Deliverance of Jonah	Jonah 2:1-10

PARABLES

OLD TESTAMENT

Jotham's parable of trees making a king	Judges 9:7-15
Nathan to David on the poor man's lamb	II Samuel 12:1-6
Woman of Tekoa and her two sons	II Samuel 14:6-11
The escaped prisoner	I Kings 20:35-40
Micaiah's Vision	I Kings 22:19-23
The thistle and cedar	II Kings 14:9
The drunkard	Proverbs 23:29-35
The sluggard and his vineyard	Proverbs 24:30-34
The unfruitful vineyard	Isaiah 5:1-6
The plowman	Isaiah 28:23-29
The eagles and the vine	Ezekiel 17:3-10
The lion's whelps	Ezekiel 19:2-9
The two harlots	Ezekiel 23
The boiling pot and its scum	Ezekiel 24:3-5
The cedar of Lebanon	Ezekiel 31
The sea monster	Ezekiel 32:1-16
The shepherds and the flock	Ezekiel 34
The valley of dry bones	Ezekiel 37
The living waters	Ezekiel 47

There are many other parables in the Old Testament, such as the faithful shepherds in Zechariah 11.

CHRONOLOGICAL TABLE OF HEBREW RULERS*
with approximate dates

THE UNITED KINGDOM

1020–1000 B.C.	Saul
1000–961 (or 1000–965) B.C.	David
961–922 (or 965–931) B.C.	Solomon

THE DIVIDED KINGDOM

	JUDAH	ISRAEL	
922 (931)	Rehoboam	Jeroboam	922 (931)
915 (913)	Abijam		
913 (911)	Asa		
		Nadab	901 (910)
		Baasha	900 (909)
		Elah	877 (886)
		Zimri	876 (885)
		Omri (Omri, Tibni 885) 876	
		(Omri 880)	
873 (870)	Jehoshaphat		
		Ahab	869 (874)
		Ahaziah	850 (853)
849 (848)	Jehoram	Jehoram	849 (852)
842 (841)	Ahaziah	Jehu	842 (841)
842 (841)	Athaliah		
837 (835)	Jehoash		
		Jehoahaz	815 (814)
		Jehoash	801 (798)
800 (796)	Amaziah		
		Jeroboam II	786 (782)
783 (767)	Uzziah		
		Zechariah	746 (753)
		Shallum	745 (752)
		Menahem	745 (752)
742 (740)	Jotham		

---

* Based upon *The Oxford Annotated Bible*, pp. 1532–33. The one system is that developed by W. F. Albright, the other (in parentheses) by E. R. Thiele.

	JUDAH	ISRAEL

	JUDAH

ISRAEL

| Pekahiah | 738 (742) |
| Pekah | 737 (740) |

| 735 (732) | Ahaz |

| Hoshea | 732 (732) |
| Fall of Samaria | 721 (723/22) |

715 (716)	Hezekiah
687 (687)	Manasseh
642 (642)	Amon
640 (640)	Josiah
609 (609)	Jehoahaz
609 (609)	Jehoiakim
598 (598)	Jehoiachin
597 (597)	Zedekiah
587 (586)	Fall of Jerusalem

←§5§→ BETWEEN
THE TESTAMENTS

ALEXANDER THE GREAT'S CONQUESTS FROM 334 B.C., when he landed at Troas, to his death in Babylon in 323, outline the era of the introduction of Greek thought into the Bible lands. His conquests revolutionized the life of the Near East, and Hellenistic culture spread through these countries rapidly. Koiné Greek (see "Ancient Manuscripts and Versions") became a language even of the Jews, for Alexander was a Greek-speaking conquerer. International trade advanced vigorously in the new cultural and political climate.

Alexander the Great and Hellenism

Ptolemy Philadelphus (285–246) is credited with the initiative in building the great library at Alexandria and in having the Jewish Scriptures put into Greek. Altogether they formed what we call the Septuagint (see chapter on "Ancient Manuscripts and Versions"), which project was in all probability started in Alexandria and finished in that general area. This was not the first translation of Scriptures—Aramaic and Samaritan renderings had been done earlier—and from that time on translating and copying the Bible became a common thing culminating in a gigantic flow of reproductions in the twentieth century A.D. in many languages (see Appendix II). The Septuagint included the Apocryphal books in addition to the Hebrew Bible: the books of the Maccabees, Tobit and Judith, the additions to Daniel and Esther, the book of Baruch and the Epistle of Jeremiah, the Wisdom of Solomon, Ecclesiasticus. (On the Apocrypha see "First Facts about

---

* Of special help in formulating this chapter was the relevant portion in "Survey of Geography, History and Archaeology of the Bible Lands," an article in *The Oxford Annotated Bible*.

the Bible," the section on the Canon.) Some of these books may be translations from Hebrew or Aramaic originals; fragments of Apocrypha texts in these languages have been recently discovered in the Dead Sea area.

The Seleucids   After Alexander, the Ptolemies of Egypt claimed Judea, and after them the Seleucids of Antioch in Syria took control. They began their rule in 198 B.C. when Antiochus the Great defeated the Egyptians. The Seleucids imposed Greek culture. Antiochus IV Epiphanes (175–164 B.C.) dedicated the second Temple in Jerusalem to Zeus Olympius in 167 B.C. With some there was no objection to this, but orthodox Jews revolted under Judas Maccabeus ("the hammer-like one") and his brothers, who were of the priestly family of the Hasmoneans (Hasmon was the ancestor of the Maccabees). His groups campaigned against the Syrians successfully and the Temple was purified in 164 B.C. (the origin of the Hanukkah festival). That the Maccabees fought for their independence is revealed in the refugee camps, caves, and forts discovered by archaeologists. Now that the Jews in Palestine were independent, the Seleucids were forced to play a more submissive role. Judas died in 160 B.C. but the Hasmoneans continued to reign until 40 B.C., thus outlasting the Seleucids who were brought to their final and complete end when Pompey made Syria a Roman province in 63 B.C. Meanwhile the Hasmonians extended their boundaries until under Alexander Jannaeus (103–76 B.C.) they controlled almost all of Palestine.

The Books of the Maccabees (in the Apocrypha), Josephus, and Archaeology (especially coinage) tell us the story of the Seleucid period. Coins reveal the drive and aspirations of the Hasmoneans who were at first recognized only as high priests and rulers of the Jews, but who, beginning with Aristobulus (104–103 B.C.), assumed the title of kings in spite of vigorous opposition from the Pharisees.

The Hasmoneans   The origin of the Hasmoneans is indicated in the paragraph above. As they conquered territory they became more ruthless, but they were weakened by growing religious and political divisions. The Sadducees, a politically minded aristocracy, were liberal in attitude and welcomed adjustment to the times. The Pharisees ("separated ones"), however, who arose in opposition to Alexander Jannaeus, sought isolation from the national life, advocated asceticism, and claimed that the present rulers were standing in the way of God fulfilling His promise through the House of David. The Pharisees revolted and Alexander Jannaeus succeeded in putting down their revolution only with great difficulty. Some 800 Pharisees were crucified and thousands of people

128

left the country. On his death-bed, Alexander told his queen (Salome), who was to rule after him, that she ought to bend every effort to make peace with the Pharisees. In the ten years of her rule (76–67 B.C.) the Pharisees were very influential. Queen Salome Alexandra appointed her elder son, Hyrcannus, high priest. After her death, a younger son, Aristobulus, attempted to become king, but did not succeed.

With these divisions and problems came internal weakening, and finally the Hasmonean dynasty fell, after which Herod the Great became king of Palestine in 37 B.C. Rome now regulated the affairs of the Jews with great seriousness. Herod married Mariamme, granddaughter of Hyrcannus, a politically wise move because it connected him with the Hasmonean family. In the course of time, Herod ruled over more area so that he controlled not only Judea but non-Jewish areas as well. He was a great builder, and redid the Temple (see chapter 9). But not even this made the Jews love him, and his evil behavior—e.g. the murder of his wife Mariamme—served only to make the wicked image of him more vivid.

Herod the Great

In his will Herod appointed his son Archelaus king; another son—Herod Antipas—he appointed tetrarch of Galilee and Peraea; still another son—Philip—he assigned tetrarch in north Transjordan and beyond. The Emperor Augustus did not confirm the appointment of Archelaus as king. He was instead made "ethnarch," a title only slightly higher than "tetrarch." Even then Archelaus reigned but nine years, after which he was exiled to Gaul in 6 A.D. by the Emperor. His territory was now ruled by a Roman governor who lived at Caesarea; in point of fact the new governor was subordinate to the governor of Syria and he was called a "procurator." Pontius Pilate, in this office from 26–36 A.D., was the fifth of these procurators.

*   *   *   *   *   *   *   *   *

During these hard times, Jews looked to the comforting hope of the Prophets whose writings had come to be read along with the Law or Torah in the synagogues. The prophetic hope was realized in Jesus of Nazareth, the central figure of the New Testament and of human history.

*Jerusalem from the Mount of Olives
looking across the Kedron Valley.*

⤚§6§⤙ BOOK BY BOOK THROUGH THE NEW TESTA- MENT ⤙

T HE NEW TESTAMENT IS ONLY ONE-THIRD THE
size of the Old, but its central figure Jesus Christ makes it
of highest value. Jesus never wrote a book, he left no
literary remains; information about Him is given by His apostles
and their disciples. Yet Jesus is the key character. Next in importance come Peter (mentioned more times than any other except
Jesus) and Paul. Paul and Luke are the chief contributors to the
New Testament literature, but a dozen men helped write the
whole.

For some 1600 years most Christians have given credence to
this New Testament of ours with its twenty-seven books which
are divided as follows:

GOSPELS   ACTS   LETTERS   THE REVELATION

There are four Gospels, one book of Acts (early Church history),
twenty-one letters by Paul, other Apostles and apostolic men, and
one Apocalypse (like Daniel in literary form). This fourfold
order is both logical and chronological. The Gospel message is
presented first (the foundation laid), the early spread of the
Gospel is related second in the Acts, the explanation of the Gospel
is elaborated next in the Epistles, and God's will for the future
of the Gospel believers rounds off the New Testament in the
book of Revelation. This arrangement is chronological too, not
in order of writing, but in subject matter. Thus, Jesus, Founder
of the faith, is revealed in the Gospels; the progress of the faith
for about thirty years after Jesus' death and resurrection is given
in the Acts; the theology of the faith is outlined in the Epistles;
the final consummation of the faith is prophesied in the Revela-

tion (Greek *apokalypsis*: "disclosure," "revelation").

Apparently the Gospels circulated individually at first, in fact until the beginning of the second century when the four were put together. Once they were sent out in a group, Acts and Luke, heretofore two parts of one work, were separated. As to Paul's works, each was kept by the individuals and communities to whom they were sent, but by the end of the first century his writings (the "Pauline corpus") were probably put together in a single "bundle" and circulated as such. Paul had covered the Gospel message both in its theological and practical aspects, and this under the inspiration of God's Spirit. At first probably just ten Epistles of Paul circulated in a group; a later three were added, the so-called Pastorals (I, II Timothy, and Titus).

Now there were in circulation two great groups of documents, the Gospels and the Pauline Epistles, and Acts served as a link between the two. Hebrews and the General (Catholic) Epistles plus Revelation were added in due course to make up the full compliment of New Testament writings.

GOSPELS: MATTHEW THROUGH JOHN

The "Synoptics"

"Gospel" is an old English word from *god spel*, "good news" or "good tidings." The Gospels are the record of "Good News" in Jesus, proclaimed and lived. The first three of the Gospels are called Synoptics (a term which originated in the eighteenth century) because they all take a common point of view and are similar in subject, order, and language. In other words, these three, summarizing the life and teachings of Jesus, frequently use the same materials. Place them in parallel columns and see this fact revealed immediately. (See also the tables of parables and miracles at the end of this section on the Gospels.)

Sources of the
Synoptics

There were sources for the Synoptic materials. Scholarly research tells us that in all probability Mark was written first. The materials in Matthew and Luke which are also in Mark undoubtedly derive from Mark. How do we know this? (1) Mark includes almost nothing (outside of details) that is not in Matthew or Luke. (2) When the order in which the material appears varies, it turns out that Luke agrees with Mark where Mark and Matthew differ, and that Matthew agrees with Mark where Mark and Luke differ. (3) Matthew and Luke never agree in the order of presentation against Mark. (4) 606 of Mark's 661 verses appear in Matthew and 380 of Mark's are found with little change in Luke. There are only thirty-one verses in Mark not found in

Matthew or Luke. In addition to these four factors, it appears that even in many details the first and third Gospels derive from Mark. Mark, then, is a major source of Synoptic information. But what of the materials common to Matthew and Luke not found in Mark? Those (over 200 verses) come from a source called "Q" (for the German word *Quelle,* "source" or "spring"). Q has never been found in a manuscript; it is simply a convenient way of indicating one common source of Synoptic information. That common source, as well as the other sources, circulated orally at first. The Jews were taught to memorize and to repeat over and again their sacred sayings. Jesus' words made such an impact on the minds and hearts of the people that they were compelled to repeat them again and again. In some such manner oral traditions grew up, were propagated, and finally set down in writing. There is evidence of sayings of our Lord (called "Logia") in written form, and perhaps more than one source of sayings was set down. When analyzed it turns out that Q is mostly sayings of our Lord anyway. The date of Q may be as early as 50 A.D. and it is thought to have originated in Antioch of Syria, cradle of Gentile Christianity (Q emphasized the Gentiles).

Irenaeus, early Church Father, gives us his view of Gospel origins:

> Now Matthew published the book of the Gospel among the Hebrews in their own dialect, while Peter and Paul were preaching the Gospel in Rome and founding the Church. After their death (departure?) Mark, the disciple and interpreter of Peter, handed down to us in writings the things preached by Peter. Luke also, the follower of Paul, put down in a book the Gospel preached by Paul. Afterwards John, the disciple of the Lord who also leaned upon his breast, also published a Gospel while residing in Ephesus in Asia.

If this account is reliable, we have further information on Gospel sources. Mark got his material from Peter, Luke some of his information from Paul. Further, Matthew put his Gospel into the Hebrew dialect (Aramaic) before it was translated into its present Greek form. John's Gospel was done last in Ephesus.

The real purpose of the Gospels was to give the plan of salvation. In fact, these four short books constitute the primary source of information about the plan of salvation. Thus, Irenaeus, referring to the Gospel writers, said, "We have learned the plan of salvation through no others than those through whom the Gospel has come down to us." Involved in salvation is the whole life of

Purpose of the Gospels

Jesus—birth, teaching, example—but the high importance of His death and passion is seen in the fact that one-third of the Synoptics and one-fourth of the fourth Gospel are given over to the cross and Jesus' preparation for the cross, all culminating in the central miracle of the Bible, the resurrection.

A portion of the Jerusalem wall showing what some say to be the "Gate Beautiful" (Acts 3:2). The gate is now sealed.

MATTHEW

Authorship and Date

Matthew ("God's gift"), whose original name was perhaps Matthias, is probably the author of the Gospel which bears his name. He was an Apostle (Matthew 10:3; Mark 3:18; Luke 6:15; Acts 1:13), and it is thought that he was the very same as Levi the publican whom Christ called in Mark 2:14 (cp. Luke 5:27). Some have suggested that he took on the new name Matthew when he gave up his old vocation. Mark tells us that Levi was the son of Alphaeus. Some have said Matthew was a relative of our Lord. Beyond these facts and suggestions little is known about him, but from the early second century there began a tradition for his authorship of the first Gospel. He may have set down part or all of his work in Aramaic first, for Papias, an early Christian writer, says, "Matthew compiled the Logia (sayings) in the 'Hebrew' (Aramaic). . . ." It was perhaps written just after 70 A.D., the date of the fall of Jerusalem which seems to be suggested in 22:7.

Destination

Matthew was the Gospel most frequently used in the early Church which included many Jewish Christians. It is clear that

Matthew was a Jew writing to fellow Jews. The following facts about the book make that clear:

(1) The numerous Old Testament references including prophecies.

(2) The emphasis upon the Kingship of Jesus.

(3) The emphasis upon the Jews as the lost sheep of Israel and Jesus' mission to them.

Key Verses

Matthew 23:37-39. "O Jerusalem, Jerusalem, killing the prophets and stoning those who are sent to you! How often would I have gathered your children together as a hen gathers her brood under her wings, and you would not. Behold, your house is forsaken and desolate. For I tell you, you will not see me again, until you say, 'Blessed be he who comes in the name of the Lord.'"

Purpose and Theme

The position of Matthew in the Canon gives away its purpose. It is the perfect link between the Old Testament and the New, because it is the most Jewish of the Gospels; and it intends to demonstrate that Jesus is the true Messiah, the fulfillment of the Old Testament prophecies. As Luke is the Gospel for the Gentiles, so Matthew is the Gospel for the Jews. Matthew used Mark's Gospel but rearranged the material and even abbreviated where he desired. The style of writing is neat, crystal clear, and orderly. An illustration of his orderliness is his more or less frequent use of threes and sevens. The genealogy of Jesus is composed of three groups of fourteen (a multiple of seven) names. There are three angelic communications to Joseph, three denials by Peter, three questions by Pilate. There are seven parables in chapter 13, and seven woes in chapter 23. (A. M. Hunter, *Introducing the New Testament* 1957, p. 59.)

A street scene in Nazareth, the humble town in which Jesus grew up.

Matthew is the only Synoptic in which the word "Church" is found: two times in the same verse, Matthew 18:17, another time in 16:18 where Jesus says, "And I tell you, you are Peter, and on this rock I will build my church, and the powers of death shall not prevail against it." Matthew sees the Church as the continuance of the Covenant people. Jesus Son of David,

135

Son of Man, Son of God, came to found the Church. It took His teaching, life, death, and resurrection to found it (this was His Messianic mission), and it will require His second coming to consummate it as the eternal Kingdom of God. Those who know divine forgiveness and fellowship are members of the Church Jesus founded.

The five great discourses of Jesus constitute an aspect of this Gospel worthy of note: The Sermon on the Mount is given in chapters 5-7; His instructions to His disciples for a missionary outreach are recorded in chapter 10 (see also Matthew 28:18-20, the "Great Commission"); the parables of the Kingdom (chapter 13); the teaching on real discipleship (chapter 18); and the teaching on the end of the age (chapters 24-25).

Outline

THE COMING OF THE MESSIAH (1:1—4:11)
> The Genealogy of Christ (chapter 1)
> The Virgin Birth (chapter 2)
> Preparation of John the Baptist, Baptism of Jesus (chapter 3)
> Satan Tempts Christ (4:1-11)

THE MESSIAH'S MINISTRY IN GALILEE AND JUDEA (4:12—20:34)
> Withdrawal into Galilee, First Disciples Called (4:12-25)
> Sermon on the Mount (chapters 5-7)
> Ten Miracles: Leper Cleansed, Peter's Mother-in-Law Healed, Storm at Sea Stilled, etc. (chapters 8-9)
> Jesus Teaches the Twelve Disciples and Sends them Out (chapter 10)
> John the Baptist in Prison, Accusations by the Pharisees (chapters 11-12)
> Jesus Teaches about the Kingdom in Parables: The Sower, Mustard Seed, Leaven, etc. (chapter 13)
> Herod Kills John the Baptist, The 5000 Fed, Peter walks on the Water (chapter 14)
> Further Accusations, The 4000 Fed (15:1—16:12)
> Peter's Great Confession (16:13-20)
> First Announcement of the Passion (16:21-28)
> Transfiguration, Demoniac Child Healed (17:1-21)
> Second Announcement of the Passion (17:22-27)
> Jesus' Instructions on Sincere Discipleship (chapter 18)
> The Question on Divorce, the Rich Young Ruler (chapter 19)
> Parables, Blind Men Healed (chapter 20)

FINAL REJECTION OF THE MESSIAH (chapters 21-25)
> Triumphal Entry, Temple Cleansed, Parable of the Wicked Husbandman (chapter 21)
> Parable of the Wedding, Increased Opposition by Pharisees, Sadducees and Herodians (chapter 22)

"Woe unto You, Scribes and Pharisees!" (chapter 23)
Predictions and Parables on the End of the Age
    (chapters 24-25)

PASSION WEEK AND RESURRECTION OF THE MESSIAH
    (chapters 26-28)
The Plot to Kill the Messiah, The Last Supper (26:1-29)
In the Garden (26:30-56)
Trial before Caiaphas, Peter's Denial (26:57-75)
Trial before Pilate (27:1-26)
Crucifixion (27:27-66)
Resurrection (chapter 28)

MARK

John Mark, cousin of Barnabas (Colossians 4:10), is the author **Authorship** of the Gospel of Mark. Tradition solidly backs this belief. Fortunately there is much more biographical information available about Mark than Matthew. He was the son of Mary, who opened her home at Jerusalem for Christian worship and conference (Acts 12:12). Some authorities believe it was in her house that Jesus and His disciples celebrated the Last Supper and where the 120 gathered on the day of Pentecost. Mark may have known Jesus; indeed, many a Bible expositor has suggested that the account in Mark 14:51, where the young man fled naked, is a concealed reference to Mark himself.

Jerusalem.
The Golden Gate
through which Christ
made His
triumphal entry.

Mark worked with Paul, Barnabas, and Peter for the spread of the Kingdom. He accompanied Paul and Barnabas for part of the first missionary journey, but deserted at Perga for some unknown reason before that journey was completed (Acts 13:13; 15:36-39). Through the centuries scholars have attempted to discover the real reason for Mark's behavior; to date no final answer or answers have come to light. Suggested reasons for the desertion—homesickness, jealousy of Paul's leadership (Barnabas and Mark were cousins), the rigors of the remainder of the first missionary journey (there were mountains ahead), and free association with the Gentiles to which Jews were not accustomed. Whatever the real reason, Paul eventually forgave Mark and even came to regard him as a very useful worker in the building of the Kingdom (Colossians 4:10 and II Timothy 4:11). Tradition says that he went to Alexandria in Egypt to found the Church there and also the well-known catechetical school where Clement and Origen were to become famous. It is thought that Mark died a martyr's death.

Eusebius, a fourth century writer, quotes Papias who wrote about 140 A.D. as saying that Mark was "the interpreter of Peter." Other ancient writers made the same observation; it definitely appears that Peter told the story of our Lord to John Mark. Moreover, it seems that Peter and Mark were very close—in I Peter 5:13 we have the expression, "Mark my son." Knowing the stories then in circulation about Jesus and having listened to Peter, Mark was led by the Spirit of God to write this brief digest of the outstanding events of our Lord's life, especially emphasizing His activities when He went about doing good.

Date

Mark is the earliest of the Gospels and is probably to be dated just after 60 A.D. We know Mark was the earliest because Matthew and Luke use Mark as a source (see introduction to the Gospels above), and John was written from Ephesus after the Synoptics were completed.

Destination

There is a long-standing tradition that Mark wrote his Gospel at Rome for Roman Christians. Unlike the Gospel of Matthew, Mark contains few references to the Old Testament. He goes out of his way to explain Jewish customs and he translates the Palestinian Aramaic expressions into Greek which was spoken at Rome in the first century. All this would suggest that he was writing to minds untutored in Jewish religion and practices. It is also true that Mark's Gospel contains more Latin words than the other Gospels. In a word, the environment of the Gospel according to St. Mark is Roman.

Mark 10:45. "For the Son of man also came not to be served but to serve, and to give his life as a ransom for many." Key Verse

Mark's Gospel is not polished in style; but, as J. B. Phillips well says, it is filled with "vivid flashes of realism." Mark paints Jesus as a rugged, very human person, but does not leave out the historic fact of the Incarnation (1:1, 11; 5:7; 9:7; 14:61-62; 15:39). Jesus' ministry is filled with works so mighty that it is clear for those who have eyes to see that the Kingdom of God is here in Him. Mark's Gospel is the Gospel of *action;* the word "immediately" appears forty times in this brief book of sixteen chapters. Mark emphasizes works more than words; his Gospel records fewer words of Jesus than the other Gospels (chapter 13 contains a collection of sayings and there are some parables in the book). The narrative was designed to appeal to the active Romans for whom he wrote. The purpose of the Gospel was to make clear the works of Jesus Christ the Son of God, and to get these down in writing before too many years passed by (it had been thirty years or more since Jesus' death and resurrection). To be reminded of our Lord's death would be a great comfort and strength for persecuted Christians in and around Rome. Without mention of the birth or childhood of Jesus (these would not be important to the slave populace of Rome), he commences his account with the appearance of the forerunner of Jesus, proceeds to John the Baptist, and then to Jesus' public ministry, passion and resurrection. Purpose and Theme

Outline

INTRODUCTION AND PREPARATION (1:1-13)

The Forerunner—John the Baptist (1:1-8)
Jesus' Baptism (1:9-11)
The Temptation (1:12-13)

JESUS' MINISTRY IN GALILEE (1:14—8:26)

First Disciples Called (1:14-20)
Many Miracles (1:21—3:12)
The Twelve Disciples Chosen (3:13-19)
Controversy with the Pharisees, Parables, Storm Quieted, Demoniac and Jairus' Daughter Healed, etc. (3:20—6:6)
The Apostles Commissioned (6:7-13)
Death of John the Baptist (6:14-29)
Feeding of the 5000, Controversy with the Pharisees, Feeding of the 4000 (6:30—8:10)
Denunciation of the Opposition, Blind Man Healed (8:11-26)

PREPARATION FOR THE PASSION (8:27—10:52)

Peter's Confession (8:27-30)

The "Gordon" site of our Lord's tomb with the ledge in front for the rolling stone.

First Announcement of the Passion (8:31-38)
Transfiguration and Demoniac Child Healed (9:1-29)
Second Announcement of the Passion (9:30-32)
Teaching on Divorce, Rich Young Ruler, etc. (9:33—10:31)
Third Announcement of the Passion (10:32-34)
Sons of Zebedee Seek First Places in Kingdom, Blind Bartimaeus Healed (10:35-52)

THE PASSION WEEK AND THE RESURRECTION (chapters 11-16)
The Triumphal Entry and Cleansing of the Temple (chapter 11)
Parable of the Wicked Husbandmen, Controversy with the Herodians and Sadducees (12:1-27)
The Great Commandment, Widow's Mite, Prediction of the Second Coming (12:28—13:37)
The Supper at Bethany (14:1-11)
The Last Supper (14:12-31)
Gethsemane and the Betrayal (14:32-52)
Trial before the High Priest (14:53-72)
Trial before Pilate (15:1-21)
The Crucifixion (15:22-47)
The Resurrection (16:1-8)
Epilogue (16:9-20)*

---

* The earliest and best manuscripts do not include the Epilogue; therefore, it is put in italics in the Revised Standard Version. True, verse 8 makes an abrupt ending, but very likely the original ending was accidentally destroyed and a later hand added 9-20 in an effort to effect a proper conclusion to the Gospel.

LUKE

Luke, the physician (Colossians 4:14), trained historian, and only Authorship Gentile writer of the New Testament, is without question the author of the Gospel which bears his name. Second century testimonies are unanimous on the point. Medical phrases, too, point to Lukan authorship. This was the first of a two volume work, Acts being the second. (Luke and Acts are, by the way, the two largest books in the New Testament.) A glance at the outset of Luke's Gospel and the beginning of the book of Acts will demonstrate his authorship of both books. We could wish for more biographical information on Luke. Aside from the "we" passages in Acts, there are only three New Testament references to him (Colossians 4:14; II Timothy 4:11; Philemon 24). Likely he was a native of Antioch in Syria; we know he was a Gentile, a doctor, a Christian, and a strong supporter of the Church.

In all probability, Luke was written just before Acts. Acts was **Date** written probably between 61 and 64 A.D. (see below under "Acts"). Since Luke used Mark as a source, it was written after Mark which was probably written just after 60 A.D. Luke is to be dated about 61 A.D.

Matthew wrote to Jews, Mark to Romans, Luke to Gentiles. **Destination** Since Luke himself was a Gentile, both his Gospel and the Acts reflect a tremendous interest in the spread of Christianity to non-Jews. In the Gospel of Luke the centurion's faith is singled out; the Good Samaritan story is told; and Jesus is traced to Adam, father of the human race, rather than to Abraham, father of the Jewish people. (See also below "Purpose and Theme.")

Luke 19:10. "For the Son of man came to seek and to save **Key Verse** the lost."

In the first instance, Luke wrote for Theophilus, a Roman offi- **Purpose and** cial. Luke wanted to let him know, in language he could under- **Theme** stand and appreciate, that Christ was the Savior of every man, not Jews only. Indeed, Gentiles are referred to over and over again: the Gospel is to be announced "to all nations," a centurion has more faith than anyone in all Israel, Jesus is "a light to the Gentiles," Samaritans (only part Jewish) are praised by Jesus.

It is generally agreed that this is the loveliest of the Synoptic Gospels; indeed, the Frenchman Renan thought it to be "the most beautiful book in the world." It is filled with poetry, imagination, stories for children (for example, chapter 15, where we

*The Church of
the Nativity
in Bethlehem, built
over the traditional
site of our
Lord's birth.*

have three stories about lost things: the lost sheep, the lost coin, the lost boy). There is a continuing tradition that Luke was a painter as well as a doctor. Whether or not this is true, it is clear that he possessed in rich measure a fine artistic sensitivity.

This Gospel is not only artistic or esthetic, it is an accurate and dependable piece of history. Luke the physician and scientist records the life of Christ with great care. Like a doctor keeping a case history, he aims to write accurately. The sources of his information were carefully chosen and sifted. He consulted Mark's Gospel and surely he talked to Mary herself. He would have spoken to the Christians at Antioch, and he was with Paul who had seen Jesus on the Damascus Road. There were other sources of information, but we can depend upon this, that even though Luke had not been an eye witness of Jesus, he did all in his power to seek out those who had seen Him in order to obtain first hand information for his Gospel. Altogether, the Gospel of Luke is a first rate life of Christ.

*The Jericho Road
winding its way
through the
Wilderness and hills
of Judea.
"Jesus replied,
'A man was
going down from
Jerusalem to Jericho,
and He fell among
robbers . . ."
(Luke 10:30).*

The doctor's heart is reflected in his Gospel in the most beautiful ways. He is concerned about the unfortunate (the penitent thief, the fallen woman), about women (the widow of Nain, Mary and Martha), about children (the birth stories—chapters 1-2). His mention of the poor, the maimed, the lame, and the blind, reflect his deep interest in those who need medical care. His many references to the healing of the sick are not surprising; in fact, twenty miracles of Jesus are cited, six of which are not mentioned in the other Gospels (the draught of fishes—5:1-11; raising of the widow's son at Nain—7:11-16; healing the infirm woman—13:10-17; healing the man with dropsy—14:1-6; cleansing of the ten lepers—17:11-19; healing the ear of Malchus—22:49-51). All of these facts suggest that a doctor is writing and thus one aspect of Luke's purpose in writing.

Great joy characterizes the Gospel. A. M. Hunter (*Introducing the New Testament*) has made the fine observation that joy comes at the beginning of the book ("Behold I bring you tidings of great joy"), in the middle ("it is fitting to make merry and be glad, for this your brother was dead and is alive" 15:32a), and at its end (the disciples "returned to Jerusalem with great joy"). It is true! One of the aims of the book is to communicate the joy and sheer happiness which is part of the Gsopel of Christ and the privilege of believers.

Moreover, Luke is the Gospel of prayer. Someone has observed that the kneeling Christ is seen in Luke more than in any other Gospel—before His baptism, on the Mount of Transfiguration, in the Garden, on the Cross, etc. Further, that only in this Gospel have we the three parables of prayer: the Pharisee and the Publican, the Friend at Midnight, and the Importunate Widow.

SALUTATION (1:1-4)   Outline

THE BIRTH AND PREPARATION OF JESUS (1:5—4:13)
    Birth of John Foretold (1:5-25)
    The Annunciation, Mary Visits Elizabeth (1:26-56)
    Birth of John the Baptist (1:57-80)
    Birth and Childhood of Jesus (chapter 2)
    Ministry of John the Baptist, Baptism and Genealogy of Jesus (chapter 3)
    Wilderness Temptation (4:1-13)

THE GALILEAN MINISTRY OF JESUS (4:14—19:27)
    Rejection at Nazareth, the Sick Healed in Galilee (4.14-44)
    First Disciples Called, Criticism by Scribes and Pharisees (chapter 5)
    Twelve Disciples Chosen and Instructed (chapter 6)
    Many Miracles and Parables (chapters 7-8)
    Feeding of the 5000, Transfiguration, First Announcement of the Passion (chapter 9)
    The Seventy Sent Out, Jesus Visits Mary and Martha, the Good Samaritan (chapter 10)
    Various Instructions and Parables (11:1—19:27)

THE SUFFERING AND DEATH OF JESUS (19:28—23:56)
  Triumphal Entry and Cleansing of the Temple (19:28-48)
  Captious Questions, Prophecy on the Second Coming
    (chapters 20-21)
  The Last Supper (22:1-38)
  Christ in Gethsemane (22:39-53)
  Trial before the High Priest, Peter's Denial (22:54-71)
  Trial before Pilate and Herod (23:1-25)
  The Crucifixion and Burial (23:26-56)

THE TRIUMPHAL RESURRECTION AND ASCENSION OF JESUS
  (chapter 24)
  The Resurrection Christ Meets the Women and the Dis-
    ciples (24:1-49)
  The Ascension (24:50-53)

JOHN

Authorship   It appears from the contents of the Gospel of John, that the author
knew Jesus personally. Tradition says he was John the beloved
disciple. Irenaeus (c. 180 A.D.), for example, wrote, "John the
disciple of the Lord, the same who reclined upon His breast,
himself also published his Gospel, when he was living in Ephesus
in Asia" (Quoted in F. F. Bruce, *The New Testament Documents, Are They Reliable?* [I.V.F., 1960], p. 51). Though some
have said another wrote the book, or collaborated with John,
there persists a strong belief that John the beloved was, in fact,
the author. The author claims that he was "the disciple whom
Jesus loved" (21:20), a phrase which seems to refer to John. See
also such passages as John 13:23; 19:26; 21:7, 24.

Date   It is safe to say that the Gospel of John was written between
85 and 110 A.D. Manuscript evidence (the John Rylands fragment
of John—see photographic reproduction in chapter on "Ancient
Manuscripts") makes it difficult to date the book later; and for a
long time scholarship has been hesitant to date it earlier than
85 A.D., though there have been a few attempts at earlier dating.
(Cp. Sir Frederic Kenyon, *Our Bible and the Ancient Manuscripts,* revised by A. W. Adams. London: Eyre and Spottiswoode,
1958, pp. 189–190.) Clement of Alexandria, a Church father, said
John wrote after the other Gospels had been produced. There is
a long tradition that John wrote his Gospel at Ephesus.

Destination   The fourth Gospel was intended not for a specific culture
group (Jews, Romans, or Greeks), but for the world, especially
the world of believers. (See purpose below.)

John 3:16. "For God so loved the world that he gave his only Son, that whoever believes in him should not perish but have eternal life."

John 20:30-31. "Now Jesus did many other signs in the presence of the disciples, which are not written in this book; but these are written that you may believe that Jesus is the Christ, the Son of God, and that believing you may have life in his name."

The Gospel of John is quite different from the first three Gospels called the Synoptics. Matthew was written to Jews, Mark to Romans, and Luke to the Gentiles; the Gospel of John was written to *everyone,* especially believers. Matthew is systematic, Mark short and rugged, Luke beautiful and John deep and full of insight. Moreover, healing events are included here which are not found in the Synoptics. Only two out of the eight miracles in John appear in the first three Gospels (the feeding of the 5000—6:5-14; Jesus walking on the sea—6:19-21). He never employs the term "miracle;" it is always "sign"—pointing to Christ as Divine (signs were proofs). When John does include materials which appear in the Synoptics (the Baptism, Temptation, Transfiguration, etc., are omitted), he usually adds a new element, as for example in John 6 (the feeding of the multitude) where the figure of Jesus as "the bread of life" is added. He also adds much new material (Nicodemus, woman at the well, Lazarus raised, and especially chapters 13-17 which tell us what happened

Excavations and reconstructions at the traditional site of St. John's burial place, near Ephesus.

Looking toward the wine-colored Church dome at Cana where Jesus turned water into wine.

on the night of the Last Supper). John includes no parables in the Synoptic sense. Altogether, John's Gospel supplements the Synoptics and completes more fully the story of our Lord.

A notable difference between John and the Synoptics is that Jesus is presented as Messiah at the very outset of the book. In the Synoptics, however, the authors *lead up* to the idea of Christ as Messiah. The outset of the fourth Gospel is different in another way, in the use of the Greek word *Logos,* a term used to convey the idea of the "Word made flesh," the Incarnate Christ.

The great themes of the fourth Gospel are light, life, love, truth, the Father-Son relationship. These are developed in two ways: by signs such as the turning of the water into wine (chapter 2), and conversations such as the one with Nicodemus (chapter 3). These great themes reflect the enormous spiritual value of the book. No New Testament work is so mystical or spiritual, and no book surpasses this one in depth of understanding. Clement of Alexandria called it "The Spiritual Gospel."

The aim of the fourth Gospel is given in the key verse, John 20:31. No other Gospel puts so much emphasis upon establishing the deity of our Lord. The Father-Son relationship is repeated again and again and again in such phrases as, "I and the Father are one." Jesus is depicted as the Light of the world, the Good Shepherd, the Door, the Vine, the Way, the Truth, and the Life. John 3:16 and 17, the best and most universally known verses of the book, reflect the author's purpose of bringing people to experimental belief in the divine Christ. This purpose is the reason the book is so widely used in evangelism and by missionaries among pagan peoples. The Holy Spirit, too, is stressed, but John's term is "the Paraclete," the "Helper." The author is intent upon conveying the truth that Christ is present with us in the Holy Spirit. John's aim was not to give the full sweep of Jesus' ministry (only a brief period of time is covered in the book); rather, it was to drive home the truth that Jesus is the Christ and that belief in Him will bring life eternal. John Calvin said of John's Gospel, It "is the key which opens the door to the understanding of the (other) gospels."

Outline

INTRODUCTION (chapter 1)
    Prologue (1:1-18)
    Ministry of John (1:19-36)
    First Disciples (1:37-51)

THE PUBLIC MINISTRY OF JESUS (chapters 2-12)
    Marriage at Cana, Temple Cleansed (chapter 2)
    Discourse with Nicodemus—"Ye must be born again" (chapter 3)
    Samaritan Woman, Nobleman's Son Healed (chapter 4)
    Impotent Man Cured, Accusation by Pharisees, Discourse on the Father and the Son (chapter 5)
    Feeding of the 5000, Jesus Walks on the Sea, Jesus the Bread of Life (chapter 6)
    Feast of Tabernacles, Opposition Strengthened (7:1-52)
    The Adulterous Woman,* Jesus the Light of the World (7:53—8:59)
    Blind Man Healed and Teaching which Followed (chapter 9)
    Teaching on the Good Shepherd (chapter 10)
    Raising of Lazarus, Mary Anoints Jesus' Feet (chapter 11)
    Supper at Bethany, Close of Public Ministry (chapter 12)

THE PRIVATE MINISTRY OF JESUS (chapters 13-17)
    The Last Supper (chapter 13)
    Jesus the Way, the Truth, and the Life (chapter 14)
    Jesus the True Vine (chapter 15)
    Final Discourse to the Disciples (chapter 16)
    Christ Prays for His Own (chapter 17)

---

* John 7:53—8:11 is perhaps misplaced or not a part of the fourth Gospel at all. It is, apparently, an authentic story. The R.S.V. translators have put it in fine print in a footnote. It occurs after Luke 21:37 in some manuscripts.

THE TRIALS AND CRUCIFIXION OF JESUS (chapters 18-19)
　The Betrayal (18:1-11)
　Trial before the Jews (18:12-27)
　Trial before Roman Authorities (18:28—19:16)
　The Crucifixion (19:17-42)

THE RESURRECTION (chapters 20-21)
　Appearance of the Resurrected Christ (chapter 20)
　Validation of the Resurrection, Peter Commanded to Feed
　　Christ's Sheep (chapter 21)

SIGNS IN WORKS
　1. Water changed to wine (2:1-11)
　2. Cleansing of the Temple (2:13-23)
　3. Nobleman's Son Healed (4:46-54)
　4. Man at Pool of Bethesda Healed (5:1-9)
　5. Feeding of the 5000 (6:1-14)
　6. Jesus Walks on the Sea (6:17-21)
　7. Blind Man Healed (9:1-7)
　8. Lazarus Raised (11:1-46)

SIGNS IN WORDS
　1. "I am the Bread of Life" (6:35).
　2. "I am the Light of the World" (8:12)
　3. "Before Abraham was, I am" (8:58)
　4. "I am the Door" (10:9)
　5. "I am the Good Shepherd" (10:11)
　6. "I am the Resurrection, and the Life" (11:25)
　7. "I am the Way, the Truth, and the Life" (14:6)
　8. "I am the True Vine" (15:1)

PARABLES IN THE GOSPELS

(1) *Found only in Matthew*

The tares	Matt. 13:24-30
The hidden treasure	Matt. 13:44
The pearl of great price	Matt. 13:45-46
The fishing net	Matt. 13:47-48
The unmerciful servant	Matt. 18:23-34
Laborers in the vineyard	Matt. 20:1-16
The man with two sons	Matt. 21:28-32
The marriage feast (given by the King's son)	Matt. 22:1-14
The ten virgins	Matt. 25:1-13
The talents	Matt. 25:14-30
The sheep and the goats	Matt. 25:31-46

(2) Found only in Mark

The blade, the ear, the full grain	Mark 4:26-29
Watch for his coming!	Mark 13:34-36

(3) Found only in Luke

The two debtors	Luke 7:36-50
The good Samaritan	Luke 10:25-37
The friend at midnight	Luke 11:5-8
The rich fool	Luke 12:16-21
The watchful servants	Luke 12:35-40
The wise steward	Luke 12:42-48
The barren fig-tree	Luke 13:6-9
The great banquet	Luke 14:16-24
The tower and counting its cost	Luke 14:28-33
The lost sheep	Luke 15:3-7
The lost coin	Luke 15:8-10
The prodigal son	Luke 15:11-32
The unjust steward	Luke 16:1-13
The rich man and Lazarus	Luke 16:19-31
The master and servant	Luke 17:7-10
The importunate widow	Luke 18:1-8
The Pharisee and the publican	Luke 18:9-14
The pounds	Luke 19:12-27

(4) Common to Matthew and Luke

House built on the rock	Matt. 7:24-27; Luke 6; 48-49
The leaven	Matt. 13:33; Luke 13: 20-21
The lost sheep	Matt. 18:12-14; Luke 15:3-7

(5) Common to Matthew, Mark, and Luke

The candle under a bushel	Matt. 5:14-16; Mark 4: 21-22; Luke 8:16-17
The new cloth on old garment	Matt. 9:16; Mark 2:21: Luke 5:36
New wine and old bottles	Matt. 9:17; Mark 2:22; Luke 5:37-38
The sower	Matt. 13:3-9, 18-23; Mark 4:3-20; Luke 8: 4-15
The mustard seed	Matt. 13:31-32; Mark 4: 31-32; Luke 13:18-19
The vineyard and husbandmen	Matt. 21:33-41; Mark 12: 1-9; Luke 20:9-16
Young leaves of the fig-tree	Matt. 24:32-35; Mark 13:28-31; Luke 21:29-33

MIRACLES IN THE GOSPELS

(1) *Found only in Matthew*
Two blind men cured	Matt. 9:27-31
Dumb spirit cast out	Matt. 9:32-33
Tax money in the fish's mouth	Matt. 17:24-27

(2) *Found only in Mark*
Deaf and dumb man cured	Mark 7:31-37
Blind man cured	Mark 8:22-26

(3) *Found only in Luke*
Draught of fishes	Luke 5:1-11
Widow's son raised from the dead at Nain	Luke 7:11-17
Woman's infirmity cured	Luke 13:11-17
Dropsy cured	Luke 14:1-6
Ten lepers cleansed	Luke 17:11-19
Malchus' ear healed	Luke 22:50-51

(4) *Found only in John*
Water made wine at Cana	John 2:1-11
Nobleman's son cured of fever	John 4:46-54
Impotent man cured at Jerusalem	John 5:1-9
Man born blind cured at Jerusalem	John 9:1-7
Lazarus raised from the dead	John 11:38-44
Catch of 153 fish	John 21:1-14

(5) *Common to Matthew and Mark*
Syrophenician's daughter cured	Matt. 15:28; Mark 7:24
Four thousand fed	Matt. 15:32; Mark 8:1
Fig-tree cursed	Matt. 21:19; Mark 11:13-14

(6) *Common to Matthew and Luke*
Centurion's palsied servant cured	Matt. 8:5; Luke 7:1
Blind and dumb demoniac cured	Matt. 12:22; Luke 11:14

(7) *Common to Mark and Luke*
Demoniac in synagogue cured	Mark 1:23; Luke 4:33

(8) *Common to Matthew, Mark, Luke*
Leper cured	Matt. 8:2; Mark 1:40; Luke 5:12
Peter's mother-in-law cured	Matt. 8:14; Mark 1:30; Luke 4:38

Tempest stilled	Matt. 8:23; Mark 4:37; Luke 8:22
Demoniacs cured	Matt. 8:28; Mark 5:1; Luke 8:26
Paralytic cured	Matt. 9:2; Mark 2:3; Luke 5:18
Jairus' daughter raised	Matt. 9:23; Mark 5:23; Luke 8:41
Woman's issue of blood cured	Matt. 9:20; Mark 5:25; Luke 8:43
Man's withered hand cured	Matt. 12:10; Mark 3:1; Luke 6:6
Devil cast out of boy	Matt. 17:14; Mark 9:17; Luke 9:37
Blind man cured	Matt. 20:30; Mark 10:46; Luke 18:35

(9) *Common to Matthew, Mark, and John*

| Christ walks on the sea | Matt. 14:25; Mark 6:48; John 6:19 |

(10) *Common to All the Evangelists*

| The five thousand fed | Matt. 14:15; Mark 6:34; Luke 9:10; John 6:1-14 |

ACTS AND LETTERS THROUGH PHILEMON

Irenaeus said,

> After our Lord rose from the dead and when they were endued from on high with power of the Spirit who came upon them, they were filled with respect to all things and had perfect knowledge and went forth to the ends of the earth proclaiming those good things which are ours from God and announcing heavenly peace to men.

This was the atmosphere of the Acts of the Apostles. These men were laid hold upon by the Spirit of God and thrust into a sinful and pagan world with astonishing dynamic to make new followers of Jesus Christ. The real resurrection of our Lord and the actual filling with the Spirit were the two great factors which caused this radical change in the Apostles. Their preaching, teaching, and living proved to be God Himself preaching, teaching, and living through them.

Steps leading up to the Areopagus where Paul was "on trial" for the faith at Athens (Acts 17).

In the first half of the Acts (chapter 1-12), Peter is the key human character. Mentioned more times than any other single figure in the New Testament outside of Jesus, his thought and preaching are preserved for us not only in the book of Acts, but also in Gospel (Mark was the interpreter of Peter) and in Epistle. Paul is the key human figure in the second half of the Acts (chapters 13-28). His preaching and thought are preserved not only in the Acts, but in Epistle form too. There is biographical information about Paul in Acts and his Epistles (the chronological chart below shows the interrelation of his journeys, imprisonment, and Epistles). He wrote thirteen Epistles, nine to churches (Romans through II Thessalonians) and four to individuals (I Timothy through Philemon). He often dictated his letters (he seems to have been nearly blind and he was often in prison), and his rugged, jagged, realistic sentences reflect the living, breathing, pulsating Apostle aflame to spread the Gospel and see people radically changed from sin to righteous living. Paul was a man who had experienced Christ (on the Damascus Road) in living encounter; he simply couldn't keep still about all this because he knew from personal experience the power of God to make bad men good. He walked, worked, wrote—he did anything and everything to tell this Good News.

A Note on the Arrangement of Paul's Letters

The letters of Paul were arranged by length rather than in their order of writing, a pattern still followed in our New Testaments. Thus letters to groups (churches) come first, those to individuals second, and within these two divisions the longest appear first with the single exception of Galatians which precedes Ephesians (Ephesians is slightly longer).

Chronological Chart

The interrelation of Paul's journeys, imprisonments, and Epistles helps provide perspective. Dates should be considered only approximate.

PAUL'S FIRST MISSIONARY JOURNEY (Acts 13-14)   47–48 A.D.
   Galatians written from Antioch in Syria
      shortly after first journey   48 A.D.

PAUL'S SECOND MISSIONARY JOURNEY
　(Acts 15:36—18:22)　　　　　　　　　　49–52 A.D.
　　I Thessalonians written from Corinth　　50 A.D.
　　II Thessalonians written from Corinth　　50 A.D.

PAUL'S THIRD MISSIONARY JOURNEY
　(Acts 18:23—21:17)　　　　　　　　　　52–58 A.D.
　　I Corinthians written from Ephesus　　54 A.D.
　　II Corinthians written from Macedonia　　55 A.D.
　　Romans written from Corinth　　57 or 58 A.D.

PAUL'S IMPRISONMENT (in Jerusalem)
　(Acts 21:18—23:30)　　　　　　　　　　58 A.D.

PAUL'S IMPRISONMENT (in Caesarea)
　(Acts 23:31—26:32)　　　　　　　　　　58–60 A.D.

PAUL'S IMPRISONMENT (in Rome)
　(Acts 27-28)　　　　　　　　　　　　　60–61 A.D.
　　Philippians written from Rome　　60 or 61 A.D.
　　Colossians written from Rome　　60 or 61 A.D.
　　Philemon written from Rome　　60 or 61 A.D.
　　Ephesians written from Rome　　60 or 61 A.D.

PAUL'S RELEASE FROM FIRST ROMAN
　IMPRISONMENT　　　　　　　　　　61 or 62 A.D.
　　Titus written from Ephesus　　63 A.D.
　　I Timothy written from Macedonia　　63 A.D.

PAUL'S SECOND IMPRISONMENT　　　　　64 A.D.
　　II Timothy written from Rome　　64 A.D.

THE ACTS OF THE APOSTLES

Authorship

Unquestionably, Luke the physician is the author of the Acts. Read the opening verses of Luke's Gospel and the opening verses of Acts and it is immediately clear that he is the author of both books. There are numerous other arguments for the Lukan authorship of Acts, one of which is that there are some fifty words in Luke which are also in Acts, but are not found anywhere else in the New Testament. Some of these reflect his medical practice; he is the only doctor who writes in the New Testament, and it is no surprise that he should use a somewhat scientific vocabulary. As in the Gospel of Luke, there is in Acts the same interest in children, women, the sick, the poor; and, of course, there is the same profound concern for his fellow Gentiles.

Date

　The Acts of the Apostles was in all probability written shortly

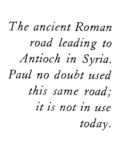

The ancient Roman road leading to Antioch in Syria. Paul no doubt used this same road; it is not in use today.

after the completion of the Gospel of Luke. If Luke were written shortly after 60 A.D., the Acts was composed not long after that. The optimistic close of Acts (the last word is "unhindered") leaves the impression that it was completed before 64 (Nero's persecution). The last event of Acts is Paul's imprisonment at Rome (c. 60–61). Thus it appears that Acts was written or completed between 61 and 64 A.D.

Destination

Though written for Gentiles generally, Luke addressed Theophilus specifically in both Luke and Acts.

Key Verse

Acts 1:8. "But you shall receive power when the Holy Spirit has come upon you; and you shall be my witnesses in Jerusalem and in all Judea and Samaria and to the end of the earth."

Purpose and Theme

The key verse outlines the entire book of Acts, a thing no other New Testament key verse does. Luke gives us this information so that the reader will know where he is going as he reads through the book. And just where is the reader going? First to Jerusalem (Chapters 1 to 7); then to Judea and Samaria (Chapters 8 to 12); finally to the uttermost parts of the world (Chapters 13 to 28). More specifically, the Gospel moves from Jerusalem to Samaria (8:5), the coast (8:40), Damascus (9:10), Antioch and Cyprus (11:19), Asia Minor (13:13), Continental Europe (16:11), and Rome (28:16).

There are one or two others reasons Acts 1:8 is unquestionably the key verse. The key word "witness" is included in the verse. All through the book, Luke attempts to show that people under the power of the Holy Spirit can witness to the saving power of Jesus Christ.

Still another reason 1:8 is the key verse is that the chief character of the book is indicated—the Holy Spirit. Someone has rightly said that this book might be called "The Acts of the Holy Spirit." While Peter is the chief human character in the first twelve chapters and Paul the leading human figure in chapters 13 to 28, it remains that the Holy Spirit is *the* chief figure of the *entire* book.

The Acts of the Apostles is the first Church history book, and it is the only such book of the New Testament. It records

Damascus' scenes: (1) the city gate leading into the Street called Straight (Acts 9:11); (2) the window through which tradition says Paul escaped in a basket (Acts 9:25; II Corinthians 11:33).

the birthday of the Church (Acts 2), the first deacons (Acts 6), the first martyr (Acts 7), etc., making the Acts a book of firsts. If we did not have this volume in our New Testament, we would be lacking a tremendous amount of information about how the Church was initiated and grew in its earliest years. The years covered in the Acts are about thirty, the period following the death and resurrection of our Lord and ending with Paul's imprisonment in Rome (c. 60–61 A.D.).

The Greek title of this book is *Praxeis Apostolon*. There are no definite articles, thus there is not sufficient evidence for the traditional title The *Acts* of *The Apostles*. As scholarly research has

Paul was at Athens, Greece. Pictured is the Erechtheum (fifth century B.C.).

pointed out, a better literal rendering of the Greek title would be *Some* Acts of *Some* Apostles.

Outline

THE ACTS OF THE APOSTLES TO THE JEWS ("in Jerusalem, Judea, and Samaria") (chapters 1-12)

The Acts of Peter (chapters 1-5)
The Promise of the Holy Spirit (chapter 1)
The Coming of the Holy Spirit (chapter 2)
The Healing of the Lame Man by the Beautiful Gate and its Results (chapters 3-4)
Ananias and Sapphira Lie to the Holy Spirit and Die (chapter 5)

The Acts of the Deacons (chapters 6-8)
The Seven Deacons Selected (chapter 6)
Stephen's Address and Martyrdom (chapter 7)
Philip's Evangelistic Activities (chapter 8)

The Acts of Peter Continued (chapters 9-12)
Saul's Conversion, Peter Heals Aeneas, Peter Raises Tabitha from the Dead (chapter 9)
Cornelius and Peter Receive Visions and Learn that the Gospel is for the Gentiles (chapters 10-11)
An Angel Releases Peter from Prison (chapter 12)

156

THE ACTS OF PAUL THE MISSIONARY TO THE GENTILES ("and to the ends of the earth") (chapters 13-28)

Paul the Traveler (13:1—21:17)
  The First Missionary Journey (chapters 13-14)
  The Jerusalem Council (15:1-35)
  The Second Missionary Journey (15:36—18:22)
  The Third Missionary Journey (18:23—21:17)

Paul the Prisoner (21:18—28:31)
  The First Imprisonment: Jerusalem (21:18—23:30)
  The Second Imprisonment: Caesarea (23:31—26:32)
  The Third Imprisonment: Rome (chapters 27-28)

ROMANS

Authorship and Date

Paul the Apostle was the author of the book of Romans. It was probably written from Corinth; Paul's stay in Greece—in Corinth at the house of Gaius (16:23)—as recorded in Acts 20:3, probably marks the period in which he wrote the letter to Rome. If so, he wrote it early in 58 or even 57 A.D., during the third missionary journey.

Destination

This book was written in the first instance to Roman Christians, though Paul had copies made by his secretary Tertius (16:22) to send to churches other than Rome. It is difficult to know how the Church at Rome was begun and established; but more than one scholar has suggested that citizens from the city of

The Appian Way still used today was travelled by Paul on his way to Rome.

*The River Tiber,
Rome.*

Rome who were at Jerusalem on the day of Pentecost (Acts 2:10) took the Gospel back to their city. It is now fairly well established that Paul was writing to both Jews and Gentiles.

Key Verses   Romans 1:16-17.

Purpose and   The key verses indicate the great purpose and dynamic behind
Theme   the writing of Romans:

> For I am not ashamed of the Gospel: it is the power of God for salvation to every one who has faith, to the Jew first and also to the Greek. For in it the righteousness of God is revealed through faith for faith; as it is written, 'He who through faith is righteous shall live.' (Cp. Habakkuk 2:4.)

Here is underscored the righteousness of God and salvation through faith. The theme is developed two ways: by a systematic and doctrinal argument (chapters 1 through 11), and by an ethical or practical application (chapters 12 through 16). The first eleven chapters comprise, along with the book of Galatians, perhaps the most authoritative source of Christian doctrine in the Christian literature; together they form a kind of final court of appeal for establishing and testing any system of Christian doctrine.

Paul develops his theme by establishing first of all the fact of the righteousness of God, that is, His moral perfection. Over against that he pits man's sin. He says if man could obey the Law of God, then he would be free from the taint of sin and thus able to come directly to God. But Paul moves on to make clear what we all know, that no one in and of himself is capable of keeping the Law of God. What is Paul's solution? The person of Jesus Christ Who bridges the gulf between the righteous God and sinful man. The atonement is the vehicle of justification. It is thus seen that salvation is the product, not of anything man can do, but of what God does in Christ. Salvation, in other words, is God's act, never man's.

St. Peter's Cathedral, Rome, named for the Apostle.

The Epistle closes by indicating how a justified person ought to live. It is not enough, says Paul, to assume the benefits of justification; one must take upon himself the responsibilities of living according to God's moral standard.

The letter terminates with news of a more personal nature including greetings. It should be noted that chapter sixteen was not included in all the copies of Romans which circulated in Paul's day, the reason being that this chapter had no relevance for groups outside Rome to which the letter was sent in the first instance.

Outline

SALUTATION AND INTRODUCTION (1:1-17)

DOCTRINAL TEACHING (1:18—11:36)
    The Gospel an Imperative (1:18—3:20)
      The Situation in the Pagan World (1:18-32)
      The Situation in the Gentile World (2:1-16)
      The Situation of the Self-righteous Jew (2:17-29)
      The Situation of the Entire Human Race (3:1-20)

    The Gospel of Justification by Faith Alone (3:21—5:21)
    Jesus Christ is Our Righteousness by Faith Alone (3:21-31)
    The Old Testament Authority (chapter 4)
    The Glorious Products of Justification by Faith alone; Adam and Christ (chapter 5)

    The Gospel of Power Over Sin in the Christian (chapters 6-8)
    New Life in Christ (chapter 6)
    Power Over Sin not Given through the Law (chapter 7)

Power Over Sin through Life in the Spirit, "More than Conquerors" (chapter 8)

The Gospel and the Jews (chapters 9-11)
God's Selection and Mercy (chapter 9)
Faith and Law, Salvation (chapter 10)
Israel's Final Salvation (chapter 11)

PRACTICAL APPLICATION (chapters 12-16)
Practical Application and the Self as Related to the Church and Humanity (chapter 12)
Practical Application as Related to Civil Governments (chapter 13)
Practical Application as Related to Questionable Practices (chapter 14)
Practical Application as Related to Joy, Peace, and Hope (15:1-13)
Paul's Plans and Closing Remarks (15:14—16:27)

I CORINTHIANS

Authorship and Date

Scholarly research and tradition tell us that Paul was the author of I Corinthians. 16:8 indicates that he wrote this Epistle from the city of Ephesus, just across the Aegean Sea from Corinth, where he resided for some two years. We have two Corinthian Epistles, though it appears that he had written another earlier than I Corinthians. Paul's stay in Ephesus began about 54 A.D. and it was during this period he wrote I Corinthians.

Destination

Acts Chapter 18 records something of the early days of the Church at Corinth which Paul established and to which this Epistle is addressed. Corinth was the largest city of Greece. It was a significant seaport and trading center, and served as the political capital of the Roman province of Achaia. It was a militarily strong city, but exceedingly wicked. The paganism of Corinth had rubbed off on the Christians, and in I Corinthians Paul attempts to come to grips with some of the problems that regularly faced his flock.

Key Verses

I Corinthians 13:1; 14:33a. "If I speak in the tongues of men and of angels, but have not love, I am a noisy gong or a clanging cymbal."

"For God is not a God of confusion but of peace."

Purpose and Theme

I Corinthians gives us a good insight into the problems of a local church in the first century. Near the outset of the book Paul launches into a forthright criticism of the party spirit in the Corinthian Church. Some, he says, announce themselves as being of

Ancient Corinth looking toward its acropolis on the hill in the background.

the party of Paul, others of the party of Apollos, others of the party of Cephas (Peter's Judaic name), and still others claimed to be of the party of Christ. Paul says divisions are nonsense and wicked. He then proceeds to another evil practice, sexual immorality. The worship of Venus (Aphrodite) included immoral acts. Paul repeatedly emphasizes the necessity of sexual purity. He discusses meat offered to heathen idols, and the difficulty involved in buying and eating such meat is dealt with. Paul also comes to grips with the matter of public worship, especially the Holy Communion. He makes clear the standards of reverence in worship and in taking the Lord's Supper. In chapters 12, 13, and 14 he treats the gifts of the Holy Spirit; the Corinthian Church had been overrun by a disorderly use of glossolalia (speaking in tongues); and he attempts to state its function along with the other gifts, but focuses in chapter 13 on the greatest of all gifts and the one most enduring, love (*agape*—the highest expression of love). Chapter 15 is the earliest account of the resurrection of our Lord in the entire New Testament. Paul concludes his first Epistle to the Corinthian Church with reference to the sick and the poor, and adds a few personal words.

Outline

SALUTATION (1:1-9)

PARTY SPIRIT REBUKED (1:10—4:21)
    Divisions in the Church (1:10—3:23)
    Defense of Paul's Ministry (4:1-21)

ANSWERS TO PERSONAL PROBLEMS (chapters 5-6)
    Immorality (chapter 5)
    Lawsuits (6:1-11)
    Fornication, the Sacredness of One's Body (6:12-20)

ANSWERS TO QUESTIONS (7:1—16:4)
    Marriage (chapter 7)
    Meat Offered to Idols, Christian Freedom (chapters 8-10)
    Problems in Public Worship (chapters 11-14)
      Covering the Head (11:1-16)
      The Lord's Supper (11:17-34)
      Tongues, the Superiority of Love (chapters 12-14)
    The Resurrection (chapter 15)
    Collections for the Saints (16:1-4)

CONCLUDING REMARKS AND BENEDICTION (16:5-24)

II CORINTHIANS

Authorship and Date   Paul is recognized as the author of this second letter to the Corinthian Church. He wrote it from Macedonia (cp. 2:13) upon the return of Titus from Corinth who brought the information that the Christians at Corinth had received Paul's earlier letter. It was written probably a few months after I Corinthians (see date of *I Corinthians* above). It should be noted, however, that chapters 1-9 are of such a different character that some scholars believe them to have been written at another time.

A road in ancient Corinth; Paul no doubt walked on this very road.

The Christians at Corinth.

II Corinthians 4:5; 5:20-21. "For what we preach is not ourselves, but Jesus Christ as Lord, with ourselves as your servants for
Jesus' sake."

"So we are ambassadors for Christ, God making his appeal
through us. We beseech you on behalf of Christ, be reconciled to
God. For our sake he made him to be sin who knew no sin, so
that in him we might become the righteousness of God."

The atmosphere of the second letter is quite different from that
of the first. In the first Paul deals with the problems in the Corinthian Church; in the second with his own ministry, feelings,
and problems. This second letter is a kind of defense of himself;
for after he wrote the first letter, in which he "scolded" the Christians at Corinth, they tended to defend themselves and undermine
Paul's authority. Through all this Paul shows a profound concern
for young Christians. It is heart warming to read of his desire to
restore to the fellowship of the Church one of its members who
earlier had had to be disciplined.

SALUTATION AND THANKSGIVING (1:1-7)

DEFENSE OF PAUL'S PERSONAL CONDUCT (1:8—2:13)

DEFENSE OF PAUL'S MINISTRY (2:14—7:4)

RESULTS OF PREVIOUS LETTER (7:5-16)

STEWARDSHIP (chapter 8-9)

DEFENSE OF PAUL'S APOSTLESHIP (chapters 10-12)

FINAL EXHORTATIONS AND BENEDICTION (chapter 13)

In I Corinthians 5:9 we see an indication of an earlier letter to
the Corinthian Church. Some scholars believe this letter is entirely
lost, others say that it is only partially lost and that a portion of it
is to be found in II Corinthians 6:14 to 7:1 and/or chapters 10
through 13.

GALATIANS

This is another of St. Paul's letters, and he probably wrote it from
Antioch in Syria in 48 A.D. shortly after his first missionary journey
(though scholars suggest dates within the ten year period, 48 to
58 A.D.).

"To the churches of Galatia" (1:2b) by which is probably meant
those founded by Paul and Barnabas on the first missionary
journey—Antioch of Pisidia, Iconium, Lystra, and Derbe (Acts
13:14—14:23)—all in the south of the Roman province called
Galatia.

Galatians 5:1. "For freedom Christ has set us free; stand fast therefore and do not submit again to a yoke of slavery."

Purpose and Theme

The clue to understanding this book is found in Acts 15, the record of proceedings at the Jerusalem Council. The question for debate at the Council was, 'Must one submit to the Jewish law, including circumcision, in order to become a Christian?' In other words, must one first become a Jew before he can become a Christian? Those who said Yes, we call legalists. Paul's answer was No. Galatians is sometimes called the Magna Charta of Christian liberty.

Evidently this very debate was carried on among the Galatian Christians. Paul attempts to settle the debate; he writes that they do not need to submit to the rite of circumcision to become Chrisians. Justification is by faith, not by acts. Naturally Paul was severely criticized by his fellow Jews for this liberal position. In his letter to the Galatians he justifies his position and underscores the doctrine of justification by faith (3:1—4:31 especially) which he developed in longer systematic form in the book of Romans. Paul adds a word of warning: even though Christians are free from irrelevant details of the Jewish law, they must produce the results of Christ-centered love which is initiated in the heart by the Holy Spirit. Paul concludes his letter with a section of practical application (6:1-10 especially). Earlier in the book he defended his apostolic authority and the truth of his instructions (1:10—2:21 especially).

Outline

INTRODUCTION (1:1-9)

DEFENSE OF PAUL'S APOSTLESHIP (1:10—2:21)

LEGALISM VERSUS CHRISTIAN LIBERTY (chapters 3-5)

PRACTICAL EXHORTATIONS (6:1-10)

CONCLUSION AND BENEDICTION (6:11-18)

EPHESIANS

Authorship and Date

Paul wrote Ephesians from Rome while he was in prison (3:1; 4:1; 6:20) in 60 or 61 A.D., about the same time he wrote Colossians. The two Epistles contain many of the same ideas and even expressions (see cross references in Revised Standard Version).

Destination

In all probability this letter was not sent to the Church at Ephesus alone, but was a kind of round robin or circular letter. Some early manuscripts exclude the words "in Ephesus" in 1:1, and there are no references in the book to Ephesus or personal greetings to the people there, even though Paul had spent a good deal of time in Ephesus (see Acts 19:9-10).

The amphitheatre in Ephesus as it appears today (compare Acts 19).

Ephesians 1:3. "Blessed be the God and Father of our Lord Jesus Christ who has blessed us in Christ with every spiritual blessing in the heavenly places."

Jesus Christ and the establishing and completing of His Church in the eternal plan of God is the theme of this Epistle. Put in simpler terms, the theme is "the Christian" (note Paul's expression "in Christ"). Christ is Savior of the world, of the whole of life, and of knowledge in all its dimensions. A great trinitarian emphasis pervades the book (1:5, 12, 13; 2:18-20; 3:14, 16, 17; 4:4-6). The Father calls people to identify with the Church, the Son redeems and forgives, the Spirit seals and guides the fellowship of believers by His indwelling presence. He refers to the Church as one and says that those who are "in Christ" enjoy a common fellowship in His Body (the Church). Note the figures for the Church: the Body of Christ (1:23; 4:16), the temple (building) of God (2:20-22), the bride of Christ (5:23-32). One gets the impression that Paul is saying to us that although people vary in their gifts and are of differing racial and cultural backgrounds, all who know Christ enjoy common privileges in Him. Note the two prayers in Ephesians (1:15-23 and 3:14-19); also the work of the Holy Spirit (e.g. 1:13-14; 4:1-16). Generally, chapters 1-3 are doctrinal, while 4-6 are practical with emphasis on the Christian's responsibility.

Outline SALUTATION (1:1-2)

THE CHRISTIAN's POSITION IN CHRIST (1:3—3:21)

THE CHRISTIAN's WALK (4:1—6:9)

THE CHRISTIAN's ARMOUR (6:10-20)

CONCLUSION AND BENEDICTION (6:21-24)

PHILIPPIANS

Authorship and Date This is another of the so-called prison (1:7, 13, 14, 16) Epistles, Paul probably being imprisoned at Rome (see the end of Acts), though the imprisonments at Caesarea and Ephesus have been suggested as possibilities. If he wrote from Rome, 60 or 61 A.D. would correspond to Acts 28:30. References to the praetorian guard and Caesar's household also make us think of Rome.

Destination The first convert of all Europe had been at Philippi in Macedonia; she was a business woman named Lydia. Here also Paul had suffered at the hands of people who misunderstood him; he had been flogged and thrown into the jail (Acts 16:25ff), but after an earthquake the jailer and his entire family were converted. The congregation at Philippi was the first established by Paul in Europe (Acts 16:11-15). With this as a background, it is no wonder Paul writes in such a personal manner (note the frequent personal pronouns).

Key Verse Philippians 4:4. "Rejoice in the Lord always; again I will say, Rejoice."

Purpose and Theme In this little book, Paul writes about a number of things in general. The initial stimulus for writing, however, seems to have been a gift sent to the imprisoned Paul by the Christians at Philippi (4:18); and, naturally, Paul wanted to thank his friends. Epaphroditus (2:25-29) had delivered the gift and he, too, returned Paul's thanks to the Philippian Church by delivering the letter. Paul's love for this Church breathes through this letter in a very beautiful way. Naturally, he desires the Philippian Church to have a high level of integrity and an aggressive program of growth. Beyond that, he encourages love, humility, unity, peace, joy. He proclaims the great fact of God and His providence (imprisonment is not necessarily bad!). He does not fail to warn the Church of legalism (compare Acts 15 and the book of Galatians) and false teachers. Paul also exhorts his friends to spiritual maturity. Philippians is a choice Epistle with the appeal to live joyfully in Christ in the midst of adverse circumstances (2:2; 4:8-14). Note the great passage on the humiliation and exaltation of Christ (2:5-11).

INTRODUCTION (1:1-11)   Outline
    Salutation (1:1-2)
    Praise and Prayer (1:3-11)
PROGRESS REPORT (1:12-30)
THE EXAMPLE OF CHRIST, HIS HUMILIATION AND EXALTATION
    (chapter 2)
BEWARE OF LEGALISM, PRESS TOWARD THE GOAL (chapter 3)
STAND FAST IN THE LORD (4:1-9)
CLOSING WORDS OF THANKS, BENEDICTION (4:10-23)

COLOSSIANS

This, like Ephesians and Philippians, is a prison (4:3, 10, 18)   **Authorship**
Epistle. It was written by Paul (1.1) from Rome, perhaps in 60   **and Date**
or 61 A.D.

Although never at Colossae, a town in Phrygia in Asia Minor,   **Destination**
Paul wrote to the Church there. No doubt he knew some of the
people there, for Ephesus was only about 100 miles away; and he
had made Ephesus a kind of center for his teaching. The Church
at Colossae had a minister in Epaphras (1:7; 4:12). Tychicus delivered the letter (4:7-8); he also delivered Paul's Epistle to Philemon (see "Philemon" below).

Colossians 1:18-20; 2:10. "He is the head of the body, the   **Key Verses**
church; he is the beginning, the first born from the dead, that in
everything he might be preeminent. For in him all the fullness of
God was pleased to dwell."

"And you have come to fulness of life in him, who is the head
of all rule and authority."

Paul's purpose in this letter is to argue against specific errors   **Purpose and**
embodied in a teaching called Gnosticism which had crept into the   **Theme**
Church at Colossae. Some teachers there claimed superior knowledge of religion (2:18), a trick of the Gnostics to make those outside the cult feel inferior and left out. The Gnostics believed in a
ladder of deities: the farther up the ladder the more power the
beings possessed. Such belief is a form of idolatry and Paul cries
out against it saying that God is the *only* supreme power and that
Jesus Christ is His Son. Paul emphasizes Christ's pre-eminence
and argues that all things find their harmony in Him and that
every problem finds its answer in Him. The Gnostics also believed
—at least some of them believed—in a kind of asceticism (isolating
one's self from the world and all luxury) (2:16, 20-23). Paul drives
home the very important point that asceticism in and of itself is

meaningless; but if refraining from giving expression to one's passions is asceticism, then that is the genuine asceticism. To refrain from using the natural gifts of God, however, is a meaningless exercise. (The asceticism of Colossae reminds us somewhat of the Essenes. See "Jewish Sects and Parties." The ritualism at Colossae [2:16-18] is also reminiscent of the Essenes.) Paul writes out of a concerned heart, and one is impressed by his utter sincerity and complete integrity. The passages on the new life through the power of the risen Christ, and the fruit of that experience, are classical (1:9-20; 2:6-7; 2:9-15; 3:1-17). Note the emphasis on doctrine (1:1—3:4) and practice (3:5—4:18).

Outline

INTRODUCTION (1:1-12)
  Greeting (1:1-2)
  Thanksgiving and Prayer (1:3-12)
THE PERSON AND WORK OF CHRIST (1:13-29)
WARNING AGAINST FALSE TEACHING (chapter 2)
THE NEW LIFE IN CHRIST (3:1—4:1)
PERSONAL GREETINGS AND BENEDICTION (4:2-18)

I THESSALONIANS

Authorship and Date

Paul, from the city of Corinth. One of his earlier Epistles, this was written in perhaps 50 A.D.

Destination

To the Christians in Thessalonica, the modern Salonika, in Greece. That Church was, of course, started by Paul (Acts 17:1-10). He had sent Timothy (3:1-3) who brought a report to Paul in Corinth; in turn the apostle writes them a letter.

Key Verses

I Thessalonians 1:9-10. "For you remember our labor and toil, brethren; we worked night and day, that we might not burden any of you, while we preached to you the gospel of God. You are witnesses and God also, how holy and righteous and blameless was our behavior to you believers."

Purpose and Theme

The atmosphere in the Thessalonian Church is best described by the word *persecution*. Paul aims to instill its members with courage and fresh conviction even though he himself had been accused wrongfully (2:3-6). As in II Corinthians, he defends his position and authority for he had been falsely criticized. He warns the Church against impurity and exhorts to love and hard work. As in II Thessalonians, I Thessalonians develops a particular eschatological idea. (Eschatology has to do with *last things,* such as the Second Coming and the winding up of history.) Paul says a word about those who have died in the Lord (4:13-18) and indi-

cates his view of the Second Coming in the last part of the Epistle
(5:1-11).

SALUTATION AND THANKSGIVING (chapter 1)

THE STATE OF THE CHURCH (chapters 2-3)
    Ministry of the Apostles at Thessalonica (chapter 2)
    Timothy Reports Progress (chapter 3)

INSTRUCTIONS TO THE CHURCH (4:1—5:11)
    Practical Instructions (chapter 4)
    On the Second Coming (5:1-11)

CLOSING REMARKS AND BENEDICTION (5:12-28)

Outline

II THESSALONIANS

Paul was no doubt writing from the same place he produced
I Thessalonians, Corinth, and a few months later, about 50 A.D.

**Authorship
and Date**

The Church at Thessalonica.

Destination

II Thessalonians 2:15. "So then, brethren, stand firm and hold
to the traditions which you were taught by us, either by word of
mouth or by letter."

Key Verse

The real thrust and purpose of this letter has to do with the
Second Coming of our Lord. A certain group in the Thessalonian
Church was so taken with the Second Coming that jobs were given
up and plans for the future dismissed. Some thought the Lord
had already come (2:2). Paul makes it clear that no man can
depend upon the absolute immediacy of Christ's return. Indeed
the "man of lawlessness" must be revealed first (2:3-8). Since we
do not know when He will come again, it is our job not to spend
time talking about the Lord's return but to work in all good conscience (e.g. 3:10) and to keep life running in a normal Christian
course. Paul writes to send appreciation of the Church members'
spiritual progress (1:3-4); to encourage them in spite of persecution (1:5-10); to correct their understanding of the Second Coming (2:1-12); and to remedy disorder in their Church (3:6-15).
I and II Thessalonians are of great help in showing us the mind
and problems of a first century local church; and they give us a
fine insight on how to handle similar problems in our own day.

**Purpose and
Theme**

INTRODUCTION (chapter 1)
    Greeting (1:1-2)
    Thanksgiving and Prayer (1:3-12)

TEACHING ON THE SECOND COMING (chapter 2)

Outline

EXHORTATIONS TO BE READY FOR CHRIST'S RETURN (3:1-15)

BENEDICTION (3:16-18)

I TIMOTHY

Authorship and Date   I and II Timothy were certainly done late in his life. I Timothy was written from Macedonia (probably Philippi) between Paul's first and second Roman imprisonments. Some scholars have questioned that he wrote I and II Timothy and Titus, but there is a long tradition favoring his authorship of all three. They are called "Pastorals" because they deal so much with the problems of a pastor and his flock. I Timothy was written about 63 A.D.

Destination   This is not a letter to a specific church or group, rather it is an ordinary personal letter. It was, of course, sent to Timothy who had a Greek father, a devout mother and grandmother (Acts 16:1; II Timothy 1:5). He was a convert of the Apostle Paul (see the story, the setting of which is Lystra, Acts 16). Timothy was very close to Paul and proved to be a valuable help in the spread of the Gospel. It appears that Timothy was in Ephesus, giving leadership to the Church in that city.

Key Verses   I Timothy 3:15; 4:12. "If I am delayed, you may know how one ought to behave in the household of God, which is the church of the living God, the pillar and bulwark of the truth."

"Let no one despise your youth, but set the believers an example in speech and conduct, in love, in faith, in purity."

Purpose and Theme   It is evident that Paul is concerned about Timothy who possessed some immaturities; and he sends warnings about erroneous teachings. It is easy, Paul suggests, for such teachings to find residence in the heart of an individual (Timothy) and in the heart of the Church. Further, Paul shared some of his beliefs and feelings about Church administration, including the selection of officers and the handling of philanthropic monies. Paul writes as a senior minister to a junior, advising on matters of public worship, qualifications for officers, false teaching, and the various groups in the Church (widows, elders, slaves, false teachers). Paul emphasizes the necessity of *godliness* in a minister of the Gospel. The book constitutes a good source of information on the problems of a first century Christian church.

Outline   SALUTATION (1:1-2)

WARNING AGAINST FALSE DOCTRINE (1:3-20)

PROPER PUBLIC WORSHIP (chapter 2)

QUALIFICATIONS FOR CHURCH OFFICERS (chapter 3)

INSTRUCTIONS ON APOSTASY (chapter 4)

CONCLUDING INSTRUCTIONS CONCERNING GROUPS AND TIMOTHY,
   A BENEDICTION (chapters 5-6)

II TIMOTHY

St. Paul, apparently from the city of Rome, about 64 A.D. This **Authorship**
book is particularly touching because it is obvious that Paul knows **and Date**
he is waiting out the last days of his life (4:6). In point of time,
this is the last Epistle he ever wrote so far as we know.

This book is written as a personal letter to Timothy who was **Destination**
still preaching in the city of Ephesus.

II Timothy 3:14-17; 4:1-5. "But as for you, continue in what **Key Verses**
you have learned and have firmly believed, knowing from whom
you learned it and how from childhood you have been acquainted
with the sacred writings which are able to instruct you for salvation through faith in Christ Jesus. All scripture is inspired by God
and profitable for teaching, for reproof, for correction and for
training in righteousness that the man of God may be complete,
equipped for every good work."

"I charge you in the presence of God and of Christ Jesus who
is to judge the living and the dead and by his appearing and his
kingdom: preach the word, be urgent in season and out of season,
convince, rebuke, and exhort, be unfailing in patience and in teaching. For the time is coming when people will not endure sound
teaching, but having itching ears they will accumulate for themselves teachers to suit their own likings, and will turn away from
listening to the truth and wander into myths. As for you, always
be steady, endure suffering, do the work of an evangelist, fulfil
your ministry."

The amazing thing is that Paul, knowing he is about to be **Purpose and**
martyred for his Lord, writes to encourage Timothy. He tells him **Theme**
to stand by the faith and to live by his convictions. Paul does not
sympathize with himself; he writes to encourage a brother. The
integrity of the Gospel and perfect loyalty to that Gospel are im-
peratives according to Paul; he lets Timothy know he must live
by this high standard. Note the personal requests at the end of the
letter.

SALUTATION AND THANKSGIVING (1:1-5) **Outline**

EXHORTATIONS TO STEADFASTNESS (1:6—2:13)

Titus

Authorship and Date Paul wrote this little book somewhere in Asia (perhaps Ephesus) between his first and second imprisonments at Rome. It was written about 63 A.D. or in the same period as I Timothy.

Destination This is sent to Crete where Titus is giving leadership to the Church on that island. Paul had visited Crete, then left and sent the letter perhaps by courtesy of Zenas and Apollos. Paul gives directions and spiritual uplift to this man Titus who was one of his converts.

Key Verses Titus 2:11-14. "For the grace of God has appeared for the salvation of all men, training us to renounce irreligion and worldly passions, and to live sober, upright, and godly lives in this world, awaiting our blessed hope, the appearing of the glory of our great God and Savior Jesus Christ who gave himself for us to redeem us from all iniquity and to purify for himself a people of his own who are zealous for good deeds."

Purpose and Theme Not unlike some passages in I and II Timothy, this little book offers guidance on the matter of Christian maturity and on the selection of Church officers and ministers. He suggests personal characteristics needed to develop a thoroughly Christian Church, and warns against what J. B. Phillips calls "counterfeit Christians."

Modern Crete, an island belonging to Greece. Paul wrote his letter to Titus who was a pastor on the island of Crete.

He has a word to say about slaves, and as usual closes with personal words and greetings. Note the emphasis on saving grace and Christian behavior (2:11-15), and Paul's own potent testimony (3:3-7). He also warns about arguing over legalism (3:8-11).

Outline

SALUTATION (1:1-4)

QUALIFICATIONS FOR ELDERS (1:5-9)

WARNING AGAINST HERETICAL TEACHERS (1:10-16)

PRACTICAL INSTRUCTIONS (2:1—3:11)

PERSONAL INSTRUCTIONS AND BENEDICTION (3:12-15)

PHILEMON

Authorship and Date

This is another of Paul's (1, 9, 19) prison Epistles and was written we think at the same time as the letters to Ephesus, Colossae (cp. Colossians 4:10-17 and Philemon 2, 23-24), and Philippi, in 60 or 61 A.D.

Destination

Philemon is an ordinary personal letter and was not intended for a church or group. The letter is directed to Philemon who was a member of the Christian community at Colossae. He had Church services in his own home as seen at the outset of this little Epistle.

Key Verses

Philemon 17-19. "So if you consider me your partner, receive him as you would receive me. If he has wronged you at all, or owes you anything, charge that to my account."

Purpose and Theme

Paul's warm heart is revealed as he writes to a personal friend, Philemon, master of Onesimus who was a runaway slave and thief. Onesimus had sought out Paul in Rome, and subsequently had not only become a stalwart Christian but a close brother in Christ to Paul. Onesimus means "useful" and apparently verse 11 is a kind of take-off or pun on the name. According to the custom of the day, Paul told Onesimus he must return to his master, but with him he sends this lovely little letter which Paul hopes will act as a kind of protection when he once again presents himself to his owner. Paul himself promises to make good any loss due to Onesimus. This story may be viewed as an analogy of redemption.

Outline

SALUTATION AND THANKSGIVING (1-7)

INTERCESSION FOR ONESIMUS (8-21)

PERSONAL GREETINGS AND BENEDICTION (22-25)

THE OTHER LETTERS THROUGH JUDE

HEBREWS STANDS by itself, its author unknown (see below), its position between the thirteen Pauline Epistles and the seven General Epistles. Hebrews underscores the superiority of Christ to persecuted Jewish Christians. The General Epistles are general in nature and were addressed to a wider group than local churches or individuals (thus their collective title). The General Letters are James, I, II Peter, I, II, III John, and Jude. Each is discussed below.

EPISTLE TO THE HEBREWS

Authorship One of the Fathers of the Church said, "Only God knows who wrote the book of Hebrews." Scholarship generally agrees with that point of view. In the days when the King James Version was produced, most people thought Paul was the author; thus the caption: "The Epistle of Paul the Apostle to the Hebrews." But since the 1611 translation of the English Bible, fewer and fewer scholars have believed that Paul actually wrote the book. There are some, however, who still hold to the Pauline authorship (the ancients along the Eastern shore of the Mediterranean and around Alexandria believed he wrote it). Others say that Paul wrote the book along with someone else (Origen believed the thoughts were Paul's, the composition and style someone else's). Still others hold that it is the product of a single pen, perhaps that of Barnabas (Tertullian thought Barnabas wrote it), Luke, or Apollos (Apollos was capable of producing the polished, Alexandrian Greek of Hebrews). The early Christians in Rome and the West did not claim to know who wrote it.

All of the other letters supposed to have been written by Paul say so in the text itself; not so with the book of Hebrews. The General Epistles (except I John) also indicate authorship in their texts. It is also true that the Greek text, in vocabulary, figures of speech, expressions, method of argument, and grammar, is frequently of a totally different character than the Epistles traditionally accredited to St. Paul.

Date It may have been written as early as the 60's A.D., but was in circulation at least by 95 A.D. The tone of the book suggests the persecution just before the fall of Jerusalem in 70 A.D.

Destination It is not known for certain to whom this book was directed. To Christian Jews, of course; the content of the book makes that clear. But to Christian Jews in what city we do not know. Jerusalem, Rome, and Alexandria have been suggested. Of these three Rome is favored by a good many scholars.

Key Verse

Hebrews 4:14. "Since then we have a great high priest who has passed through the heavens, Jesus, the Son of God, let us hold fast our confession."

Purpose and Theme

The author is writing to a group of persecuted Christian Jews who, because they are in the minority and are suffering, are tempted to deny their faith. He argues that the Person about whom the Jewish Scriptures and prophecy spoke is definitely Jesus the Christ. Who else could it be, argues the author, when He is superior to His predecessors and to angels? The New Covenant which Jesus came to bring and demonstrate is superior to the Old Covenant and Law of the Jewish Scriptures. The author's logic is clear; if the new is superior to the old, then why lapse back into the old? Besides, there are far richer resources in knowing Christ than simply in knowing the Old Testament Law. In Hebrews we have the longest continuous argument of any book in the entire Bible; the argument aims to show the pre-eminence of Christ and His faith over the Jewish faith. The book closes on a level of exhortation in terms of Christian responsibility and practical application of the Gospel. The great faith chapter ("the hall of fame" —chapter 11), and the author's view of Jesus Christ, "the same yesterday, today and forever" (13:8), have been an inspiration to Christians in all ages.

Outline

INTRODUCTION (1:1-3)

SUPERIORITY OF CHRIST TO ANGELS (1:4—2:18)

SUPERIORITY OF CHRIST TO MOSES (3:1—4:13)

SUPERIORITY OF CHRIST THE HIGH PRIEST TO THE OLD TESTAMENT PRIESTHOOD (4:14—10:18)

Christ and Aaron (4:14—5:4)

Christ and Melchizedek (5:5—7:28)

Christ and the New Covenant (8:1—10:18)

PRACTICAL APPLICATION (10:19—13:17)

Exhortation to Steadfastness (10:19-39)

Examples of Faith (chapter 11)

Further Practical Exhortations (12:1—13:17)

CONCLUSION AND BENEDICTION (13:18-25)

Authorship   A long tradition says that James the Just, brother of our Lord and bishop or overseer of the first Church at Jerusalem, was the author of this little volume (108 verses). He has been called "James the camel-kneed" because tradition says he prayed so much he produced callouses on his knees. There are in the New Testament three different persons by the name of James: James the son of Zebedee, sometimes called James the Great; James the son of Alpheus; and James the brother of our Lord, sometimes called the Just or Less. It is James the Just to whom the Church accredits this book.

Date   It is thought by many that this is the earliest book of the New Testament (others say Galatians is earliest). It could be dated in 50 or 51 A.D. or earlier.

Destination   This is addressed to the "twelve tribes in the dispersion." Very likely that means simply to the Jews scattered by persecution. These were the ancient displaced persons. They are known to the scholars as the Jews of the dispersion, though it should be realized that there were several so-called dispersions in Jewish history.

Key Verses   James 1:27; 2:20. "Religion that is pure and undefiled before God and the Father is this: to visit orphans and widows in their affliction, and to keep oneself unstained from the world."

"Do you want to be shown, you foolish fellow, that faith apart from works is barren?"

Purpose and Theme   This letter has sometimes been called the Proverbs of the New Testament because of its pithy, straightforward, homiletic statements. James is straightforward indeed when it comes to exposing sin, especially those subtle sins such as pride, gossip, aloofness, materialism, and practical atheism (belief in God without acting like it). There have always been those in the Christian Church who have respected this letter for its balance and sanity. Justification by faith alone (not highlighted in James) is one thing, but proving it by works is the acid test. This "acid test" James makes perfectly clear: "faith without works is dead." Note the emphases on pure religion (1:27), the claims of Christ (1:1; 2:1, 7), and individual regeneration (1:18, 21). There are fifty-four commands in this short book. Compare the ethical teaching of James with the Sermon on the Mount (Matthew 5-7).

Outline   SALUTATION (1:1)

THE TEST OF FAITH (1:2-27)

FAITH AND WORKS (chapter 2)

On Controlling the Tongue (chapter 3)

Reproofs Against Worldliness (4:1—5:6)

Admonitions to Holy Living (5:7-20)

I Peter

Authorship and Date

This letter from Peter (1:1) was probably written in Rome. Babylonia is used as the symbol of Rome. It is thought this letter was sent from Rome to Asia Minor between 62 and 69 A.D.

Destination

It will be noticed at the very outset that this book, like that of James, is addressed to the displaced (scattered) Jews. Specific places in Asia Minor are indicated (1:1).

Key Verses

I Peter 4:12-13. "Beloved do not be surprised at the fiery ordeal which comes upon you to prove you, as though something strange were happening to you. But rejoice in so far as you share Christ's sufferings that you may also rejoice and be glad when his glory is revealed."

Purpose and Theme

I Peter reminds us somewhat of Hebrews because the people to whom it was sent suffered a great deal of persecution. The book is concerned with the Christian's attitude or frame of mind in the midst of suffering; and Peter, in the spirit of a good pastor, sends hope and encouragement. To be a part of the sufferings of Christ (4:13) will prove the reality of their faith (1:6, 7). The Christian family and the Christian citizen are discussed. There are some interesting theological statements interspersed in the book— for example, that Christ, after his death, preached to the imprisoned spirits. Note the emphasis on God's saving act in Christ (1:3-12) and on holiness (1:13—2:10)

Outline

Salutation (1:1-2)

Suffering and Salvation (1:3-12)

Suffering and Holy Living (1:13—3:22)

Rejoicing in Suffering (chapter 4)

Exhortations to Elders and Other Church Members (5:1-11)

Personal Remarks and Benediction (5:12-14)

II Peter

Authorship and Date

There is considerable question as to the authorship. Ancient and contemporary research tends away from the idea that Peter was the author. A quick look at the book of Jude will show striking similarities to II Peter (cp. Jude 4-16 and II Peter 2:1-8), and the style is quite different from I Peter. Couple those two facts with a third, that the occurrences of the book suggest events after Peter's death, and it is clear why scholars tend to be unwilling to credit this book to Peter. A second century figure may have written under Peter's name (1:1) to gain prestige, a common device in ancient times. There is however, a possibility that Peter wrote part of it, and there is a school of thought that says he wrote all of it. Arguments for Petrine authorship are: there is a long Church tradition that Peter wrote it; the difference in style can be explained (he had a different secretary, he wrote to a different group, etc.); 1:1 may not have been added but put there by Peter himself.

It is probably impossible to date the book, but the tendency in current scholarship is to place it in the early second century.

Destination Apparently this letter was addressed to a local Church, but to what Church we do not know.

Key Verse II Peter 2:1. "But false prophets also arose among the people, just as there will be false teachers among you, who will secretly bring in destructive heresies, even denying the Master who bought them, bringing upon themselves swift destruction."

Purpose and Theme Somewhat apocalyptic in character, this book affirms the Second Coming of our Lord; it also cries out against the evils of heresy and teachers of error. There are practical statements (e.g., 1:2-7; 2:9) in the book as well as exhortations to develop a store of knowledge. The Christian faith is very real and important.

Outline SALUTATION (1:1-2)

EXHORTATIONS TO RIGHTEOUS LIVING (1:3-21)

WARNINGS AGAINST FALSE TEACHERS (chapter 2)

THE SECOND COMING OF THE LORD (3:1-17)

BENEDICTION (3:18)

I JOHN

Authorship and Date Tradition says that John the beloved, a member of the apostolic circle, was the author of this book. There are in the New Testament five men called John: John the Baptist; John the father of Simon Peter; John a member of the Sanhedrin (Acts 4:6); John Mark; and John the Apostle. It is the last of these five who was the author of this letter known as I John. Apparently John did his writing as an old man, perhaps in the early 90's A.D.

Destination Written from Ephesus, this little letter was probably a circular to be read by the individual Churches round about that great city of Asia Minor.

I John 5:11-12. "And this is the testimony, that God gave us eternal life and this life is in his Son. He who has the Son has life; he who has not the Son has not life." Key Verses

The emphases of love, righteousness, the spiritual life, etc., remind us of the Gospel of John. The view of sin is reminiscent of that Gospel, too. The emphasis upon love is beautiful indeed, and notice, too, the relation of obedience to love. Love is the opposite of fear, John observes further. Jesus Christ is, of course, very important to the author and he makes clear his belief that He was a real man who came to bring Life. The clear teaching on the new birth is driven home by the idea that it is quite possible for man to live in union with God. Warnings against false teachings are included; in this regard note the affirmation of 4:2 (cp. II John 7). **Purpose and Theme**

Outline

INTRODUCTION (1:1-4)

LIGHT AND DARKNESS CONTRASTED (1:5—2:29)

LOVE EVIDENCED IN OBEDIENCE (chapters 3-4)

ETERNAL LIFE THROUGH CHRIST (chapter 5)

II JOHN

Tradition says the same man who wrote I John wrote II John. Probably about the same time as I John.
To a local church ("The elect lady") and its members ("her children"). (See verse 1.) **Authorship Date Destination**

II John 9-10. "Any one who goes ahead and does not abide in the doctrine of Christ does not have God; he who abides in the doctrine of Christ has both the Father and the Son." **Key Verses**

This is one of the shortest books of the New Testament. It reminds us of II Peter in its denunciation of heretical teachers, and it is reminiscent of I John in its underscoring of the doctrines of Christ and Christian love. Verses 4 and 12 are warm personal statements to the "lady and her children." **Purpose and Theme**

Outline

GREETING AND PRAISE (1-4)

THE OLD COMMANDMENT OF LOVE (5-6)

RECEIVE NOT FALSE TEACHERS (7-11)

PERSONAL MESSAGES (12-13)

III JOHN

Authorship The same as that of I and II John.

Date About the same as that of I and II John.

Destination This book is addressed to one Gaius; but who was Gaius? Nobody really knows. This was a common name used several times in the New Testament. Gaius may have been an active leader in a local church, a church John had either visited or heard about.

Key Verse III John 11. "Beloved, do not imitate evil but imitate good. He who does good is of God; he who does evil has not seen God."

Purpose and Theme Apparently John is attempting to get across the idea that there is a vast difference between good and bad behavior, between poor and good conduct. He illustrates this by contrasting Diotrephes, a bad character (he "liked to put himself first," verse 9), and Demetrius, a good character. There is also in this letter a wholesome emphasis upon prayer, faithful work in the Church, and Christian integrity.

Outline

GAIUS: WALKS IN THE TRUTH (1-8)

DIOTREPHES: OPPOSES THE TRUTH (9-11)

DEMETRIUS: COMMENDED BY THE TRUTH (12)

CLOSING REMARKS (13-15)

JUDE

Authorship and Date Tradition says that Jude, brother of our Lord (Matthew 13:55), was the author of this book. Jude or Judas was a common name used several times in the Bible; but this particular Jude was the brother of James. He was not a believer until after the resurrection (John 7:5; Acts 1:14). It is impossible to know precisely when this book was written. The years between 70 and 80 A.D. may be suggested.

Destination To what church this was written we do not know, but apparently it was a congregation suffering temptation and heretical teaching. This could have been intended for more than one church, indeed perhaps for the Church in general.

Key Verse Jude 3. "Beloved, being very eager to write to you of our common salvation, I found it necessary to write appealing to you to contend for the faith which was once for all delivered to the saints."

Purpose and Theme This letter reminds us of II Peter and II John in its warning against heresy or false teaching. If the content of heretical teaching is not emphasized, the character of heretics is. Immorality (4, 7, 16), covetousness (11, 16), rejection of authority (8, 11), worldliness (they are "devoid of the Spirit"—vs. 19)—these are the signs of those who breed a contentious spirit. Their doom is like that of Sodom and Gomorrah (7). It is clear that a Jew is writing—for one thing there are references to Jewish literature. Fidelity to the faith "once for all delivered to the saints" (3) is underscored, and no one should overlook the well-known and magnificently beautiful doxology (24-25), a great ascription of praise.

Outline

SALUTATION (1-2)

ADMONITIONS TO CONTEND FOR THE FAITH (3-4)

EVIDENCE OF GOD'S JUDGMENT IN THE PAST (5-13)

ASSURANCE OF GOD'S JUDGMENT IN THE FUTURE (14-19)

FURTHER ADMONITIONS TO HOLD FAST (20-23)

BENEDICTION (24-25)

THE REVELATION

KNOWN AS "The Revelation to John," there is a long tradition that John the beloved disciple is the author of this book; the Muratorian fragment (c. 170 A.D.), for example, ascribes it to St. John, and Justin Martyr even earlier (135) believed him the author. It is traditional that he was the author of five New Testament books: the Gospel of John, I, II, and III John, and the Revelation. When he wrote Revelation, he was a prisoner on the Island of Patmos, a prisoner because of his faith in Christ (1:4, 9; 22:8). Well known among the Christians of Asia Minor, he was called a "prophet" in his own day (22:9). He wrote his book in the late 80's or early 90's A.D.

Authorship and Date

To the seven churches of Asia Minor mentioned in the book: Ephesus, Smyrna, Pergamos, Thyatira, Sardis, Philadelphia, and Laodicea.

Destination

Revelation 1:1a, 5b-6. "The revelation of Jesus Christ, which God gave him to show to his servants what must soon take place."

Key Verses

"To him who loves us and has freed us from our sins by his blood and made us a kingdom, priests to his God and Father, to him be glory and dominion for ever and ever."

The author is writing to persecuted Christians and is using a code. The purpose of the code is to protect the Christians because outright Christian literature and the propagation of the Gospel were outlawed in many places in the ancient Roman Empire.

Purpose and Theme

Scholars have spent a great deal of time attempting to decode the book. One recent theory is that this is a drama intended to be put on the stage; and that if the book is examined as a drama, the strange and figurative language is illumined and makes sense. Another theory is that this is a series of visions about the past; another that it is a series of visions about the future. Still others believe that the great thrust of the book has to do only with the then present age. But even more important than theories of interpretation are the great themes of the book which come through clearly. These themes are:

Christ and His Church
God's divine purpose in history
God's presence in His Church even in persecution
The triumph of the saved
The wrath of God
The judgment of God

1:1a should be especially noted—"The Revelation of Jesus Christ"—for herein lies the great heart throb of the writer. He wants to reveal Jesus, Redeemer and Conqueror of evil and only solid hope of the future. Toward the end of the book Christ is revealed as coming again with the armies of heaven (19:11-21), establishing His Kingdom and judging at the Last Day on the great white throne (20:1-15), and as creating a new heaven and a new earth (21:1-8). The city of God is described in 21:9—22:5. At the end there is a lovely attitude toward the worship and

A scene from ancient Smyrna, one of the seven churches of Revelation (Revelation 1:11).

adoration of God, and this prayer should be on every true Christian's lips, "Even so, come Lord Jesus" (22:20).

INTRODUCTION AND REASON FOR WRITING (chapter 1)   **Outline**

LETTERS TO THE SEVEN CHURCHES (chapters 2-3)

   Ephesus (2:1-7)

   Smyrna (2:8-11)

   Pergamus (2:12-17)

   Thyatira (2:18-29)

   Sardis (3:1-6)

   Philadelphia (3:7-13)

   Laodicea (3:14-22)

VISIONS OF HEAVEN (chapters 4-5)

THE SEVEN SEALS (chapters 6-7)

THE SEVEN TRUMPETS (chapters 8-11)

SIGNS OF THE END (chapters 12-14)

THE SEVEN VIALS (chapters 15-16)

JUDGMENT FALLS ON BABYLON (ROME) (chapters 17-18)

THE TRIUMPH OF CHRIST (19:1—22:5)

   The Marriage Supper of the Lamb (chapter 19)

   Satan Bound (chapter 20)

   The New Heaven and Earth (21:1—22:5)

EPILOGUE AND BENEDICTION (22:6-21)

CHRONOLOGICAL TABLE
OF NEW TESTAMENT RULERS*
with approximate dates

EMPERORS OF ROME

Augustus (Octavius)	27 B.C.–A.D. 14
Tiberius	A.D. 14–37
Caligula	A.D. 37–41
Claudius	A.D. 41–54
Nero	A.D. 54–68
Galba; Otho; Vitellius	A.D. 68–69
Vespasian	A.D. 69–79
Titus	A.D. 79–81
Domitian	A.D. 81–96

---

* Based upon *The Oxford Annotated Bible*, p. 1534.

CHRONOLOGICAL TABLE
OF NEW TESTAMENT RULERS
with approximate dates

RULERS OF THE HEROD LINE

Herod the Great (king of the Jews)	37–4 B.C.
Archelaus the ethnarch (Judea)	4 B.C.–A.D. 6
Herod Antipas the tetrarch (Galilee and Perea)	4 B.C.–A.D. 39
Philip the tetrarch (Ituraea, Trachonitis, and other places)	4 B.C.–A.D. 34
Herod Agrippa I the king (Ituraea, Trachonitis, and other places; 41–44 Judea, Galilee, Perea)	A.D. 37–44
Herod Agrippa II the king (Ituraea, Trachonitis, and other places; 56 or 61–c. 100 portions of Galilee and Perea)	A.D. 53–c.100

PROCURATORS OF JUDEA
(AFTER ARCHELAUS TO HEROD AGRIPPA I)

Coponius	A.D. 6–8
M. Ambivius	A.D. 9–12
Annius Rufus	A.D. 12–15
Valerius Gratus	A.D. 15–26
Pontius Pilate	A.D. 26–36
Marullus	A.D. 37
Herennius Capito	A.D. 37–41

PROCURATORS OF PALESTINE
(HEROD AGRIPPA I TO THE REVOLT OF THE JEWS)

Cuspius Fadus	A.D. 44–about 46
Tiberius Alexander	A.D. about 46–48
Ventidius Cumanus	A.D. 48–52
M. Antonius Felix	A.D. 52–60
Porcius Festus	A.D. 60–62
Clodius Albinus	A.D. 62–64
Gessius Florus	A.D. 64–66

PART THREE

OUR BIBLE: PERSONS, PLACES, THINGS

The earliest likeness of Paul known to exist, found in an underground room in Rome, and dating at the end of the second century or beginning of the third century A.D.

The earliest likeness of Peter known to exist, found in an underground room in Rome, and dating at the end of the second century or beginning of the third century A.D.

⋅§7ξ⋅ PERSONS: THUMBNAIL SKETCHES OF MAJOR BIBLE PERSONALITIES

THIS IS A SELECTED LISTING OF BIBLE PERSON-
alities; time and space do not permit all figures to be treated.
These are thumbnail sketches, not complete histories. They
are arranged alphabetically for convenient reference.

* * * * * * * * * *

AARON

Aaron, whose name means "uncertain," was the eldest son of
Amram and Jochebed, of the tribe of Levi. He was the brother of
Miriam and Moses, husband of Eusheba, and father of four sons.
Moses entreated God to let Aaron be his prophet or mouth. God
granted this request and Aaron joined Moses. At Moses' command,
Aaron performed miracles with his rod (Exodus 7:12 ff, etc.). He
helped to hold up Moses' arms at the battle of Amalek, so the
"rod of the Lord would be lifted up." Aaron and his sons were
anointed priests (Exodus 29:9), but Aaron alone was anointed high
priest, which office he held for almost forty years. At his death he
was succeeded by his third son, Eleazer. Although Aaron feared
God he had one great flaw, he weakened in the moment of temptation. When Moses was on Mt. Sinai, Aaron permitted the people
to make an idol of gold. Aaron joined Miriam in scorn of Moses
for his marriage to an Ethiopian wife. At times he had little faith
and doubted God's power. As punishment he was never permitted
to enter the Promised Land. He died at 123 years of age. (Numbers 33:38-39.)

ABRAHAM

Abraham is known as the divinely appointed founder of the
Hebrew religion. Son of Terah, he was born at Ur of the Chaldees
(now in Iraq). Abraham married Sarai, his half-sister (Genesis

11:29-31). God appeared to him and told him to go to Canaan where he would be the founder of a great nation (Genesis 12:1-2). Abraham took his wife, his nephew Lot, and a group of servants and started out by faith. God again appeared to him giving him the promise that his people would have the whole land. Abraham went to Egypt during a famine and returned to Canaan very rich. Separated from Lot, he later rescued him from Sodom, the city destroyed by God. In his impatience for the fulfillment of the promise of God, Abraham had a son, Ishmael, by the maid Hagar. When Abraham and Sarah were quite old, God kept his promise of a son. He gave them Isaac, their only son. Abraham's great test was the command to offer Isaac as a sacrifice to God. Because he was faithful, God provided a substitute sacrifice for Isaac. Abraham died at the age of 175. He is known as a hero of faith (Hebrews 11:8-13).

ADAM

Adam was the first man and God gave him dominion over all creatures, care of the Garden of Eden, and eternal life. The first sin was Adam's disobedience to God by eating fruit of the tree of the knowledge of good and evil (Genesis 2:17). Adam and his wife Eve were driven out of the Garden of Eden and punished with labor and brief life. They had three sons—Cain, Abel, and Seth. Adam lived 930 years and his life is recorded in Genesis 1-5, but he is also mentioned in other parts of the Bible. Paul contrasted him to Christ: Adam fell, sin and death came into the world; but Christ, " 'the second Adam' was righteous and through him eternal life was provided" (I Corinthians 15:22).

AGRIPPA I, and II, HEROD

A grandson of Herod the Great, Agrippa I ruled as a king in Palestine. He had James put to death and he himself was eaten by worms (Acts 12). His son Agrippa II was king of certain areas of Northern Palestine, and it was he Paul addressed in Acts 25:13f.

AHASUERUS

Ahasuerus is the name of four Median and Persian kings in the Bible and Apocrypha. In Tobit (14:15) of the Apocrypha, Ahasuerus (or Astyages) is mentioned with Nebuchadrezzar in reference to the destruction of Nineveh (612 B.C.). In Daniel (9:1), Ahasuerus (or Cyaxares) is named the father of Darius the Mede (or Astyages, about 594 B.C.). In Ezra (4:6), Ahasuerus (or Cambyses, son of Cyrus) is identified as the king of Persia (529–521 B.C.). Darius Hysaspis reigned from 521–485 B.C. His son, Xerxes, also called Ahasuerus, reigned from about 485–465 B.C. The book of Esther tells much about this illustrious king who married Esther (Esther 1:1f). His son, Artaxerxes I (464–424 B.C.), is mentioned in the books of Ezra and Nehemiah.

AMOS

Amos, a contemporary of Isaiah and Hosea, was the earliest of the minor prophets. He was the son of Nahum and father of

Mattathias in the genealogy of the Saviour (Luke 3:25). As a Judean, who was born into the middle or lower class of society, Amos lived in Tekoa in the Southern Kingdom, six miles south of Bethlehem. His home town was inhabited chiefly by shepherds. He owned a small flock of sheep (Amos 1:1) and was a caretaker of sycamore trees (Amos 7:4). Amos was a "gatherer" of sycamore fruit. In the East fruit ripens, drops to the ground, and is then "gathered"—it is not generally "picked" as in the West. He may also be called a "pincher" of sycamore fruit because the fruit was thus irritated to speed up the ripening process. Though he had no training in the prophetical schools, he was called of God to prophesy in Israel (Amos 7:15) during the reigns of Uzziah of Judah and Jeroboam II of Israel. He went to Bethel to rebuke her sins, but was compelled to return to Judah by the high priest, Amaziah (Amos 7:10-17), who got the order for his expulsion from King Jeroboam. After going home, Amos put into writing the substance of his speeches, and the roll thus written is the earliest book of prophecy that has come down to us.

ANANIAS, THE DISCIPLE

Ananias of Damascus saw a vision from God asking him to baptize Saul of Tarsus. He first hesitated because of Saul's reputation, but reassured by God, he went to Saul and laid his hands on him. Saul received his sight and was later baptized (Acts 9:10-19). One tradition says Ananias was killed by the sword, another that he was stoned to death after being tortured by Lucian, a ruler of Damascus.

ANANIAS, WHO CHEATED GOD

As a Christian belonging to the infant Church, Ananias made an agreement with his wife Sapphira to give only part of their land profits to a general fund. Peter openly condemned him for holding out on God and Ananias fell to the ground dead. The people of the Christian community at Jerusalem set apart their property to the work of furthering the Gospel and giving aid to the needy. The contributions were intended for sacred purposes. Since Ananias' act was related to religious affairs, he lied to God and was guilty of sin (Acts 5:1-11). (See "Sapphira.")

ANDREW

Andrew was the first called of Jesus' disciples. He was reared in Bethsaida of Galilee where he and his brother Simon Peter were fishermen. Upon the testimony of John the Baptist, Andrew persuaded Peter to accompany him to hear Jesus. As an Apostle, Andrew is mentioned several times in the New Testament: at the feeding of the five thousand (John 6:8) he told Jesus of the lad with the five loaves and two fish; in John 12:20-22 he introduced some Greeks to Jesus and in Mark 13:3, along with Peter, James and John, he wanted Jesus to give further details on the destruction of the Temple; at Pentecost he was in the Upper Room with

ANTIPAS

James and the other Apostles (Acts 1:13). Tradition says Andrew was crucified on a cross at Patrae of Achaia, but this is not certain. (See Herod Antipas)

APOLLOS

Apollos was born of Jewish parents in Alexandria, Egypt. He was a devout person, "learned in the Scriptures" (Acts 18:24); however, he knew only the teachings of John the Baptist. Apollos met two tentmakers, Aquila and Priscilla, who told him more about God. After their instruction he went to Achaia for two years and taught what they had told him. Later he became a teacher in Corinth after Paul left. Here factions arose in the Church, one group claiming Paul as their leader, another claiming Apollos, another claiming Cephas (Peter), and still another Christ. This situation was a cause of Paul writing his First Epistle to the Corinthians, in which he told them to unite "in the same mind and the same judgment" (I Corinthians 1:10). The last mention of Apollos is made in Titus (3:10).

AQUILA

Aquila was a Jewish tentmaker who became influential in the Christian Church during its early days. After the Emperor Claudius ordered all Jews living in Rome to leave, Aquila and his wife Priscilla went to Corinth (Acts 18:2-3). There they met another tentmaker, Paul of Tarsus, whose primary occupation was spreading the Gospel of Christ. They became friends, and Aquila and his wife were converted to Christianity before Paul left Corinth. They were known as zealous Christians (I Corinthians 16:19; Romans 16:3-4), accompanied Paul to Ephesus, and later returned to Rome where their house was a meeting place for the young Church (Romans 16:5). Afterwards, they returned again to Ephesus to continue Gospel work and that is the last known of them. (See "Priscilla.")

ARTAXERXES I

(See "Ahasuerus.")

BALAAM OF PETHOR

Balaam, the son of Beor, was a non-Israelite prophet from Pethor, a city in Northern Mesopotamia. Well known for his powers as a sooth-sayer, he was employed by the king of the Moabites to curse Israel. God intervened, with the use of an ass (Numbers 22:23-30), and Balaam blessed the Israelites instead of cursing them. He predicted a magnificent future for the very people he was called to curse. Later a battle was fought against the Midianites. Balaam sided with the Midianites against Israel and was killed (Numbers 31:8).

BARNABAS

Barnabas, living in Jerusalem at the time of the founding of the Church, was a Levite of Cyprus. He was one of the first converts to Christianity and a cousin to John Mark (Colossians 4:10). His real name was Joseph (or Joses), but he was known as Barnabas by the Christians because it meant "the Son of Encouragement" (Acts 4:36). We first hear of Barnabas when he sold one of his Cyprian fields and gave the money to the Christian community. He also supported Paul and his work, though later they separated (Acts 15:36-39). He is described as a "good man and full of the Holy Spirit." He was kind, sympathetic, and understanding towards everyone he met. He is mentioned by name twenty-nine times in the New Testament. Tradition says he was the father of the orthodox Church of Cyprus.

BARTHOLOMEW

Bartholomew, the son of Talmai, and also one of the disciples, was born in Cana of Galilee. He is referred to as Bartholomew in Matthew 10:3; Mark 3:18; Luke 6:14; and Acts 1:13, and also as Nathanael in John 1:48. John gives us the only insight into his personality. Nathanael was calm, peaceful, and retiring. He was inclined to meditate on the things of the Lord (John 1:48-49). He first hesitated about accepting Jesus as the Saviour because he could not see how anyone so extraordinary could come from Nazareth, a town adjacent to his rural home in Cana (John 21:2). John referred to Bartholomew as Nathanael ("God has given"). He was constantly coupled with another disciple and friend, Philip (Matthew 10:3; Mark 3:18; Luke 6:14; John 1:45).

BELSHAZZAR

Belshazzar was the King of the Babylonian Empire during part of the captivity of the Jews. When a former king had conquered Judah, he had taken the gold and silver vessels from the Temple. Belshazzar used these vessels for serving dinner wine. A hand appeared and wrote on the wall, and Daniel was the only one who could interpret the writing which foretold the fall of the Empire and the death of the King at the hands of the Medes and Persians (Daniel 5:5-30). The event came about in 538 B.C.

CAESAR, AUGUSTUS

Augustus Caesar was the follower and heir of Julius Caesar. His real name was Octavius but he was given the name of Augustus after attaining supreme power as Emperor. He is mentioned in Luke 2:1 as having decreed that "all the world should be taxed." This seems to be the only reference to him in the Bible. He died in 14 A.D., having reigned since 27 B.C. (Claudius Caesar is also mentioned in the New Testament—Acts 11:28; 17:7; 18:2.)

CAIAPHAS

Caiaphas was a high priest who played an important part in the trial of Jesus. When Jesus was brought before Caiaphas two false witnesses said, "This fellow said, 'I am able to destroy the temple of God, and to build it in three days'" (Matthew 26:61). Christ did not answer. Then Caiaphas demanded that Jesus tell whether He was the Christ or not. To this Jesus answered, "You have said so" (Matthew 26:64). Then He was accused by Caiaphas of blasphemy, and sent to Pontius Pilate.

CALEB

Caleb of the tribe of Judah was one of the twelve spies sent by

Moses into Canaan. Ten of these spies reported that the Children of Israel could not possess the land. Caleb with Joshua disagreed and said, "Let us go . . . at once, and possess it; for we are well able to overcome. . . ." Because of their good report, God spared them from the punishment He imposed upon the rest of murmuring Israel, and they were allowed to enter Canaan (Numbers 14:24). At the time of the report, Moses promised Caleb Hebron and its surrounding hills as an inheritance. Forty-five years later, at the age of eighty-five, Caleb claimed Hebron. Joshua granted it to him because he had "wholly followed the Lord God of Israel."

CLAUDIUS LYSIAS Claudius Lysias was a military tribune holding the chief command in Jerusalem. His main task was that of keeping order at the time of the great Jewish festivals. During an uproar Lysias arrested the Apostle Paul, thinking him to be the leader of a band of assassins. Later Paul was arrested again; this time ostensibly for mentioning the word "Gentile" in a speech (Acts 22:21). He was sent before the Jewish Council which plotted to kill him. Claudius discovered the plot and sent Paul under guard to Caesarea where the guards handed him over to Felix the governor. He greatly admired Paul because he "was born a citizen." Claudius Lysias is referred to in Acts 21:31; 22:24; 23:26-30. The last reference is the letter he wrote to Felix explaining his action.

CORNELIUS Cornelius of Acts 10 was an Italian Centurion stationed at Caesarea. This devout man had a vision in which he was told to send for Peter in order to learn more about God. Peter, who simultaneously had a vision which showed him that the Gentiles were not unclean, went to Cornelius and told him about Jesus and His mission on earth. As a result of this visit, Cornelius became one of the first Gentiles to be converted and to receive gifts of the Holy Spirit under the ministry of Peter. (Acts 10:44 has been called the Pentecost to the Gentiles.) Cornelius believed in God and was allowed to worship in the synagogue. He did not follow all of the Jewish customs; he was not circumcised.

CYRUS THE GREAT Cyrus the Great was the founder of the Persian Empire, which at his death extended from the Mediterranean to ancient Bactria in Asia. He defeated both Lydia and Babylon with intentions of invading Egypt and India. Upon entering Babylon with no resistance, he was hailed as the "Bringer of Peace" by the natives of the strife-worn city. Later he aided the Jews by warding off their oppressors, returning the captives and exiles to their homeland, and rebuilding the Temple in Jerusalem. He was killed in battle in 530 b.c. Cyrus is referred to in Isaiah 44:28; II Chronicles 36:22; Ezra 1; 3:7; Daniel 1:21; 6:28; 10:1.

DANIEL Little is known of Daniel's parentage. He was taken to Babylon in 604 B.C. and trained for the king's service. During this training Daniel and three young friends refused to eat food offered to the idols (Daniel 1:8) and they requested a change of food. After a test was given the request was granted, for these young Jews were found to be in better physical condition than those who ate of the king's food; also, they passed all others in learning and knowledge. Daniel interpreted a dream of Nebuchadrezzar, revealing the future of his empire. Daniel also had visions of the world's future. Moreover, he interpreted the handwriting on the wall for Belshazzer, son of Nebuchadrezzar. By his rivals he was cast into the lions' den for his faithfulness in prayer to God (Daniel 6:10-24). This scheme to get rid of Daniel failed because of his great faith. Daniel was a prophet who furthered the cause of God.

DAVID In Hebrew the name David means "beloved." Chief sources for the life of David are Samuel and Kings. David, the son of Jesse, was born in Bethlehem. He was the youngest of eight brothers and spent his youth as a shepherd. Samuel was sent of God to anoint one of Jesse's sons as king in Saul's place. Rejecting the elder sons, he anointed David. David then resumed his duties as shepherd until King Saul heard of David's genius for music and poetry. Saul took him into his court where he became the friend of Jonathan, Saul's son, and the husband of Micah, Saul's daughter. These new relationships were extremely important to David's future safety. In Saul's palace he learned much of court life and the military, all of which helped prepare him to be king. When David, in his youth, slew Goliath, he won enormous popularity, but also the wrath of Saul from whom he had to flee for years. David ruled Judah at Hebron for seven and a half years before finally gaining the throne of all Israel. He reigned from about 1000–961 B.C. His achievements include (1) moving the ark back to Jerusalem, (2) uniting the twelve tribes, (3) establishing the capital at Jerusalem, (4) making plans for the Temple. David died at seventy and was buried in the "City of David," Jerusalem.

DEBORAH Deborah was a prophetess who dwelt between Ramah and Beth-el in Mt. Ephraim where she judged Israel (Judges 4:5). The people had sunk into a state of total discouragement under the oppression of the Canaanites. Deborah inspired the people and summoned Barak to lead the forces against Sisera and his allies. At the battle of Kedesh, the Canaanites under Sisera were defeated. The details of this deliverance are given in the Song of Deborah and Barak (Judges 5).

DORCAS Dorcas (also known as Tabitha which means "gazelle") was a Christian woman from Joppa whom Peter raised from the dead (Acts 9:36-43). She was loved by all and is noted for good deeds and works of charity, especially for the garments she made. When Peter raised her from the dead, the news was spread near and far and many found Christ as a result.

ELI (See "Hannah" and "Samuel.")

ELIJAH Elijah the Tishbite, probably born in the town of Tishbet in Galilee, was a man of the outdoors (II Kings 1:8) and was a great speed runner (I Kings 18:26). He predicted a drought (I Kings 17:1) as a penalty for Israel's idolatry (I Kings 18:18). During this drought, Elijah was fed by ravens at the Brook Cherith (I Kings 17:5-6) and when the brook dried up, he was fed by a widow (I Kings 17:10-16). In a contest on Mt. Carmel the prophet proved that the Lord, not Baal, was the true God (I Kings 18:20-39). Jezebel, King Ahab's wife, then sought to kill Elijah and he fled across the desert to Mt. Horeb where the Lord sustained him forty days and nights (I Kings 19:15-17). At Mt. Horeb, God, "in a still small voice," told Elijah to anoint Hazael as king of Syria, Jehu as king of Israel, and Elisha as his own prophet (I Kings 19:12-17). Like Enoch (Genesis 5:24), Elijah was translated to heaven without dying.

ELIPHAZ "Eliphaz the Temanite" was one of Job's three "comfortors." After seven days and nights of silence and Job's complaints, Eliphaz spoke condemning Job's attitude and underscoring the greatness, majesty, and purity of God. The point in all of his speeches is the false idea that suffering is punishment for sin. See Job 2:11; 4:1—5:27; 15; 22. (See the Book of Job, Chapter IV.)

ELISABETH Elizabeth was one of the women closely associated with Jesus. She was the wife of Zacharias and the mother of John the Baptist (Luke 1:5, 57-63). A notable act of her life was the blessing of Mary as "The Mother of my Lord". (Luke 1:43). Although little is said about her, she was regarded as righteous and obedient to God.

ELISHA Elisha, "the son of Shaphat of Abelmeholah" (I Kings 19:16), was the disciple and successor of the prophet Elijah. Elijah "found Elisha . . . who was plowing with twelve yoke of oxen before him, and he was with the twelfth. Elijah passed by him and cast his mantle upon him" (I Kings 19:19). This was a sign symbolizing Elijah's adoption of Elisha as his son and successor in the prophetic office. Elisha left his family and was with Elijah six or eight years before the latter left the earth. Elisha's career was marked by merciful deeds and incessant activity. His only aim was to complete Elijah's reforms of renewing ancient truths and ridding his people of paganism. He was often called "the man of God" (II Kings 4:9; 5:15). Some of his miracles include increasing the widow's oil (II Kings 4:1-7); curing gourds of poisonous effects (II Kings 4:38-41); and causing an axhead to float in water (II Kings 6:1-7). At least two of his miracles resemble some that Jesus performed: multiplying bread (II Kings 4:42-44) and curing Naaman's leprosy (II Kings 5:1-14).

ENOCH

Enoch was Jared's son and Methuselah's father (Genesis 5:18, 21). In the genealogy recorded by St. Luke, he has a place among the ancestors of Christ (Luke 3:37). Enoch was a man in contrast to his age. In a day when "the wickedness of man was great in the earth," Enoch "walked with God" (Genesis 6:5; 5:24). Of each of his predecessors is the record "and he died;" yet of Enoch is the remarkable expression "and he was not, for God took him" (Genesis 5:24). This simple yet forceful statement is the origin of the statement in Hebrews, "By faith Enoch was taken up so that he should not see death; and he was not found, because God had taken him" (Hebrews 11:5).

A curious Jewish tradition purports Enoch to be the inventor of astronomy, letters, and arithmetic. He lived 365 years.

EPAPHRAS

Affectionately called by Paul "our beloved fellow servant" and "faithful minister of Christ" (Colossians 1:7), Epaphras founded, and was later the first bishop of the Church at Colossae. His encouraging personal report of the Colossians' "faith in Christ Jesus" and "love in the Spirit" strengthened Paul during his first Roman imprisonment. The phrase used by Paul, "my fellow prisoner in Christ Jesus" (Philemon 23), may refer to an actual imprisonment of Epaphras (although the allusion may be to "spiritual" rather than actual "physical" captivity). Epaphras' zeal led him to evangelize such neighboring towns as Laodicea and Hierapolis (Colossians 4:12-13). Joining in Paul's greeting to Philemon, he reveals his constant concern for members of the Body of Christ. According to tradition, Epaphras suffered martyrdom at Colossae.

EPAPHRODITUS

Epaphroditus is mentioned by Paul in his letter to the Philippians who had sent him as a messenger to serve the Apostle in Rome (Philippians 2:25). His dedication to the service of the Christian Church was shown through his anxiety at not being able to help either Paul or his home Church while he was extremely ill in Rome. As soon as Epaphroditus had recovered, Paul made plans for his return to Philippi, and entrusted to his care the letter to the Philippian Church. Modern scholars agree that Epaphroditus should not be confused with Epaphras who was connected with the Church at Colossae and mentioned in the book of Colossians.

ESAU

(See "Jacob.")

ESTHER

A Jewess of the tribe of Benjamin, Esther was an orphan adopted and reared by her cousin Mordecai. Because of her extreme beauty and poise she was chosen queen by Ahasuerus. When the lives of her countrymen were endangered by Haman's planned slaughter, she was willing to risk her own life in an attempt to change the edict. Her courageous character and personal charm brought Ahasuerus to add to Haman's decree a statement permitting the Jews to defend themselves. The Jewish victory was commemorated by the Feast of Purim (Esther 9:17—10:3).

EVE She was the wife of Adam and the first woman according to Genesis. Eve ate of the tree of knowledge, thus yielding to temptation and sin. She tempted Adam to do the same. She was punished by pains in childbirth. Eve is referred to by Paul in the New Testament (II Corinthians 11:3; I Timothy 2:13). Genesis 3:20; 4:1.

EZEKIEL Jewish tradition says that Ezekiel, one of the last of the Old Testament prophets, wrote the book of Ezekiel. He was a descendant of a priestly family, and as a young man preparing for the priesthood, was among the Jews who were taken to Babylonia when Nebuchadrezzar captured Jerusalem. Ezekiel was called by God to be a "watchman" (Ezekiel 3:17) over the Jews in captivity, to encourage them and to help them better understand God's plan and purpose. The Jews longed to return to their home in Jerusalem, but Ezekiel gave them a "vision of God" and helped them endure their suffering. God promised Ezekiel that the Jewish people would return to Jerusalem after seventy years of captivity. He prophesied the destruction of Jerusalem; and after the destruction Ezekiel prepared the Jewish people for the new generation by reconstructing Israel's religious thoughts as to the freedom and responsibility of the individual, and the meaning of true repentance.

EZRA Ezra was a Jewish priest in exile in Babylonia when Cyrus conquered Babylonia in 538 B.C. He was appointed leader of the Jews in that country and received a commission to take the Jews back to Jerusalem. He did in fact lead many Jewish priests and Levites back to their holy city. Ezra's main purpose was to put the Law back into effect and to establish it as the supreme authority in civil and religious affairs. Arriving in Jerusalem, he was grieved to find that some of the Jews had taken foreign wives, which God had forbidden (Ezra 9:1-3). But as a result of his influence foreign wives were cast out (Ezra 10:17). God used Ezra to give the Law authority it had not previously had; indeed, the Jewish people to this day follow some of the lines laid down by Ezra. He was a prayerful man who used the power God gave him to re-establish the Jewish people as the true nation of God.

FELIX, ANTONIUS Felix was the Roman Procurator of Judea, an appointment made by the Emperor Claudius. He rose from slavery, having been freed by Claudius Caesar. His rule in Judea was one of constant disorder and disaffection. He was the husband of three queens, one a daughter of King Agrippa. As Procurator he was usually cruel and unjust, committing many hateful crimes while in office. The New Testament speaks better of him (Acts 23:24—24:27) than do most history books.

Festus was the successor of Felix in the government of Judea. He was appointed by Nero about the year 60 A.D., and died not long after. He is mentioned only in connection with Paul; he presided at his hearing in Caesarea (Acts 25). Festus was a man of good character and probably would have set Paul free had he known the issues and tactics of Paul's accusors. Festus is known as one of Rome's better officials. He succeeded in ridding the country of robbers and settling the agitation of the time.

FESTUS, PORCIUS

The Epistle of III John is addressed to Gaius. Little is known about him, but some have identified him with Gaius of Macedonia (Acts 19:29), Gaius of Derbe (Acts 20:4), or Gaius of Corinth (I Corinthians 1:14; Romans 16:23).

GAIUS

Julius Annaeus Gallio was the Roman proconsul of Achaia. In a religious dispute, the Jews took Paul to be judged by Gallio. Gallio said he would have no part in the dispute and dismissed the case (Acts 18:12-16). There are several conflicting theories pertaining to the death of Gallio. Tradition says he was killed by order of Nero with his "brother," the philosopher Lucius Annaeus Seneca. Julius Annaeus was adopted into the Gallio family, and history does not relate clearly whether he was the real or stepbrother of Seneca. St. Jerome claimed Gallio committed suicide in 65 A.D.

GALLIO

The Jewish teacher of Paul (Acts 22:3) and a person held in high respect (Acts 5:34), he was a grandson of the well-known Jewish rabbi, Hillel. His objective attitude toward Christians was indeed commendable and courageous (Acts 5) and helped save the day for the early Church.

GAMALIEL

One of the great figures of the Old Testament, his story may be read in full in Judges 6-8. The sign of the fleece, the defeat of the Midianites by only three hundred divinely picked soldiers who used pitchers and torches, and Gideon's refusal of a crown (the first recorded attempt toward a monarchy in Hebrew history)—all are part of the story of this godly judge of Israel.

GIDEON

Habakkuk was the eighth of the minor prophets. Little is known about his personal life, although it is inferred, since he is termed "the prophet" (Habakkuk 1:1), that he held a recognized position as a religious leader. It is also thought from the expression "on my stringed instruments" (Habakkuk 3:19) that he was a member of the Temple choir. He delivered his prophecy about

HABAKKUK

the twelfth or thirteenth year of Josiah (629 or 628 B.C.). He cried out against the social evils of his day and against the Chaldeans with whom God was displeased. He was the first to use the phrase that the Apostle Paul and Martin Luther made famous, "the just shall live by faith" (Habakkuk 2:4).

HAGAR

Hagar was an Egyptian woman in the service of Sarah, Abraham's wife. Sarah, thinking she could have no children of her own, proposed that Abraham should take Hagar as his concubine (Genesis 16:3). Subsequently, Hagar fled into the wilderness due to Sarah's jealousy and harshness. She obeyed an angel who appeared to her in the wilderness and returned to her mistress. After her return she gave birth to Ishmael, Abraham's son. (See "Ishmael.")

HAGGAI

Haggai was the Old Testament contemporary of Zechariah, who prophesied in the sixth century B.C. Cyrus, king of Persia, in the first year after his conquest of Babylonia in 537 B.C., issued a decree permitting the return of the Jews and the rebuilding of the Temple. In Ezra 2 it is recorded that 42,360 Jews returned; the building of the altar and laying of the foundation for the Temple is mentioned in Ezra 3 and 4. Haggai found the people in Palestine feeble, discouraged, and lax in their religious observances. His task was that of encouraging them to rebuild the Temple and to renew a vigorous worship.

HANNAH

Hannah was the first and most loved of the two wives of Elkanah of Ramah. Her barrenness was the cause of much sadness to her, especially when Peninnah, the second wife, tormented her about it. One year when the family was in Shiloh offering their yearly sacrifices, she was especially bitter and began to weep because she had no child. She promised the Lord that if He would send her a male child she would give him to God. Her prayer was answered and she gave birth to Samuel (which means "God hears"). As soon as Samuel was weaned she brought him to the Temple to be trained and to serve Eli the priest (I Samuel 1:24-28). Once a year, when Hannah came to offer the yearly sacrifices, she would bring Samuel a robe which she had made. For her obedience God blessed Hannah with three sons and two daughters. Hannah's song of praise at Samuel's dedication is believed to have been known by Mary, the mother of Jesus, because it is similar to the one Mary sang when she told Elizabeth about her heavenly visitor. Old Testament reference: I Samuel 1-2.

HEROD AGRIPPA

(See "Agrippa, Herod.")

HEROD ANTIPAS

Herod Antipas was the son of Herod the Great, and ruler of Galilee and Peraea at the time of Jesus' death. When he married his niece Herodias, he aroused the distrust of the Jews. This brought on a war with King Aretas IV in which Antipas lost his army. John the Baptist had rebuked Antipas for living illegally with Herodias. For this Herodias sought revenge and had Antipas put him in prison. At her instigation her daughter Salome tricked Antipas into beheading John (Matthew 14:1-12). Jesus described Herod Antipas as "the fox." Later, at the review of Jesus' trial, he asked to be shown a miracle and was refused. In an attempt to gain more power and prestige, he went to Rome where he was accused by Herod Agrippa I of conspiring against the Romans. He died in 39 A.D.

HEROD THE GREAT

Herod, an Idumaean descendant of Esau, began the rule of Judea in 37 B.C. and died 4 B.C. Jesus was born during his rule (Matthew 2:1; Luke 1:5). He divided his kingdom into four natural states for tighter government control, giving local authority to his politically loyal friends. He erected a new maritime city on the Mediterranean and named it Caesarea after Caesar who had appointed him king. Although spiritually and morally heathen, he maintained a domestic peace by enforcing a police state. He pacified the Jews with tax reform and the rebuilding of their Temple at Jerusalem. (For more information see Chapter V.)

HEROD PHILIP II

(See "Philip the Tetrarch.")

HEZEKIAH

An eighth century B.C. figure, Hezekiah succeeded his father, King Ahaz of Judah, to the throne at the age of twenty-five. He reigned for twenty-nine years in Jerusalem. Hezekiah is remembered for cleansing the Temple, executing moral and religious reform, restoring the worship of Jehovah, and celebrating the great fourteen-day Passover (it had been previously neglected). Also he revived the use of David's and Asaph's psalms and was responsible for the completion of a collection of Solomon's Proverbs. Hezekiah contributed greatly to the prosperity of his people and kingdom through the rapid progress of public improvements, the reformation movement from idolatry, and the overthrow of the Assyrian power in Judea. During the union against Assyria, he was attacked by a fatal disease; but he made a remarkable recovery through prayer and was granted a fifteen year extension of life. Hezekiah followed the will of God and lived his latter years in peace. The story of King Hezekiah may be found in II Kings 18-20; Isaiah 36-39; and II Chronicles 29-32.

HOSEA

Hosea—the name comes from the Hebrew word meaning "help"—the son of Beeri, was the first of the minor prophets and the last prophet of Northern Israel. His prophecy comes shortly after Amos, toward the end of the reign of Jeroboam II (c. 786–746 B.C.). He worked for national unity, opposed foreign alliances, and demanded a just public administration. He was a sensitive and tenderhearted man, craving love and fellowship. Hosea 1-3 relates the story of his marriage to Gomer and her unfaithfulness to him. This story gives us insight into the feelings of God toward unfaithful Israel. Hosea prophesied against the people of Israel, whom he scolded and threatened for their idolatry and wickedness. He earnestly pleaded for repentance as the only means of warding off the evils overhanging their country. Hosea reveals the Lord's readiness to forgive and his yearning desire to save his people. (See Hosea in Chapter IV.)

ISAAC Isaac was born to Abraham and Sarah as the fulfillment of God's divine promise to them, and he spent his early years in or near Beersheba. Abraham did not hesitate to obey God's command even when he was commanded to offer Isaac as a sacrifice (Genesis 22). God intervened, however, and Isaac's life was spared. In fulfillment of Abraham's wishes Isaac married Rebekah, a granddaughter of Abraham's brother, and they had two sons, Jacob and Esau. Rebekah and the younger son, Jacob, tricked Isaac into giving the blessing to Jacob rather than Esau (Genesis 27). This provoked a long-time enmity, but the two sons were finally reconciled. Isaac is remembered especially for the fact that he carried over the divine blessing of the covenant from Abraham to Jacob.

ISAIAH Isaiah, the son of Amoz, was born into a family of high social rank as shown by his access to the court and the king. He became court preacher, married, and had two sons. Chapter six of the book of Isaiah tells of his call to the prophetic office in which he was active from approximately 740–700 B.C. He accepted this call even though he knew it would be a fruitless work. He had the assurance from God that from the fallen kingdom a new one would rise in which God would reign. He died during Manasseh's reign. He is the best known of Israel's prophets and is well known for his Messianic passages (Isaiah 7:14; 11; 53; etc.). (See Isaiah, Chapter IV.)

ISHMAEL Ishmael was the son of Abraham by Hagar, Sarah's Egyptian maid whom she gave to Abraham for a second wife. Ishmael was used by Abraham as a way of fulfilling God's promise of a child. Later God's promise was truly fulfilled through the birth of Sarah's child Isaac. Ishmael was banished along with Hagar to the wilderness of Beersheba till both were perishing of thirst. An angel of God directed Hagar to water and thereby the lives of the two were preserved. Ishmael grew up in the wilderness of Paran, south of Canaan, married a wife from Egypt and in the fulfillment of a promise made by God to Abraham became the progenitor of twelve princes who became the Ishmaelites. He had a daughter who married Esau. Ishmael took part with Isaac in burying Abraham. References: Genesis 16; 17; 21; 25.

The Lord revealed to Rebekah that she would give birth to twin sons who were to become significant for two great nations— Esau was the father of the Edomites, Jacob carried on the line of the Jewish nation and was a forebear of Jesus. Esau was the first twin to be born, grew to become a skillful hunter, and became Isaac's favorite. Jacob, quiet and inoffensive, became Rebekah's favorite. After coming home from hunting, hungry, Esau begged Jacob for food. Jacob stated that the only way he would feed him was to surrender his birthright. Esau consented (Genesis 25:33). While Esau was hunting again, Rebekah persuaded Jacob to pass himself off as Esau and go to his nearly blind father and obtain the birthright blessing. After Jacob succeeded, Esau discovered what had happened and resolved to kill his selfish brother after his father died.

To allow time for the quarreling man to cool, Jacob fled to Haran. While on his journey he had a vision in which a ladder connected earth and heaven, angels ascended and descended, and God assured him of the Covenant blessing (Genesis 28:12-15). While working for his uncle Laban, Jacob served fourteen years for the hand of Rachel in marriage, and six for a payment in cattle. During this time he married three other women. After some years, believing that Laban and his sons were envying his prosperity and turning against him, Jacob grew alarmed, and fled with his wives and possessions toward Canaan. Three days later Laban discovered Jacob's disappearance; Laban's men caught up with him about a week later, but God saved him from injury, and the meeting became the occasion of a treaty. A heap of stone was erected and a covenant meal was eaten to establish the agreement that neither party should pass that point to attack the other. Before Jacob crossed the Jordan River, he met Esau who forgave him of his past wrongdoing. Jacob had been trusting in his own strength for success. While wrestling with God, he learned that his own strength was of no power and that he must pray for His blessings. References: Genesis 25-34.

James, the son of Mary and Joseph (Matthew 13:55; Mark 6:3), was not one of the twelve Apostles (Matthew 10:2-4), nor was he at first a believer in his brother Jesus (John 7:5). But after the resurrection he came to believe, probably through a special manifestation of the risen Lord. (Christ manifested Himself to the five hundred, and "he was seen of James" [I Corinthians 15:7].) He received the title of Apostle (Galatians 1:19), occupied a place of leadership in the Church at Jerusalem (Galatians 2:9, Acts 15), and, with the elders, received Paul upon his return from his third missionary tour (Acts 21:18). He is the author of the Epistle which bears his name. It has been inferred that he was married (I Corinthians 9:5). James was surnamed "the Just" by the ancients on account of his eminent virtue. Tradition says he was stoned by religious leaders.

JAMES, THE SON OF ALPHAEUS

James was the son of Alphaeus and Mary, who was supposed by some to be the sister of Jesus' mother, which would make James a cousin to Jesus. James was one of the twelve Apostles (Matthew 10:3; Acts 1:13). He was called James "the Less" or "the Little" possibly because he was short of stature. James had some brothers but it is not known for sure how many or who they were, possibly Joseph (Matthew 27:56) and Matthew (Mark 2:14).

JAMES, THE SON OF ZEBEDEE

James, son of Zebedee and Salome, elder brother of John, was one of the earliest disciples of Jesus. James' call was given by Jesus as He walked by the Sea of Galilee. James immediately forsook his fishing business and followed him. Jesus surnamed James and John, Boanerges or sons of thunder (Mark 3:17). Along with Peter and John, he was one of Jesus' three intimate Disciples. James was the first of the Twelve to suffer martyrdom; he was slain in the early days of the Apostolic Church by King Herod Agrippa I about 44 A.D. (Acts 12:2).

JEHOIACHIN

Jehoiachin was a king of Judah and son of Jehoiakim. His father was slain by King Nebuchadrezzar who allowed Jehoiachin to reign in his father's place. (He reigned but three months in 598 B.C.) Jehoiachin and his people were subsequently taken captive to Babylon. The fall of Jerusalem took place about 597 B.C. Jehoiachin was imprisoned for thirty-seven years. At the age of fifty-five he was released from prison. Jehoiachin is believed to have had children, but there is no mention of them in the Bible. There is very little known of Jehoiachin's family. References: II Kings 24; II Chronicles 36.

JEHOIAKIM

Jehoiakim, the son of King Josiah of Judah, was successor to the throne when Pharoah-necho put his brother Johohaz in chains about 609 B.C. Unlike his father, Jehoiakim imposed direct taxation, constructed idols and introduced heathen religion. Jeremiah, a prophet of God, witnessed to him, warning that his godless rule would lead to the destruction of Jerusalem, but Jehoiakim paid no heed. Then Nebuchadrezzar over-powered Pharoah-necho, placing the rule of the empire in the hands of the Chaldeans. After rebelling against Nebuchadrezzar, Jehoiakim was forced from his throne and replaced by Jehoiachin, his son (II Chronicles 36:8). It is not known whether he was murdered, but it is told that his body was pulled outside of the city gate and left there, thus having the "burial" of an ass.

Jeremiah was born in the seventh century B.C., in Anathoth, which is not far from Jerusalem. At twenty years of age the Lord called him to be a prophet. He prophesied of the Judgment of Jerusalem to a people of hardened heart and unreceptive ears. Standing faithfully under desperate and crushing circumstances of persecution, Jeremiah saw his nation change from a prosperous position under King Josiah to a state of wickedness under the leadership of four godless kings who raised up idols and continued to lead the people astray. Helplessly, he witnessed the Babylonian invasions and finally—the fulfillment of his prophecy—the fall of Jerusalem. For his safety, Jeremiah was persuaded to go to Egypt by the pleas of sympathizers. He preached for about fifty years. He is identified with the Old Testament book which bears his name.

Jeroboam, a resident of Zereda, was the son of Nebat of the tribe of Ephraim. He worked on the construction of fortifications during the reign of Solomon. Recognizing Jeroboam's ability, Solomon appointed him overseer of the house of Joseph. Because Jeroboam disliked the tyranny of Solomon and because a prophet foretold that God would establish him a kingdom, Jeroboam rebelled, forming plots against Solomon. For this, Solomon sought Jeroboam's life, and the latter was forced to flee to Egypt. With Solomon's death Jeroboam returned, finding Solomon's son Rehoboam the new king. To try to alleviate heavy taxes imposed at this time, Jeroboam became spokesman for the people. Rehoboam, however, denied all requests and the ten northern tribes revolted, electing Jeroboam their king. His reign lasted from about 922 to 901 B.C. His rule, however, was dominated by his own interests. To prevent the people from returning to Jerusalem for their yearly pilgrimage, he revived two old shrines at Bethel and Dan (I Kings 12:26-30). He also set up golden images, and the name of Jeroboam is a byword for wickedness because of the idol worship he initiated.

Jethro, the priest of Midian, was a man of strength, spiritual depth, and wise judgment. He is perhaps best known for his relationship with Moses, having provided him refuge and work in his flight from Egypt. Moses tended Jethro's flocks for forty years and married his daughter Zipporah. When called by God to return to Egypt, Moses took Zipporah and his two sons, but soon returned them to her father's care. After crossing the Red Sea, Jethro brought them back to Moses. He then taught Moses legislative and judicial procedures in leading the children of Israel, stressing that all law must be given by God and entrusted only to men of ability, piety, integrity, and truth (Exodus 18:19-23). Jethro has also been called Reuel.

JOB   Job is referred to in Scripture as a perfect and upright man who feared God. He was wealthy and lived in the land of Uz. In the midst of his abundant life, God sent tribulation: he lost his wealth, his family was destroyed, and his health failed. In all this Job had patience and unswerving trust in God, even amidst the accusations of his friends. More affliction came to Job but the account says, "the Lord blessed the latter days of Job more than his beginning" (Job 42:12). Though he suffered greatly, he could say, "I know that my redeemer liveth" (Job 19:25). The book of Job tells the story in epic form. (See Job in Chapter IV.)

JOEL   The prophet Joel was the son of a man called Pethuel. Joel was probably brought up in Judah and it is clear that he prophesied in Jerusalem. There is some debate about just when Joel lived and prophesied; probably it was in the ninth century B.C. Two calamities gave rise to Joel's literary output, the one was a locust plague, the other a severe drought. The prophet challenged the people to prayer and fasting. Perhaps some of the people responded, for towards the end of the book of Joel there is a spirit of optimism.

JOHN THE APOSTLE   John the Apostle, son of Zebedee and Salome and the brother of James, was by trade a fisherman until called by Christ to follow Him. Tradition assigns John the role of the youngest Apostle as well as one of the best remembered. John the Apostle is said to be the author of five New Testament books: the Gospel of John, the three Epistles of John, and the Revelation or Apocalypse. Of the twelve Apostles, John, Peter, and James were the closest to Christ. These three were with Him at the raising of Jairus' daughter, on the Mount of Olives, in Gethsemane, etc., but John alone was at the cross when his Lord was crucified and it was there Jesus commanded him to care for Mary, Jesus' mother, which he did till her death. John's closing years were spent in Ephesus, and it was there he apparently wrote his Gospel. A pillar in the Jerusalem Church, he was exiled to the Isle of Patmos where he wrote the Revelation. References: Mark 3:17; 14:33, Luke 5:10, Acts 3, etc.

JOHN THE BAPTIST   John the Baptist, known as the forerunner of Christ, was born three months before the birth of Jesus Christ, to a priest named Zacharias and his wife Elizabeth (Luke 1:5-25, 57-80). Upon reaching manhood John chose to spend his time in the wilderness preaching about Jesus who would presently come to the Jews. Except for his dress, a garment of camel's hair bound by a leathern girdle, he was a second Elijah proclaiming the message of repentance, "Repent ye, for the kingdom of God is at hand" (Matthew 3:2). Josephus, an ancient historian, acclaims John the Baptist "an excellent man, who admonished the Jews to come to baptism, practicing virtue and justice toward all men and piety toward God." Jesus Himself also praised John. Born c. 4 B.C., John was beheaded about 29–30 A.D. by Herod Antipas for speaking out against Herod's marriage to his sister-in-law, Herodias (Matthew 14:1-12).

JOHN MARK

The first reference to John Mark is in the Acts of the Apostles (Acts 12:12). He was the son of a certain Mary of Jerusalem and was a cousin of Barnabas. Mark accompanied Paul and Barnabas on their first missionary journey. Prior to the second journey a sharp difference arose between Paul and Barnabas over John Mark which eventually resulted in their separation, Barnabas siding with Mark (Acts 15:37-39), because Mark had turned back from the journey (Acts 13:13). Paul later had considerable faith and trust in John Mark, for when he writes to the Colossians (Colossians 4:10) and to Philemon (Philemon 24), Mark is in Rome and his presence there seems to be a solace to Paul. A strong tradition of the early Church says that John Mark was a companion of Peter also. Ten or twelve years elapsed between the last reference to John Mark in Acts and the first reference to him in the Epistles. It is believed that he accompanied Peter during these years. There is evidence that he was with Peter during the Apostle's last years and that Mark is telling Peter's story in the Gospel of Mark. (See the book of "Mark," Chapter VI.)

JONAH

Jonah ("dove") was the son of a certain Amittai. He appears unique among the Hebrew prophets in that his primary purpose does not seem to have been preaching to Israel. The Lord told him to go to Nineveh to warn the people that He would destroy their city (Jonah 1:1-2). Instead of obeying God, Jonah sailed for Tarshish. A great storm arose and Jonah told the men to cast him overboard, for *he* was the cause of the storm. God prepared a great fish to swallow him. He finally repented and the Lord caused the fish to vomit him up on dry land (Jonah 2:10). Having learned his lesson, Jonah now went to Nineveh and warned the people and they repented. Jonah is considered a type of the Christ because of the reference to his being in the fish's belly three days, just as Christ was in the grave three days (Matthew 12:40).

JONATHAN

Jonathan ("gift of Jehovah") was the heir apparent and eldest son of King Saul. He is first known as the hero of the War of Michmash, in which he brought victory to Saul almost single handed (I Samuel 13-14). Greatly loved by his people, he was athletic, handsome, a brilliant military leader, and was one of the most beautiful characters of all Bible history. He is best remembered for his unusually devoted friendship with David, which "passed the love of women," under the most trying circumstances (I Samuel 18-20). He was even willing to sacrifice his claim to the throne in favor of David. When David was exiled and persecuted by Saul, Jonathan remained loyal to his friend. At his death in the Battle of Mt. Gilboa he left one son, Mephibosheth, and was buried at Zelah in Benjamin (I Samuel 31:1-3).

JOSEPH Joseph was the son of Jacob and Rachel. Jacob loved Joseph more than his brothers because he was the son of his old age, and he gave him a coat of many colors. Joseph was hated by his brothers who plotted against him. They sold him into slavery for twenty pieces of silver (Genesis 37:28). But Joseph had faith in God and would not sin; the Lord was with him and he became the interpreter of Pharoah's dreams in Egypt. Joseph predicted a famine, was made a governor in Egypt, and gathered surplus food-stuffs of the good years into the great storehouses. Joseph's brothers came from the land of Canaan to buy food during the famine. He forgave his brothers and treated them well; Jacob joined them in his last years and the family was reunited (Genesis 45-46).

JOSHUA The hero of the book of Joshua and the son of Nun, Joshua ("Jehovah is salvation") was first the trusted aide and minister of Moses. Israel's armies were led by him in a great victory over the Amalakites at Sinai (Exodus 17:8-16). Representing the tribe of Ephraim among the twelve spies sent into Canaan, he and Caleb alone urged the people to possess the land through faith in God (Numbers 13:6, 8; 14:6, 38). A long life and succession to Moses were to be his reward for this. At Moses' death he led the Children of Israel over the Jordan into the Promised Land (Joshua 1-6). Under his leadership Jericho and the surrounding country were conquered, the land was divided, and the cities of refuge established (Joshua 7-21). He died at the age of 110 and was buried at Timnathserah.

JUDAS ISCARIOT Judas Iscariot was one of the twelve Disciples of our Lord (Mark 3:19). Nothing is known about him prior to his discipleship. Judas served as treasurer for the Apostolic circle, but grew covetous of the money he handled and his dishonesty and unfaithfulness led him to sell his Master. Previous to the Passover, Judas went to the chief priests and agreed to betray Jesus for thirty pieces of silver (Matthew 26:15). During the Passover Satan entered into him and he left the feast. The betrayal of Christ took place following the Lord's Supper in the Garden of Gethsemane (Matthew 26:47-50). After the crucifixion, Judas confessed his crime and attempted to return the money to the priests. The priests refused his offer, and Judas, feeling remorse for his crime, went out and hanged himself (Matthew 27:3-5; Acts 1:15-20).

There is little information about Jude. Actually there were many people in New Testament times with the same name. The Jude referred to here was the brother of Jesus and author of the little book that bears his name. Like his brothers, he did not believe in Christ until after the resurrection. Later, however, he portrayed himself as a "servant of Jesus Christ" (Jude 1). The spiritual relation of Christ, through James, was more important than his relationship to Christ in the flesh. Jude did not claim to be an apostle. He evidently was married. According to tradition, he preached in Mesopotamia and later became a martyr.

The name Lazarus is an abbreviation of Eleazar meaning "God has helped." Perhaps Jesus' closest non-disciple friend, Lazarus and his two sisters, Mary and Martha, lived in Bethany. After his death, Lazarus, being of a wealthy family, was given a fine funeral and buried in the family tomb in Bethany. Jesus raised him after he lay dead four days in the summer heat (Luke 11:1-46). The resultant conversion of many people caused jealousy in the Sanhedrin. Tradition says that Lazarus was thirty years old when Jesus raised him and that he lived an additional thirty years. Some records say that Lazarus preached in France after his resurrection from the dead. (The Lazarus of Luke is a different figure.)

Leah ("weary"), Jacob's first wife, was less desirable because she lacked physical beauty. Leah's father, Laban, tricked Jacob into marrying her instead of Rachel for whom he had worked seven years (Genesis 29). Leah bore Jacob six sons and a daughter (Reuben, Simeon, Levi, Judah, Issachar, Zebulu, and Dinah); her handmaid bore Gad and Asher (Genesis 30:10-13). *The Midrash* (an ancient exposition of Jewish Scriptures) regards her as a good and honorable woman, even though disliked by Jacob. She was buried in the family tomb of Machpelah in Hebron and most likely did not go to Egypt with Jacob.

(See "Thaddaeus.")

While Lot, the son of Haran and nephew of Abraham, was living in Egypt with Abraham, their prosperity caused disputes among some of their herdsmen. To settle the disagreements, Abraham decided to let Lot have his choice of one-half the land, either the fertile Jordan or the less desirable Canaan. Lot chose the former. God sent two angels to Lot, now a resident of the wicked city of Sodom, who told him to take his family and flee before He destroyed the city. They fled at the last possible moment, but his wife turned to a "pillar of salt" (Genesis 19:26) because she did not heed God's command not to look back at the city. Lot and his family escaped to the mountains. His two daughters bore him the fathers of the tribes of Moab and Ammon (Genesis 19:27-28). New

LUKE

Testament references: Luke 17:28-32; II Peter 2.7 f.

Luke, mentioned only three times by name in the New Testament (Colossians 4:14; Philemon 24; II Timothy 4:11), was a well-educated Greek physician who wrote the Gospel of Luke and the Acts of the Apostles. Luke 1:2 reveals that the physician was not "an eyewitness and minister of the word from the beginning;" apparently he joined Paul's company at Troas (Acts 16:10) and sailed with them to Macedonia. He was Paul's friend and traveling companion, remaining with him about nine years. Paul refers to him as the "beloved physician," and II Timothy 4:11 gives our last glimpse of his faithful friend. (See Luke, Chap. VI.)

LYDIA

Lydia, a Jewish proselyte and seller of purple from Thyatira, was a worshiper of God at Philippi who resorted to the riverside as a place of prayer. Here it was that Paul and his companions found Lydia, a ready listener, whose heart was opened by the Lord (Acts 16:14). She and her household believed, were baptized, and became the first converts of Paul in Europe. She became known as the hostess at Philippi when, eager to show her gratitude, she housed the Apostles after their imprisonment (Acts 16:15). Lydia, a proper name commonly borne by women of that time, may have been derived from the district Lydia. Since we know that a Church did grow up after the first conversion, Lydia became the key to a new way of life for Philippi and for Europe. (See "Claudius.")

LYSIAS, CLAUDIUS

MALACHI

The name Malachi signifies "angel of Jehovah." Malachi is believed by some as merely the name of the Old Testament book written by Ezra, while most other sources state that he is the last of the prophets. His messages were clear and clean-cut, encouraging the dispirited people of Israel. Little is known about him except that he was a prophet who preached and wrote.

MARK

(See "John Mark.")

MARTHA, SISTER OF MARY AND

Martha, the sister of Mary and Lazarus (John 11:1), was an admirable woman and a devoted friend of Jesus. Martha's home was in Bethany where she, as older sister, took over the responsibilities of the house. She is referred to in the raising of Lazarus from the dead in Bethany. In this incident Martha, upon hearing that Jesus was coming, went to meet him. At this time Jesus made his great statement concerning eternal life (John 11:20-27). (See "Lazarus.")

LAZARUS

MARY OF BETHANY

Mary, the sister of Lazarus and Martha, appears only briefly in the Scriptures. She and her sister Martha appear in the Gospel of Luke as receiving Christ into their home. Mary sat at Jesus' feet listening eagerly to the words He spoke while Martha was busy serving. Jesus commended Mary for having "chosen that good part," the "one thing needful" (Luke 10:42). Mary is next mentioned at the raising of Lazarus. As soon as Martha heard Jesus was coming, she ran to meet Him, but Mary remained in the house until Jesus called for her. Both the sisters said to Him, "Lord, if thou hadst been here, my brother had not died" (John 11:21, 32). Even though Lazarus had been dead four days, Christ raised him again to life and many Jews who had followed Mary believed. John states that this was the same Mary who anointed the Lord at the last feast of Bethany.

In the little town of Magdala (now Mejdel), which had a reputation for wealth and immorality and was located three miles from Capernaum on the Northwest shore of the Sea of Galilee, Mary Magdalene was born. She may have been the Mary out of whom Jesus cast seven devils (Mark 16:9); there is doubt that she was the woman in Luke 7:37 who washed Jesus' feet with ointment and tears. Mary Magdalene must not be confused with Mary of Bethany who was the sister of Martha and Lazarus. First Scriptural mention of her is made in Luke 8:2 where with certain other women she ministered to Jesus. Mary Magdalene was probably among the women in Luke 23:49 who saw the crucifixion, for we find that later (Mark 16:1) she went with Salome and Mary the mother of Jesus to anoint Jesus' body in the tomb. However, the tomb contained not the body of Jesus but angels. When Jesus appeared to her at the empty tomb, she mistook Him for the gardener until He spoke her name. He charged her to go and tell the other disciples that He would soon ascend to God (John 20:11-18). After this incident the Scriptures are silent concerning Mary Magdalene.

Mary was the wife of Cleophas (Clopas); he in turn was brother of Joseph, husband of Mary the Virgin. Mary is primarily remembered as a member of a group of women which viewed the crucifixion, followed the funeral procession, and was a spectator at the burial of Christ (Matthew 27:56, 61). She was among the very first to bear spices to the tomb to anoint the body of her dead Lord. However, upon reaching the tomb her sorrow turned to joy because her Lord had risen.

Mary, mother of John Mark and aunt of Barnabas (Colossians 4:10), made her home available as a worship center. It was perhaps the scene of the Last Supper and possibly of Pentecost. It is also recorded that Peter went there from prison (Acts 12:12). Moreover, Mary was a woman of character and probably a widow of comfortable circumstances, owning her home and having servants (Acts 12:13). The home of Mary is said to have been located on the southern end of Mount Zion, which was a residential area in

MARY MAGDALENE

MARY, MOTHER OF JAMES AND JOSES

MARY, MOTHER OF JOHN MARK

the time of Jesus.

In the city of Nazareth there was a virgin named Mary who was engaged to a man called Joseph of the lineage of David. An angel of the Lord revealed that because she had found favor in God's sight she had been chosen to become the virgin mother of the One who would save Israel from its sins (Matthew 1:18-21). Mary spent three months of her pregnancy with Elizabeth, her cousin, who was to become the mother of John the Baptist. When the time approached for the birth of Jesus, Mary and Joseph were required to travel to Bethlehem for the purpose of taxation (Luke 2:1-5). It was there at Bethlehem that Jesus was born in a rude stable (Luke 2:6-7). Jesus' public ministry began with a miracle in Cana of Galilee where Mary sent men to Him to replenish the wine at a wedding feast (John 2:1-11). Mary witnessed the crucifixion of her son. While on the cross Jesus asked John, His beloved disciple, to take the place of a dying son in Mary's life and asked Mary to transfer her motherly affection to John (John 19:25-27). After Jesus' Ascension, Mary continued as a devout believer of the Way, and is last seen as one of the Upper Room company (Acts 1:14). Tradition has it that she went to Ephesus, to live near John, where she spent her last years.

Matthew, or Levi, is recognized primarily for his authorship of the Gospel of Matthew. He was the son of Alphaeus and lived in Capernaum where he served as tax collector at the local custom house. Though a publican himself, Matthew was not as wealthy as those Roman publicans who rented the business of tax collecting to resident deputies such as Matthew. Matthew relates his call to discipleship in Matthew 9:9: "As Jesus passed on from there, he saw a man called Matthew sitting at the tax office; and he said to him, 'Follow me.' And he rose and followed him." (Two parallel accounts of Matthew's call are found in Mark 2:14 and Luke 5:27-28.) It was the feast that Matthew then prepared for Jesus that provoked the Pharisees to ask Jesus why he ate and drank with tax collectors and sinners. There is no other direct mention of Matthew in the New Testament except in the listing of the Apostles in Luke 6:15. It is believed that Matthew preached in Judea for twelve to fifteen years and then went as an evangelist to foreign nations, where he died either in Ethiopia or Macedonia.

The only Biblical account of Matthias is found in Acts 1:15-26. In the Circle of the Twelve he filled the place left vacant by Judas Iscariot. Joseph Barsabbas was also considered for the position. Presenting the two men to the Lord, they prayed that God would determine through the casting of lots who was to be chosen. The lot fell on Matthias, and "he was enrolled with the eleven apostles" (verse 26). Nothing definite is known about Matthias after this event, though an apocryphal book was published under his name.

Melchizedek is mentioned twice in the Old Testament (Genesis 14:18; Psalm 110:4). He was both an ancient king and a priest "of God Most High" (Genesis 14:18). After a battle, Abraham was met by him with the kind offer of bread and wine. As both king of righteousness and king of peace Melchizedek became the eternal representative and symbolic head of the highest order of Levitical priesthood, and Hebrews depicts Christ as a High Priest after the order of Melchizedek (Hebrew 5:6).

Methuselah lived when the earth was vile and full of wickedness. The name means "released from death." He was the son of Enoch and the grandfather of Noah. According to Scriptures he was the oldest man who ever lived. At the age of 187 he became the father of Lamech. He was 969 years old when he died (Genesis 5:27).

Micah was a contemporary of Isaiah and Hosea, having lived in the eighth century B.C. His name means "who is like Jehovah," and he was perhaps the first man to prophesy or warn of the destruction of Jerusalem. During his time there was a great deal of sin in both Israel and Judah, and Micah attacked the sin in men of all walks of life. He dealt primarily with social morality and personal religion; he underscored justice, kindness and humility. Micah's message was heard throughout Israel and Judah despite the fact that he spent the majority of his time in western Judah. His earnestness and truth are seen in his fervent style. He foretold that Jesus would be born in Bethlehem (Micah 5:2). Micah 6:8 is one of the great texts of the Bible: "He has showed you, O man, what is good; and what does the Lord require of you but to do justice, and to love kindness, and to walk humbly with your God?"

Moses, a Levite, was born to Amram and Jochebed at Heliopolis, a famous city in lower Egypt. He was adopted by Pharaoh's daughter and educated "in all the wisdom of the Egyptians" (Exodus 2:1-15). He became a man "mighty in words and deeds." This first period of his life closed with the killing of the Egyptian and the resulting exile in Midian (Exodus 2:15—4:31). During his exile (a forty-year period) he married Zipporah, a daughter of Jethro. Moses came to the burning bush as a shepherd and received a call from God. When he returned to Egypt he became the emancipator and governor of Israel (a forty-year period). Moses, leader of the Exodus (Exodus 5:1—15:21), brought the people to Sinai by way of the Dead Sea (Exodus 15:22—19:2). There he became the Lawgiver (the Ten Commandments are recorded in Exodus 20:1-17 and Deuteronomy 5:6-21). He led the Israelites from Sinai to the borders of the Promised Land, but he died at Nebo. Moses was a great prophet, general, administrator and legislator, statesman, lawgiver, liberator, author, poet, and a Hebrew historian.

NAAMAN Naaman, whose name means "pleasantness," lived in the ninth century B.C. He was a military officer in charge of his ruler's (Ben-Hadad's) army and was highly respected by his countrymen. It is odd that a man with such a high position could have leprosy, but Naaman did. His wife's handmaid, an Israelite, told him of a wonder worker in her home land who could heal. Naaman finally found Elisha and was told to bathe in the Jordan River seven times (II Kings 5:10). It took awhile for this proud man to follow Elisha's instructions, but when he did he was cleansed (II Kings 5:14). Naaman was a sincere and gracious man and tried to shower the prophet with gifts. He recognized the power of Elisha's God and took Him as his own Lord.

NAHUM One of the minor prophets, his name means "compassionate." Practically nothing is known of his personal life. He is called "the Elkoshite" which refers to his native village of Elkosh, perhaps in Galilee. It is believed that his prophecy was written sometime between 661 and 612 B.C. (see "Nahum" in Chapter IV). He describes the judgment of Nineveh about which his contemporary, Zephaniah, also prophesied. Nahum's prophecy is especially interesting because he foretells the fall of Nineveh which actually took place in 612 B.C. (chapters 2-3).

NAOMI Naomi was the wife of Elimelech of Bethlehem, and the mother of Mahlon and Chilion. Her history is interwoven with that of her daughter-in-law Ruth. Naomi went with her husband and sons into Moab because of famine in Palestine. Her sons married Moabite women, Ruth and Orpah. Within ten years the men died, leaving Naomi and her two daughters-in-law. She decided to return to Bethlehem and encouraged the daughters to return to their respective home countries. Orpah returned, but Ruth, being very devoted, went to Bethlehem with Naomi. Ruth uttered the beautiful and classic words, "Entreat me not to leave you or to return from following you, for where you go I will go, and where you lodge I will lodge; your people shall be my people, and your God my God . . ." (Ruth 1:16). Naomi's name means "pleasantness" or "delight." However, upon her return to Bethlehem, when asked, "Is this Naomi?" she answered, "Call me not Naomi, call me Mara, for the Almighty hath dealt very bitterly with me." The name Mara she desired to be called means "bitterness."

NATHAN Nathan was a Hebrew prophet who lived in the time of David

and Solomon and served as their chief spiritual advisor. He was David's consultant in the building plans of the Temple at Jerusalem. When David had committed adultery with Bathsheba, Nathan rebuked him for his sin (II Samuel 12:1-10)—"thou art the man"—and told him of the message from the Lord that he could not now build the Temple. He is last mentioned in the Bible (I Kings) in connection with the future kingship of Solomon and the thwarting of the plans of David's older son Adonijah to make himself king.
(See "Bartholomew.")

NATHANAEL

Nebuchadrezzar, the second king of Babylon, reigned from 605 B.C. to 562 B.C. During his reign he conquered Judah and took the Jews captive. He constructed brick streets, great walls, moats, dams, temples of gold and cedar, and beautiful bronze statues. The strangest and most beautiful architectural accomplishment of his reign was the famed hanging gardens of Babylon. Nebuchadrezzar is the king who put Shadrach, Meshach, and Abednego into a fiery furnace for not worshipping his idol; when the fire did not harm the men, Nebuchadrezzar honored them and their God (Daniel 3:28-30). He had strange dreams which he could not understand and he called on Daniel to interpret them.

NEBUCHAD-
REZZAR

Nehemiah, the son of Hacaliah, held an important position as a young boy: it was his honor to be cup bearer to King Artaxerxes of Persia (464 B.C. to 424 B.C.). Nehemiah found favor with the King and asked his permission to go to Jerusalem to help his countrymen rebuild the walls which had been destroyed by Nebuchadrezzar. The King gave his permission and appointed Nehemiah governor of the province of Judea. He also gave Nehemiah letters to the governors of provinces to assist him in going from place to place in safety. A letter to Asaph asked for wood from the King's forest to make beams for the gates of the fortress of the Temple, for the walls of the city, and for the house which Nehemiah would occupy (Nehemiah 1:7-8). But "when Sanballat the Horonite and Tobiah the servant, the Ammonite, heard this, it displeased them greatly that someone had come to seek the welfare of the children of Israel" (Nehemiah 1:10). After renovating the city, Nehemiah established religious and social reforms, assisted by Ezra the priest and scribe. Nehemiah reigned periodically as Governor of Judea until his death.

NEHEMIAH

Nicodemus, a Pharisee, was a member of the Sanhedrin and a ruler of the Jews. His story is told only by John. Nicodemus requested a meeting with Jesus. Nicodemus was confused when Jesus told him he must be born again; he took the re-birth in its literal sense rather than its spiritual. Jesus went on to explain the

NICODEMUS

meaning (John 3:5-8). Although this meeting with Jesus seemed to be fruitless, it appears that Nicodemus stood in Jesus' defense at the Feast of Tabernacles when the Sanhedrin was against him (John 7:50-52). When Jesus died, Nicodemus provided Christ with "the mixture of myrrh and aloes" (John 19:39). This may have labeled him as being a follower of Christ; if so, he was at last a "born again" Christian.

NOAH   Noah, the preacher of righteousness, is mentioned in nine books of the Bible (Genesis, I Chronicles, Isaiah, Ezekiel, Matthew, Luke, Hebrews, I and II Peter). His story is told in full in Genesis 5-10. Noah was a descendant of Adam by Seth, the son of Lamech, and the father of Ham, Shem, and Japheth. The age in which Noah lived was one of religious indifference and defiance to God. Noah is remembered especially as he relates to the story of the flood. At the age of 480 years Noah was instructed by God to build an ark in which he and his family and every kind of animal, clean and unclean, would find security from the destructive flood waters caused by forty days rain. Noah and his family and the animals entered the ark 120 years later. The rains came and the earth was covered by water. When the waters subsided a year later, the ark rested on Mt. Ararat. Noah sent out a raven and a dove to determine how far the water had recessed. The second time the dove was sent out it did not return, so Noah knew the ground was dry. One month later he and his family and the animals left the ark, and Noah offered burnt sacrifices on an altar. God gave the rainbow as a symbol of His promise never again to destroy the earth by water. Noah lived 350 years after the flood and died at the age of 950 years.

OBADIAH THE PROPHET   Regarding the person and circumstances of this prophet's life, little is known. (See Obadiah, Chapter IV.) A dozen Old Testament figures are known by the name "Obadiah."

ONESIMUS   Onesimus was the escaped slave of a Greek Christian named Philemon. After escaping to Rome Onesimus met Paul and was converted to Christianity. Paul then sent Onesimus back to Philemon with a letter (the book of Philemon) explaining Onesimus' conversion and asking Philemon to receive Onesimus as a new brother in Christ. (See Philemon, Chapter VI.)

PAUL   Paul was born a Roman citizen in Tarsus of Cilicia. His family was of the tribe of Benjamin and he was brought up a Pharisee. He studied under Gamaliel (Acts 22:3) and was highly educated (he knew several languages and was conversant with Hebrew and Greek literature). Saul, which was his name in the Hebrew language, was a great persecutor of the Church, evidence of which was his approval of Stephen's death (Acts 7:58—8:1), but Stephen's victorious death made its impression on him. He was converted later on the road to Damascus after being struck blind (Acts 9:1-19; 22:5-16; 26:12-18). He recovered his sight when the Holy Spirit filled him. Shortly after he went to Arabia (Galatians 1:17). He was the great world missionary of the New Testament, and in Gentile territory he used his Roman name Paul. Paul's three missionary journeys are recorded in Acts and his work was in Asia Minor, Greece, and Rome. He suffered intense persecution (imprisonment, stoning, beating, etc.), but nothing stopped him from his ministry of preaching, healing, Church building, and writing. Imprisoned for extended periods in Rome, tradition asserts he died a martyr by beheading in Rome about 64-67 A.D. He is the author of most of the New Testament Epistles. Paul has been called the most powerful human personality of the New Testament, and certainly his love chapter (I Corinthians 13) is unsurpassed (J. B. Phillips' rendering of it is one of the great masterpieces of twentieth century English literature). There is an ancient and traditional description of Paul which says "he was a man small in size, with meeting eye-brows, with a rather large nose, baldheaded, bow-legged, strongly built, full of grace, for at times he looked like a man, and at times he had the face of an angel."

PETER, SIMON

The name Peter means "stone." He was a brother to Andrew and son of Jona (or Johanan). A native of Bethsaida, he is pictured as a rugged fisherman. He is mentioned more times than any other figure in the New Testament, aside from Jesus. Married, he was nonetheless one of the twelve Disciples. He denied Jesus at the time of the crucifixion (Matthew 26:73-75). Jesus saw him after the resurrection (see I Corinthians 15:5—Cephas is another name for Peter). In the Acts of the Apostles, he is the dominant character and Apostolic leader in the first part of that book, chapters 1-12. He addressed the Disciples about a man to take Judas' place and preached to the crowd at Pentecost (Acts 2). He was the instrument of many cures (e.g., Acts 3) and conversions to Christ (Acts 4). He even raised a woman (Dorcas) from the dead. He had the courage to preach to the Gentiles in Cornelius' house (Acts 10). His acts and good works were too numerous to list here. He influenced Mark's Gospel—in fact, he told the story which Mark reduced to written form. He is the author of I Peter and tradition says of II Peter too. His great confession (Mark 16:16) stands out as a high point in the New Testament. When Herod nearly succeeded in taking his life, he escaped by the hand of the Lord (Acts 12:1-17) and was not mentioned again in Acts except for chapter 15 (the Jerusalem Council). The image that has come down through history is that of a man of impetuous but sincere

PHILEMON

action. Tradition says he died crucified upside down at Rome.

Philemon was a Christian of Colossae, and a leader of the Church in that city. He was a man of property and influence. Also, he was regarded as a man with a high and noble character, generous toward his friends and the poor, and had a sympathizing and forgiving spirit. Philemon was a friend and probable convert of Paul. Onesimus, a slave of Philemon, robbed his master and fled to Rome, where he became a convert of Paul. Paul then made intercession to Philemon for Onesimus, requesting forgiveness and acceptance as a brother in Christ. It is not known whether or not Philemon showed charity toward Onesimus, but we may suppose he did. The story of Philemon and Onesimus is told in the little Epistle by Paul called "Philemon." Tradition says Philemon died a martyr under Nero.

PHILIP THE APOSTLE

Philip the Apostle was from Bethsaida on the Sea of Galilee, also the city of Andrew and Peter. Jesus called him to be a disciple and he followed immediately inviting Nathanael to meet Jesus and His company. He was among the followers of Jesus at Calvary and met with those in the Upper Room following Jesus' Ascension. After Pentecost Philip continued to preach.

PHILIP THE EVANGELIST

Philip was always ready to witness for his Lord. From the fact of his being appointed as one of the seven deacons (Acts 6:5), we know he was honest and Spirit-filled (Acts 6:3). Philip ministered in Samaria where he performed miracles that drew attention away from Simon Magus, a sorcerer. Philip proceeded to preach to the crowds, leading many to Christ. The well-known story of Philip and the eunuch is also significant. Philip, on seeing the eunuch reading Isaiah 53, asked if he understood the Scripture. The eunuch invited him to expound it and was then converted (Acts 8). This story should be studied for its lessons in personal evangelism. Nothing is said of Philip's family antecedents, but Acts 21:8 mentions four "unmarried daughters, who prophesied." Philip is chiefly remembered as a preacher and evangelist.

PHILIP THE TETRARCH

Philip the Tetrarch or Herod Philip II (4 B.C.–34 A.D.) was a son of Herod the Great and Cleopatra of Jerusalem. He was the most noble member of the Herod family. Philip ruled the northeastern part of Palestine. His territorial improvements were general. He also built the city of Caesarea Philippi and rebuilt Bethsaida. Philip was a willing and just judge; when he traveled, he took along his tribunal to expedite efficient judgment of complaints. After Philip's death his territory became part of the Province of Syria.

PONTIUS PILATE

Pontius Pilate was the Roman procurator of Judea at the time of Christ's crucifixion (Matthew 27:2; Mark 15:1; Luke 23:1;

John 18:28-29). He was personally responsible to Emperor Tiberius for the finances and for the civil, military, and criminal jurisdiction of his Judean province. Pilate is best known for his role in the trial and crucifixion of Jesus. He tried to release Jesus but the people demanded the release of the thief Barabbas instead. In condemning Him, Pilate acted against his conscience and the warning of his wife. He called Christ the King of the Jews. It is believed that Pilate was dismissed from office by Vitellus, a ruler in Syria, for the murdering of many Samaritans. On his way to trial in Rome the emperor died and it is thought that Pilate somehow escaped at that time. No further mention seems to be made of him in history.

PRISCILLA

Priscilla, or Prisca, was the wife of Aquila, a tentmaker, with whom she is always mentioned (Acts 18:2, 18, 26; Romans 16:3; I Corinthians 16:19; II Timothy 4:19). When Paul was in Corinth he stayed with them, and they in turn traveled with him as far as Ephesus. Paul always spoke highly of her and the zealous work she was doing in advancing Christianity. Her homes in Corinth, Ephesus, and Rome were the meeting places of the early churches in those cities. She and her husband helped in the theological training of Apollos. It has been suggested, though without proof, that she and her husband were the co-authors of the Epistle to the Hebrews. (See "Aquila.")

RACHEL

Rachel, whose name means "ewe," was the younger daughter of Laban (Genesis 29:6). Her husband Jacob worked seven years for her hand in marriage, but was tricked by Laban into marrying Leah, the older daughter; so Jacob had to work seven years more for Rachel. She was barren for several years and then bore Joseph. When Jacob left the service of Laban, Rachel stole her father's teraphim (images) which she hoped would bring prosperity to her and her husband. The first impression of Rachel is favorable; she is attractive in person, manner, and address, and quick to stir Jacob's affections; but this opinion is changed when she stole and lied about her father's teraphim. Rachel died at Benjamin's birth, and her burial place is near Bethlehem. References: see Genesis 29-35.

REBEKAH

Rebekah was the daughter of Bethuel, the sister of Laban, the wife of Isaac and the mother of Jacob and Esau. She was discovered by one of Abraham's servants and consented to become the wife of Isaac (Genesis 24). Rebekah remained childless for twenty years but finally had twin sons, Jacob and Esau. In Genesis 27 we see that Rebekah led her favorite and younger son, Jacob, to deceive Isaac by falsely receiving Isaac's blessing. She then had to send Jacob to Mesopotamia to escape the wrath of Esau. Rebekah died before Isaac and was buried in Abraham's tomb, the cave of Machpelah near Hebron.

REHOBOAM   Rehoboam became king upon the death of his father Solomon. Due to unwise and unpopular taxing policies, a political division occurred in the united kingdom. The nation separated, with ten northern tribes forming the nation of Israel. Rehoboam with the tribes of Judah and Benjamin remained in control of the capital city, Jerusalem, and formed a new nation, the southern nation of Judah. During Rehoboam's reign, with the nation now divided, Egypt was able to invade and capture Jerusalem and carry away the Temple treasury. During Rehoboam's reign (c. 922–915 B.C.), the Hebrew nation began its decline.

REUEL   (See "Jethro.")

RUTH   Ruth, her name signifying "companion" or "attachment," was a Moabite woman who became the ancestress of David, Mary, and Jesus Christ. She married Mahlon after he, his parents, Naomi and Elimelech, and his brother Chilion, had been driven from their home in Bethlehem because of famine. The men died, leaving Naomi, Ruth and Orpah, Chilion's wife. Naomi decided to return to Bethlehem, and Ruth, being very devoted, went with her. They arrived in Bethlehem at the beginning of the barley harvest. Ruth gleaned the fields to earn support for Naomi and herself. There she met Boaz, a relative of Naomi, who treated her kindly and soon fell in love with her. Boaz purchased Mahlon's share of the ancestral estate, thus according to the Hebrew law (Deuteronomy 25:5-10) he was able to marry her. Their first-born son was Obed, who was the father of Jesse and the grandfather of David. Reference: the book of Ruth.

SAMSON   Samson was born a Nazarite and received great strength when he took the Nazarite vow never to cut his hair. His feats of strength were spectacular; killing 1,000 Philistines with the jawbone of an ass (Judges 15:16), carrying off the gates of Gaza (Judges 16:3), etc. Samson had a weakness for women and Delilah, a Philistine, was his favorite woman. She was paid by Philistine lords to discover the secret of Samson's strength. Discovered, they cut off his hair while he slept, and then took him captive, tortured him and put out his eyes. Samson's hair grew back and while the Philistines mocked him at a great banquet, he prayed to God for strength. Receiving strength, he pushed over the pillars which supported the roof of the feast room and everyone including Samson was killed (Judges 16:29-30).

SAMUEL   When Samuel was born to Elkanah and Hannah (I Samuel 1:20)), the twelve tribes of Israel had been in Canaan for a little over three hundred years. There was great discontent and strife among the tribes. The priesthood was racked with sin and incompetency; and aging Eli, as their judge, was unable to cope with the problems confronting his nation. As a young child Samuel was taken by his mother Hannah to Eli the priest and dedicated to the service of Jehovah. This was the fulfillment of a promise that Hannah had made to God when she was praying for a son. Samuel grew to manhood in the service of the priesthood. When Eli died from shock upon hearing of the slaying of his irresponsible sons, it was Samuel who took his place as the priest of Israel. He was Israel's first prophet and the last of the judges. His birthplace, judicial residence, and burial place were all at Ramah, about six miles from Jerusalem. During his ministry—which spanned part of the lives of Eli, Saul, and David—God chose Samuel as His main instrument in dealing with sinful Israel. He united the twelve tribes into a kingdom under Saul, led the Hebrew army to victory over the Philistines, established the government of Israel, and served as judge.

Sapphira (an Aramaic name meaning "beautiful") was the wife of Ananias and accomplice in the sin for which they both died. Upon the sale of their property, they retained the profit rather than giving it to the Church, and then denied the act. When Ananias was confronted by Peter concerning the sale, he lied and was immediately struck dead. About three hours after the death of her husband, Sapphira entered quite unconscious of what had happened. Questioned by Peter as to the price obtained for the land they had sold, she repeated the lie of her husband and exposed herself to the fate of Ananias. Peter replied to her, "How is it that you have agreed together to tempt the Spirit of the Lord? Hark, the feet of those that have buried your husband are at the door, and they will carry you out." On hearing these words she fell dead at his feet (Acts 5:7-10).

SAPPHIRA

Sarah (the Hebrew name for "princess") was the wife of Abraham and mother of Isaac. Her name was originally Sarai. There is little known of her birth or parentage because the Scriptures do not contain an account of her early history. It is believed by many historians that she was related to Abraham through his father, but this is not certain. When Sarah was unable to give Abraham a son, she presented to him her Egyptian handmaiden Hagar to be the mother of his children. Hagar gave birth to Ishmael. But God promised Sarah a son, even though she was past her time. God's promise was fulfilled when Sarah gave birth to Isaac. As the two sons grew, Ishmael began to mock Isaac and Sarah demanded that Abraham send Hagar and her son away. Assured by God that Sarah was right, Abraham did as he was commanded. Thirty-seven years

SARAH

after the birth of Isaac, at the age of one hundred and twenty-seven, Sarah died at Hebron. She was buried in the cave of Machpelah. References: Genesis 20-23. (See "Abraham" and "Hagar.")

SAUL Saul was the first king of Israel, the son of Kish and a member of the tribe of Benjamin. According to II Samuel 1:23 he was of great physical stature; he was "head and shoulders taller than the rest of the people." For some time Israel had wanted a king; and finally the people demanded one. Samuel was asked to appoint the king. God revealed to Samuel that a man called Saul would come to him and that this man was God's choice as king. All went well until Saul's self-will caused him to commit sin. (An example is recorded in I Samuel 15.) God commanded Saul to invade Amalek and to "utterly destroy it." But Saul did not completely destroy the country; in fact, his army brought home cattle and the king—the cattle supposedly as sacrifices, the captured king to display (Saul was proud). It is possible for a man to have the blessing of God and to walk with God, yet fall short of the assigned goal. Even though Saul was chosen by God, he fell because of self-will and sin. He died by his own hand, but only after he had consulted the Witch of Endor. At the end of his life Saul said, "I have played the fool;" but another Saul—Saul of Tarsus—said at the close of his life, "I have fought the good fight."

SILAS Paul's missionary companion, taking Mark's place on the second journey to Macedonia and Corinth (Acts 15:22-40; II Corinthians 1:19), he was also known as Silvanus (I Thessalonians 1:1; II Thessalonians 1:1). He may have been Peter's secretary or amanuensis (I Peter 5:12). Tradition says he died in Macedonia.

SIMEON WHO BLESSED JESUS Simeon ("hearing") was typical of the Jewish people in that he was obedient to the Law of Moses and also he was looking forward to the coming of the Messiah. He was promised by God that he should not see death until he had seen the Christ. He was in the Temple when Mary and Joseph brought the Child, according to the Law, to be circumcized. Simeon, directed by the Holy Spirit, knew that the Child was the Anointed One of God and dedicated Him to God's service (Luke 2:33-35).

SIMEON, SON OF JACOB AND LEAH Simeon was the second son of Jacob and Leah. His name is derived from Shama, the Hebrew word "to hear." He is mentioned twice in the Old Testament. In Genesis 42:24, Simeon was required by his brother Joseph to stay in Egypt as security so that the others could return with Benjamin. He is mentioned again as killing the Shechemites to avenge the rape of his sister Dinah. For this he is cursed by Jacob (Genesis 49:5-7). As a result, his descendants, though of the twelve tribes of Israel, were scattered and eventually absorbed by the tribe of Judah.

"Simon the Cananaean," was one of the twelve Apostles (Matthew 10:4; Mark 3:18), otherwise described as Simon Zelotes (Luke 6:15; Acts 1:13). The latter term is peculiar to Luke. He is not to be identified with Simon the brother of Jesus. There is not a great deal known of Simon, in fact practically nothing. He belonged to the Zealots, an intensely nationalistic sect, quite different from the Publicans. Jesus chose a Zealot and a Publican (Matthew), from bitterly rival factions, to be brothers in Him and in His work.

SIMON THE CANANAEAN

This Simon was a Jew from the trading town of Cyrene located on the northern coast of Africa. As he was coming into the city of Jerusalem he was compelled by Roman soldiers to help carry the cross of Jesus to Golgotha. The incident is recorded in Matthew 27:32, Mark 15:21, and Luke 23:26. Being from Africa, Simon may well have been a Negro or dark-skinned man.

SIMON OF CYRENE

Simon Magus (Simon the Magician or Sorcerer) had such a bewitching influence over the people of Samaria that they recognized him as a "great power" of God. He was "converted" and baptized after observing the miracles performed by Philip. When Peter and John came to Samaria, laying their hands on new converts that they might receive the Holy Spirit, Simon was greatly impressed and asked to buy this power. Peter sternly rebuked him declaring that his heart was not right with God, and that he was still "in the gall of bitterness and in the bond of iniquity." Taking the rebuke meekly, he begged the Apostle to pray that none of these evils befall him (Acts 8:9-24). The buying and selling of Church offices—a notorious evil of the Middle Ages especially—is known as Simony after Simon Magus.

SIMON MAGUS

Solomon (meaning "peaceful") or Jedidiah (meaning "beloved by Jehovah"), was the youngest son of King David and Bathsheba. As a young king, Solomon went before God not to seek life, wealth, or victory, but to ask for wisdom which he received and for which he is remembered. Solomon's first wife was an Egyptian princess, but it is said that he had 700 wives and princesses and 300 concubines. Besides being noted for his wisdom and his women, Solomon is also remembered for his writings, including poems and proverbs; his wealth; his success in commerce; his magnificent buildings which include the Temple, palaces, and other structures; and for his fortification of Jerusalem and other towns. During his forty year reign (c. 961–922 B.C.), Solomon did much for his country through commerce and wealth, but he also allowed it to fall into ruin. Pagan temples were built and his army was left untrained. After experiencing a life of wealth and luxury,

SOLOMON

Solomon left his heir, Rehoboam, with only a shell of a once great empire. The story of Solomon is told in I Kings 1-14, also II Chronicles 1-13.

STEPHEN   Stephen was the most prominent of "the seven" chosen to serve as deacons (Acts 6). He went beyond these duties, however, and became a powerful preacher. When Stephen gave his remarkable defense (Acts 7) in which he summarized the heart of Old Testament history, the Jewish leaders—after he pointed the finger of guilt at them—were so provoked that they seized him, dragged him out of the city, and stoned him. Stephen was the first martyr of the Christian Church. Because of Stephen's testimony, many were converted and added to the Church. Among them was Saul of Tarsus, who had witnessed Stephen's irresponsible death.

THADDAEUS   Thaddaeus (also known as Lebbeus), a little known disciple of Jesus (the name "Thaddaeus" occurs in Matthew 10:3, Mark 3:18), is thought to have been born in Odessa. Tradition says further things about him: that he came to Jerusalem where he was baptized by John the Baptist, that he then began his ministry, that he returned to his home town of Odessa to preach the Gospel, and that he died and was buried in Beirut. There is some confusion about his name, but from comparison of Matthew, Mark, and Luke, it seems scarcely possible to doubt that the three names Lebbeus, Judas the brother of James, and Thaddaeus belong to the same person.

THOMAS   Thomas, one of the Apostles of Jesus Christ, is mentioned in all the Gospels, but in the closing scenes of John he becomes a prominent figure. It is believed that his name was Judas, but that he was called Thomas to distinguish him from the other two named Judas. The recently discovered Gospel of Thomas identifies him as Didymus Judas Thomas, but the Old Syriac Version of the Gospels says he was "Judas not Iscariot" (John 14:22). The word "Thomas" is Aramaic for twin and "Didymus" is Greek for twin. Three main traits of Thomas are brought out by John. Thomas was inclined to think that bad situations were worse than they really were, but he possessed a loyalty that made him steadfast in spite of danger. This is shown in John 11:16 when he urged the Disciples to accompany Christ to Judea even though there was Jewish hostility. Thomas refused to believe that Jesus had risen until he was able to see the nail prints for himself (John 20:28). Tradition declares that he was a missionary and founder of the Church of Mar Thoma in India, and that he died a martyr. It is also said that he wrote an apocryphal gospel.

TIMOTHY   Timothy was born in Lystra, the son of a Greek father and Jewish mother, Eunice (Acts 16:1; II Timothy 1:5). Eunice and her mother, Lois, were Christians (converted on Paul's first visit to Lystra) who instructed Timothy in the Scriptures as a youth. On Paul's second visit he saw great possibilities in Timothy, wanted to use him, and to alleviate Jewish prejudices had him circumcised (Acts 16:3). Timothy accompanied Paul on part of his Macedonian tour. When Paul went to Athens he was immediately sent back to visit the Thessalonian Church. During Paul's long stay at Ephesus, Timothy "ministered to him" and was sent ahead of him to Macedonia and to Corinth to remind the Corinthians "of my ways in Christ" (I Corinthians 4:17). At Rome Timothy was with Paul during his imprisonment, when the Apostle wrote some Epistles. Timothy himself was apparently imprisoned for a time (Hebrews 13:23). Ancient legends claim that Timothy was bishop of Ephesus (cp. I Timothy 1:3), and that his death was caused by his denouncing the feast of Diana for its licentiousness. Timothy is mentioned in II Corinthians, Titus, Galatians, Acts, and of course I and II Timothy which are addressed to him. It is interesting that Paul's last letter (II Timothy) is directed to him.

TITUS

Titus was one of Paul's most trusted assistants. He was of Greek parentage (Galatians 2:3) but otherwise of unknown origin. He was converted under the Apostle Paul. This Gentile went with Paul to Jerusalem in order to resist the demand of the Jewish Christians for the circumcision of the Gentiles (Galatians 2:1). His strength of character is shown by the fact that he was trusted to be sent to Corinth to collect money for the poor Jerusalem Church, and he was sent to Crete when problems arose there (Titus 1:5). Subsequently, he apparently went to Dalmatia (II Timothy 4:10) on the eastern shore of the Adriatic Sea. Titus is mentioned in II Corinthians, Galatians, II Timothy and, of course, Titus.

UZZIAH, KING OF JUDAH

Uzziah (eighth century B.C.) was elected tenth king of Judah by the people. He began his reign at age sixteen with successful military campaigns against his father's enemies. Uzziah conquered the Arabians and Ammonites, warred successfully against the Philistines and stormed the cities of Ashdod, Gaza, and Jabneth. He fortified and provided Jerusalem with war equipment. Under Uzziah's rule, the kingdom of Judah prospered. Uzziah sinned by offering incense on the altar of God and was struck with leprosy (II Chronicles 26:19-21).

XERXES

(See Ahasuerus.)

ZACCHAEUS

Zacchaeus was a well-known tax collector in Jericho and is referred to in only one place in the New Testament, Luke 19. When Jesus came to that city, Zacchaeus, who was a small man, had to climb up into a sycamore tree to see over the throng of people. Upon seeing him Jesus commanded that he come down so that he could go home with him for dinner. Because tax collectors had a bad reputation, the people were amazed at Jesus' invitation. But the Lord's presence made a different man of Zacchaeus. To live up to his name, which in the original means "pure," Zacchaeus promised to give half his goods to the poor and to those from which he had taken anything unjustly he promised to restore them fourfold (Luke 19:8). Salvation was brought to the house of Zacchaeus and he later became a disciple.

ZACHARIAS

Zacharias was a priest of the course of Abijah, one of the twenty-four priestly divisions since the time of Chronicles. These divisions took turns serving in the Temple. On the day which Zacharias had been assigned, he went to the Temple to perform the duty of offering incense in the Holy Place. While there an angel of the Lord appeared and announced that his wife was going to have a son. Zacharias and his wife were aging, she had been barren all her life, and Zacharias doubted the angel and asked for a sign. He was immediately struck dumb and recovered his speech only after having named the child John at his circumcision. This child was John the Baptist who came to prepare the way for Jesus Christ, the Messiah. Reference: Luke 1.

ZECHARIAH THE PROPHET

Zechariah wrote the book of the Old Testament that bears his name. He prophesied at the same time as Haggai. The great goal of Zechariah's ministry was to encourage those who were rebuilding the Temple and thus his messages are intensely inspirational. Zechariah says that the building of God's house is essentially a spiritual work and it is to be done "not by might, nor by power, but by my spirit, saith the Lord" (Zechariah 4:6). In chapters 1-6 the prophet outlines eight visions he was given in the night, all aimed at encouraging the people to have faith that God is with them in their task of rebuilding the Temple. Towards the end of the book we have remarkable prophecies of the Messiah: the betrayal of Christ for thirty pieces of silver (11:12-13), the piercing of His side (12:10), the pouring forth of His blood for the sins of mankind (13:1), the nail prints (13:6), the scattering of the disciples (13:7), the destruction of Jerusalem in the New Testament period (14:2), and the second coming of our Lord (14:4). In 9:9-10 we have the Triumphal Entry prophesied in these magnificent words: "Rejoice greatly, O daughter of Zion! Shout aloud, O daughter of Jerusalem! Lo, your king comes to you; triumphant and victorious is he, humble and riding on an ass, on a colt the foal of an ass. I will cut off the chariot from Ephraim and the war horse from Jerusalem; and the battle bow shall be cut off, and he shall command peace to the nations; his dominion shall be from sea to sea, and from the River to the ends of the earth."

"And he did that which was evil in the sight of the Lord." Thus could be summarized the life and reign of Zedekiah, the last of the kings of Judah (he reigned 597-587 B.C.). At the age of twenty-one he was placed on the throne by Nebuchadrezzar, King of Babylon. The anger of the Lord was kindled against Zedekiah as he ignored Jeremiah the prophet. Rebelling against Nebuchadrezzar, he later laid siege to Jerusalem. In the eleventh year of Zedekiah's reign, as famine prevailed in the city, Zedekiah and his army deserted the people and fled to the plains of Jericho. Subsequently he and the army were captured. His sons were killed before his very eyes and he himself was blinded, then put in a Babylonian prison. References: II Kings 24:17—25:7.

ZEDEKIAH (MATTANIAH)

Zephaniah ("hidden of Jehovah" or "Jehovah hides or protects") is thought to have been a great-grandson of Hezekiah. He prophesied during the reign of Josiah (640–609 B.C.) (Zephaniah 1:1). He prophesied the utter desolation of Judea for their idolatry and neglect of the Lord. Zephaniah was a priest and it was his duty to punish false prophets. After the capture of Jerusalem, Zephaniah was taken to Biblah in the land of Hamath and slain by the Babylonians.

ZEPHANIAH

Zerubbabel is the supposed son of Shealtiel of the tribe of Judah and in the line of David. He and Joshua led the first colony of Israelitish captives to Jerusalem from Babylon in 536 B.C. In Jerusalem he restored the observance of sacred Jewish practices including public worship and the Feast of Tabernacles. The book of Ezra tells of Zerubbabel's refusal to aid the Samaritans in rebuilding a Temple. They were angered and caused disruption in the construction after two years and two months of work (Ezra 4). He finally finished the Temple after a seventy year period. The fate of Zerubbabel is unknown, but it is thought that he became king of Judah and was conquered by the Persians.

ZERUBBABEL

*The ruins of ancient Jericho from the west,
old city wall in foreground.*

✑8✑ PLACES: GEOGRAPHY & ARCHEOLOGY

O N A CLEAR DAY ONE CAN STAND IN THE viewing area on the Mt. of Olives, 2,650 feet above sea level, and look far enough west to see the glistening Mediterranean Sea. Nearer, and just below the Mount, is the Garden of Gethsemane, and just west of the Garden is Jerusalem, a city divided today by Jews and Arabs as Berlin is divided by Russians and the free world. Minarets, the Dome of the Rock (a mosque on the ancient Temple site), and Christian crosses all rear their heads in Jerusalem, Jordan. (Jordan as a whole is only fourteen per cent Christian.) On the Jordan side of the city are excavations at the Biblical Pool of Bethesda; and the Fortress of Antonia, in operation in Jesus' day, has been fairly well outlined very near the general area of the Via Dolorosa or "way of the cross."

Walls and a no-man's land separate Jerusalem, Jordan from Jerusalem, Israel, and entrance is through the Mandalbaum Gate with strict regulations. On the Israeli side Dead Sea Scrolls are on display. Also on that side are the traditional place of the Last Supper, of Pentecost, and the tomb of David, greatest of Israel's kings. Israel extends beyond the city west to the Mediterranean, and of course north and south. The dominant impression given by this new country of Israel (established in the late 1940's), is *energy*, reflected in new institutions of learning, and millions of new trees. Here is a new nation with all the vigor of youth, and

A Birds-Eye View of Palestine and Bible Lands

---

*For information in chapter viii, I am especially indebted to the article in *The Oxford Annotated Bible* (1962) entitled, "Survey of the Geography, History, and Archaeology of the Bible Lands."

Looking toward the Mt. of Olives through Arabic arches on the ancient Temple site, Jerusalem.

the prophecy of Isaiah—"the desert shall blossom as the rose"—is coming true.

Looking east from the Mt. of Olives, one can see the Dead Sea in the distance, and behind it very faintly the Mountains of Moab where Moses viewed the Promised Land from Mt. Nebo just before Joshua took command (Deuteronomy 34:1). From Mt. Nebo one can see Palestine in full view on a clear day. Much nearer than the hills of Moab and the Dead Sea is Jericho in the rich Jordan Valley. The city, with its present-day population of 10,000, is identified by its palm trees, groves of citrus, banana trees, and adjacent refugee (Arab) camps. Not far from the present site

The entrance to the pool of Bethesda, Jerusalem. This is the authentic site.

of Jericho are the excavations of the ancient town of Jericho (built several times and not always on the same spot), which recent excavations suggest goes back as far as 7,000 B.C. The Spring of Elisha, across the road from the excavations, to-day serves some 85,000 people (Elisha is said to have purified the spring with salt—II Kings 2:19-22). Overlooking Jericho is the Mt. of Temptation, thought to be in the general area of

Jesus' forty day period of temptation in the wilderness.

Whether one looks east or west from the Mt. of Olives, barren hills are in view. Nestled in the hills is an occasional village; one such is Bethany where a Church stands over the traditional place of Martha and Mary's home. Near the Church is a cave tomb said to be the one from which Lazarus was raised. Aside from the occasional village, there is not much greenery to the east until the hills of Judea level out into the Jordan Valley. That Valley is some sitxy-five miles long and supplies a good share of Jordan's food. The area east of the Jordan is known as the Transjordan, still part of the modern nation of Jordan, and it is bounded by Syria, Iraq, and Saudi Arabia.

Jericho, the city of palm trees, with the Spring of Elisha in the foreground. The excavations of ancient Jericho sites are adjacent.

Looking south from Mt. Olivet is parched hillscape and then there is the great desert expanse known as the Negeb which separates Palestine from the countries north of the Red Sea. Arabia, the Sinai Peninsula, and Egypt are south of the Negeb, all mentioned in the Bible. It is now known that the Negeb was heavily populated during the patriarchal and Israelitish periods.

Far north are Lebanon ("wide mountains") and Syria, Lebanon the home of Byblos (see "Ancient Manuscripts and Versions") and Tyre and Sidon of ancient Phoenicia, Syria the country that housed Antioch (now in Turkey) where followers of Christ were first called Christians. Antioch was the third largest city of the ancient Roman world; today it is a small town. Syria's capital is Damascus, with a present-day population of 500,000. Perhaps the oldest city in continuous existence, its origins go back to 6,000 B.C.

The Lebanon Mountains (along the coast) and Anti-Lebanon Mountains form a valley between them that leads eventually into the Jordan Valley. The Orontes River flows generally north and south, though it actually flows west when it goes through Antioch. (After flowing north, the river bends so that it flows in a southwesterly direction to the sea.) The highest point in the general area of Palestine is Mt. Hermon (9,232 feet), its peak being a boundary between modern Lebanon and Syria, the west slope belonging to Lebanon, the east to Syria. It is snow-capped the year around and springs and streams from it feed into the Lake of Galilee (known variously as the Sea of Galilee, Gennesaret, the Sea of Tiberias— Tiberias is on the Lake—etc.). Much farther south it flows into the Dead Sea, the lowest spot on earth, 1,285 feet below sea level. Swimming in the Dead Sea, it is impossible to sink because of the heavy salt and mineral content. It is one of the richest spots on earth in natural resources.

The Jordan River is famous for its historic events: John baptized Jesus in it; it parted to let the Israelites cross; Naaman was cured of leprosy upon washing in it seven times. Today at the traditional site of Jesus' baptism, its width is an easy stone's throw; in Jesus' day it was much wider and deeper, and in Moses' time still larger. North of Lake Galilee it is a half to two-thirds of a mile wide, and its banks are lined with oleander, tamarisk, and other flora typical of the Holy Land. It is a major source for irrigation.

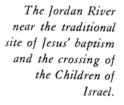

The Jordan River near the traditional site of Jesus' baptism and the crossing of the Children of Israel.

A main street in ancient Ephesus.

North of Lebanon and Syria is Turkey, extending east and west. Paul's missionary journeys took place north and west into Asia Minor; the seven Churches of the book of Revelation are far west and St. John lived and died in that area at Ephesus, which city is rich in archaeological finds (see photographic illustrations Chapters VI and VIII). Across the Aegean Paul went into Europe, going to Greece (where such Biblical cities as Corinth and Athens can still be seen), and north and west to Rome (where remains of the Forum and Colosseum still stand). Outside Rome is the Appian Way, used by Paul and twentieth century travelers too.

Near the Way are catacombs, underground tombs used by early Christians. The Island of Cyprus ("copper"—which was exported from there in ancient times), located east towards Syria, and Crete in the southern Aegean, were not left out of the missionary program of early Christianity. Delphi, Corinth, Ephesus, Malta, Thessalonica all hold inscriptional evidences or parallels of Biblical facts, places, or events.

Back in Palestine, Jesus was born in Bethlehem ("House of Bread") of Judea, not far from Jerusalem; He was reared north

Looking through a skylight from a catacomb used by early Christians. Christians sometimes worshipped in catacombs, underground tombs.

Excavations of a luxurious synagogue built 1800 years ago in Capernaum. This synagogue was built on or near the site of one which Jesus knew.

of Judea in Nazareth of Galilee. Outside Bethlehem is the "Shepherd's Field" of the Christmas story, and Rachel's tomb. David's ancestors lived in Bethlehem, and there Helena, Constantine's mother, built the Church of the Nativity over the supposed site of our Lord's birthplace (a cave). One gets the impression from a visit to the places associated with Jesus in Bethlehem and Nazareth, that He was brought up in very humble circumstances indeed (the traditional site of Joseph's carpenter shop in Nazareth reflects very poor circumstances, as do aspects of the Biblical story itself).

Between Judea and Galilee was Samaria, east of Samaria Peraea, and north of Peraea and south of the Lake of Galilee was the Decapolis ("ten cities"). At the foot of the Galilean hills is the great Valley of Esdraelon (Jezreel or Armagedon) from which Mt. Carmel can be seen. In this valley many battles were fought. It communicates with the Plain of Acco and then the Jordan Valley. Cana (where Jesus turned water into wine and where today there is a church with a wine-red dome), Endor (associated with the witch in the King Saul story), Tabor (at the foot of Mt. Tabor, which is perhaps the Mt. of Transfiguration), Nain (where Jesus restored the widow's son), and Capernaum (where an ancient and luxurious synagogue was excavated), are all in Galilee. South and west of Galilee are the ruins of ancient Caesarea—not to be confused with Caesarea Philippi, which is north and inland.

Altogether, Palestine is made up of coastal plains, the central hill territories, a chain of valleys, the plateau of the Transjordan, and desert. Villages, towns, and cities are in abundance (the Bible mentions over 600 places west of the Jordan). Nomadic life continues to this day, the nomads grazing their sheep and goats wherever there is a patch of green, and living in tents, rough houses, or even caves. The donkey, costing the equivalent of seven to fifteen dollars, is the chief mode of transportation for the poor peasant, though horses are used by the military and others, and the automobile is fast finding its place. Roads north and south, east and west, make travel possible. The road leading from Jerusalem to Jericho over the Judean hills was made famous by Jesus' story of the Good Samaritan; today the "Good Samaritan Inn" stands at the summit of the passage between Jerusalem and Jericho, and a traditional robbers' cave is nearby. (The Inn is occupied by the Jordanian militia, and was built by Crusaders.) The climate of Palestine and area is very like that of California, dry and sunny. The Jordan Valley reminds one of Imperial Valley in its rich productivity. The flora—figs, grapes, poplar, olives—are also similar to California's.

The People

The Canaanites were the people conquered in the time of Joshua. They were mostly of Semitic origin, though there is evidence of the infiltration at an early date (second millennium B.C.) of non-Semites, as for example the Horites from the Upper Euphrates and the Hittites from whom Abraham purchased the cave of Machpelah (Genesis 23—Machpelah became the chief burial place of the Patriarchs). Archaeological evidence indicates Mediterranean influences in Canaanite art as early as 1500 B.C. By 1400

The traditional robbers' cave near the Good Samaritan Inn. (Compare Luke 10.)

people from the Aegean area had come into Palestine and areas
south. The Philistines, Israel's great enemy during a large part of
the Old Testament era, came from Crete. They had settled in
numerous places in Palestine even before the Israelitish conquest.
Abraham and the first Jews appear to have descended from the
Arameans who came to Syria and Mesopotamia from the Arabian
desert-fringe. Branching off from Abraham's line were estranged
groups such as the Moabites and Ammonites (whose father was
Lot), the Arabs (whose father was Ishmael), and the Edomites
(whose father was Esau).

*Crusader
constructions at
the port of
Biblical Caesarea
on the Mediterranean
Coast.*

**The Canaanites
and Archaeology**

Archaeology and research have unearthed a good deal of information about the Canaanites. Their period (3200 to 1200 B.C.)
is called the Bronze Age. They set up city-states (mentioned in the
Old Testament and in the letters dug up at Mari), their plan
having been to decentralize. Their towns were used as market
places, defense, and administrative centers. Canaanite towns were
built in high places to strengthen defense, and twenty acres was
usually considered ample for the construction of a town. Methods
of fortification were given a great deal of thought; in addition to
the elevation of the town, huge stones at the foot of embarkments,
walls of mud-brick, and towers were all used. In larger towns there
was an acropolis. City gates were planned with care; they were
constructed of wood, bronze, and stone. The huge doors were of
wood, the hinges of bronze which pivoted in stone sockets. The
approach up to and outside the gate was used for a market, open
air court, or meeting place for the town council.

Water was supplied the Canaanite cities by springs, wells, aqueducts, and cisterns. Aqueduct tunnels were dug under the city

234

walls, connecting springs with the city, and the springs themselves walled in against enemy attack. Cisterns were what they are today, reservoirs formed to collect rain water. (There is evidence of rock-cut cisterns near Beersheba in pre-Canaanite times.) Wells in and out of the cities were dug in the hope of continuous water supplies (the custom in the Near East is for a single well to supply several homes).

As to worship, each city-state had its religious center or centers. The famous "high places" were outdoor enclosures. In them were pillars or stones (*massebah*) in which Canaanites believed divinities lived. Sometimes there were rows of stones; these stood for the families or distinctive groups which worshipped. A sacred tree or wooden post (*asherah*) symbolized much the same thing as the *massebah*. A well or basin for purification rites, and a stone altar were also found in high places. Sometimes a temple took the place of or supplemented the high places. A Canaanite temple was found at Ai, one of the cities captured early in the Hebrew conquest. Canaanite religion is seen in temple excavations at Lachish, Megiddo, and Shechem, and in representations of Baal (e.g. on a cylinder from Bethel dated c. 1300 B.C.). The Ras Shamra finds tell us something about Canaanite religion too: Baal was a storm god; emphasis on war, "sacred" sexual expression, and the consequent social maladjustment, constitute some of the information.

The Canaanites buried their dead in caves. If there were no caves, they dug them eight to ten feet deep to contain one or more burial units. The dead were laid out on stones (in contrast to pre-Biblical Phoenicians who buried their dead in huge clay jars). The dead were provided with objects familiar to them in everyday life, plus weapons and provisions for their journey into the world beyond. (Egyptians put provisions with their dead for the same reason.) The Tell el-Amarna documents—about 350 of them—throw light on Palestine and Syria from about 1400–1360 B.C. For one thing, the disintegration of Egyptian control before the conquest by Israel is indicated. The tablets are written in a Babylonian dialect.

The founders of Israel, taking their start with Abraham ("the Father of the Jewish nation"), are called Patriarchs. The name applies specifically to Abraham, Isaac, Jacob (Israel), and Jacob's twelve sons for whom the twelve tribes of Israel are named.* While archaeology has helped our understanding of the Patriarchal era, Genesis remains the chief source of information. The service

The Fathers of Israel

---

* If Levi, which was not a geographical unit, is counted, there were thirteen tribes.

of archaeology has been this, that the essential reliability of the historical accounts has been confirmed repeatedly (this is true for a large part of the Old Testament, but especially of the Patriarchal period), and our knowledge of the general cultural situation of the day has been enriched. Two or three examples will suffice. At Mari, near the River Euphrates and in Syria, 20,000 tablets were found in a dialect very like that spoken by the Patriarchs. They give us a rich store of geographical, historical, and religious information on Mesopotamia. At Nuzi (in Iraq) 20,000 clay tablets in a Babylonian dialect and in cuneiform script provide us with strong parallels to Patriarchal customs and culture. A very interesting parallel in a Nuzi text is the indication of an exchange of birthright as in the Esau story. At Ras Shamra (Ugarit on the Syrian coast north of Lebanon) tablets also provide parallels to the Patriarchal age.

The Patriarchs or Fathers were not settled; they were in transit, nomadic people camping here and there. They moved with their animals (a chief source of sustenance), finding grazing space where they could. Genesis gives us the major camp sites of the Patriarchs and their families: Shechem was the first stop in Canaan (Genesis 12:6-7); second, a spot between Bethel and Ai, where Abram and Lot parted company (Genesis 12:8; 13:3-11); Mamre, where God appeared to Abraham (Genesis 13:18); Beersheba in the Negeb (Genesis 21:25-34).

Joseph, one of the Patriarchs, was sold ruthlessly into Egypt, a Bible story well known. This was the beginning of a Jewish migration to that great and ancient country. All of the elements of that story can be paralleled on wall paintings or reliefs from Egyptian antiquity: slavery, want and famine, caravans, etc. In fact, tomb paintings at Beni-hasan in Middle Egypt show a caravan of Semitic immigrants in multi-colored robes being introduced to a ruler.

The Period of Moses Moses was raised up by God to deliver His people from Egyptian slavery. The Hyksos rulers preceded the return of the national Egyptian dynasty. The Hyksos had treated the Jews well compared to the nationals who subjected them to the slavery well known by every Sunday School boy. Under God, Moses, of the tribe of Levi, took the children of Israel across the Red Sea and on to Mt. Horeb (Sinai) where God gave them a Covenant. (Today Mt. Sinai is the site of a Russian Orthodox monastery and houses many rare Christian documents, now photographed and preserved in microfilm. Some of the greatest manuscript discoveries of all times have been made here: see the chapter on "Ancient Manuscripts and Versions.") At Horeb the decalogue (Ten Commandments) was revealed to Moses by God, also details of the Law. In many respects the Mosaic Law reminds us of the Code of Hammurabi who was a king of Babylon (c. 1792–1750 B.C.). That code is recorded on an eight foot stele of black diorite (discovered in 1902 at Susa) and is housed in the Louvre, Paris. The language of the code is Akkadian. It is divided into 282 paragraphs which deal with criminal, civil, and commercial law. There is a strong sense of justice, as in the Mosaic code, though, surprisingly enough no reference to homicide in general. The similarities between the Mosaic and the Hammurabi codes is explained by the universal similarity of crimes, but the whole atmosphere of the Hebrew Law is more humane than that of the Babylonian.

As to religion, morality took on a practical aspect and worship was centered in the Ark of the Covenant, the symbol of God's presence among His people. The Ark was a wooden chest in which were stone tables of the Law.

Moses wandered with his people through the desert, wilderness, and wastelands, but his disobedience prevented him from taking Israel into the Promised Land. He only got a look at it from the hills of Moab.

Archaeologists have unearthed several Canaanite cities destroyed in the thirteenth century B.C.; thus, some scholars have dated the conquest under Joshua about this time. The conquest itself is outlined in the book of Joshua. They took a route down Moab, then across the Jordan, and captured Jericho and Ai (modern archaeology has excavated both these cities). From thence Joshua fought here and there over Canaan, succeeding now, failing then, but Jerusalem (ancient Jebus after the Jebusites) was not permanently in the hands of the Israelites until David's time. **The Period of Conquest**

The settlement of the tribes is outlined in Joshua 13-21 and may be seen best on a Bible map of Palestine for the period under Joshua and the Judges. With the settlement, the nomadic life of the Jews was lessened, for the groups were now identified with assigned territories. But they were forced to live with the Canaanites whom they had only partially conquered. This influenced Israel's religion, and domestic life too, for there was intermarriage. This whole miserable tale of attempted co-existence is reflected in the book of Judges.

Subsequent to the period of the judges, Israel, against the strong warnings of the last Judge Samuel, started a monarchy (Moses had held out for a theocracy). The Canaanite kings had lorded it over the Jews who maintained a humble tenant-estate program of overseeing; and Ammon and Moab in the Transjordan, and the Arameans in Syria had their kings too. Partly to **The Monarchy** keep up with their neighbors and partly to unify Israel, Saul was made king. He had a rough job: from the west the Philistines attacked, from the east the Ammonites. The Philistines organized into a five-city federation, with cities at Ashdod, Ashkelon, Gaza, Gath, Ekron. Archaeology and research make it clear that the Philistines aimed to conquer the whole of Palestine: their pottery found in many places, proves just how wide an area they had infiltrated. Further, it is clear that they were the first in Palestine to use iron and they had a monopoly on it, a product not used in Palestine before twelve hundred B.C. (but there is evidence of metal around 4,000 B.C.). Iron gave them an economic superiority the Israelites found difficult to conquer. Houses and pottery of the Israelites during the period of the Judges reflect circumstances inferior to the Philistines.

Saul established his capital in Gibeah in Benjamin. The foundations of his palace-fortress have been unearthed five miles north of Jerusalem. At Gibeah life was simple, though there is evidence of some iron weapons. Saul did well with a great many odds against him, until he began to follow a pattern of disobedience against God. His end came in a battle in the Plain of Esdraelon where his son Jonathan died too.

Before 1000 B.C. David was made king and he reigned in Hebron for seven years, after which he moved the capital to Jerusalem which he had taken from the Jebusites. At Jerusalem he ruled the Northern tribes as well as Judah and Benjamin. Under David, the Ammonites were defeated and the Philistines driven back.

The outstanding achievement of Solomon was the building of the first Temple on what was to become the traditional site in Jerusalem, which today holds not a temple (two temples were built after Solomon) but a mosque. Victory over the Philistines made possible the development of Phoenician trade; Hiram of Tyre provided craftsmen, and timber came from Lebanon (I Kings 5:1-12) for the Temple. Solomon built storage space for treasures along the sides of the Temple. The art of the Temple—cherubim, palms, designs—has parallels in the contemporary art of Samaria, Ras Shamra, and other places. But the Temple was by no means the only thing that proved Solomon's progressive and creative leadership. Archaeological evidence has shown his interest in the military horse (at Megiddo stables for 500 or more horses were found—cp. I Kings 9:15, 19).* An increased use of iron is evidenced and iron and copper mines have been unearthed in the

---

* Some scholars suggest that the stables date in the reign of Ahab, a century after Solomon.

Negeb. Ruins of a smelting plant were discovered near Agaba. Further, he established a naval base at Elath (Eziongeber). He had a fleet operated by Phoenician sailors which plowed the seas to Arabia, India, and east Africa bringing back gold ("gold from Ophir" was inscribed on a pot discovered), peacocks, ivory, jewels, etc. (I Kings 9:26-28; 10:22). His improvement in building engineering is evidenced not only in the Temple, but in the residences of district governors at Megiddo and Hazor, and

Cedars of Lebanon of which only a few remain today. Solomon used timber from Lebanon to build the Temple.

also in the huge storage granaries at Lachish and Bethshemesh.

The schism of Jeroboam, while it only reflected the hostile feelings of the Israelites, did in fact separate North (Israel) and South (Judah) into what Biblical history calls the divided monarchy. Rehoboam succeeded Solomon about 931 B.C., but his overtaxation angered the north and Jeroboam seceded with ten tribes. Judah held the seat in the line of David; the north had its independence. Jeroboam fortified Shechem and made it the first capital of the North (I Kings 12:25). Later the capital was moved to Tirzah where it stayed until Omri made the capital Samaria (I Kings 16:23, 24). From then on Israel and Samaria were, for all practical purposes, interchangeable terms. Tirzah was eventually abandoned, though reoccupied as a governor's residence about 800 B.C. At Samaria Omri possessed improved communications with Phoenicia and her ports. Accordingly, trade flourished. An open cistern or pool has been found at Samaria (cp. I Kings 22:38), and in Jehu's reign (842 or 841) defense walls were constructed which stood until the middle of the second century B.C.

Archaeology has revealed further information about Samaria. Its foundations have been exposed and it is known that the whole area was surrounded by a double wall. In a room of the king's palace were found carved ivory plaques, partly guilded, partly inlaid, which had been used to decorate wood furniture. This art shows Egyptian, Oriental, and Mediterranean influences. Storehouses containing broken jars with Hebrew writing on them, indicate the jars were filled with oil and wine delivered in payment of taxes. These jar inscriptions are valuable for the Biblical scholar

The Divided Monarchy

because they tell us the tax districts of the Northern kingdom. Like Samaria, Mizpah and Gibeah were well fortified, the two being frontier towns at the time of the divided monarchy.

In Judah the economy was still dominantly rural. Uzziah (Azariah) dug cisterns and built towers in the countryside (II Chronicles 26:10). Shops were set up in Jerusalem, Hebron, and Lachish. But relations between Israel and Judah were uneasy. Now there was open hostility, now hidden plots against each other, and rarely there were confederations for protection against a foreign power (e.g. Ahab and Jehoshaphat united against the Syrians, I Kings 22:29-40). The alliance of Jehoshaphat and Jehoram against Mesha (II Kings 3:4-7) is recorded on the Moabite Stone discovered in 1868 and now housed in the Louvre, Paris.

Israel had a standing quarrel with Damascus over Gilead, but once Israel and Syria united to fight Assyria though to no avail. The progress of the Assyrians in the Near East is spelled out in Biblical and cuneiform texts, from the battle of Qarqar on the Orontes (when Ahab and the Syrians were defeated in 853) to the tribute exacted from the last king of Israel. Finally, there was the long siege of Samaria by Shalmaneser V. Sargon II, who succeeded his brother, won final victory and Samaria fell in 722 B.C. Subsequently large numbers of Israelites were deported, being replaced by Babylonians (II Kings 17:24). This event is proved archaeologically by the evidence of Assyrian and other foreign pottery which was brought in, and by the evidence of fewer inhabitants and lower economic standards.

Judah, too, had her problems with Assyria. The campaign of Sennacherib, Sargon's successor, is recorded on a hexagonal prism of clay in Assyrian cuneiform. In 701 Assyria besieged and captured Lachish. A bas-relief (c. 690 B.C.) from the palace of Sennacherib at Nineveh, pictures prisoners going into captivity by ox cart. Some reliefs of the fall of Lachish are in the British Museum, and the Biblical accounts of the same event is in II Kings 18. Meanwhile Hezekiah worked to strengthen Jerusalem. He made a tunnel aqueduct chiselled through the solid rock to bring water 1700 feet into the city from the Virgin's Spring (II Kings 20:20; II Chronicles 32:30). An inscription in Hebrew, discovered in 1880, relates the details of the project. In due course Jerusalem was surrounded by the Assyrian militia, but the city was miraculously saved and the Assyrian soldiers died *en masse* (II Kings 19:35). This event, however, did not stop Assyria from subsequent attacks on Judah. Judah thought of protection through Egyptian alliances which were continuously opposed by the prophets. In due course Assyria fell (612 B.C.) and the Neo-Babylonian empire was ushered in. The new power followed the Assyrian tradition and besieged Judah. Nebuchadrezzar recaptured Lachish, which in the meantime had been recaptured by Judah. In 1935 the ruins of Lachish yielded letters in ancient Hebrew script which referred to events preceding the siege of the city in 588 B.C. Jerusalem finally fell and the Temple was destroyed in 586 or 587 B.C. The creative and intelligent Jews were deported, the commoners left under the rule of Babylonian governors.

The Exile meant a complete readjustment, as deportation always does. The Jews were forced to leave their homes, give up deeds to property, and settle in a quite foreign land. Once adapted to the new environment, however, the Jews proved their independence and creativity by entering the professions, involving themselves in international trade, and working in and with the banking systems. Archaeologists have discovered contracts inscribed on tablets in Neo-Babylonian cuneiform that give evidence of this involvement in business and the professions.

Upon the release of the Jews under Cyrus in 538, some were so well situated in business and the professions, and had their own homes—in a word, they were so well settled—that many did not leave for Jerusalem and the homeland. From now on there would in fact be Jews in places other than Judah; but the reverse was true too, that from now on there would be a more or less continuous stream of Jews returning to their homeland, and that is true even today. Archaeology shows that Judah was not repopulated as in the former days until the third century B.C.

Cyrus, king of Persia, freed the Jews from Babylonish rule. Jews went back on a volunteer basis, but with Persian guards. Some of the earliest coins known to have been made in Palestine had the word *Yehud* ("Judah") inscribed on them. These Hebrew coins began to appear in the fifth century and were in abundance by the third century. Jar handles, too, were inscribed sometimes; examples: *Yhd* ("Judah"), *Yrslm* ("Jerusalem"). Archaeological and textual evidence point to this, that the Jewish exiles concentrated in Jerusalem and also parts southwest of Jerusalem. Southern Palestine came to be known as Idumea, for the Edomites had settled there after the Babylonian conquest.

The first great achievement of the returning exiles was the reconstruction of the Temple, known as the Second Temple. The building had begun and was to be finished, under Zerubbabel, Persian appointed governor of Jerusalem and Jew of the royal line, but subsequent interruptions delayed its completion. Finally, in 516 B.C. and during the reign of Darius, it was finished.

The second great achievement was the reparation of the walls of Jerusalem under Nehemiah. Men were organized into groups. Each group was responsible for completing the repairs of an assigned portion. The walls were completed, celebration of which event took place in 444 B.C. The work had been strongly opposed by the Samaritans and the Ammonites. The Samaritans were the descendants of the people put in Israel by the Assyrians and some remaining Israelites. They took up the Jewish religion and still exist today (see section on the Samaritan Pentateuch in the chapter on "Ancient Manuscripts and Versions").

The New Testament Era

Augustus became emperor of Rome in 27 B.C. Palestine and surrounding territories were left under the control of local rulers. From 37–4 B.C. Herod I (the Great) was king of the Palestinian area. His building programs included country fortresses and palaces, south of Jericho a winter palace, public buildings in Ashkelon (Herod's birthplace) and Samaria (here he made a temple to the Emperor Augustus). At Samaria he also rebuilt the city walls in part and reinforced them with towers. Further, he gave Samaria a stadium and renamed the city Sebaste. He also built residences at Bethlehem, called the Herodium, and Herod made considerable structural alterations at Antipatris and Caesarea. He built a huge fort at Masada. He supplied Jerusalem with water by an aqueduct from springs south of Bethlehem. A fortress in Jerusalem was rebuilt in style, with residential quarters attached. But his chief construction project was the rebuilding of the Temple, the "Third Temple" or the "Temple of Herod." He surrounded it by extensive courtyards lined with porches. (For more on the period between the Testaments, see Chapter Five.)

After Herod's death in 4 B.C., Palestine was ruled by tetrarchs: Archelaus (4 B.C.–6 A.D.) ruled over Judea and Samaria; Herod Antipas (4 B.C.–39 A.D.) over Galilee and Peraea; Philip (4 B.C.–34 A.D.) over the districts of Iturea and Trachonitis, southeast of Mt. Hermon. Palestine was unified again under Herod Agrippa I, who built the third wall of Jerusalem and ruled the tetrarchy of Philip from 37 A.D., Galilee from 39, Samaria and Judea from 41, until his death in 44 A.D. Little is known of his period archaeologically, though it is known that his sister Bernice, according to her own inscription, restored buildings at Caesarea built by Herod the Great. Later Herod Agrippa II acquired the tetrarchy of Philip and several Galilean towns in the 50's A.D. to about 100. At interim periods the regions were ruled by the Emperor's deputy from Syria, while Samaria and Judea were placed under the Roman procurator at Caesarea on the coast.

Such was the period of Jesus. For a long time there has been a debate over the site of Jesus' death and resurrection. The Church

The "Gordon" site of Golgotha, the "place of the skull" (Matthew 27:33).

of the Holy Sepulcher in Jerusalem marks the traditional spot of His death, but outside the walls of the city stands today a hill that assumes the shape and appearance of a skull. This hill, say some, is the true Golgotha. Very near this hill is an open tomb, discovered by General Gordon in 1883, which shows the place for a rolling stone; this site is said to be the place of the resurrection and today a garden is kept up by a private, evangelical concern in the "garden tomb" area. A number of tombs closed by the "cartwheel" stone have been found dating to Roman times. Interestingly enough, a number of tombs examined in 1945 by E. L. Sukenik, have the word "Jesus" on them and may refer to Christ and may be early (before 50 A.D.) Christian burial places. Many other grave inscriptions carry names like Simon, Lazarus, Judas, Ananias and Joseph, which shows the popularity of these names found also in the New Testament.

The Jews revolted against the Romans in 66 A.D. The Jews had some successes at first, but Jerusalem was finally taken and the Temple destroyed for the last time in 70 A.D. Coinage suggests Jewish attitudes before 70 A.D.: they made silver coins to prove their independence from Rome. But as the Jews lost ground, the coins were poorer in quality and more scarce. Some time after 70 A.D. Roman coins (inscribed: *Iudaea capta*) marked the Roman

Interior of the Colosseum, Rome, completed only a few years after the deaths of Peter and Paul.

victory. The Temple destroyed in 70 A.D. is identified with few archaeological finds, though the warning sign on the entrance to the inner Temple area (Gentiles would die for entering) was discovered in a Greek inscription in 1871 (see Acts 21:28). Another such warning sign was discovered in 1935. In addition to the Pool of Bethesda (John 5:2) mentioned earlier, the Pool of Siloam (John 9:11) has been located south of the Temple site. Incidentally, the wall of Sychar near Shechem (John 4:5, 6) is still used.

Matson Photo Service, Los Angeles

*Air view of the Jerusalem Temple area from the north,
the village of Siloam in the background.*

~§9§~ THINGS

A. The Tabernacle, Temples and Synagogue;
B. Musical Instruments; *C.* Jewish Feasts
and Festivals; *D.* Jewish Sects and Parties;
E. The Sanhedrin; *F.* Plants and Animals,
including Birds; *G.* Time, Measures, Weights
and Money ह~

A. THE TABERNACLE, TEMPLE, AND SYNAGOGUE

THE TABERNACLE, MADE AT THE COMMAND OF   **Tabernacle**
God, was a rectangular tent supported by a wooden frame-
work. Covered with cloth and animal skins, it was movable;
the responsibility for setting it up, taking it down, and moving it was
given to the Levites. Once set up, the Pillar of Cloud rested over it.

Two rooms, one smaller and the other larger, made up the
inner area which was surrounded by the Court of the Tabernacle.
The smaller room was known as the Holy of Holies; it was entered only on the Day of Atonement and then by the high priest
alone. In the Holy of Holies was the Ark with its mercy seat and
cherubim; all were covered with gold. The larger room was the
Sanctuary or "Holy Place" in which was the altar of incense, table
of showbread, and golden candlestick. The Sanctuary was used for
daily worship. The two rooms were separated by a heavy veil.

Upon entering Canaan, Joshua had the Tabernacle set up at
Shiloh; while there, living places for the priests were added to it.
Bible descriptions of the Tabernacle are found in Exodus 25-27, 30,
36-40.

There were three Jewish Temples, all in Jerusalem and all on   **The Temple**
the same general site.

The first was Solomon's. Forbidden by God to construct the   **(a) Solomon's**
Temple, David had hoped to build it and had gone so far as to   **Temple**
collect materials and purchase the site (I Chronicles 22:7-8; II
Samuel 24:18-35). King Solomon commenced the construction program in the fourth year of his reign and completed it about seven

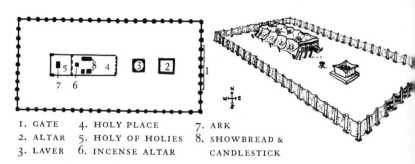

Left: The floor plan of the Tabernacle. Right: Reconstruction of the Tabernacle.

1. GATE	4. HOLY PLACE	7. ARK
2. ALTAR	5. HOLY OF HOLIES	8. SHOWBREAD &
3. LAVER	6. INCENSE ALTAR	CANDLESTICK

years later. It was built in the general area where today the mosque known as "The Dome of the Rock" stands. Archaeology has unearthed no remains of Solomon's Temple.

Solomon's Temple is described in I Kings 6-7 and II Chronicles 3-4. (There are definite similarities to Ezekiel's temple—a vision which never became reality—recorded in Ezekiel 40-43.) It was rectangular and faced east and west. Its dimensions were modest: the inside measurements were about ninety feet long and thirty wide. An altar of bronze for burnt-offerings was located in the inner court (I Kings 8:22, 64; 9:25). The bronze laver ("brazen sea"—I Kings 7:23-26) was a huge basin fifteen feet in diameter resting on bronze oxen arranged in four groups of four each, the groups facing north, south, east, and west. The brazen seat stood between the bronze altar and the porch. On the later removal of the oxen, see II Kings 16:17.

The entrance to the Temple was graced by decorated doors bordered by twin pillars of bronze called Jachin and Boaz (I Kings 7:21; II Chronicles 3:15-17). Through the doors was the porch, then the Holy Place, and finally the Holy of Holies. The porch was fifteen feet long and thirty wide; the Holy Place, where ordinary

A seven-branched candlestick is seen on this Corinthian capital from the ruins of a synagogue in Capernaum. Such candlesticks were used in the tabernacle.

The Matson Photo Service, Los Angeles

rituals took place, was sixty feet long and thirty wide, and it was separated from the porch by wooden (cypress) doors. The Holy Place was lighted by windows located near the ceiling (I Kings 6:4), and in this room could be seen the incense altar, table of showbread, five pairs of lampstands—all covered in gold. Wooden doors (also of cypress) led into the Holy of Holies which appears to have been entered only once a year at the

Reconstruction of Solomon's Temple.

Feast of Atonement. This room, thirty feet in all directions—thus a perfect cube—housed two cherubim of wood fifteen feet in height, and the Ark of the Covenant. Left and right wings of the cherubim met in the center and under them was the Ark (I Kings 6:23-28); the outside wings touched two sides of the room. God's presence in the Holy of Holies was symbolized by a cloud (I Kings 8:10f).

Walls, doors, and paneling were overlaid with gold. Much cedar from Lebanon was used, and Phoenicians helped in the construction (I Kings 5:10, 18; 7:13-14). None of the stonework was visible; gold and decorations were to be seen everywhere. Rooms in upper stories in all probability housed priestly garments, and were used as safe deposits for the offerings.

The floor plan of Solomon's Temple resembled the figure below.

Unfortunately, Solomon's Temple suffered abuse. Shishak of Egypt confiscated Temple treasures (I Kings 14:26)—this while Solomon's son, Rehoboam, was on the throne. Treasures of the Temple were, in later years, used to buy off enemies (I Kings 15:18; II Kings 16:8, etc.). Moreover, paganism (idols, a foreign altar) crept into the sacred House (II Kings 16:17; 21:4; 23:1-12). In the seventh century Josiah repaired the Temple, the people giv-

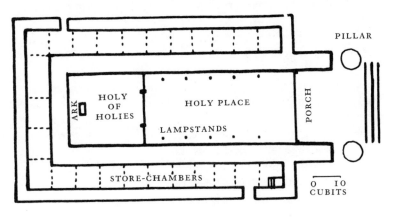

The floor plan of Solomon's Temple.

249

ing the needed funds to make this possible (II Kings 22:4). In the sixth century its precious possessions were thoroughly confiscated and the Temple itself destroyed by Nebuchadrezzar. The spot, however, remained sacred in the minds of Jews (Jeremiah 41:5).

(b) The Second Temple (Zerubbabel's Temple) After the Exile in Babylon, faithful Jews rebuilt the Temple. This second Temple stood for upwards of 500 years. Some treasures which Nebuchadrezzar had taken off were brought back by returning exiles in about 537 B.C. Cyrus gave permission to rebuild the Temple. The book of Ezra tells the story (see also Haggai, Zechariah, Nehemiah). Zerubbabel, governor of Jerusalem, gave support to the project and thus the Second Temple is sometimes known as Zerubbabel's Temple. Opened in 515, it was about ninety feet long and seventy feet high. In the apocryphal book of I Maccabees, a description of the furnishings is to be found (I Maccabees 1:21; 4:49-51). However, the Ark of the Covenant could not be put back in the new Temple because it had been lost during the Exile and was never found; the Holy of Holies thus remained empty. Only a curtain separated the Holy of Holies from the Holy Place. In the Holy Place a seven-fold candelabrum stood in the place of Solomon's ten lampstands. But the new House of God was definitely inferior in beauty and perfection to Solomon's though it was generally the same size. The Second Temple was desecrated in the second century B.C. (I Maccabees 1:54), but shortly after was purified by the Maccabees (I Maccabees 4:36-59) who also fortified it against enemy armies.

(c) Herod's Temple A political maneuver, the third and last Temple was built by Herod the Great. Actually, the project was one of *reconstruction,* not the putting up of an entirely new building, though the whole Temple area was considerably extended, the grounds being about 1,500 feet by 1,000 feet. The construction was begun in 19 B.C. and completed in the main ten years later, though labor on the structure continued for some time (cp. John 2:20). The completed floor plan looked like the drawing on page 251.

The huge Temple area was enclosed by stones as long as fifteen feet and about four feet in height. No wonder they were called "wonderful stones" (Mark 13:1)! Remains of the wall are still there; so also remains of some of the gates. The east gate may have been the Beautiful Gate of Acts 3; the decorations on the doors were done in Corinthian art forms in bronze. In the northwest corner the Fortress of Antonia was located; here the procurators took up residence when in the city and here also soldiers were kept on duty to quiet any riot that might arise (such as in Acts 21).

Along the outer rim of the Temple area (but within the walls) there was a portico; the south and east sides were known respec-

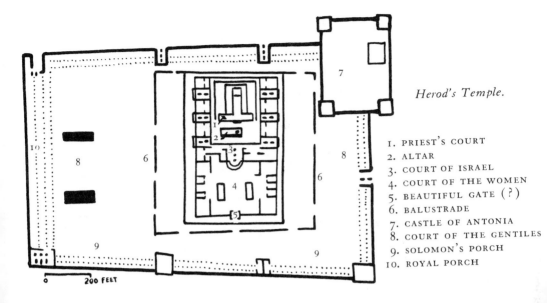

Herod's Temple.

1. PRIEST'S COURT
2. ALTAR
3. COURT OF ISRAEL
4. COURT OF THE WOMEN
5. BEAUTIFUL GATE (?)
6. BALUSTRADE
7. CASTLE OF ANTONIA
8. COURT OF THE GENTILES
9. SOLOMON'S PORCH
10. ROYAL PORCH

tively as the Royal Porch and Solomon's Porch (Acts 3:11). In the porch areas money-changers had their tables (John 2:14-16), and here too the scribes argued and taught. On the other side of the portico all the way around was the Court of the Gentiles. Between the Court of the Gentiles and the inner part was a balustrade with warning signs in Greek and Latin to the effect that Gentiles who crossed the balustrade would suffer the death penalty. Two such plaques have been discovered.

Just inside the Court of the Women were coffers for collecting money for expenses of the services (Mark 12:41-44). Inside the Priests' Court was the altar made of rough stone. The general plan of the Temple itself followed that of Solomon's. The veil of Matthew 27:51 and Mark 15:38 divided the Holy Place from the Holy of Holies or inner sanctuary. The Holy Place was sixty feet long, thirty wide, and sixty high; the inner sanctuary was thirty feet square and sixty feet high. There were three stories of rooms along the north, south and west sides.

The Temple's finished and perfected beauty was to be admired for only a brief period, for in 70 A.D. the Romans destroyed the Temple (which has never been rebuilt) and carried off (to Rome) gold furnishings to symbolize their military victory.

Synagogue

The word "synagogue" means "bringing together," "a gathering." Its origins are lost in the mists of time, but it is probable that it existed during the Exile. By that time the Jews would have wanted central meeting houses, especially because use of the

Temple in Jerusalem was no longer possible. It is even possible that synagogues or their forerunners existed earlier than the Exile. The earliest archaeological evidence, however, is third century B.C., and consists of inscriptional information about an Egyptian synagogue near Alexandria. The phrase in Psalm 74:8—"the meeting places of God"—may be a reference to synagogues.

It appears that at one time it was the custom to build synagogues on hills. However, by New Testament times they were constructed when possible by rivers (Acts 16:13), no doubt because of the convenience for administering purification rites.

Architectural design usually included three front doors and a vestibule with pillars which led into the rectangular sanctuary. The sanctuary also included pillars. A gallery was reserved for the women who were not allowed to sit with men on the ground floor of the sanctuary.

The furnishings included a curtained-off alcove or closet for the keeping of the linen-covered Torah (Law) scrolls. On the platform sat the elders, and on it too was a kind of reading desk from which a man expounded the Scriptures in a sitting position. Lamps, trumpets, and horns (used on special days) were also included in the furnishings.

The worship of the synagogue included a lengthy prayer by an assistant, during which the congregation stood facing Jerusalem. Seven members of the congregation came forward to read the assigned passages for the day. It was the custom to read the Torah all the way through every few years, but other parts of the Old Testament were used too. During the New Testament era, each verse was read in Hebrew then translated into Aramaic. Following the assigned readings a passage from the Prophets was chosen at will and read, after which it was explained by a volunteer or someone called upon (Mark 1:21, 39; Acts 13:5; etc.). Finally a benediction was offered, often by a priest. Only gradually were the items of worship taken over by officials (cp. Acts 13:15; Luke 4:20; Acts 22:19). Synagogue worship, unlike Tabernacle and Temple worship, made the oral word, instead of ceremony, central; this fact served to stimulate a livelier spiritual climate.

B. MUSICAL INSTRUMENTS

MUSIC, BOTH sung and played, is mentioned frequently in the Bible; indeed, the Bible reflects a fine sensitiveness to music and its beauty. Tradition says Jubal was "the father of all those who play the lyre and pipe" (Genesis 4:21). It was a symbol and expression of joy at feasts, festivals, and weddings. It was enjoyed by kings and queens, and even the shepherd had his lyre. David organized a choir and orchestra (I Chronicles 15:16-24); there was antiphonal singing of the Psalms; and the book of Psalms (the hymnal of the ancient Hebrews) refers to making a "joyful noise before the Lord." Music figured into the battles of the day, too.

What was the music like? Actually, no one knows, but if it were anything like the music of the Near East as we know it today, it would sound strange to our Western ears since it is built on a different scale than ours. What did the instruments look like? The answer to that is obscure too, but the derivation of the names of the instruments, discoveries of ancient Near Eastern instruments and pictures, plus a little imagination help in the attempt at reconstruction.

Bells

There were several kinds of *bells* employed in Bible times. Small tinkling bells were worn as adornments by women on wrists and ankles to attract attention and admiration (Isaiah 3:16-18). Golden bells were attached to the bottom of the high priest's robe as ornamentation and also to announce his entrance and exit (Exodus 28:33-35). Bells were often attached to horses as ornaments and also to help the owner find a strayed animal.

Castanets

II Samuel 6:5 is a possible reference to *castanets,* a musical instrument which David and his musicians played. This instrument takes its name from the word "castanea" (chestnut), for in ancient times two chestnuts were attached to the fingers and beaten together to make music. Later castanets were made from small, spoon-shaped cymbals. In Egypt they were made of metal, bone, and wood. Psalm 150:5 may be a reference to castanets.

Coronet

A hollow, curved horn, the *cornet* was originally made from an animal's horn, later of metal. Psalm 98:6; Daniel 3:5, 7, 10, 15. (See also Horn.)

Cymbals

Cymbals, used especially in Old Testament times in festivals and ceremonies (I Chronicles 15:19; Ezra 3:10), were of several types (see illustrations). Some were concave plates of brass usually clanged together or beaten. Others were conical or near-conical with handles and were clanged together vertically. There was even a type scraped together. David and the Israelites played the cymbals and other instruments while the ark was being taken to Jerusalem (II Samuel 6:5). The only time cymbals are mentioned in the New Testament is in the great love chapter, I Corinthians 13 (vs. 1). Psalm 150:5.

Drum (Hand Drum)

The hand *drum* resembled a tom-tom and consisted of a wooden hoop with skins pulled across the frame. It is associated with praise and merrymaking, and is translated variously as timbrel, tabret, and tambourine. Exodus 15:20; Judges 11:34; Psalm 68:25. (See also Timbrel.)

Dulcimer

The word *dulcimer* in Daniel 3:5, 10, 15 probably refers to the bagpipe and is so translated in the R.S.V. The dulcimer, however, was a resonance box with strings stretched across it, and was played with small hammers.

Flute

The *flute* is mentioned in Daniel 3:5, 10, 15; Judges 5:16, etc. Some flutes were simply straight pipes with holes, others had two parallel tubes (one provided melody, the other a kind of accompaniment); some were like bagpipes, and still others resembled the modern flute which moves along the lower lip. They were constructed of wood, bone, or metal. They were used in orchestras, at funerals, and especially at festive occasions such as weddings.

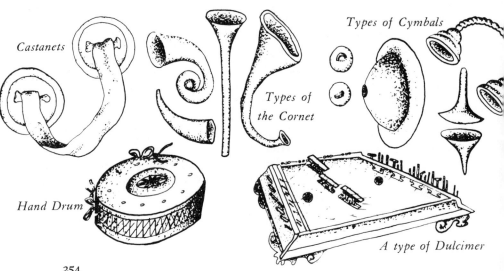

Castanets

Types of Cymbals

Types of the Cornet

Hand Drum

A type of Dulcimer

The first instrument mentioned in the Bible (Genesis 4:21), the *harp* was made of wood (cypress or almug). Small and stringed, it was usually carried about and played with the fingers or a plectrum. It had perhaps eight or ten strings and varied in size and shape. David soothed King Saul with his harp music (I Samuel 16:16). It was used in Temple worship and at various festivals. Some have suggested that its origin was in Syria. The Egyptians had a harp which was as tall as a man.

Harp

The ram's *horn* (sometimes a cow's horn) was a simple wind instrument which produced a series of tones used as signals or flourishes. It is sometimes known as a trumpet or cornet in the Bible. Joshua 6:4, 6, 8, 13.

Horn (Ram's Horn)

The *lyre* consisted of five or more strings stretched across a more or less rectangular frame. The strings are said to have been made from the small intestines of sheep. Only one note could be played on each string. The lyre was very much like the harp. I Samuel 16:23.

Lyre

(See Pipe below.)

Oboe

The word for *Organ* is translated "pipe" in the R.S.V. (Genesis 4:21; Job 21:12; Psalm 150:4). Precisely what the instrument was is unknown. It is clear that it was totally unlike our present-day organ; perhaps it was in fact a kind of pipe or woodwind instrument; some have suggested it was a *group* of wind instruments.

Organ

The term probably signifies an oboe or is perhaps a general word for reed and even flute-like instruments. The shepherd had a *pipe* which he probably made himself; it was a simple reed, sometimes with more than one hole, made of wood, ivory, or bone. Genesis 4:21; Job 21:12; Psalm 150:4.

Pipe

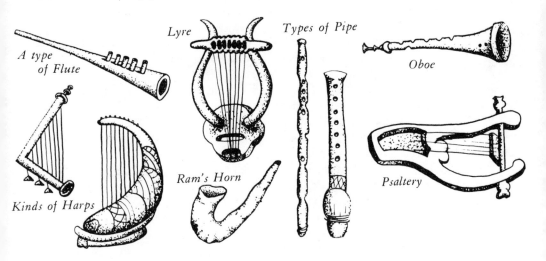

A type of Flute — *Lyre* — *Types of Pipe* — *Oboe* — *Kinds of Harps* — *Ram's Horn* — *Psaltery*

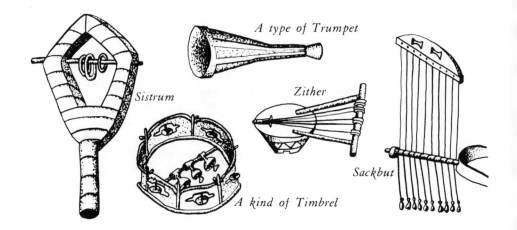

A type of Trumpet

Sistrum

Zither

Sackbut

A kind of Timbrel

Psaltery

The *psaltery* of ancient Israel was a harp-like instrument (it is sometimes translated harp or lyre) used for worship and at festive gatherings. It was plucked with the fingers, not a plectrum. Some have suggested that its Hebrew name meaning "bottle" is descriptive of the shape of the instrument. It may have been of Phoenician origin. I Samuel 10:5; II Chronicles 5:12; Psalm 71:22.

Sackbut

Also translated "trigon," the *sackbut* was a portable, harp-like instrument which was tied to the player's waist and held upright as he walked and played. It varied in the number of strings and was considered by the Greeks and Romans a luxury item in Oriental musical instruments. It is mentioned in Daniel 3:5, 7, 10, 15 only. It was in Nebuchadrezzar's orchestra.

Sistrum

The Hebrew word for *sistrum* comes from the verb "to shake." Metal rings were strung across a wire within a frame and a jingling sound resulted when the instrument was shaken. The only possible reference is II Samuel 6:5.

Tambourine

(See Drum and Timbrel.)

Timbrel (Tabret)

A round, drum-like instrument, the *timbrel* or tabret (or tambourine) was a symbol of joy. A single skin was usually stretched across one end of the frame, and sometimes metal discs were attached to the outside. As the player beat on the drum end, the discs would jingle adding to the gaiety of the occasion. Exodus 15:20; I Chronicles 13:8; Psalm 81:2. (See also Drum.)

Trumpet

Usually made from the horn of a ram or goat, this instrument is variously translated "ram's horn," "cornet," "*trumpet.*" It was used for giving signals in war as in the case of Gideon (Judges 7:16-23). Another type of trumpet was straight and made of metal. Moses was instructed by God to make two trumpets of silver

(Numbers 10:1-10). Trumpets are mentioned in Revelation 8:2, and I Thessalonians 4:16 (cp. Matthew 24:31 and I Corinthians 15:52) speaks of "the trumpet of God" at the Second Coming.

The Hebrew word translated *zither* means "ten." It was similar to a lyre or harp and may be referred to in the Bible in the expression, "an instrument of ten strings." Psalms 33:2; 144:9.

Zither

C. JEWISH FEASTS AND FESTIVALS

CELEBRATED ANNUALLY and known today as Yom Kippur, the *Day of Atonement* was an important high Sabbath in Jewish religious life. No work was done on this day, and regular morning and evening sacrifices were offered as well as expiatory sacrifices for the priesthood, sin offerings for the people, and burnt offerings for both priests and people. The blood of an animal was shed to atone for the sins of the priests and people. Exodus 30:10; Leviticus 16; 23:27-32; Numbers 29:7-11.

Atonement

The *Feast of Dedication* was primarily a New Testament festival in honor of the purifying of the Temple by Judas Maccabeus in 164 B.C. after its desecration by Antiochus Epiphanes. It is also known as the Feast of Lights since each evening the Temple and houses were illuminated with lamps, lanterns, and torches. The festival lasts eight days and is known today as Hanukkah. John 10:22.

Dedication

The *Fast of the Fifth Month* (9th Abh) is celebrated for several reasons: (1) The first Temple was destroyed by Nebuchadrezzar on this day; (2) The second Temple was destroyed by Titus on the same day of the year; (3) It is said that on this day Jehovah forbade the children of Israel to enter the Promised Land (Numbers 14:29-31); (4) 9th Abh is also considered the anniversary of the capture of the city of Bether by the Emperor Hadrian.

Fifth Month

(See *Pentecost*.)

The *Fast of the Fourth Month,* celebrated on the 17th of Tammuz, commemorated several events. On this day the Israelites made the golden calf, and Moses broke the Tables of Law on the same day of the year (Exodus 32:19). Daily sacrifices ceased on this day during a shortage of cattle prior to the destruction of Jerusalem, and Jerusalem is said to have been beseiged by Nebuchadrezzar on the 17th of Tammuz.

First Fruits

Fourth Month

(See *Dedication*.)

The *year of Jubilee* occurred after a lapse of seven Sabbaths of years, or forty-nine years. This fiftieth year was a time of rest

Hanukkah

Jubilee

and redemption for Israel. The Law provided rest for the soil during this year, and no man was allowed to sow or reap (Leviticus 25:11). In addition, if a man, through poverty, had sold certain property and that property had not been redeemed, it reverted back to him at no cost during the year of Jubilee. The law further provided that during this year any Israelite who had become a slave through debt was to be freed with his family. Thus the year of Jubilee was one of freedom and deliverance to the poor and rest from work for all of Israel. Leviticus 25:8-55; 27:17-24.

Lights (See *Dedication*.)

New Moon The *New Moon* marked the beginning of a new month and was thus celebrated as a division of time. On the thirtieth day of the month watchmen were posted on the hills of Jerusalem to watch for the appearance of the new moon. As soon as it could be seen, the men hurried into the city to the Sanhedrin from which formal announcement was made. The day was then celebrated with special sacrifices and feasting. Exodus 40:2, 17; Numbers 10:10; 28:11-14; Psalm 81:3; Amos 8:5; Colossians 2:16.

New Year (See *Trumpets*.)

Passover The *Passover* was the most important of the great Jewish feasts for it commemorated Israel's deliverance from the last plague visited upon the Egyptians and their freedom from bondage to Egypt. The Passover was instituted when God commanded the head of each household to sprinkle blood on the doorposts so that when the death angel passed over, the first-born child in each house would be spared. The Passover was celebrated on the 14th of Nisan and was followed by the Feast of Unleavened Bread. Exodus 12; 13:1-10; Leviticus 23:5-14; Numbers 9:2-14; Mark 14:1; Luke 2:41; John 19:14.

Pentecost Second in importance among Jewish festivals, *Pentecost* was celebrated fifty days after Passover and commemorated the conclusion of harvest and the offering of the first fruits on the altar. No work could be done, and various offerings were presented to Jehovah in thanksgiving for the harvest. Exodus 22:29; 23:16, 19; Leviticus 23:10-21; Numbers 28:26-31; Deuteronomy 16:9-12. In the New Testament Pentecost is particularly associated with the descent of the Holy Spirit. Acts 2; 20:16; I Corinthians 16:8. Pentecost is also known as the Feast of Weeks or the Day of First Fruits.

Purim The feast of *Purim* as recorded in Esther 9:26, 31 was instituted by Mordecai, at the suggestion of Esther, to commemorate the deliverance of the Jews of Persia from the plot of Haman to have them murdered. The 14th and 15th of Adar were kept as days of feasting and joy, and gifts were exchanged and given to the poor. See the Book of Esther.

(See *Trumpets*.)

Rosh Hashanah

The seventh day of every week was rigidly observed by the Israelites as a day of rest. No work of any kind was permitted, for the *Sabbath* was to be a day set apart unto the Lord. Exodus 20:8-11; 31:12-17; Leviticus 23:1-3.

Sabbath

Every seventh year was set apart as a *Sabbath Year*. All cultivation and tillage of the soil ceased for this one year, and anything growing spontaneously during the year was for the free use of the poor, servants, and the like. See Leviticus 25:2-5. There was no danger of lack of food, since God promised that the sixth year would provide enough for three years. Debts were to be postponed or remitted, and the Law was to be read before the people at the Feast of Tabernacles (Deuteronomy 31:10-13).

Sabbath Year

The third most important of the great annual feasts, the *Feast of Tabernacles* was celebrated from the 15th to the 22nd of Tishri. It was a harvest festival and commemorated the beginnings of the wanderings in the wilderness. Booths made from branches were constructed throughout the city, and everyone born an Israelite was compelled to live in one of these booths for the duration of the festival as a reminder of God's protection during the wilderness wanderings. The Feast of Tabernacles also marked the completion of the harvest of fruit, oil, and wine, and the conclusion of the festal year. Exodus 23:16; 34:22; Leviticus 23:34-36, 39-44; Numbers 29:12-40; Deuteronomy 16:13-15; 31:10-13; John 7:2.

Tabernacles

The *Feast of Trumpets,* celebrated on the first day of the sabbatical month Tishri, marked the beginning of the Jewish civil new year. It was set aside as a day of rest and spiritual employment along with feasting and the blowing of trumpets. This was a sacred month with the Day of Atonement following on the tenth and the Feast of Tabernacles on the fifteenth. The Feast of Trumpets is known today as Rosh Hashanah. Leviticus 23:24-25; Numbers 29:1-6.

Trumpets

The *Feast of Unleavened Bread* followed directly after the Passover and lasted from the fifteenth to the twenty-first of Nisan. Its name is derived from the fact that only unleavened bread could be used for baking during these seven days. On the first and seventh days of the feast, the people rested from work and held a holy convocation in celebration of their historic deliverance from Egypt. On the second day, the first sheaf of the new barley harvest was waved as an offering to the Lord. Exodus 12:15-20; 13:6-8; Deuteronomy 16:3-8; Matthew 26:17; Mark 14:1, 12; Luke 22:1, 7; Acts 12:3; 20:6.

Unleavened Bread

(See *Pentecost*.)

Weeks

Woodcarrying It appears from Nehemiah 10:34 and 13:31 that certain days were set aside as a *Feast of Woodcarrying* on which the Israelites gathered wood for the Temple. It was principally a day of picnicing and was probably held on the twenty-first of Abh and the twenty-first of Elul.

CALENDAR OF JEWISH FEASTS AND FESTIVALS

Festival	Hebrew Date	English Date
Purim	14th-15th Adar	February-March
Passover	14th Nisan	March-April
Unleavened Bread	15th-21st Nisan	March-April
Pentecost	5th Sivan	May-June
Fourth Month	17th Tammuz	June-July
Fifth Month	9th Abh	July-August
Woodcarrying	21st Abh	July-August
Woodcarrying	21st Elul	August-September
Atonement	10th Tishri	September-October
Tabernacles	15th-22nd Tishri	September-October
Dedication	25th Kislev	November-December

D. JEWISH SECTS AND PARTIES

Essenes THOUGH NOWHERE mentioned in the New Testament, the Essene party is thought to have originated about the second century B.C. The name "Essenes" means "saintly," and, according to Philo, the group numbered about 4000. The Essenes lived for the most part along the west shore of the Dead Sea, far removed from the distractions of the rest of the world. An ascetic community, the Essenes frowned on marriage and considered themselves the true remnant of God's people. They shared all things in common (cp. the early Church, Acts 4:32-37), renouncing riches and luxury of any kind. Their theological beliefs were similar to those of the Pharisees. The discovery of the Dead Sea Scrolls has shed new light on the beliefs and practices of the Essenes (cp. *The Manual of Discipline* found near Qumran).

Herodians The Herodians were chiefly a political rather than a religious party. They take their name from the Herod family whom they favored as ruler of the Jewish nation, and whose cause they tried to promote. Mentioned only three times in the Bible, the Herodians sided with the Pharisees against Jesus, whom they regarded as a common enemy, in an attempt to trick Him into sedition against Rome, or at least to discredit Him among the Jews (Matthew 22:15-22; Mark 12:13-17). Mark 3:6.

Pharisees

Although tendencies characteristic of the Pharisees can be traced back to post-exilic days under Ezra and Nehemiah, the Pharisees did not become a distinct party until the last half of the second century B.C. They first became known as Separatists because of their opposition to the heathenizing influence of Antiochus Epiphanes, and later were given the title "Pharisees" meaning "the separated ones." The chief characteristic of the Pharisees was their strict observance of the Law. Their emphasis was on the *letter,* rather than the *spirit* of the Law. For this reason the name Pharisee became synonymous with "hypocrite" (see Jesus' denunciation in Matthew 23). Their basic teachings included belief in (1) Divine Providence, (2) angels and spirits, (3) immortality of the soul, (4) resurrection, (5) future rewards and punishments, and (6) a literal Messianic reign on earth. They avoided all possible contact with the heathen and were noted for their pride and self-righteousness. Mark 7:1-13; Luke 14:1-6; Acts 23:6; 26:5; Philippians 3:5.

Sadducees

The term Sadducee comes from the Hebrew word meaning "righteousness" and is also associated with the family of Zadok for whom the party is thought to have been named. The Sadducees became a distinct party about the same time as the Pharisees—the last half of the second century B.C. Composed primarily of priests from wealthy, aristocratic families, the Sadducees had little influence among the common people. The teachings of the Sadducees are most often contrasted with those of the Pharisees since their beliefs seem to have been at opposite ends of the theological pole. The Sadducees denied immortality, resurrection, angels and spirits, and the possibility of future rewards and punishments —all basic tenets of the Pharisaic faith. They further denied Divine Providence, holding that man's actions depend upon his own free will. Mark 12:18-27; Acts 23:6, 8.

Scribes

From early times scribes played an important part in Jewish religious life. Primarily priests by profession, in pre-exilic times scribes served simply as secretaries handling correspondence and bookkeeping for the king (e.g., II Samuel 8:17). Later they began copying the Law and various sacred writings and eventually became scholars in religious matters (Ezra 7:11). Gradually they separated themselves from the priestly class and became official interpreters of the Law (see Luke 5:17—"doctors of the law"— and Matthew 23:7—"rabbi"). Mark 12:28; Luke 10:25; 20:39.

Zealots	Also known as the Cananaeans, the Zealots formed themselves into a party under Judas the Galilaean about A.D. 6. Their name comes from a Hebrew derivative meaning "jealous." Chiefly political in nature, the Zealots were radical Jewish nationalists who favored armed rebellion against Rome. They were extreme in their hatred and instigated frequent uprisings. It appears from Luke 6:15 that Simon "who was called the Zealot" was a member of this party before he became one of Christ's disciples. See also Matthew 10:4; Mark 3:18.
Addendum on the Assassins (Sicarri)	Known also as the Sicarri or "dagger-men," the Assassins were a group of militant Jewish nationalists who attacked with daggers those whom they considered enemies of the nation. Some appear to have been followers of an Egyptian who came to Jerusalem 54 A.D. claiming to be a prophet. Paul was mistaken for their leader in Acts 21:38.

E. THE SANHEDRIN

WHEN THE Sanhedrin was started is unknown. An old tradition says it originated with Moses and his seventy assistants who were elders (Numbers 11:16-24). Ezra reorganized a Sanhedrin group after the Exile, says the tradition. Apparently the number of men varied, but its full size of seventy or seventy-one members was fixed after Ezra. By that time both Sadducees and Pharisees were included in it. Of the Sadducees, there were those termed "the souls of the Sanhedrin," men who were either former High Priests or candidates for the office of High Priest. The Pharisees or doctors of the Law were stronger in influence than the Sadducees in our Lord's day. "Elders" were those Sanhedrin members who were neither Sadducees nor Pharisees. The scribes were the legal experts (Matthew 26:57). Joseph of Arimathaea was a member of the Sanhedrin. Methods of selecting its membership varied over the centuries.

The president of the Sanhedrin was the High Priest; thus Caiaphas was president at Jesus' trial and Ananias at Paul's trial (Acts 23:2). Generally speaking, the territory over which the Sanhedrin had power was limited to Judea, although Jews everywhere respected its authority and were influenced by it (Acts 9:2). Roman authority did not rob it of its essential power; it was the supreme court of the Jews (Matthew 26:59, Mark 14:55, Luke 22:66, John 11:47, Acts 4:15, 5:21ff, 6:12ff, 22:30, 23:1ff, 24:20.— In Matthew 5:22 "Sanhedrin" means simply any court of justice). The Sanhedrin had its own police force, authority to arrest, try

(Matthew 26:57ff, John 19:7, Acts 4, Acts 22-24), and execute all penalties with the exception of the death penalty (except when a Gentile passed the barrier into the forbidden part of the Temple [Acts 21:28ff—see the discussion on the Temple, chapter 9]). Even with the death penalty, it could pass judgment and ask for ratification by the procurator. When the death penalty was considered, the youngest members of the Sanhedrin had to vote first (voting was by standing) so as not to be influenced by the position of the older men, and it was a rule that the total vote must be two more than half the number. When sentence of death was passed, it was supposed to be carried out the following day; therefore, such sentence was never passed on the day before the Sabbath, for it was against Jewish Law to execute a person on their holy day. The only case of capital punishment in the New Testament is the death of Jesus (Stephen's death was a case of mob violence). Sessions were not to be held on Feast days or on the Sabbath (the Sanhedrin met on regular days, but which days we do not know). It was the policy of the Sanhedrin that always the benefit of the doubt be on the side of the accused; this is one reason we know that Jesus' trial was a miscarriage of justice.

During sessions, the group sat in a semi-circle and thus could see each other. Two secretaries stood in front, one recording the statements made in favor of the one on trial, the other the statements made in opposition to him. Students of Law, who were aspirants to seats on the Sanhedrin, attended the sessions as learning experiences. The court's quorum was defined as twenty-three members.

F. PLANTS and ANIMALS, including BIRDS

PLANTS OF THE BIBLE

Acacia The *acacia* tree is especially valued in Bible lands because of its use in construction work. Its wood is durable and was used in building the ark of the Covenant and the tabernacle (Exodus 25:5, 10; 26:26). Acacia is found particularly in the Jordan Valley. It produces leaves with small leaflets and flowers round like a ball.

Algum The *algum* tree grows abundantly on the mountains of Lebanon and Gilead and reaches a height of sixty-five feet. The fruit of the algum is black and globular, and the tree itself grows in the shape of a pyramid. King Solomon makes reference to the algum (or Grecian juniper as it is also called) in connection with the building of the Temple (II Chronicles 2:8).

Almond   The *almond* tree is well known to Bible lands. Its beautiful pink and white flowers usher in spring each year; indeed, they precede spring, coming out in January or February. The almond grows wild but is also cultivated for its fruit which is well liked by Orientals. The tree grows to almost three times the size of a man in height. Passages which refer to the almond include Jeremiah 1:11, where it is used as a figure of speech; Ecclesiastes 12:5, which refers to its flowers. Aaron's rod was a branch from an almond tree (Numbers 17:8). Flowers from the almond were used as decorations for the Hebrew sanctuary. Almond kernels are famous throughout the world for the oil which they produce; one hundred and fourteen pounds of the fruit yield about fifty pounds of oil. Genesis 43:11.

Almug   Also known as red sandalwood, the *almug* was a sweet-smelling durable timber used in the construction of Solomon's Temple. The almug tree grows to a height of about twenty feet, and its red (or white) wood was used for making musical instruments in Bible times. The wood was imported from southern India. I Kings 10:11-12.

Aloe   The *aloe* of the New Testament is a succulent plant with thick, fleshy leaves and a tall stem from which hang many bell-shaped flowers. A substance known as aloin was taken from the leaves and mixed with perfumed incense for purifying the bodies of the dead. Nicodemus carried such a mixture when he came to the

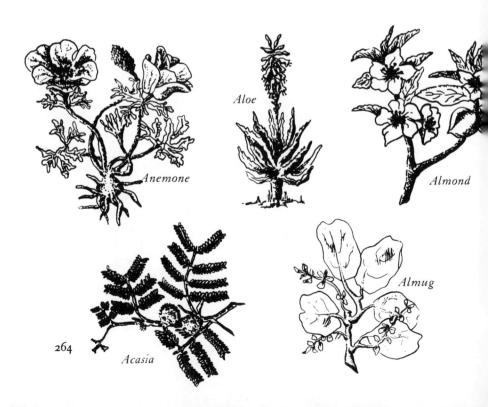

Aloe

Anemone

Almond

Almug

264

Acasia

grave of Jesus (John 19:38-40). The *aloe* of the Old Testament (Psalms 45:8; Proverbs 7:17) was very valuable; and, known also as eaglewood, it grew to a height of one hundred and twenty feet. Its wood was highly esteemed, and the soft inner wood was often used as a setting for precious jewels.

It is possible that the "lilies" of Matthew 6:28 and Luke 12:27 **Anemone** are *anemones* which grow in abundance in Palestine. The flowers of the anemone, ranging from crimson to purple, make a colorful sight in springtime. The plant itself reaches a height of six inches.

The *apple* tree may or may not be referred to in the Scriptures; **Apple** it is difficult to translate the Hebrew word. Possibilities are Proverbs 25:11; Song of Solomon 2:3, 5; 7:8; 8:5; Joel 1:12. Some say Proverbs 25:11 should be translated apricots since true apples were of poor quality. There is, of course, no textual basis for believing that the tree of knowledge, the forbidden fruit, indicated in Genesis 2 and 3 was an apple. The apple tree is rarely cultivated in Palestine today.

There are several kinds of *balm* mentioned in the Bible. Myrrh **Balm** is one of them. Jeremiah speaks figuratively of a "balm of Gilead" (8:22). Today there is found in quantity around the Dead Sea, a balm which grows to a height of twelve to fourteen feet; it is an evergreen shrub with white blossoms and apple-like fruit. Gum resin extracted from the bark of one type of balm was used for medicinal purposes until the seventeenth century. Genesis 37:25.

A staple cereal, *barley* has been cultivated universally from **Barley** ancient times. It is sown in late fall and gathered in the spring at the Passover season. At the feeding of the five thousand Jesus blessed the lad's five barley loaves (John 6:1-13). We assume that the lad was probably poor because coarse barley bread sold at least twice as cheaply as the fine wheat bread (II Kings 7:1, 16, 18). Barley is also mentioned in connection with the plagues (Exodus 9:31), Ruth's gleanings (Ruth 1:22, 2:17, 23; 3:2, 15), the Passover (Leviticus 23:10), and in many other instances.

Whether the *box* tree is actually mentioned in the Scriptures **Box** is not known, but some scholars say it is referred to in Isaiah 41:19; 60:13; and Ezekiel 27:6. It flourished in Lebanon and Cyprus. The box is useful as an ornamental shrub, and its durable lumber is suitable for construction purposes.

The *broom* is a flowering desert tree highly valued as fuel. **Broom** Its flowers and fruit resemble that of the pea, and it is also used for shade. I Kings 19:4.

The *bulrush* (papyrus) is a familiar sight along the Nile in **Bulrush** ancient Egypt. Its tall stems provided material for making the earliest form of paper, known as papyrus. The pith of the stem was cut into strips which were laid together to form flat sheets. (See "Reed" and chapter on "Ancient Manuscripts and Versions.") Bulrushes are thought of especially in connection with the story of the child Moses who was hidden in a basket among the bulrushes (Exodus 2:1-10).

Calamus *Calamus* is not native to Palestine but was imported from India and Arabia. It is of the reed or cane family and is mentioned in Song of Solomon 4:14 and Ezekiel 27:19. Strong smelling oil was taken from its root.

Caper The *caper* grows abundantly in Palestine. It is a prickly bush, and the flower bud was used as a digestive aid. It was also used as a stimulant. Some say it is mentioned in Ecclesiastes 12:5.

Carob The *carob* tree grows to a substantial height, perhaps forty feet, and produces long, black, bean-like pods which are fed to animals. In the story of the prodigal son, the husks fed to the hogs were likely carob pods (Luke 15:16). The carob is well known in Bible lands and has been used for medicinal purposes. The bean pod grows to a length equal to the span of a normal adult hand.

Cassia The *cassia,* something like the cinnamon tree, has many uses. The bark is fragrant and is often mixed with other spices. Buds are used as a seasoning for food. A substance made from the pods and leaves of the cassia was a chief article of commerce in Bible times (Ezekiel 27:19). See also Exodus 30:24.

Cedar The brown berried *cedar* reaches a height of twenty feet and was used for sacrificial purposes in Temple worship. It grows on high, rocky mountains and bears a small orange-like fruit. The different *cedar of Lebanon* is a stately evergreen which often reaches a height of one hundred and twenty feet. It exudes a sweet-smelling resin which is noticeable even when walking through a grove of cedars. Its cone takes three years to mature, and cedar wood is particularly durable. It was used in the construction of the Temple (I Kings 6-7) and in the making of furniture and boats. The cedars of Lebanon (today only a few hundred are left) symbolize, among other things, strength, beauty, nobility, goodness, and the Messiah. (Ezekiel 17:22-24; I Kings 5:6, 8-9; 9:11; Jeremiah 22:7.)

Chestnut (See "Plane.")

Cinnamon While the *cinnamon* tree did not grow in the Holy Land itself, it was imported from Arabia and Ceylon for its cinnamon (extracted from the inner bark) and its sweet smell (it is referred to as a kind of perfume in Proverbs 7:17 and Revelation 18:13). It is also used as a figure of speech (Song of Solomon 4:14) and is mentioned in connection with holy oil (Exodus 30:23).

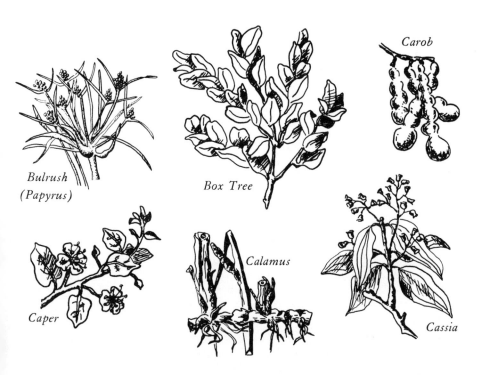

Bulrush
(Papyrus)

Box Tree

Carob

Caper

Calamus

Cassia

Whether the *citron* is actually mentioned in the Bible is not known. Some scholars believe that Leviticus 23:40 is a reference to the citron fruit rather than to the apple or apricot. The tree grows to two or three times the height of a man. The leaves look like those of the lemon or orange trees. The actual fruit resembles a lemon but is larger and its exterior is not as smooth.

Citron

A member of the carrot family, *coriander* has leaves like parsley, white or pinkish flowers, and a rounded gray seed which contains a valuable oil used for flavoring. It grows wild in the Mediterranean area, and has long been used for culinary and medicinal purposes; it is also used as a perfume. Bread, cakes, and meat are often flavored with it. Numbers 11:6-9 records its use among the Israelites. See also Exodus 16:31.

Coriander

A small delicate plant, the *cummin* was frequently grown and cultivated in Palestine. Jesus referred to it (Matthew 23:23). The fruit of the plant is valuable for medicinal purposes, while the seeds are often crushed and mixed with bread and meat as a spice. The fruit is harvested by beating the stocks with a stick (Isaiah 28:27).

Cummin

The *cypress* is a common evergreen seen in southern Europe and is a landmark in the Holy Land. Today thousands of cypress are used as windbreaks. A beautiful and graceful tree, it is useful

Cypress

for its hard and remarkably durable lumber. (One ancient historian said the cypress doors on the Temple of Diana at Ephesus were like new after 400 years!) Cypress wood is mentioned in reference to construction work in the Sanctuary (I Kings 6:15-35). It was also used in the building of ships. There are many references to the cypress in Scripture (Isaiah 55:13; 60:13; Hosea 14:8, etc.).

Fig   The *fig* is referred to at least fifty times in the Bible—the famous fable of Jotham (Judges 9:7) is an example. The tree is a common sight in Palestine. Fruit is seen on the tree for about ten months of the year; it comes in three stages: late autumn, green winter, and first-ripe. When Jesus cursed the fig tree (Mark 11:13), it was the season for neither first-ripe nor late autumn fruit; he thus expected green figs. The fig has been used for medicinal purposes (Isaiah 38:21); the tree is frequently employed as a figure of speech in the Scriptures (Matthew 7:16); Adam and Eve used the leaves, large and broad in size, to make coverings for themselves (Genesis 3:7); and the fruit is eaten dried or fresh, in cakes or in mixtures.

Fir   The pine or *fir* of the Holy Land is a cone-bearing tree which grows to a height of some sixty feet. Several species are found on Mt. Lebanon. In ancient times it was a symbol of nobility, and its timber was used in the construction of temples and houses. It is probably referred to in Isaiah 60:13, and some say in I Kings 5:10 and Isaiah 37:24.

Flax   *Flax* was an important plant in ancient Israel and Egypt because it was commonly used to make linen. The plants were pulled up, allowed to dry in the sun (Joshua 2:6), and then soaked in water until the outer layer decayed. Next the inside of the stem was combed and the individual threads peeled from the stalk. These fine threads were now ready to be woven into linen. High Priests wore linen clothes (Exodus 28:6), the curtains of the Tabernacle were made of it (Exodus 26:1), but Jews were forbidden to wear a piece of clothing made of both wool and linen (Deuteronomy 22:11). Flax is referred to a number of times in the Bible. See Exodus 9:31; Proverbs 31:13; etc.

Frankincense   The *frankincense* tree grows primarily in India and northern Arabia. Its wood is hard and durable and the juice or resin of the tree is used as incense. The name frankincense means "free lighting." The wise men brought gifts to the Christ Child: gold, frankincense, and myrrh (Matthew 2:11).

Gall   The *gall* mentioned in Matthew 27:34 in connection with the crucifixion was, say some, the juice of the opium poppy. (Cp. Mark 15:23 and see under "Myrrh.") This juice is a kind of narcotic which produces a sleep so heavy as to render the person insensible. Jesus refused the mixture of gall and wine choosing rather to remain conscious during his suffering. Gall also refers to anything bitter or poisonous (Acts 8:23). As poison, it is sometimes translated "hemlock."

Garlic

The *garlic* of the Bible times looked much like ours today. It was used for flavoring and as a staple food among the Israelites, and was greatly missed on their journey to the Promised Land (Numbers 11:5).

Gourd

Standing some ten feet high, the *gourd* was a large bush with rich green or bronze leaves, and fruit which is first gray-green and then turns to a bright red. An oil was taken from the tree and used as fuel for lamps. A gourd (some say a castor oil plant) was provided as shade for the prophet Jonah in Jonah 4:6-10. II Kings 4:39.

Grape

(See "Vine.")

Hemlock ("Poison Hemlock")

A biennial, the *hemlock* produces a poisonous, oily substance which was sometimes given prisoners under the death penalty. The plant reaches a height of about five feet, and its leaves resemble that of a fern. It should be called "poison hemlock" to distinguish it from the true hemlock. The poison is extracted from the root (cp. Deuteronomy 29.18) and Socrates probably

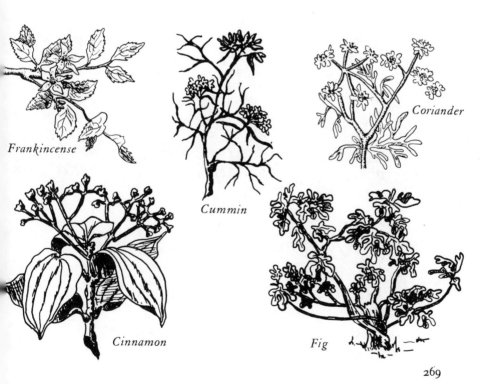

Frankincense

Coriander

Cummin

Cinnamon

Fig

died of this plant. Passages referring to poison have sometimes been identified with this plant (Psalms 69:21) and with gall (see "Gall").

Henna

The *henna* shrub is referred to only once in the Old Testament, Song of Solomon 1:14, though some have thought that Song of Solomon 4:13 is also a reference to it. It grows in Judea and produces white scented flowers. A powder made from dried henna leaves can be used to color the hair or fingernails in reddish and yellowish hues.

Hyssop

There are two types of *hyssop* referred to in the Bible. The hyssop of the New Testament is a tall, yellow-green plant with strong stems and ribbon-like leaves. The grain of this hyssop is also known as "Jerusalem corn" and is a main part of the Palestinian diet. A sponge filled with vinegar was placed on hyssop and given to Jesus at the crucifixion (John 19:29). The hyssop of the Old Testament was of the mint family and entirely different from that mentioned above. This plant has hairy stems with small leaves and bunches of golden flowers. It was used by the Israelites at the Passover to sprinkle blood over the doorposts (Exodus 12:22), for cleansing lepers (Leviticus 14:4), and for other rites of purification ("Purge me with hyssop and I shall be clean." Psalms 51:7).

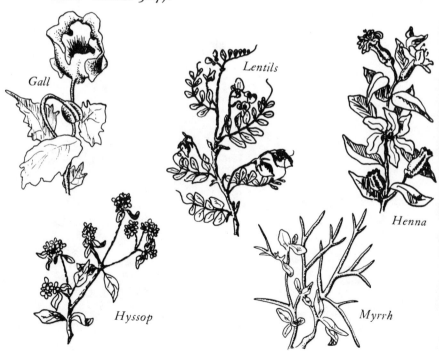

Gall

Lentils

Henna

Hyssop

Myrrh

The *juniper* looks very much like the cypress. The "shrub" (R.S.V.) of Jeremiah 17:6 is thought by some authorities to be the juniper.

As the Israelites murmured against Moses they reminded him of the things in Egypt they missed. "We remember . . . the *leeks* . . ." (Numbers 11:5). A favorite vegetable in Palestine, the leek resembles the onion and is consumed in great quantities. It was also used for medicinal purposes.

Looking something like a pea, the *lentil* is used as a cereal and for making bread. It grows in abundance in Palestine. Jacob gave Esau "bread and pottage made of lentils." Genesis 25:34; II Samuel 17:28; 23:11; Ezekiel 4:9.

There are several plants referred to as *lilies* in the Scriptures. The "lilies by the rivers of waters" (of the apocryphal Ecclesiasticus 50:8) are known today as the iris. Its flowers are pale yellow or lavender and the bulb was often dried and placed in linen chests or hung among garments to add perfume. It was also used for medicinal purposes. The "lilies of the field" (Matthew 6:28) perhaps refers to the anemone (see "Anemone"). Yet another lily is that mentioned in Song of Solomon 5:13. With bright red flowers and a clear green stalk, this lily was a symbol of loveliness. It is also known as the Scarlet Martagon, and its Hebrew name "shushan" is given to musical instruments.

The *mint* of Palestine was used in some forty-one medicinal remedies, as a perfume (Greek: "sweet-smelling") in Jewish synagogues, and as a flavoring in meat dishes. There are three varieties of mint in Palestine: garden mint, peppermint, and pennyroyal. Mint grows wild on banks and in ditches. Matthew 23:23; Luke 11:42.

Possibilities of reference to the *mulberry* are II Samuel 5:23-24; Luke 19:4. The mulberry in ancient times was cultivated for its fruit. It is not very plentiful in Palestine today and is raised only for ornamentation. In Syria the white mulberry is used for the raising of silkworms and has been for hundreds of years, though not in Bible times.

Mustard grows wild in Palestine and is also cultivated. It has yellow flowers and its leaves are used as a vegetable. The seeds provide powder for seasoning purposes and the making of poultices for treating some illnesses. Jesus refers to this plant in his famous parable about the mustard seed (Matthew 13:31-32) and in a great statement about faith (Matthew 17:20).

The mention of *myrrh* quickly brings to mind the visit of the magi who brought gifts of "gold, frankincense and myrrh" (Matthew 2:11) to the Christ Child. This myrrh is the resin or drip-

Juniper

Leeks

Lentils

Lilies

Mint

Mulberry

Mustard

Myrrh

pings of a thorny bush which has thin, papery bark, and was gathered and sold as a spice or medicine, also for use in cosmetics and perfume, and in the making of holy oil for anointing (Exodus 30:23:33). It was imported from Arabia and Africa and does not grow in Palestine. It was used as a salve for anointing the dead (see John 19:39-40). According to Mark 15:23 a mixture of wine and myrrh was offered Jesus on the cross (see "Gall"). The myrrh of Genesis 37:25 and 43:11 is probably the "lot," a small plant which grows in abundance in Palestine with a profusion of colorful flowers resembling wild roses. Its resin is also used for perfume.

Myrtle   The *myrtle* is well known in Palestine and is an evergreen. Isaiah uses it to symbolize the promised Messiah (Isaiah 41:19; 55:13). The myrtle is also referred to in Nehemiah 8:15; it was used in making booths or huts at the Feast of Tabernacles (feast of booths). It was a sign of glory to the Greeks. Esther's Hebrew name, Hadassah (Esther 2:7), meant "myrtle."

Oak   The *oak* is referred to frequently in the Bible (Genesis 35:4; Ezekiel 27:6; Zechariah 11:2). Many species grow in Palestine and it had a variety of uses including shade and lumber. In some religions it was considered sacred. The oak symbolized power and strength (see, e.g., Isaiah 2:13; Amos 2:9).

Olive   The *olive* tree is plentiful in the Holy Land and highly valued. Its fruit is widely consumed. Olive oil is a source of revenue, an aid in cooking, and is used for fuel in lamps. The wood of the olive tree is yellowish in color and has a beautiful grain. Olive trees grow best in dry, gravelly soil, and this makes it remarkably well suited to the Near and Middle East. It grows to a very great age, and even now in the Garden of Gethsemane ("garden with the olive press"), we are told, some of the olive trees were planted hundreds of years ago. It takes at least ten years for the first harvest, and the finest fruit does not appear until the tree is thirty years old. The tree varies in height and sometimes reaches thirty-five or forty feet. Harvesting takes place in the September to October period. The olives are shaken or beaten from the tree and gathered rather than picked. In Bible times, olives that remained on the tree were for the "sojourner, the fatherless, and the widow" (Deuteronomy 24:20; cp. Isaiah 17:6; 24:13). The olive and its oil (extracted with primitive stone crushing equipment) are common figures of speech in Scripture, symbolizing prosperity, joy and vitality. The Mt. of Olives (Mt. Olivet) overlooking old Jerusalem is, with its sun-bathed and rocky soil, an ideal place for olive trees which still grow there. Genesis 8:11; Psalms 55:21; Proverbs 5:3; Hosea 14:6.

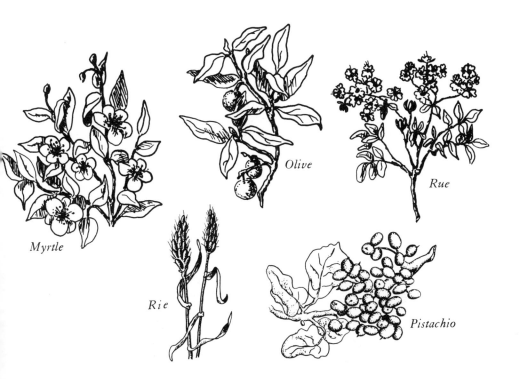

Myrtle

Olive

Rue

Rie

Pistachio

One of the refreshing sights in the Jordan Valley is the graceful green date *palm*. There are a great many species but the date palm is the only kind that prospers in the Holy Land. Its fruit is nowhere mentioned directly in the Bible, but a great deal of reference is made to the beauty of the tree and to the use of its branches. See, for example, John 12:13, the famous passage on the Triumphal Entry. Numbers 33:9; II Chronicles 28:15; Revelation 7:9.

Palm

(See "Bulrush" and "Reed" and chapter on "Ancient Manuscripts and Versions.")

Papyrus

(See "Fir.")

Pine

There is only one reference to the *pistachio* nut tree in the Bible, Genesis 43:11. It is rare in Palestine today.

Pistachio

Modern scholarship tends to associate the chestnut with the *plane* tree referred to in Scripture. A tree much desired for shade, it grows particularly in Syria and along the coast of the Mediterranean. It has vinelike green leaves and small globular fruit covered with spikes. The bark peels annually; the Hebrew word for this tree means "peeling off." Genesis 30:37; Ezekiel 31.8.

Plane

A wild shrub native to Persia and Syria, the *pomegranate* has spreading branches, dark green, shiny leaves, and bright red, wax-like flowers. The fruit is dark red in color, about the size of an orange, and has a thick skin covering a juicy pulp and many

Pomegranate

seeds. The blossoms were used as a medicine for treating dysentery, while the fruit is a refreshing delicacy to desert dwellers. The pomegranate has been used as a symbol by several religions; it symbolizes life and fertility in the Christian tradition. High priestly robes were decorated with pomegranates (Exodus 28:31, 33-34). Numbers 13:23; Deuteronomy 8:8; Song of Solomon 6:11; 7:12.

Poplar The *poplar* grows to a height of thirty to sixty feet and is native to Palestine and Syria. The underside of the green leaves is white; the tree's Hebrew name comes from a root meaning "to be white." The poplar is a familiar sight in the Holy Land. Genesis 30:37; Hosea 4:13.

Reed Several varieties of *reed* grow along river banks and lake fronts in Palestine. One species is a tall plant which has a lustrous purple head of blossom and resembles a plume. In antiquity, pens were often fashioned from reeds, and the stem, which grows to ten or twelve feet high, was used as a measuring device (Ezekiel 40:3). Papyrus is a reed used for making "paper" (see chapter on "Ancient Manuscripts and Versions") and boats (Isaiah 18:2). Many a sermon has been preached on the classic text, Isaiah 42:3.

Rie The *rie* of Bible times was probably spelt, a grain resembling wheat which grows in very poor soil. It was useful, though an inferior grain. Isaiah refers to it (28:25) and in Ezekiel we see it included in a formula for making bread (4:9). It is also mentioned in connection with the seven plagues (Exodus 9:32).

Rose There are many plants referred to as *"rose"* in the Bible. The "rose growing by the brook" of Ecclesiasticus 39:13 is the oleander, a tall flowering shrub which was poisonous. The rose of Isaiah 35:1 refers to a plant with a bulb and is thought to be the narcissus, a flower with a bright yellow bloom growing wild in desert areas of Palestine. The "rose of Sharon" (Song of Solomon 2:1) has reference to another bulb-growing plant, a kind of tulip. It is native to the plain of Sharon—it is sometimes called the Sharon tulip—and has bright red flowers. The rose bush as such is not mentioned in the Bible. The name Rhoda (Acts 12:13) means "rose."

Rue Mentioned only once in the Bible, *rue* was nevertheless of great worth. It was used as a disinfectant, as flavoring in cooking, and was contained in some eighty-four medicinal remedies. The rue plant grows five feet tall and has clusters of bright yellow flowers at the top of its stems. Luke 11:42.

Rush The soft or bog *rush* of the Holy Land grows along the edges of streams and rivers. It has flowers and its grasslike leaves are used for making baskets, wicker chair seats, etc. Many species grow in Bible lands. Job 8:11; Isaiah 35:7.

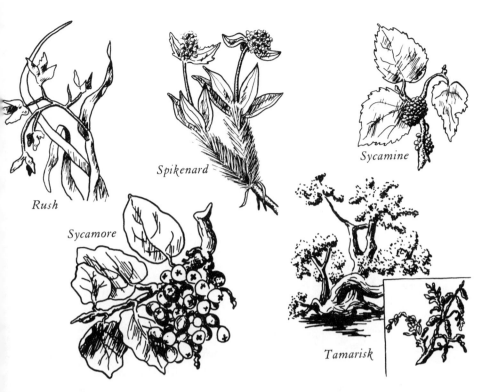

Rush

Spikenard

Sycamine

Sycamore

Tamarisk

(See "Almug.")

A derivative of the oak tree, the *scarlet* is a large evergreen shrub closely resembling a holly tree. Its shoots are the breeding ground of an insect from which a scarlet dye is taken. The bark of the tree yields a dye which turns black when soaked in boiling water. Its leaves are small and spiny and it bears small acorns. Leviticus 14:51.

A source of costly perfume, *spikenard* was imported from northern India, and one pound of it sold for the equivalent of nearly a year's wages for a daily laborer. It is a small plant with hairy stems from which the rosy red, sweet-smelling ointment is obtained. It was treasured in Old Testament times (Song of Solomon 1:12 and 4:14), and Mary anointed Jesus with spikenard (Mark 14:3-6; cp. Matthew 26:6ff, John 12:1ff).

The *sycamine* is like the black mulberry and its fruit, closely resembling the blackberry, comes in clusters like grapes. The leaves were used as food for silkworms by the Chinese. Jesus refers to the sycamine tree in a lesson on faith (Luke 17:6).

Unlike the so-called *sycamore* tree well known in the West, the sycamore of the Holy Land is a fig producing tree, and its greenery resembles the mulberry (the fruit is sometimes called "mulberry fig"). Its branches grow close to the ground so that even a short

Sandalwood

Scarlet

Spikenard

Sycamine

Sycamore

man like Zaccheus could latch onto a low branch and climb up into the tree (Luke 19:1-4). The sycamore produces yellowish fig-like fruit with dark spots, less tasty than the fig but plentiful, and was widely eaten especially by the poor. This fig-like syca-more grows in Egypt (Psalms 78:47) as well as in the Holy Land. The prophet Amos was a "dresser" of sycamore trees (Amos 7:14), which means, among other things, that he pricked the skin of the fruit to force ripening. Today a needle with hypodermic action is used. I Kings 10:27; I Chronicles 27:28; Isaiah 9:10.

Tamarisk

The *tamarisk* tree abounds in many species in the Mediter-ranean area. It has graceful, curved branches, small leaves, pink flowers, and can grow to a very great size. It was regarded as a sacred tree in the Old Testament. Arabs consider it sacred today; according to a legend, it says "Allah, Allah" as the wind blows through it. Genesis 21:33; I Samuel 22:6; 31:13.

Tares

One of the most destructive weeds of the Holy Land, it is almost impossible to tell the difference between *tares* and wheat in the early stages of growth. A fanning or sifting process is used to separate the tares from the wheat at harvest, the tare seeds being lighter and smaller. The seeds often contain a poisonous fungus which when eaten is harmful to human beings, causing dizziness (French for tares is literally "drunkenness"), nausea, and some-times death. Job 31:40; Matthew 13:24-30, 36-43.

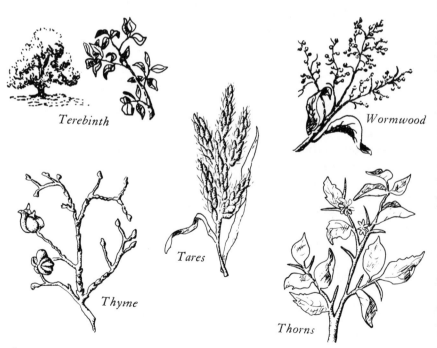

Terebinth

Wormwood

Thyme

Tares

Thorns

The *terebinth* (holm oak) tree is common in the Holy Land. **Terebinth**
Its branches remind one of the spreading chestnut, and it may
reach a height of fifty feet. It provides shade, produces a turpen-
tine, and was considered a sacred tree. The seed of its fruit can be
eaten. Absalom was caught in the branches of what was perhaps
a terebinth tree (II Samuel 18:9, 10). Under terebinth and other
trees, worship both good (Genesis 12:6) and unacceptable (Hosea
4:13) took place. Isaiah 6:13.

A common sight in Palestine, the *thistle* is a tall weed with **Thistles**
mauve or yellow flowers, depending upon the species, and a spiny
stem. The shores of Lake Galilee know a variety that grows as
high as thirteen feet. Thistle seeds are often seen floating in the
wind. "Thorns and thistles" go together as figures in the Bible
(Hebrews 6:8), and Jesus made a now famous statement about
thorns in the Sermon on the Mount (Matthew 7:16; Genesis 3:18;
Hosea 10:8).

There are several species of *thorn* plants in the Holy Land. **Thorns**
The "crown of thorns" placed on Jesus' head at the crucifixion
may have been the "Christ" or "Jerusalem" thorn, a native of
Palestine. It has small white flowers which grow in close proximity
to the long, sharp thorns which often inflict a wound. The thorn
of Matthew 7:16 is different; it is perhaps the variety that produces glossy orange berries about the size of small plums. Thistles
were planted as hedges to protect crops from destruction by cattle
and camels. Still another type is the buckthorn, a small evergreen
tree also used for making hedges. Thorns were used as kindling
under cooking pots (Psalm 58:9). The Old Testament abounds in
reference to them as figures (II Samuel 23:6; Ezekiel 28:24;
Hosea 2:6).

A small hardwood evergreen, the *thyine* is native to the Atlas **Thyine**
Mountains in Libya. Its wood is valuable as a building material,
including furniture, and was also burned as incense. Resin obtained
from the tree is used as varnish when dissolved in wine. Revelation 18:12.

A common type of agriculture in the Holy Land was that of **Vine (Grape)**
raising the *vine* or *grape*. Grapes are harvested from July through
October. Bunches of grapes were put into a wine press and the
juice made into wine and vinegar. The Bible cries out against
drunkenness (Isaiah 28:1; Hosea 4:11). Grapes were also eaten
fresh, dried (I Samuel 25:18), or in cakes (Hosea 3:1). There are
many references to grapes and their cultivation in the Bible
(Genesis 40:10-11; Song of Solomon 2:13, 15; Isaiah 5:2-7; Jeremiah 8:13). Israel is symbolized by the vine (Hosea 10:1). Jesus
said, "I am the true vine, and my Father is the husbandman,"

then adds that His disciples are the branches (John 15:1-8). Moreover, the Old Testament sees the vine as a symbol of forgiveness (Joel 2:19) and the New as a symbol of our Lord's blood through which forgiveness is obtained (I Corinthians 11:25).

Walnut   Song of Solomon 6:11 is apparently the only reference to the *walnut* in the Bible. Walnuts were abundant in Bible times but today they are rare.

Wheat   A common grain throughout the world, Biblical references to "corn" usually mean the cereal *wheat*. The wheat of Genesis 41:1-7 bears seven ears (spikelets) on one stock and is harvested in June. Ezra 7:22; Psalm 81:16; etc.

Willow   The *willow* tree is common to almost every country. It grows near water (Isaiah 44:4) and has a long, narrow leaf which is green on top and white underneath. A bitter juice extracted from the shoots was used as a substitute for quinine. The willow of Psalm 137:1-5 probably refers to the aspen, a tall tree with crisp leaves which hang down and sway back and forth as if "weeping." There are a number of species of willow in the Holy Land.

Wormwood   The *wormwood* tree produces a bitter juice in which connection it is usually mentioned (Deuteronomy 29:18; Jeremiah 23:15; Revelation 8:10-11). The leaves are used medicinally, and it produces small, greenish-yellow flower heads. Several species of wormwood grow in Palestine.

ANIMALS

Ant   There are several kinds of *ants* in Palestine, but reference is made to the ant only in Proverbs 6:6-8 and Proverbs 30:24-25. It is the wisdom of the ant that is underscored in these two passages.

Asp   The *asp* is a snake, perhaps the Egyptian cobra. It is poisonous and now rare in Palestine. Deuteronomy 32:33; Job 20:14, 16; Psalm 58:4; 91:13; Isaiah 11:8.

Ass   (See Donkey.)

Bat   The *bat* is referred to in Leviticus 11:19, Deuteronomy 14:18, and Isaiah 2:20. In the Leviticus and Deuteronomy passages the bat is considered an unclean animal, thus one not permitted to be eaten. Bats are numerous in Palestine and thrive especially well in hot or warm climates. Several species have been identified in Palestine.

Bear   Now almost extinct in Palestine, *bears* in Biblical times were plentiful. The books of Revelation and Daniel mention bears in connection with visions (Daniel 7:5; Revelation 13:2); David encountered bears (I Samuel 17:34, 36, 37); Isaiah refers to the bear within a Messianic context (Isaiah 11:7); a well-known proverb refers to it (Proverbs 17:12). The bear was used as a figure of speech by prophets and poets (Isaiah 59:11; Lamentations 3:10; Amos 5:19).

Bee

The four references to *bees* in the Bible are in Deuteronomy 1:44; Judges 14:8; Psalm 118:12; Isaiah 7:18. Honey, of course, is referred to more frequently; Samson's connection with it is well known (Judges 14:8, 9, 18). The Palestinian bee is small and plentiful, and its honey has been cultivated over the centuries. The reddish clay beehives are seen to this day in Palestine. The name Deborah means "bee."

Boar

Numerous in Palestine, the *boar* (same as "pig" in Hebrew) is nonetheless referred to in the Scriptures only once, Psalm 80:13. It was an impure animal, and apparently well known for damaging prepared agricultural lands and forbidden to be eaten. (See Pig.)

Boar

Bull

The animals of the bovine family are referred to frequently in the Scriptures. The *bull,* the cow, the heifer, cattle, these terms appear again and again. This is only evidence of the fact that the bull or the cow was greatly respected by the Palestinian people. And well it might have been for here was a source of meat and leather, and in the case of the cow, milk. Cows and bulls also provided labor aid in agricultural duties. A few of the many references to the bull or cattle are Numbers 7:3; Deuteronomy 22:10; 25:4; I Samuel 6:7; I Kings 12:28; 19:19; II Kings 10:29. The *calf* was frequently used in sacrifice (Genesis 18:7; I Samuel 28:24; I Kings 1:9, etc.).

(See Bull.)

Calf

Camels are, of course, numerous in the Bible lands and have been over the centuries. Like the donkey, it is a sure-footed animal, a beast of burden, though not adapted to mountainous regions. To this day the visitor to the East sees frequently this "ship of the desert" making its slow, plodding way across the hot sands. Genesis 12:16; 24:30; I Kings 10:2; II Kings 8:9; Isaiah 30:6 are but a few of the references to the camel, though the Israelites did not always make very great use of it. It can carry huge loads over a continuous thirty mile journey. Females give up to one and a half gallons of milk daily, from which butter and cheese can be made. It provides good leather and some eat its meat (though Israelites were forbidden to do so, Leviticus 11:4). The New Testament refers to the camel in Matthew 3:4 and Mark 10:25.

Camel

Cow	(See Bull.)
Dog	The *dog* has always been well known in the Eastern countries. Employed as a guard and often as a sheep dog, it was considered helpful by Israelites but not appreciated as in the West today. In fact, Israelites held the dog in disrespect when not in the role of guardian. The Bible refers to dogs some forty times (e.g., Exodus 11:7; Job 30:1; Isaiah 56:10). There were many wild dogs (as well as tame ones) in Palestine; voracious creatures, they traveled *en masse* devouring the filth of the streets as they went (Psalm 59:14-15); and they even consumed corpses (I Kings 14:11; 16:4; 21:19, 23). A rather jackal-like creature with a wolf-like tail, the untamed dog was not pleasant company (the Israelites did not pet even the tamed dog), though he could be scared off rather easily as a rule. It was an insult to be called a dog (II Samuel 16:9).
Donkey (Ass)	The *donkey* or ass is mentioned over one hundred times in the Bible. Even to this day it is one of the most commonly seen animals in Palestine, indeed in all of the Bible lands. Passages which refer to the ass are Exodus 13:13; 20:17; 21:33; Isaiah 1:3; 30:24, etc. Generally speaking, donkeys have been more plentiful than horses in the Bible lands. They are sure-footed and easily cared for. Land owners usually possessed a number of them. It should not be overlooked that Jesus rode a donkey at the Triumphal Entry. (Mark 11:2f).
Dromedary	The *dromedary* is a camel with one hump. (See Camel above.)
Fish	*Fish* and fishing are mentioned in the Bible, but specific kinds or species are not generally indicated. Jesus must have respected fishermen for He chose men from the trade to be among His disciples. The fish was the symbol of early Christians; known as the ICHTUS (Greek for fish), the letters of that word stood for JESUS CHRIST, SON OF GOD, SAVIOR. Jewish law forbade eating some kinds of fish including certain mollusk forms or shellfish. On the other hand, "ceremonially clean" fish was a regular part of the diet of Jews (Matthew 7:10; 14:19ff; John 21:9). The Dead Sea can sustain no fish (the Jordan's fish die upon reaching the Dead Sea), but the Mediterranean and Lake Galilee continue to provide fish as in Bible times.
Flea	The *flea* is common in the Middle East and is a plague to both man and beast. It inflicts an irritating bite which usually causes swelling and itching. David compares himself to a flea in I Samuel 24:14. The flea is also mentioned in I Samuel 26:20, though this may not be a correct translation.
Fly	*Flies* are not referred to frequently in the Old Testament (instances: Ecclesiastes 10:1 and Isaiah 7:18). However, they are ever present in the Near and Middle East as anyone knows who has

traveled there. One of the plagues (Exodus 8:21f) was flies or some type of insect (the Hebrew is not specific here). In Bible lands flies are the carriers of eye disease and are frequently seen resting on the corners of the human eye.

Fox   Two species of *fox* lived in Palestine, a larger and a smaller. Nehemiah 4:3; Song of Solomon 2:15; Lamentations 5:18; Ezekiel 13:4; Luke 9:58; 13:32; Matthew 8:20 are examples of references to the fox in the Bible. Foxes are thought of as tricky. Jesus called one of the Herods (Herod Antipas) a fox (Luke 13:32).

Frog   *Frogs* are rarely mentioned in the Bible. The plague of frogs in Egypt—the second plague—is referred to in Exodus 8:1-15 (also in Psalms 78 and 105). The frog is mentioned once in the New Testament (Revelation 16:13) as a symbol of impurity.

Gazelle   There are several species of *gazelle* in Palestine and they are frequently hunted. It was considered meat for eating (Deuteronomy 12:15, 22). A graceful creature, its name was sometimes given to Jewish girls, as seen in the story in Acts 9:36ff (*Tabitha* is Aramaic and *Dorcas* Greek for Gazelle). Its grace coupled with its agile ways, make it a lovely figure of speech (Proverbs 5:19; Song of Solomon 2:9, 17; etc.).

Gazelle

Goat   The *goat* is referred to many times in the Bible (e.g., Leviticus 1:10; Numbers 7:17, 23). It was used for a sacrifice (recall the "scapegoat"). Jesus mentions it in a parable (Matthew 25:31-46), and it is used as a figure of speech now and again in the Old Testament (Ezeikel 34:17; Daniel 8:5; etc.). Female goats produced milk from which cheese and butter were made, its meat was edible, and the skin could be used for making clothes or bottles.

(See Kid.)

Grasshopper   (See Locust.)

Hare   The *hare* is referred to only twice in the Bible (Leviticus 11:6 and Deuteronomy 14:7). It is called an unclean animal. There are a number of species in Palestine.

Hart (Stag)   Only remains of the bones of the *hart* exist today because it is now extinct in Palestine. It was perhaps something like the deer and its flesh could be eaten (Deuteronomy 14:5). It moved with lightning speed, and because of its beautiful and quick movements

Hart

it was a particularly appropriate figure of speech (e.g., Genesis 49:21; II Samuel 22:34; Proverbs 5:19; Isaiah 35:6). The most famous passage in the Scriptures on the hart is in Psalm 42.

Heifer The *heifer* is referred to now and again in the Old Testament. It was respected and used as a figure of speech (Jeremiah 46:20; Hosea 10:11). It was sometimes employed as a plow animal (Judges 14:18) and for other reasons, also for sacrificial purposes (Deuteronomy 21:3). The "red" heifer's ashes were used in purification rites (Numbers 19:2-22; 31:23).

Hornet Exodus 23:28; Deuteronomy 7:20; and Joshua 24:12 are the three passages in the Bible in which *hornets* are mentioned. It is said to have been sent as a kind of plague against the enemies of Israel. Hornets are plentiful in Palestine.

Horse The *horse* is mentioned in Scripture a great number of times (e.g., Genesis 41:43; 47:17; Revelation 9:7). It was a symbol of war because it was used to pull military chariots and was ridden in battle. The Bible writers say again and again that victory in battle will be due to God not horses; therefore, we do not read that the Jewish people used them nearly as much as their pagan neighbors. At the Triumphal Entry, Jesus did not ride on this symbol of war, but on the peaceful donkey. Most of the passages about the horse are in the Old Testament. It is, for example, mentioned in the story of Elijah's ascent to Heaven (II Kings 2:11). The book of Revelation refers to the horse (6:2-8; 9:16-19; 19:11-16; cp. the visions in Zechariah 1:8; 6:2-8), the book of James to the horse's bit (James 3:3); otherwise, the New Testament practically ignores this animal.

Hyena Common to Palestine, it is, however, rarely mentioned in the Bible. I Samuel 13:18 (the "valley of hyenas") is one of the rare references. Some think Jeremiah refers to the *hyena,* a carnivorous animal, in Jeremiah 12:9.

Jackal

Still seen in Palestine, it inhabits desert places particularly and is a carnivorous animal. Biblical references to *jackals* are frequently figurative as in Isaiah 13:22 and Psalm 44:19.

Kid

The *kid,* a young goat, is referred to many times in the Old Testament and was considered excellent meat, tender because of its youth. Kids were sometimes offered as sacrifices, even as Passover sacrifices, though the use of lambs was customary. Among the references to kids are Genesis 27:9; 37:31, and Isaiah 11:6. The latter is a Messianic passage.

(See Goat.)

Lamb

The *lamb* is referred to more or less frequently in the Bible and it appears in both the Old and New Testaments. The skipping lamb is a symbol of joy (Psalm 114:4, 6); gentleness and innocence are also symbolized by it (Isaiah 53:7). It was of course used in sacrifice; in fact, no Israelite festival took place without the offering of a lamb. Over one hundred lambs were used at the Feast of Tabernacles! Jesus Himself was called the Pascal Lamb. The picture of blood pouring forth from a lamb is still used to represent our Lord's redemptive work.

Leech

There appears to be only one passage in the Bible where the *leech* is referred to, Proverbs 30:15. Precisely what is meant by the leech here is difficult to say, but the implication of greediness is clear enough.

Leopard

This is a carnivorous animal which exists in Palestine in one area and another. *Leopards* are used figuratively in the Old Testament by the prophets (Jeremiah 13:23; Habakkuk 1:8; Isaiah 11:6, etc.). Daniel speaks of it in 7:6, and in the book of Revelation we have a leopard rising from the sea (Revelation 13:2).

Jackal

Hyena

| Leviathan | The meaning of the word *leviathan* varies. Job 41 and Psalm 74:14 probably have reference to the crocodile, while the leviathan of the sea in Psalm 104:26 may be the whale. There is an allusion to a mythological dragon in Isaiah 27:1. |

Leviathan
: The meaning of the word *leviathan* varies. Job 41 and Psalm 74:14 probably have reference to the crocodile, while the leviathan of the sea in Psalm 104:26 may be the whale. There is an allusion to a mythological dragon in Isaiah 27:1.

Lion
: The king of the beasts is mentioned over one hundred times. Today there are no *lions* in Palestine; but during Bible times there were a good many, and they were rightly considered dangerous. Samson is said to have torn a lion (see Judges 14:5, 6); David defended his flock from the lion (I Samuel 17:34); and the prophet Amos refers to the beast (Amos 3:12). His malpractices, his roarings, his avaricious appetite, his hideouts are all referred to in the Holy Scriptures. The lion is compared to the Devil in I Peter 5:8 where Peter visualizes Satan as being like a lion who prowls and roars seeking whom he may devour. The lion is frequently used as a metaphor in the Bible (Ezekiel 1:10; Daniel 7:4; Hosea 5:14; Revelation 4:7). The expression "Lion of the tribe of Judah" is in reference to Christ (see Revelation 5:5 and compare Genesis 49:9).

Lizard
: Nowhere in the New Testament do we find the *lizard* mentioned. However, in the Old we have reference to the "great lizard" (Leviticus 11:29). Leviticus 11:30 and Proverbs 30:28 may also be references to it.

Locust (Grasshopper)
: *Locusts* or grasshoppers are found in the Scriptures many times. Its presence is common in Palestine. The coming of locusts *en masse* is said to be the judgment of God (Deuteronomy 28:38). Then as now, these insects formed clouds heavy enough to cover the sun. In thirty minutes they were capable of stripping trees and crops of all fruitage and foliage. It is no wonder Joel likens an invading army to grasshoppers (Joel 2:1f). Some species were and are used for eating and in cooking.

Mosquito
: There are only two passages in the Bible that refer to *mosquitos*, Exodus 8:16-19 and Psalm 105:31. Some scholars have the idea that in the Exodus passage "mosquitoes" ought to be translated "lice," but apparently the majority of translators prefer the term "mosquito." Aaron illicited the third plague by striking the dust; the dust particles were translated into mosquitoes which pestered both human beings and animals in the land of Egypt (Exodus 8:16-19).

Moth
: The East is no stranger to *moths*. Its damage to cloth and materials of many kinds is frequent. The Old Testament uses the moth as an analogy (Job 4:19; Psalm 39:11; Hosea 5:12, etc.). The New Testament admonishes, "Do not lay up for yourselves treasures on earth, where moth and rust consume and where thieves break in and steal, but lay up for yourselves treasures in heaven,

where neither moth nor rust consumes and where thieves do not break in and steel" (Matthew 6:19-20). See also Luke 12:33 and James 5:2.

Mouse

The words *mouse, rats, mice* come from the same Hebrew word. In the Scriptures they are considered unclean animals (Leviticus 11:29; see Isaiah 66:17 where the author cries out against pagan rites involving the eating of mice). In I Samuel 5:6 and 6:4 we read about an epidemic of mice striking the Philistines which may have been bubonic plague. The collapse of Sennacherib's army (II Kings 19:35 and Isaiah 37:26) was possibly the result of a plague brought by vast numbers of mice (the historian Herodotus believed rodents the cause of the army's downfall).

Mule

There are a number of references to *mules* in the Old Testament (e.g., I Kings 18:5; Ezra 2:66; Psalm 32:9; Zechariah 14:15). Mules were used for military purposes and also as beasts of burden. The story of Absalom's death while riding a mule will be recalled (II Samuel 18:9). It is thought these animals were not original to Palestine but bred in other countries and imported.

Pig

Pork was not allowed for meat eating purposes by the Jewish nation. In 1962 new laws against raising pigs were passed in Israel. Jesus tells the story of the prodigal son and has the poor young man, at the end of himself, feeding swine. Jesus uses swine or the *pig* here for a very special reason, to show that the prodigal was in fact in a most miserable and impure situation. Foreign cults used the pig for ritual purposes (Isaiah 66:17), and this may have been one reason it was considered unclean, though of course pork spoils readily in warm weather without refrigeration and is often a carrier of parasites. Herds of pigs are mentioned in Matthew 8:30; Mark 5:11; Luke 8:32; 15:15. Jesus used a strong statement when He said, "Do not cast your pearls before swine" (Matthew 7:6). It is of further interest that the Mohammedans as well as the Jews do not permit the use of pork.

Ram

The *ram* was used as an animal of sacrifice, particularly the sacrifice of atonement (Leviticus 5:15 and other passages). Trumpets were made from rams' horns (Leviticus 25:9; Joshua 6:4). In Daniel the Medes and the Persians are compared to the ram (Daniel 8:3-4, 20).

Rat

(See Mouse.)

Scorpion

The *scorpion* is used both literally and figuratively in the Bible. There are several species, some of which are found in Palestine, others in adjoining countries. The scorpion is equipped

Scorpion

to sting animals and human beings; the sting is painful, though, contrary to popular opinion, seldom fatal. Deuteronomy 8:15 and Ezekiel 2:6 are among the few Old Testament references to the scorpion. In the New Testament Jesus refers to it in Luke 10:19 and 11:12. It is also mentioned in Revelation 9:3, 5, 10. The area southwest of the Dead Sea is called the "Ascent of the Scorpions."

Serpent The *serpent* or snake is used both figuratively and literally in the Bible. One or two species such as the asp or cobra and the horned viper are referred to, but generally speaking, the serpent is mentioned without reference to specific type. Its characteristics are seen as analogous to character traits of the human being or the Devil. They are deceptive, dragon-like, crawling, poisonous, cunning. The brazen serpent (II Kings 18:4) was a kind of symbol. Moses' rod became a serpent (Exodus 7:9). (See Viper.)

Sheep *Sheep* are frequently referred to in the Scriptures. They are used as metaphors in a great many passages, perhaps the Twenty-Third Psalm being the most famous. The sheep was considered of great value to the native Palestinian because it produced so many things: meat, milk, skins, and wool. The tail, weighing up to fifteen or twenty pounds, was considered a delicacy. Deuteronomy 32:14; Isaiah 7:21; I Samuel 25:18; Amos 6:4; Proverbs 27:26 are a few of the many references to sheep. Sheep have always been raised in Palestine.

Spider Isaiah 59:5 and Job 8:14 make reference to the spider's web as a figure of speech. The translation of Proverbs 30:28 varies, but some versions use the word *spider*. Aside from these references, no mention is made of this organism in the Bible, though it exists in many species in Bible lands.

Viper There are several species of *viper* in the Palestinian area, although the Greek word translated viper usually covers all poisonous snakes. Acts 28:3-6 records the incident of Paul's encounter with a viper on the island of Malta. Jesus called the Scribes and Pharisees "a generation of vipers" (Matthew 12:34; 23:33). (See Serpent.)

Wolf The *wolf* has been and still is plentiful in Palestine. Shepherds hate the animal because of its ferocity. Frequently used as a figure of speech in the Bible, Isaiah spoke of the Messianic day when the wolf and the lamb would live together (Isaiah 11:6; 65:25). Jesus refers several times to wolves (Matthew 7:15; 10:16; Luke 10:3; John 10:12). St. Paul in his famous address to the Ephesian elders makes it clear that there will be "wolves" who will try to snatch the members of the Church from the fold (Acts 20:29).

Worm Usually when the term *worm* is used in the Bible it has reference to larvae, of one and another kind of insect, which eat away at food, foliage, diseased areas of the human body, and corpses. Acts 12:23 is a case in point.

BIRDS

The Bible makes many references to birds. One obvious reason is that Palestine itself is rich in birds. The Bible frequently uses them as figures of speech (the eagle, the sparrow, etc.). It is difficult, however, to identify with certainty some of the birds of the Bible.

The *bittern* may be referred to in Isaiah 14:23; 34:11; and **Bittern** Zephaniah 2:14. It belongs to the same family as the heron and the egret and lives in marshy regions. It is distinguished by its mournful call usually heard only at night. When angry the bittern ruffles its neck feathers and extends its plumage.

The *cock* and the *hen* are mentioned several times in the New **Cock** Testament. Matthew 26:34, 74-75 is in reference to Peter's denial of Christ. Cocks were bred in ancient times to serve as alarm clocks (thus the cock became a symbol of watchfulness), and by Jesus' day eggs were used as food in Palestine (Luke 11:12). Mark 13:35 mentions the "cockcrow" which was the third watch of the night (midnight to three a.m.). Jesus' concern for Jerusalem is compared to a hen's care for her chicks (Luke 13:34; Matthew 23:37).

The *cormorant* is listed among the impure birds in Leviticus **Cormorant** 11:17 and Deuteronomy 14:17. A large web-footed bird, it is commonly seen along the Jordan River and the Sea of Galilee. It lives on fish.

There is some uncertainty as to the exact meaning of the word **Crane** translated *"crane"* in the King James Version (Isaiah 38:14; Jeremiah 8:7). At any rate, the crane is a tall wading bird which migrates to Palestine and southern countries in the winter. It is similar to the white stork.

Dove is the poetic term for pigeon, and doves are referred to **Dove** instead of pigeons in the Bible. There are several species in Palestine. It was used as a sacrifice for purposes of purification. Since they were less expensive than animals, the Law provided that poorer people could substitute two doves in certain instances. It is interesting that the parents of Jesus were among those who used doves instead of animals (Luke 2:24). One of the most famous statements about the dove is, ". . . Be wise as serpents and innocent as doves" (Matthew 10:16). In the Christian religion the dove has been used by artists as a symbol for many things—for peace, for hope, for the Holy Spirit (because at Jesus' baptism

Heron

Hoopoe

Kite

Osprey

Eagle

a dove appeared, Matthew 3:16; Mark 1:10; Luke 3:22; John 1:32).

The *eagle* is referred to a number of times in the Holy Scriptures. There are several species in the Palestinian area. The meat of the eagle was not allowed for eating according to the Jewish Law. It lends itself as a figure of speech because of its grace in flight, its creativity in protecting and feeding itself, and its skill in caring for the young. Ezekiel and Revelation both include references to the eagle (Ezekiel 1:10 and Revelation 4:7). Christian artists have used it in sculpture and painting as a symbol (for St. John the Evangelist, etc.).

Gull

The *sea gull* is considered one of the unclean birds according to Leviticus 11:16. Deuteronomy 14:15 may refer to the gull. It is a web-footed creature that can be seen on the shores of Lake Galilee as well as the Mediterranean.

Hawk

Three references to the *hawk* are to be found in the Old Testament (Leviticus 11:16; Deuteronomy 14:15; Job 39:26). Some scholars believe that another bird—perhaps the falcon—is referred to in the Hebrew. This is a bird of prey and its flesh was forbidden by the Law. It is frequently seen in Palestine.

Hen

(See Cock.)

Heron

It is not known for certain that the Hebrew word frequently translated *heron* is in fact in reference to the heron. But the heron may be the bird of Leviticus 11:19 and Deuteronomy 14:18. It lives in marshes and looks something like a stork. It may be seen along the shores of Lake Galilee.

Hoopoe

The *hoopoe* is mentioned in Leviticus 11:19 and Deuteronomy 14:18. This bird has a long curved beak, and on its head there is a crest which can spread out like a fan. It is seen in Palestine in spring and summer.

Kite

It is not known for certain whether the *kite* is referred to in the original Hebrew, but Deuteronomy 14:13 is thought by some scholars to be a reference. Job 28:7 may also refer to the kite. There are several species in Palestine (black and red species are

Partridge

Quail

Raven

common), and they are said to have extraordinarily sharp vision.

Osprey While translators are not certain that the *osprey* is referred to in the Old Testament, some think that in Leviticus 11:13-19 and Deuteronomy 14:12-18 there are references to this bird. It is a bird of prey, has a hooked beak, is rather large, and has a sizeable wing spread. It is sometimes known as a "fishing eagle." It is not too common in Palestine.

Ostrich The *ostrich* existed in greater quantity in Bible times than today. It is referred to a number of times in Scripture (Job 30:29; Isaiah 13:21; Jeremiah 50:39; Micah 1:8, etc.). The ostrich is used as a figure of speech now and again. A large bird, it can run at high speeds. The eating of its flesh was forbidden (Deuteronomy 14:15).

Owl The *owl* is referred to now and again in the Holy Scriptures. It is probably one of the unclean birds, though there are translation difficulties in the Leviticus 11 and Deuteronomy 14 passages. The owl definitely lives in Palestine and builds its nest in areas near villages, preferably in olive trees. There are several species of owls in the Holy Land—the "great owl" and the "little owl," for example.

Partridge The *partridge* is a common bird in Palestine but is referred to only twice in the Scriptures (I Samuel 26:20 and Jeremiah 17:11). Certain species breed in the mountains. Some kinds are smaller than others and they vary in color. Partridges are seen in deserts and near the Dead Sea.

Peacock The *peacock* is referred to, in connection with Solomon who imported it from Ceylon or India, in I Kings 10:22 and II Chronicles 9:21. No other place in the Bible makes mention of this bird.

Pelican *Pelicans* are seen frequently in Palestine, especially along Lake Galilee where they fly in large flocks. Whether or not it is definitely referred to in the original Hebrew is a matter of debate among scholars. Possibly it is mentioned in Leviticus 11:18; Deuteronomy 14:17; Psalm 102:6; Isaiah 34:11; and Zephaniah 2:14.

Quail It will be recalled that the Israelites fed upon *quail* (Exodus 16:13; Numbers 11:31-33, etc.). The quail is in fact a very edible creature, though it must be consumed in moderation. Its migratory pattern is most interesting: Making its exit from Europe in the fall, it proceeds to the Mediterranean area, and thence to Africa where it settles until spring. In flight it is sometimes carried along by the wind and usually flies at low altitude in large flocks.

Raven The *raven* is referred to on a number of occasions in the Holy Scriptures. In Luke 12:24 Jesus said, "Consider the ravens: they neither sow nor reap. . . ." In Song of Solomon 5:11 the raven is referred to, and of course in the story of the prophet Elijah by the Brook Cherith we have faithful ravens supplying him food. (See picture of the Brook Cherith, Chapter IV.) There is also mention of it in the flood story (Genesis 8:7). The raven is black, is sometimes a bit on the mean side, and lives in lonely areas. It feeds on a variety of things and even eats the eyes of the dead and of living young animals.

Sparrow In the Bible, *sparrow* sometimes refers to the larger family of birds which includes all of the so called passerines (sparrow-like birds—robins, finches, etc.), but usually the sparrow as such is intended. Jesus Himself refers to the sparrow (or sparrow-like birds) in the classic verse, "Fear not, therefore; you are of more value than many sparrows" (Matthew 10:29, 31; Luke 12:6, 7). Psalms 84:3; Proverbs 26:2.

Stork The Hebrew word for *stork* means "pious" or "kind." This no doubt comes from the fact that it is extraordinarily kind to its young. According to the Jewish Law the stork could not be eaten. In a few passages the stork is mentioned (Leviticus 11:19; Deuteronomy 14:18; Psalm 104:17; Jeremiah 8:7; Zechariah 5:9). There are at least two species of storks; one, interestingly enough, is a wild black bird; the other is the familiar white creature which may be seen going north along the Jordan Valley in March and April.

Swallow It is not known for certain whether the Hebrew refers to the *swallow;* but frequently four passages in the Old Testament have been translated by the term swallow (Psalm 84:3; Proverbs 26:2; Isaiah 38:14; Jeremiah 8:7). The swallow is well known to the people of the Holy Land.

Vulture The *vulture* is a rather large bird of prey. It is sometimes compared with the eagle (Matthew 24:28 is translated both "eagles" and "vultures"). It is known to the people of the Holy Land, and Job 39:27 is very likely an authentic reference to the vulture, though the R.S.V. translation is "eagles."

G. TIME, MEASURES, WEIGHTS, AND MONEY

TIME

The Jews counted their days from one sunset to the other, thus **Day** making the advent of darkness the beginning of a new *day*. Even to this day Jewish holy days, including the Sabbath, begin at nightfall. Naturally there was the more colloquial use of the term "day," which referred generally to that twelve-hour period when the sun is up. (See Week.)

The *days of the week* possessed no particular names among the ancient Jews except for the Sabbath (sundown Friday to sundown Saturday). They did use a term called "the day of preparation" which was the day just before the Sabbath.

The Bible frequently refers to the term *evening* and appar- **Evening** ently this was a significant time of day for Jews and their families. Jewish sacrifices and special days frequently took place at evening. It was a time of worship and a period when the family could be together as a unit. It was also the period of the "cool of the day" when the soft breezes arose and during the hot summer months provided the relief for which every resident of Palestine and the Near and Middle East thirsted.

In the Old Testament the term *hour* does not appear to have **Hour** reference to a specific duration of time as it does in modern thinking. As a matter of fact, the term is used only five times in the Old Testament, each time in the book of Daniel (Daniel 3:6, 15; 4:19, 33; 5:5). In the New Testament the term is used many times but with a quite different meaning; whereas in the Old Testament the term refers not to a specific segment of time, in the New Testament it frequently refers to one of the twelve hours in the day (John 11:9). The Babylonians were the first to divide the day into twelve hours. The Greek and Roman civilizations followed the twelve hour scheme and thus it came to be employed by the New Testament writers. The third hour of the day was considered to be approximately 9:00 in the morning, the sixth hour noon, the ninth hour 3:00, etc. Numerous references to the hours of the day are found in the New Testament: Mark 15:25, where it indicates that Jesus was crucified at the third hour; Acts 10:30, where the text reads that Cornelius was praying at the ninth hour; etc. It is of further interest that the length of the hours in the New Testament times varied from 49 to 71 minutes.* The reason for this is obvious. The days are longer

---

* W. Corswant, *A Dictionary of Life in Bible Times*. London: Hodder and Stoughton, 1960, p. 149. Data used in section G based on Corswant.

or shorter according to the season; and each day was divided into twelve parts from sunup to sundown.

Month

Jews divided their calendar into twelve months very much as we do in modern times. Each *month* began with the appearance of the new moon and consisted of 29/30 days, depending upon the length of each lunar cycle. Occasionally it was necessary to add a thirteenth month since the solar year contains about eleven more days than the lunar year. For many centuries the Jews have used the Babylonian calendar for naming their months.

MONTHS OF THE YEAR

Jewish Term	*English Term*
1. Nisan	March-April
2. Iyyar	April-May
3. Sivan	May-June
4. Tammuz	June-July
5. Abh	July-August
6. Elul	August-September
7. Tishri	September-October
8. Marhesvan	October-November
9. Kislev	November-December
10. Tebet	December-January
11. Sebat	January-February
12. Adar	February-March
Ve'adar	Intercalary month

Night Watch

In the Old Testament the *night* was divided into three *watches* of four hours each: the "first watch" (Lamentations 2:19); the "middle watch" (Judges 7:19); and the "morning watch" (I Samuel 11:11). Psalm 63:6 refers to the "watches of the night." In the New Testament the length of the watches followed the Roman pattern, so that the night was divided into four watches of three hours each. Thus we have the evening watch, the midnight watch, the cockcrow watch, and the morning watch, all of which are mentioned in Mark 13:35.

Seasons

The year in Palestine is divided into two great *seasons*, the warm season and the wet. The warm season or summer lasts from the middle of May to the middle of October and provides the necessary sunshine for the harvesting of crops. The wet season lasts the remaining six months of the year.

Sundial

The *sundial* is referred to twice in the Old Testament, II Kings 20:11 and Isaiah 38:8. No precise description of this time-telling device is given us, but in the Isaiah passage the "steps of Ahaz" are referred to in terms of the position of the shadows on the steps, which apparently served as a method of telling time.

Time

Generally, exact ideas of *time* were not held by the Hebrew people as by modern man. Time was a very general thing, frequently a state of being more than real chronology (e.g., a man was evidently said to be forty years of age as long as he was in the full vigor of mature life). For generalized use of numbers see Judges 3:11; 4:3, etc. At other times in the Bible, time indications were more specific ("But on the first day of the week . . . they found the stone rolled away . . ." [Luke 24:1-2]). The Greeks and Romans were more exact in time keeping than the Hebrews.

Week

The days of the *week* were unnamed in the ancient Jewish economy save for the expression "first day," "second day," "third day," etc. In all probability the Jews followed a seven-day week pattern, though some have suggested, a ten-day week. Doubtlessly the phases of the moon determined this, but there have been suggested theological reasons for this, too, such as the sacredness of the number seven in Jewish thought and the Genesis account of creation in six days with rest on the seventh.

Year

The new *year* in the Jewish calendar begins in the autumn, the first day of their month being Tishri (Tisri), which corresponds generally to the period from the middle of September to the middle of October. The ancient Hebrew year may have had 354 days as over against our 365. The eleven days differential made it necessary for a thirteenth month to be added every two or three years (see above under "month"). This was eventually changed so that only twelve months were observed every year.

MEASURES

Generally speaking, units of measure in the Jewish literature of ancient times is only approximate. The human anatomy constituted a basis for measures and the *fingerbreadth* was considered the smallest measure, about three-fourths of an inch. Put four fingerbreadths together and we have a *handbreadth* or palm which equaled about three inches. The *span* was another unit of measure and this was the hand opened wide, the measure between the thumb and the little finger constituting a unit. This was equal to about nine inches. The span is mentioned in such places as Exodus 28:16 and Isaiah 40:12 (poetic use of the term). The *cubit* was still another unit and was arrived at by measuring the length of the area between the elbow and the tip of the middle finger. Naturally this varies in size between persons and this accounts for the fact that the "ordinary" cubit was about eighteen inches

Fingerbreadth

Handbreadth

Span

Cubit

and the "great" cubit about twenty-one inches. The cubit is mentioned in II Chronicles 3:3 and elsewhere in the Old Testament, and in the New Testament in Matthew 6:27, Luke 12:25, John 21:8, and Revelation 21:17.

Bath

A *bath* was equal to 6.073 gallons. It is a term used to measure liquids such as water, wine, or oil. The bath corresponds generally to the dry measure unit called the ephah.

Cor

The *cor* is a unit for measuring both liquid and dry measure. It is equal to about six and one-half bushels of dry measure or slightly under sixty-one gallons of liquid. Wheat and flour were counted by cors in the Old Testament (I Kings 4:22; 5:11).

Ephah

The *ephah* is equal to three seahs or 20.878 quarts. It was an ordinary measure for dry or solid materials. (Cp. "Bath" above.)

Fathom

This, of course, is a measure of depth (Acts 27:28) and was approximately six feet. It was supposed to be equal to the span of two arms stretched out and was a Roman unit of measure.

Furlong

A *furlong* was approximately 606 feet, though it varied somewhat. The New Testament uses the term several times, for example Luke 24:13, John 6:19, Revelation 14:20. The Greek term for furlong is *stadion* from which we get the word stadium. Foot races were run in the stadium and the track itself was sometimes called the "stadion."

Hin

The *hin* is a measure used by ancient Jews to denote liquid capacity, and was the equivalent of about one gallon. It is referred to in such passages as Exodus 29:40, Numbers 15:4, Ezekiel 4:11.

Homer

The *homer* is supposedly equal to what a donkey could carry and that amounted to approximately six and one-half bushels. It is also equal to the cor.

Kab

The *kab* was equal to four logs or 1.349 quarts. It is mentioned only in II Kings 6:25 in connection with a famine.

Line

There is apparently no precise length that can be assigned to the *line* of the Old Testament. This was, of course, a string or rope-like device for measuring; but sometimes it was also employed to determine to what extent an area was level. Lot lines are suggested or referred to in the Bible (Psalm 16:6 may be a reference to lot lines).

Log

In Old Testament times, while solid measures were not always precise and consistent, generally speaking the *log* was equal to about sixty-seven percent of a pint. Leviticus 14:10.

Mile

The *mile* was about 4,879 feet. It comes from the word *mille* meaning one thousand (double) steps, and was used by the Romans as a measure of road lengths—"milestone." It was supposed to be equal to eight furlongs.

The Jewish Law permitted only a limited amount of travel on the Sabbath Day and that was approximately one-half to three-fourths of a mile. Acts 1:12.

Sabbath Day's Journey

The *seah* is a measure for dry or solid materials only, such as flour or grain (see Genesis 18:6 and I Samuel 25:18). It equals one gallon and five pints.

Seah

This unit of measure is still used in Syria today and is supposed to be equal to the amount of ground a pair of oxen yoked together can plow in a single day.

Yoke

WEIGHTS

The *mina* was equal to fifty shekels or about twenty ounces. Minas are mentioned in the Old Testament (e.g. Ezekiel 45:12). It is Summarian in origin and was a weight employed to measure particular kinds of merchandise, especially valuable metals which, at least on some occasions, were used for money. The mina later came to be considered a unit of money.

Mina

The only weight mentioned in the New Testament is the Roman *pound* (John 12:3; 19:39). It was equal to .72 pounds or eleven and one-half ounces.

Pound

We usually think of the shekel as denoting money, but in the first instance the Hebrew word from which we get *shekel* indicated the *weighing* of money (*saqal*—"to weigh"). Thus, prior to the time of coinage, merchandise was bought and sold by the sheer weight of gold and silver (that is, a quantity of it). Apparently the Israelitish scheme for weights was derived from the Babylonian in which, according to Corswant, *A Dictionary of Life in Bible Times,* "each weight was sixty times greater than the preceding one" (p. 296). As a weight the shekel was equal to about 0.4 ounces.

Shekel

The Hebrew *talent* was derived from the Babylonian talent and originally denoted a measure of weight, though later it came to be a unit of money. It was equal to 75.558 pounds. In the New Testament it is related to Greek money units. (See under Money.)

Talent

MONEY

The Jews have not always purchased with coins. The earliest method was apparently primitive bartering; after that silver or gold was weighed out in terms of shekels (see "shekels" above). Not until after the Exile did the Jews have coinage. After the second century B.C. the Jews made their own coins. Up to that time they used the coins of foreign countries (of Phoenicia and

Rome, e.g.). When they did make their own coins they did not put the faces of rulers or kings upon them, but symbols close to their own hearts such as an ear of corn, a bunch of grapes, or a candle. Inscriptions were also included on the coins and these referred frequently to Israel's deliverance.

Even after coinage, money was sometimes weighed out as well as counted because the coins did not always weigh the same.

Daric (Dram)

The *daric* (or dram) (Ezra 2:69; 8:27, etc.) is perhaps the oldest type of coinage employed in the Old Testament. It was gold and was initiated by Darius I. The King's picture was on the face of the coin.

Denarius

The *denarius* was a Roman unit and was used commonly in silver in Palestine beginning about the first century B.C. It was worth approximately sixteen cents, just about what an ordinary laborer would earn in a day (Matthew 20:2). The denarius is mentioned in Matthew 22:19 and Luke 10:35, among other places, though it is translated "penny" in the King James Version.

Didrachmon (Didrachma)

The *didrachmon* was a silver coin and was Greek. It is mentioned in the New Testament (Matthew 17:24) and was valued at approximately thirty-two cents or equivalent to the Jewish half-shekel (silver). This was the amount of money every Jew was taxed annually for Temple upkeep.

Drachme (Drachma)

This was a Greek silver coin common in ancient times. The *drachme* is referred to by the historian Luke (Luke 15:8-9). It was worth approximately the same as a denarius or about sixteen cents.

Dram

(See *Daric.*)

Farthing

The Jewish lepton, translated "mite" or *"farthing,"* was worth one-eighth of a cent. A farthing would purchase two sparrows (Matthew 10:29; Luke 12:6).

Lepton

(See *Mite.*)

Mina

Of Summarian origin, the *mina* (mna) was at first a unit of weight but later came to be a unit of money like the talent. It appeared in either gold or silver and was valued at about sixteen dollars. The word translated "pound" in I Kings 10:17, Luke 19:11-28, etc. appears to refer to the mina.

Mite (Lepton)

The *mite* (lepton) was a bronze Jewish coin. It was the smallest unit of money used at the time of Jesus and was worth about one-eighth of a cent. Mark 12:42.

Quadrans

A small, bronze, Roman coin, the *quadrans* was worth about one-fourth of a penny. Possible references are Matthew 5:26 and Mark 12:42.

Shekel

Originally a unit of weight in ancient Israel, the *shekel* was later used as money. References are made to half-shekels, quarter-shekels, and one-twentieth-shekels. We do not know its exact value, but silver shekels were thought to have been equal in value to one-fifteenth of a gold shekel. II Samuel 14:26; Ezekiel 45:12; etc.

The *stater,* a Greek coin, is referred to in Matthew 17:27. It was equal to four drachmas and was also known as the Tetra-drachma. Its value is estimated at sixty-four cents. **Stater (Tetradrachma)**

Originally a unit of weight, the *talent* later became representative of a large sum of money. It came either in silver or gold. The value of the talent is difficult to estimate, but it was probably worth about $960. **Talent**

APPENDIX I

THUMBNAIL SKETCHES OF SIGNIFICANT PERSONALITIES IN CHURCH HISTORY

CHURCH HISTORY is divided into three periods:

Ancient: From the close of the New Testament to Gregory Great (590 A.D.).

Medieval: From Gregory Great to Martin Luther (1517).

Modern: From Luther and the Reformation to the present.

In these thumbnail sketches, selections have been made with these periods in view and with the following emphases:

In the Ancient period: The Church Fathers especially, those men who pioneered and in many cases established policy and doctrine.

In the Medieval period: Represented by those men who are remembered for their devotion to Christ, interest in learning, or practical leadership.

In the Modern period: Represented particularly by the Protestant Reformers and prominent leaders or founders of Christian movements and denominations.

In selecting the men to be sketched, the needs of the laymen have been kept in view; in other words, the more obscure figures have been excluded. In no sense is this a definitive listing. No living person has been sketched. Nor are there representatives of the modern cults (Mary Baker Eddy, Charles Taze Russell).

In keeping with the purposes of the *Handbook of the Bible,* a number of the men who figure in the history of Biblical scholarship and translation (Jerome, Wyclif, Coverdale, Erasmus) have been included. All are listed in alphabetical order.

à Kempis, Thomas

(See Thomas à Kempis.)

Abelard, Peter
(1079-1142)

The Frenchman who put reason before faith ("I understand in order to believe") and is contrasted to Anselm who put faith before reason ("I believe in order to understand.") A zealous, hot-headed, impetuous philosopher, he was frequently condemned by his peers for his belief. His works include some hymns, and *Sic et Non* ("Yes and No" or "Pros and Cons") in which he quoted contradictory statements of the Church Fathers with no attempt to reconcile them. Doubting, said Abelard, makes one inquire and so leads to the truth.

Albright, Jacob
(1759-1808)

Founder of the Evangelical Church which was an offshoot of Methodism, Albright established his denomination for the express purpose of evangelical leadership among the Germans in America. The Evangelical Church has now merged with the United Brethren to form the Evangelical United Brethren denomination. (See Philip Otterbein.)

Ambrose
(c.339-397)

Ambrose was appointed governor in Northern Italy with his residence at Milan. The Bishop in that city died. Factions arose over theology and Ambrose went to settle the dispute when a child cried, "Ambrose, the Bishop." The people joined in the clamour and eight days later he was consecrated Bishop, having been baptized in the meantime. He gave himself to the study of theology and was made a "Doctor" of the Church. Interested in music, he apparently had a part in developing the chant now known as "Ambrosian." The great Augustine was converted under his stirring preaching.

Amman, Jacob

The organizer of the Amish Brethren for whom the group is named, Jacob Amman, was an Alsatian Mennonite of the late seventeenth century. Amman represented the strictest expression of the Mennonites, believing that non-conformists should be dismissed from Church membership (I Corinthians 5:9-11). Today there are several Amish groups in America. Two groups are well known, the Conservative Amish Mennonite Church and the Old Order Amish Mennonite Church. They are characterized by their plain clothing, "Pennsylvania Dutch," and opposition to higher education, telephones, cars, etc.

Andrewes, Lancelot
(1555-1626)

A prominent clergyman appointed (1607) to help make the Authorized Version of the Bible (1611). His area of translation included the Pentateuch and Joshua through I Chronicles. Andrewes stands out as a preacher and bishop too. He wrote against the Roman Catholic Church and his ninety-six sermons are outstanding, also his prayers which have been published in our own day.

St. Anselm was born in northern Italy. From his mother he acquired an interest in religion and at twenty-seven he entered a monastery of the Benedictine Order, the Abbey of Bec in Normandy.

Anselm
(1033-1109)

On September 5, 1093, Anselm was made Archbishop of Canterbury, England. Called to this high office, he spent himself in the service of God laboring for the welfare of others, the advancement of learning, and the proper recognition of the Church. In his writings he dealt with the nature and existence of God (God could be proved by reason), and the Incarnation and atonement. (See also Abelard.)

He is remembered primarily for one thing, the false doctrine named for him called "Arianism." He believed that because Christ is the Son of God, He must have been younger than the Father and was a creature rather than a divinity. Only God the Father is eternal, he said. Controversy over this doctrine was a major factor in causing Constantine to call the first ecumenical council in Church history at Nicaea in 325. The council condemned the view of Arius and formulated a statement of Christian belief which became the basis for the Nicene Creed.

Arius
(c.250-c.366)

Founder of the Dutch reformed movement in Protestant theology known as Arminianism, he was born in Holland and preached and taught there. John Wesley preached the free salvation Arminius taught. Arminius opposed Calvinistic predestination, against which he advanced the doctrine of free will. His complete *Works* have been published in the twentieth century.

Arminius, Jacobus
(1560-1609)

Born in England, he was appointed Wesley's "general assistant" in America. At the historic Christmas Conference of 1784, the Methodist Episcopal Church in America was formed; Asbury and Thomas Coke were elected joint superintendents. He preached some 16,500 sermons, traveled on horseback about 6,000 miles each year, and presided over 224 annual conferences. His salary was $64 per year, he had no place to call home, and was never married. He ended his American ministry with 695 preachers and 214,235 members, and has been called the "Father of American Methodism."

Asbury, Francis
(1745-1816)

Athanasius, a great defender of the faith against Arianism (which limited Christ), has been labeled the "Father of Orthodoxy." Much of his life was spent escaping those who wished to do away with him. He forcefully backed the orthodox creed at the Council of Nicaea (325 A.D.). The redemption and salvation

Athanasius, Bishop
of Alexandria
(c.296-c.373)

of man, said Athanasius, demanded that God had not only revealed Himself to man through Christ, but had become man in Christ. This was very much the New Testament viewpoint. He dealt with the relationship of God to the creation and the universe: God is Creator, Ruler, and Sustainer. His *On the Incarnation of the Divine Word* is a classic.

Augustine of Hippo (354-430) Bishop of Hippo in Africa and one of the "Doctors" of the ancient Church, he was perhaps the first since St. Paul to state clearly the doctrine of free grace (forgiveness is the free gift of God). He knew this truth not only from the Bible but from experience as well, for he had been saved out of an exceedingly sinful life. He believed he had nothing to do with his salvation, that it was all of God. The prayers of his mother Monica, the preaching of Ambrose, and the reading of Romans (especially Romans 13:13) were God's instruments in his salvation. He believed in irresistible grace (predestination) and he opposed Pelagius whose belief was in the direction of man saving himself. His writings include *On the Trinity, The Confessions* (his spiritual pilgrimage), and the *City of God* (the Church is eternal).

Basil of Caesarea (c.330-379) Basil of Caesarea, sometimes called "the Great," was educated in Constantinople and Athens. Strongly drawn to monasticism he lived for a time as a monk. Even today, many of the monastic communities of the Eastern Orthodox Church use as a guide the rules he set up. A natural leader, he wrote extensively, improved the liturgy of the Church, was a pioneer in the monastic movement in Asia Minor, and fought Arianism (see Arius). Made bishop of Caesarea in Cappadocia, he founded near the town a huge institution which housed a monastery, hospital, elementary school, and a kind of hotel. (The institution was known as the "Basileum.") Welfare work was his special concern at Caesarea, and he, with his brother Gregory of Nyssa and Gregory Nazianzon, were known as the "Great Cappadocians."

Baxter, Richard (1615-1691) Richard Baxter was born in November of 1615. His education during younger years was primarily from illiterate drunken instructors. Three years of training at Wroxeter ended in his quitting at the age of nineteen, almost destitute of mathematical and physical science and ignorant of Hebrew and Greek. He later repented of his neglect of scholarship. He says, "As to myself, my faults are no disgrace to any university: for I was of none." But later he did have access to a great library and apparently took advantage of it. Baxter tried law as a profession but soon revived his original intention of becoming a minister of the Gospel. Baxter was ordained in 1638 and not long afterward became a nonconformist and was alienated from the Church of England. In 1647

Baxter was forced into retirement because of ill health. Upon his recovery in 1649 he continued to preach and was severely beaten and jailed many times for his views. His *The Reform Pastor* is a classic. When someone whispered of the good he had done by his books while Baxter was on his deathbed, he faintly answered, "I was but a pen, and what praise is due to a pen?"

He was sent to be reared in a monastery at age seven and was ordained deacon at nineteen and priest at thirty. A life-long thirst for knowledge is evidenced by his tireless study, teaching, and writing. His best known work is the *Ecclesiastical History of the English Nation,* and he is known as the "Father of English History." But he is also remembered for his translation of the Gospels and Psalms into Anglo-Saxon.

Bede ("The Venerable")
(c.673-735)

Famous minister of Plymouth Church (Congregational), Brooklyn, New York. A brilliant preacher and orator, he cried out against slavery and carried a considerable influence in political matters. He wrote numerous books including a life of Christ and sermons.

Beecher, Henry Ward
(1813-1887)

Benedict of Nursia gave his life to improve monastery life. Educated in the city of Rome, the serious-minded Benedict renounced the evils of the city and became a hermit. His fame for piety spread and about 529 he founded a new monastery on the hill of Monte Cassino, halfway between Rome and Naples, and remained there until his death. The regulations of this ideal monastic community were set forth by Benedict in the *Rule.* In the seventy-three chapters of the *Rule* Benedict dealt with such subjects as work, worship, study, and discipline.

Benedict of Nursia
(c.480-c.543)

In 1114 Bernard founded a new monastery in a wild valley called Wormwood, and the rude structure was given the name Clairvaux (clear valley). In his lifetime this Frenchman founded one hundred and sixty such monasteries where the discipline was rigid. Bernard was a preacher and leader in the Crusades and had great influence in the Church. His devotional meditations are still read and appreciated; his hymns—especially "Jesus, the Very Thought of Thee"—are still sung.

Bernard of Clairvaux
(1090-1153)

Beza was a French Protestant theologian converted from Roman Catholicism. His early life was not a model of purity, but a severe illness brought him to his senses. He sacrificed his fortune and devoted his life to the Reformed Church. He was a close friend and associate of Calvin in Geneva, and became his biographer and successor. Beza presented the famous Codex D, a Greek-Latin manuscript of the New Testament, to Cambridge University, and the Codex is named for him.

Beza, Theodore
(1519-1605)

Born in England, he is remembered in Church history as "the

Boniface (Winfrid)
(c.675-c.754)

apostle of Germany." His call to preach overseas was genuine, for though he was at first denied permission to go, he persisted and went to Rome where he was granted his wish to spread the gospel among the heathen tribes of Germany. He it was who sowed the seed of Christianity beyond the Rhine River. He made many converts, was a good organizer, and became the first archbishop of Mainz. He died a martyr's death.

Booth, William
(1829-1912)

The founder of the Salvation Army was born in England. He became one of the most important figures in the fight to bring assistance and salvation to the needy and destitute, not only in London, but the whole world. Educated by a private theological tutor of the Methodist Connexion Church, he began his ministry at the age of fifteen in the open air. He pursued evangelistic work and in 1865 founded in London an organization called "The Christian Mission for the Amelioration of the Condition of the Destitute and Vicious Population of the Eastern Portion of London." By 1878 the organization was known as "The Salvation Army." His daughter Evangeline was active and well known in Salvation Army work. His writings include *Salvation Soldiery* (1890), *In Darkest England and the Way Out* (1890), and *Religion for Every Day* (1902).

Brewster, William
(c.1560-1644)

Sometimes called "Elder Brewster" because he was the Ruling Elder of the Plymouth Colony. He was also the Teacher and Preacher until 1629. He is remembered for his spiritual leadership of the Pilgrims who crossed the ocean on the Mayflower (1620).

Brooks, Phillips
(1835-1893)

Phillips Brooks, American clergyman and author, was rector of famed Trinity Church, Boston, and in 1891 was consecrated bishop of Massachusetts. An overseer and preacher at Harvard for many years, he greatly influenced the religious life of the students. He died, unmarried, January 23, 1893. Besides his published sermons are his Bohlen lectures at Philadelphia Divinity School on *The Influence of Jesus* (1879) and his Lyman Beecher lectures at Yale, *Lectures on Preaching* (1877). He is best known and loved for his Christmas carol, "O Little Town of Bethlehem."

Brother, Lawrence
(c.1605-1691)

His real name was Nicolas Herman, sometimes known as "Brother Lawrence of the Resurrection." A mystic and a monk, he was also manager of the monastery kitchen; and he stated in *The Practice of the Presence of God* (a series of letters to a friend, afterwards edited and made into a priceless devotional book) that even while he heard the clanging and clattering of the pots and pans in the kitchen, he never once forgot God.

Browne, Robert
(c.1550-c.1633)

Robert Browne is remembered as a leader of the English Separatists known as Brownists. He was the first Englishman to

304

express the doctrine of complete separation of Church and State. Today he is generally considered the founder of Congregationalism because of his clear, pioneer outline of Congregational Church government.

He is best known for his *Pilgrim's Progress*. In a day of illiteracy in England, he learned to read and write. His wife introduced him to two devotional books which influenced him to give up amusements and swearing. Subsequently he began to preach, though he suffered extended imprisonment because he was a Dissenter (one not a member of the Church of England). When his wife died, he was left with four children, one of whom was blind. In 1659 he remarried. In prison he wrote his *Pilgrim's Progress*, a work which has had an enormous sale. His *Holy War* and *Grace Abounding to the Chief of Sinners* (a truly great spiritual autobiography) are also well known.

Bunyan, John (1628-1688)

The French Protestant who organized the Reformation in Geneva and founded "Calvinism." Calvin and his co-worker, Farel, were expelled from the city for being too strict. For the next three years he was the minister of a French congregation and lecturer in the theological school in Strasburg. He returned to Geneva in 1541 and by 1555 won the city to his way of thinking. He set up a theocratic regime along Old Testament lines and for fourteen years until his death was the sole ruler of the town. Under Calvin, the Church had the right of excommunication and power over the private lives of the citizens of Geneva. Calvin wrote extensively: commentaries on most of the New Testament books, documents on the Reformation, a treatise on predestination, etc. In 1559 he founded the Academy of Geneva which became the University of Geneva. His most enduring literary work was the *Institutes* which today is still the highest authority in many Protestant churches.

Calvin, John (1509-1564)

His father Thomas worked out the principles upon which he founded the Disciples of Christ. His movement has been known as the Campbellites. Born in Ireland and educated at Glasgow, he came to America and settled in Virginia. He came to believe firmly in immersion. He founded a college, published some sixty volumes, did editorial work, and there stands to his memory today a great denomination.

Campbell, Alexander (1788-1866)

Sometimes called the "Father of the Modern Missionary Movement," he was mainly responsible for the first foreign missionary society in England, the Baptist Missionary Society. He was a poor English shoe cobbler who, against great odds, went out to India. There he applied himself to language study and translated the whole Bible into Bengali, Hindi, Sanskrit, and Marathi.

Carey, William (1761-1834)

305

| Cartwright, Peter (1785-1872) | One of the most picturesque of American Methodist preachers, he traveled thousands of miles on horseback declaring the Gospel. He is supposed to have received more than 10,000 members into the Methodist Church, to have baptized over 12,000 people, and to have preached some 15,000 sermons. He was a rough and ready preacher. His autobiography, reissued in 1954 by Abingdon Press, is one of the delightful stories of frontier American Methodism. |

Cartwright, Peter
(1785-1872)

One of the most picturesque of American Methodist preachers, he traveled thousands of miles on horseback declaring the Gospel. He is supposed to have received more than 10,000 members into the Methodist Church, to have baptized over 12,000 people, and to have preached some 15,000 sermons. He was a rough and ready preacher. His autobiography, reissued in 1954 by Abingdon Press, is one of the delightful stories of frontier American Methodism.

Cartwright, Thomas
(1535-1603)

Once described as "the head and most learned of that sect of dissenters then called Puritans," Thomas Cartwright spoke out boldly against the polity (government) of the Church of England and believed that the reformation of the Church had not gone far enough. In addition to opposing ceremonies and vestments, he advocated the appointment of elders for discipline in each parish, the election of pastors by their people, and the abolition of such offices as archbishop and archdeacon. To avoid arrest, Cartwright retired to the Continent and became minister of the English residents at Antwerp and then Middleburg. After about ten years he returned to England where he was persecuted, being put into prison twice. In the main, the Presbyterian Churches of Great Britain and America still stand by his principles.

Chalmers, Thomas
(1780-1847)

Born in Scotland, he was preacher, teacher, and philosopher. While preparing a series of articles on Christianity for the *Edinburgh Encyclopedia,* he discovered a great hidden reality in Christ and was genuinely converted. Following a pastorate in the Tron Church, Glasgow, he became Professor of Moral Philosophy at the University of St. Andrews. In 1828 he was appointed to the chair of Theology at the Divinity College, Edinburgh. Dismayed by certain principles and practices of the National Church, in 1843 he led four hundred ministers out of the State Church and organized the first General Assembly of the Free Church in Scotland, which Church has since been reunited with the mother body. *The Works of Dr. Chalmers* has been published in twenty-five volumes.

Chrysostom, John
(c.347-407)

Born at Antioch, Syria, Chrysostom is remembered as a Christian writer and commentator (he did the *Homilies*), but especially as an eloquent preacher who won many to Christ (he was given the name "golden-mouthed"). While Bishop of Constantinople he was exiled. During a third exile he died.

Clarke, Adam
(c.1762-1832)

Clarke, perhaps the greatest Methodist since Wesley, was born in Northern Ireland. Influenced by John Wesley, he became a Methodist preacher and served in such places as the Channel Islands, the Shetland Islands, and London. Three times (1806, 1814, 1822) he was chosen president of the Methodist Conference. Clarke was a student of the classics, the Church Fathers, Oriental languages, and natural science. His best known work is his eight volume commentary on the Bible, still in print.

A Congregational minister, Clarke founded the Christian Endeavor Society for youth in 1881. He traveled over the world in the interests of this organization and published books to forward its cause. "C. E.", as it is called, is still in operation in a number of denominations.

Clarke, Francis E. (1851-1927)

Clement of Alexandria, Egypt, was a teacher of Origen and advanced the so-called Logos theology, the belief that Jesus Christ was actually Incarnate God. Origen followed him as head of the famed catechetical school of Alexandria. Clement's *Stromateis* ("carpet-bags" or "patch work") is a work of theology. He knew how to turn the simple Church tradition into a scientific theology.

Clement of Alexandria (c.150-c.215)

One of the "Apostolic Fathers," he was bishop of Rome from c. 90–100 A.D. He did an epistle to the Corinthian Church which is still in existence, and other literature has been accredited to him. His epistle throws light on very early Church history and the New Testament.

Clement of Rome (?-100)

John Colet was an English theologian and classical scholar, who was born about 1466 and died in 1519. He became Dean of St. Paul's Cathedral, London, and was also founder of St. Paul's School. It is believed that he studied at Magdalen College, Oxford, and later in Paris and Italy. He was the intimate friend of Erasmus and More, and one of the main promoters of the Renaissance and indirectly of the Reformation. Colet did not directly advocate the Reformation (he was a priest and never actually gave up Catholicism), but he did promote various reforms. Some called him a heretic because of the views he held. When his father died, Colet became the master of a vast fortune. He used part of his money to found a new school in St. Paul's Churchyard without restriction as to nationality. He aimed to provide a sound Christian education and knowledge of Greek and Latin. He is especially well known for his *Expository Lectures on Romans*.

Colet, John (c.1466-1519)

An early saint of Ireland, he was a missionary to Scotland where his preaching and exemplary life resulted in the conversion of king and people. He made his headquarters the Island of Iona, and from there gave leadership to many churches in Ireland and Scotland. In both these countries he founded churches and monasteries.

Columba (521-597)

The "Great" Emperor of Rome whose Edict of Toleration gave freedom to Christians. He called the first great Church Council at Nicaea in 325. A warrior of skill, he was spurred on to military victories by a vision in the sky: "In this sign (the cross) conquer." He brought Church and State together. Constantine encouraged the copying of the Scriptures.

Constantine (c.272-337)

307

Coverdale, Miles (1488-1568)

Miles Coverdale lived when those opposing Roman Catholicism were being actively hunted down. He became enthusiastic for Church reform especially on two issues, confession and images. Forced to leave England, he went to the Continent and there worked on an English translation of the Bible. He left his name in the hearts of Christians as a pioneer in the field of English Bible translation.

Cowman, Charles E. (1868-1924) and Lettie B. (1870-1960)

In 1901 Charles E. and Lettie B. Cowman felt God's call and left a lucrative executive position with the Western Union Company. Without any financial backing or the support of a mission board they travelled to Japan. Their goal, "the evangelization of the world in our generation," began with the 57,976,322 people of the "land of the rising sun." They conceived and initiated the first blanket literature crusade in the history of missions. In the following five years every one of the 10,320,000 homes of the Mikado's empire had been visited and a Christian witness together with a Gospel portion of God's Word had been left. This grass-roots literature distribution campaign (described as "the greatest piece of intensive missionary work since Pentecost") is credited with giving the impetus to the Christian Church in Japan.

From this beginning has grown the world-wide effort of the Oriental Missionary Society.

At age fifty-four, after the premature death of her husband, Lettie B. Cowman began the most fruitful years of her life. At an age when most women seek retirement, she became President of the Oriental Missionary Society and was active as a world traveler, lecturer, writer and source of inspiration to young people.

Lettie B. Cowman's devotional classics in leterature include STREAMS IN THE DESERT, SPRINGS IN THE VALLEY and MOUNTAIN TRAILWAYS FOR YOUTH. Subsequently the Cowman Foundation and the Cowman Publishing Company were formed to carry forward her goal of literature distribution both in the United States and abroad.

Theirs was a life of prayer, faith, and devotion characterized by an unyielding trust in the God of the impossible.

Crammer, Thomas (1489-1556)

Thomas Crammer gained the favor of Henry VIII by preparing a work on divorce which would allow the king to be released from his marriage to Catherine of Aragon. This led the king to consecrate him Archbishop of Canterbury in 1533. Later, under Edward VI, Crammer worked in favor of the Reformation. Queen Mary hated him, tried him for treason and heresy, imprisoned and condemned him to death. Crammer aided in the circulation of the Bible, the sanctioning of marriage for priests, and the replacement of the mass by the Protestant Lord's Supper. He was the principal author of *The Book of Common Prayer*, the chief influence of the Episcopal Church throughout the world.

Hostile to bishops and Puritans, he became an Independent, led an army which defeated Charles I, and became ruler (Protector) of England. As Protector, he tolerated all except Catholics, Anglicans, and extremists. He attempted a national Church of Calvinistic belief which included Baptists, Presbyterians, and Independents.

Cromwell, Oliver (1599-1658)

His enthusiasm and ability, together with his contribution of money to the relief of the poor and other good causes, led to his being made bishop of the Church in Carthage in 248 (crowds besieged his house until he consented to be bishop). He was banished and later beheaded (September 14, 258), the first African bishop to die a martyr. He wrote on theology and practical matters, advanced the ideas of the authority of bishops and Rome as the principle Church, and stressed infant baptism and penance as means of grace.

Cyprian (200-258)

A pioneer in, and generally considered the founder of, the Plymouth Brethren, he believed strongly in individuality and in the leadership of the Holy Spirit. He took a "dispensational" viewpoint on the Scriptures. Because of conscientious scruples he left the Church of Ireland believing that denominational distinctions and a regular ministry should be discarded. He formed an association in Dublin in 1828 and another in Plymouth from which came the name "Plymouth Brethren" in 1830. In England some of the Brethren were called "Darbyites." He did a translation of the Bible and wrote a five volume work, *Synopsis of the Books of the Bible*. In all, his writings constitute some thirty-two volumes. Today there are eight Plymouth Brethren groups, distinguished by Roman numerals I–VIII. Each believes a Bible theology but differs in minor points, usually of Church government. There is no Church membership in the sense of "joining an institution." In everything the aim is to set up the Church on strictly New Testament lines.

Darby, John Nelson (1800-1882)

He made clear that the Greek of the New Testament was not some "special" language for the elite but the language of everyday life. This discovery was a major factor in leading to the movement of modern speech translations of the Bible (Moffatt, Weymouth, Phillips, etc.). His *Light from the Ancient East* shows the bearing of papyri and inscriptions on the New Testament. He is remembered, too, for his work on Paul and Luke-Acts.

Deissman, Gustav Adolph (1866-1937)

Scotsman James Denney was born at Paisley to a family belonging to the Reformed Presbyterian Church. At the age of twenty, he, with a large majority of the members of the denomina-

Denney, James (1856-1917)

tion, joined the Free Church of Scotland. He was educated at Glasgow University and Glasgow Free Church College. After eleven years pastoral work, he returned to Glasgow Free Church College as Professor of New Testament. Later he was made principal of this college, a position he held until his death. Although Denney did admirably as pastor and preacher, his main title to remembrance is in the field of theology with special emphasis on the Atonement. His *The Death of Christ* is a well-known book on the Atonement, as is *The Christian Doctrine of Reconciliation,* and *The Atonement and the Modern Mind.* Denney contributed to *The Expositor's Bible* the volumes on Thessalonians and II Corinthians, and to *The Expositor's Greek New Testament* the work on Romans. His life has been done by T. A. Walker, *Principal James Denney, D.D.*

Drummond, Henry (1851-1897)

Born in Scotland, he lectured and wrote on religion and natural science; worked with university students; was associated for a time with D. L. Moody in evangelism and Bible teaching; and is especially remembered for his short but powerful commentary on I Corinthians 13, "The Greatest Thing in the World."

Eckart, Meister (1260-1327)

Meister Eckart was a Dominican monk and a mystic. He later taught at the College of St. James in Paris and engaged in Church work. In 1307 he was appointed Vicar-general of Bohemia with power to institute some monastic reforms. Because of his inclination toward the "Brethren of the Free Spirit" (a mystical group), Eckart brought on himself the displeasure of the Church, and was accused of heresy and tried in 1326. Refusing to recant he appealed to the Pope, who condemned as heretical seventeen out of twenty-eight points acknowledged by Eckart. During the proceedings he died. He is properly considered by many as the father of modern mystical pantheism, and he believed in the "Divine Spark" theory. Today the larger part of his works are lost, and others are only partially edited. He wrote in both the German and Latin languages.

Edwards, Jonathan (1703-1758)

One of the great minds of American history, he entered New Haven College (Yale) at the age of thirteen, pursued theological studies and became a minister. In 1735 there occurred in his parish at Northampton, Massachusetts, a great spiritual awakening which spread over New England. At this time he did more than any other American clergyman to promote doctrinal purity, and he was a strong Calvinist. He was convinced that it was wrong to permit unconverted persons to partake of the Lord's Supper; this and other things resulted in his dismissal from his pulpit in 1750. On September 26, 1757, he was elected President of Princeton. One week following his inauguration he was inoculated for smallpox (he cooperated in an early experiment) and four weeks later died as a result of the inoculation. A systematic theologian, his most important works are *A Divine and Supernatural Light Imparted to the Soul by the Spirit of God, Five Discourses on Justification by Faith, A Treatise Concerning Religious Affections,* and *Freedom of the Will.*

Desiderus Erasmus Roterodamus the Dutchman was the great interpreter of Humanism to his age. Satirical (*In Praise of Folly*) yet devout, he published the first printed edition of the Greek New Testament (1516), also an edition of the Latin New Testament which Cambridge students waited in line to purchase. At least one student was converted reading his Latin Testament. He was an ordained priest of the Roman Catholic Church which he criticized but never left. He knew intimately the progress of the Reformation but never joined Protestant forces. In addition to translating and editing the New Testament, he put it into paraphrases which were enthusiastically received, and in 1548 a translation of them was made in English and put in every parish Church alongside the Bible.

Erasmus (c.1466-1536)

The "Father of Church History" (the *Ecclesiastical History* is a pioneer work), he was probably born in Palestine and became Bishop of Caesarea. He was influenced by Origen, and at the Council of Nicea in 325 submitted the first draft of the creed which was later adopted with changes. The Arians with whom he had earlier sympathized were apparently denying the real divinity of Christ and now he voted against them. He is best known for giving the world historical information about the early Church, and his *Life of Constantine* is valuable source material.

Eusebius of Caesarea (c.260-340)

Figuring strongly in the revivalist movement of America, he was a lawyer turned evangelist; thousands were won to Christ in the 1830's, 40's, and 50's. He founded Oberlin College, wrote *Lectures on Revivals,* and did a two volume work, *Lectures on Systematic Theology.* His life has been written by Richard Ellsworth Day in a book entitled *Man of Like Passions* and by V. Raymond Edman, *Finney Lives On.*

Finney, Charles G. (1792-1875)

Born in Switzerland, Fletcher moved to England and became a defender of Arminianism and by this advanced materially the Wesleyan cause. In 1760 he became vicar of Madeley, England, where he preached until his death. He was active in Lady Huntingdon's College at Trevecca, Wales, and establised Sunday Schools for children. As a writer he is remembered especially for his *Checks to Antinomianism.*

Fletcher, John William (1729-1785)

An Englishman, he was the founder of the Quakers (Society of Friends). In 1648 he began his public ministry in market places,

Fox, George (1624-1691)

fields, and even in some church buildings. His preaching was strong and moved many to accept genuine religion, though he was often arrested for his preaching. The name "Quakers" was given in derision because Fox told a justice to "tremble at the word of the Lord." He married one of his early converts, Margaret Fell. He died in London on January 13, 1691, having preached with great power two days before. The presence of the "Inner Light" in the individual, he taught, should guide one's faith and actions. His *Journal* is the classic of Quakerism.

Francis of Assisi
(1181-1226)

Francis was the son of a rich cloth merchant of Assisi, Italy, but he gave up the ease and luxury of his home to become a mendicant (begging) monk. While worshipping in church one morning he heard the call of God; henceforth, he set out to save souls. He gathered round him a little band of like-minded followers. As he went from place to place preaching—Rome, France, Spain, Eastern Europe, and Egypt—his associates increased by the scores. The Order of Franciscans was organized. He wrote hymns and a number of books. *The Little Flowers of St. Francis* is a devotional gem.

Gregory I
(540-604)

Gregory ("the Great") was born in, and became the pope of, Rome. When he took over the Papacy, he found Italy in a time of crisis and to effect relief assumed control of the army, repaired the walls and the aqueducts of Rome, fed the starving people from the granaries of the Church, and appointed governors over several Italian cities. In so doing he established the political and social powers of the Papacy far beyond former limits. Conversions were among his greatest successes in England through his missionary program. Gregory I was a strong preacher and a learned writer. He developed and established the veneration of relics, the doctrine of Purgatory, and "Gregorian" chant. In fact, a good many main lines of distinctive Roman Catholic belief and practice were fixed by him.

He is one of the four "doctors" of the Western Church.

Gutenberg, Johann
(c.1396-1468)

Gutenberg was born in Mainz, Germany. He trained as a goldsmith and moved to Strasburg where he apparently taught the art of printing to a few men. Returning to Mainz, he formed a copartnership with Johann Fust, and when he became insolvent, surrendered most of his property to Fust. It was about this time that the 42-line (Gutenberg) Bible was printed. It is now generally believed that the first movable-type printing press was built in Mainz and that the Bible (Latin Vulgate) was the first book produced on the press. This particular Bible is known as the "Mazarin Bible" and was published before 1456. (See Chapter III.)

Henry VIII
(1491-1547)

The King of England who broke with Rome and founded the

Church of England. His divorce was the excuse, not the real cause, of the break; the English people were ready for Reformation. He said the Church was under the authority of the King of England, not the pope of Rome. The Church of England is known by the name Episcopal in America.

Some say he was the pope who marks the turning point from the Dark Ages to the better Medieval period. It is true that he, with others, hit concubinage in the clergy, and the buying and selling of Church offices (simony). Henry IV, Emperor of Germany, had assumed authority for the Church (he had made Church appointments); thus, Hildebrand dismissed him from the Church. Henry repented (in the snow, as the legend goes) and was forgiven only to persecute the very man who had forgiven him. He went on abusing the Church and Hildebrand died in exile.

Hildebrand (Gregory VII) (c.1020-1085)

He is celebrated for his work on the *Laws of Ecclesiastical Polity* (eight volumes) which contains some of the finest English ever penned. This work was designed to answer Presbyterian attacks on the polity and customs of the Church of England. It asserts the right of a broad liberty on the basis of Scripture and reason.

Hooker, Richard (1553-1600)

A Bohemian reformer before the Reformation, he was a leading proponent of the writings of Wyclif and was strongly opposed for this position. He was a fearless preacher, cried out against the sins of clergy and Church, condemned the sale of indulgences, rejected purgatory and the worship of saints. He exalted the Scriptures as Wyclif had done. Emphasis on the Scriptures made available for everyone, was a characteristic of the Reformation. He was tried in 1414, imprisoned, named a heretic, and burned at the stake, but his martyrdom advanced the cause of reformation and political revolution in Bohemia.

Huss, John (c.1371-1415)

Bishop of Antioch in Syria, he was known by Polycarp who knew the Apostle John. His writings provide us with useful information about the New Testament and the early Church. He was the first writer outside the New Testament to describe Christ in terms of current philosophy and the first outside the New Testament to mention the Virgin Birth. He was opposed to false doctrine and Church divisions, believed in the authority of the Church and wished for a martyr's death. It is probable that he met a martyr's death in the amphitheatre in Rome.

Ignatus of Antioch (c.50-117)

Founder of the Society of Jesus (Jesuits), he began his career as a soldier, was wounded, challenged to Christian service and became a "soldier" for Jesus Christ. His was a disciplined concept of Christianity. A faithful band of ten followers were gathered,

Ignatius Loyola (1491-1556)

and formed the nucleus of the Society of Jesus, a movement which has been marked through its history by missionary endeavor and the founding of colleges and universities.

Innocent III (1160-1216)

While he was pope the Papacy reached its highest point of power; he insisted upon and obtained absolute and final authority over the Church. He also involved himself in politics and became the real ruler of a share of Europe. Had his movement continued, a Christian commonwealth, with the pope as its head, would have been the result. But this movement was brought to a halt by a stronger movement, nationalism.

Irenaeus (c.140-200)

Born in Asia Minor, Irenaeus was influenced early in life by Polycarp who knew the Apostle John. Irenaeus is an important witness to the beliefs and events of the Ancient Church. He became bishop of Lyons in Gaul. Instrumental in the battle against major false doctrines, he wrote *Against Heresies*. By some he is considered the first writer of the post-Apostolic period to deserve the title of theologian.

Jerome (342-420)

He is known particularly for his translation of the whole Bible into Latin. It is called the *Vulgate* and is still the authoritative text for the Roman Catholic Church. Through his knowledge of Greek and Hebrew, St. Jerome introduced the treasures of the Eastern Church to the West. About 382 he traveled to Bethlehem where he spent the rest of his life. There he did Bible commentaries and a host of other works including the Vulgate.

Jowett, John Henry (1864-1923)

Born in Halifax, England, he was educated at the University of Edinburgh and Oxford and was widely known for his preaching. He served as minister of St. James Church, Birmingham, England, Fifth Avenue Presbyterian Church in New York City, and was Lyman Abbott lecturer at Yale in 1912.

Justin "Martyr" (born c.100)

Born of pagan parents, he nonetheless became a strong supporter of Christianity. In Rome he lectured in a classroom of his own. He suffered the death of a martyr and is thus known as Justin "Martyr." His writings, *Apology* and *Dialogue*, show him Christian and theologian and provide valuable information on the life of the Christian Church in the middle of the second century and on the history of the New Testament writings. Justin is said to be the first of those who have tried to reconcile Christian and non-Christian culture.

Kenyon, Sir Frederic George (1863-1952)

A great believer in the truth of the Bible, Sir Frederic Kenyon was born in London, England, and educated at New College, Oxford. He joined the staff of the British Museum in 1889 and served there in various capacities until his retirement in 1930. He is known particularly for his publications of classical texts and as a renowned Bible scholar who produced *Our Bible and the An-*

cient Manuscripts and other books.

Kierkegaard, Danish philosopher and theologian was a founder of modern existentialism and a revolutionary figure in the history of Protestant Christianity. The title of his work *Either/Or* indicates the center of his thought, his insistence on the choice which each individual must make between Christ and the world. He believed all attempts at providing "proofs" of Christianity were fundamentally irreligious; one must take the "leap" of faith. "Purity of heart," said Kierkegaard, "is to will one thing." He died in Copenhagen.

Kierkegaard, Soren Aabye (1813-1855)

John Knox, father of the Protestant Reformation in Scotland, was a close friend and associate of John Calvin and worked with him in Geneva for a time. The Scottish Reformed Church, under Knox's leadership, took on an organization without bishops; this was the beginning of Scottish Presbyterianism. Among his publications are, *An Answer to a Scottish Jesuit, History of the Reformation Within the Realm of Scotland,* and *First Blast of the Trumpet Against the Monstrous Regiment of Women.*

Knox, John (1505-1572)

His father was E. A. Knox, D.D., a bishop in the Church of England and humorist (verse and parody) who became editor of *Punch* in 1932. E. A.'s son, Ronald, was converted to Roman Catholicism in 1917 and ordained Priest in 1919. He became Catholic Chaplain at Oxford in 1925, and during his life held other important posts. He wrote detective tales for pleasure (as did Dorothy Sayers). Known as a defender of the faith, he was an apologist, preacher, and writer. He is remembered as a Bible translator.

Knox, Ronald A. (1888-1957)

A Dutch theologian and statesman, Abraham Kuyper was born in Holland and became a convert to strict Calvinism. He held several pastorates and was professor of systematic theology at Free University in Amsterdam for many years. He was the founder of the Free Reformed Church and fought against liberal theology in Holland.

Kuyper, Abraham (1837-1920)

In 1726 he wrote the first of his practical treatises on "Christian Perfection" which impressed Wesley and the early Methodists. John and Charles Wesley became his disciples. Law influenced John to go to Georgia as a missionary. The works of William Law were collected in nine volumes (1762). The *Serious Call* (1728) is his best known work.

Law, William (1686-1761)

The first pope of Rome actually to get anything like universal recognition as supreme ruler of the Church in the line of Peter. Leo gave an orthodox definition of the person of Jesus Christ which was adopted by the Council of Chalcedon (451).

Leo, The Great (c.390-461)

A many talented Scot who was a pioneer missionary and ex-

Livingstone, David (1813-1873)

plorer in Africa. A student of both theology and medicine, he spread the Gospel and healed the sick. His travels figure in the establishing of an African geography and he helped stop slavery. He died on his knees praying for his African friends.

Luther, Martin (1483-1546)

The "Father of the Protestant Reformation," Martin Luther was born in Germany. He entered an Augustinian monastery and was ordained a priest. The inner peace he sought came as a result of meditations on Romans 1:16-17; he discovered that sinners receive justification only by *faith,* not by human works. Luther attacked the Roman Church in connection with the indulgences issued by Pope Leo X. He posted his "95 Theses" October 31, 1517, in which he distinguished true repentance from mere penance. The theses were freely circulated, and before the end of the year they were being read and discussed widely. The pope accused him of false doctrine and eventually he was dismissed from the Church. His translation of the Bible (with the help of his nephew Melanchthon), his hymns, and the two catechisms (for instruction in the distinctive Protestant doctrines) are among his works.

Machen, J. Gresham (1881-1937)

Machen taught at Princeton Theological Seminary until he felt compelled to leave because of the influx of liberal attitudes. He founded Westminster Theological Seminary in Philadelphia (1929), and was active in forming the Independent Board of Presbyterian Foreign Missions which was founded in opposition to policies of the Board of Foreign Missions (Presbyterian Church). His better known writings include *The Origin of Paul's Religion* (1921), *Christianity and Liberalism* (1923), *The Meaning of Faith* (1925), *The Virgin Birth of Christ* (1930). His life has been written by Ned B. Stonehouse.

Makemie, Francis (1658-1708)

Makemie founded the first American presbytery in Philadelphia, 1706. Because of the significance of this historic act, he is sometimes called the founder of American Presbyterianism. A devout and energetic man, he was an evangelist in America for a time, preaching from South Carolina to New York.

Manes (c.215-275)

One of the early rivals of Christianity, Manes was born probably at Seleucia-Ctesiphon, capital of the Persian Empire. He received his first vision at about the age of twelve and from there developed a religion of dualism and asceticism which spread rapidly throughout Egypt, Rome, Africa, and Turkey. He stressed the idea of a conflict of light and darkness and practiced severe asceticism. He was put to death while in prison. Followers of Manes are known as Manichaeans. St. Augustine was a Manichaean for several years before his conversion to Christianity.

Martin of Tours (c.315-401)

Bishop of Tours in France, he appealed to the common man

and made many converts. He destroyed pagan temples and put up Christian churches in their place. Fantastic numbers of people came to see him and when he died, it is said, some 2,000 monks followed him to his grave.

Melanchthon is said by some to be second only to Luther in importance as a German Reformer. His knowledge of Greek made him invaluable to Luther in translating the Bible. He wrote considerably in the areas of theology, history, and philosophy. He did a pioneering work in the field of systematic Reformation doctrine.

Melanchthon, Philip (1497-1560)

Scottish Reformer who followed John Knox and carried his torch, Andrew Melville was principal of Glasgow University where he enlarged the curriculum and drew students from all quarters, overflowing longtime empty classrooms. In 1580 he went to the University of St. Andrews, becoming principal of St. Mary's College. As moderator of the General Assembly of the Scottish Church he took an active part in establishing the Presbyterian form of government. Under Melville's leadership, the General Assembly gave full authority to presbyteries as ecclesiastical courts and ratified the Presbyterian *Second Book of Discipline.* He suffered exile and imprisonment for his views. Released in 1611, he retired to France, becoming a professor of Biblical Theology, and there died at the age of 77.

Melville, Andrew (1545-1622)

A native of Glasgow, Scotland, James Moffatt was a New Testament and Church History scholar particularly known for his translation of the Bible. He edited a complete commentary on the New Testament in seventeen volumes. His Bible translation is written in colloquial style and has had wide circulation. He died in New York.

Moffatt, James (1870-1944)

Dwight L. Moody, an American evangelist, was born at Northfield, Massachusetts. Before becoming a Congregational lay evangelist, he formed a class for poor boys in Chicago, which later grew into a large Sunday School. He was a pioneer in the American YMCA. Though a pastor in Chicago for a time, he was never ordained. Joined by Ira David Sankey, a Gospel singer, the two went to England and Scotland where great religious awakening occurred. Upon their return to America, large meetings were held throughout the country. He founded the Bible Training Institute in Chicago (now Moody Bible Institute). He published *How to Study the Bible, Men of the Bible, Weighed and Wanting, Arrows and Anecdotes,* and other sermons and lectures.

Moody, Dwight Lyman (1837-1899)

An American Methodist layman who never submitted to ordination, he was one of the great Christian voices of the generation just past. He promoted with great enthusiasm foreign mis-

Mott, John R. (1865-1955)

sions among young people. He was active in YMCA, the Student Volunteer Movement, and the ecumenical movement among missionaries. A man of deep spirituality and fervent prayer life, he had a wide influence through his books, lectures, preaching, and personal counseling. His biography has been done by J. B. Matthews and G. M. Fisher.

Muhlenberg, Henry Melchior (1711-1787) The "Father of the Lutheran Church in America," he was a warm-hearted Christian sent by the German Pietist Franke to give guidance to the Lutheran Churches of eastern Pennsylvania. Actually, he worked from New York to Georgia. He founded the first Lutheran synod in America. A man of many talents, he organized churches, educated ministers, and produced hymn books. His *Journals* constitute an important source on American Lutheranism.

Müller, George (1805-1898) Born in Prussia, he became known as the founder of the large orphanage near Bristol, England. His prayer life was remarkable, for he firmly believed that prayer was the answer to temporal need and he refused a fixed salary. He traveled and preached in many lands including Germany and America, and his orphanage is one of the great miracles of the modern Church. His life has been written by A. T. Pierson, *George Müller of Bristol and His Witness to a Prayer-Hearing God* (1899).

Newton, John (1725-1807) Born in London, Newton lost his mother when very small and went to sea at an early age with his father. He was a wicked young sailor, cursing and swearing being second nature to him. He became captain of a slave ship, and an awful storm at sea was the beginning of his return to God, or rather, as Newton puts it, "God's return to me." He served two churches as an ordained minister in the Church of England at Olney, England, and St. Mary Woolnoth, London. As preacher, hymnwriter (he helped break down the resistance to hymn singing), letterwriter, and counselor he saw scores converted and helped many a young minister to a more spiritual ministry. He was a pioneer in missions and helped materially to abolish slavery. He was, in fact, the leader of the Evangelical Party within the Church of England. His works include the *Olney Hymns*—some of the hymns were written by his friend William Cowper—and *An Authentic Narrative,* the unbelieveable autobiography of his early life. Among his better known hymns are "Glorious Things of Thee are Spoken," "How Sweet the Name of Jesus Sounds," and "Amazing Grace."

Origen (182-253) He may be called the "Father of systematic theology," for his book, *On First Principles,* was the first major attempt at making a systematic theology. He followed his teacher, Clement, as head of the catechetical school at Alexandria, Egypt. He advanced the doctrine of the Incarnation, and his influence was greatly felt in his own day as it is in ours. Origen produced over 6,000 works including commentaries on the Old and New Testaments, and the *Hexapla* (a "six" column work) which provided a Greek translation of the Old Testament. The columns of the *Hexapla* Bible were Greek, Hebrew in Greek characters, the Septuagint, and three versions of the Septuagint. It is only in fragmentary existence now but was used by Old Testament textual scholars.

Coming to America from Germany in 1752, he went to Pennsylvania to work with German speaking people. Like most of the missionaries from Germany, he was a Pietist; that is, one who insists on an inner spiritual experience. Otterbein worked for a time in Baltimore as a pastor, came in close touch with Asbury, assisted at the latter's ordination, and in 1800 formed, with Martin Boehm and eleven others, a new denomination along Methodist lines known as the "United Brethren in Christ." The name came from the expression, "we are brethren," with which Otterbein greeted Boehm after hearing him preach for the first time. Jacob Albright, also a German pietist, founded a similar body, the Evangelical Association (Church); it merged with Otterbein's group in 1946 to form the Evangelical United Brethren Church.

Otterbein, Philip William (1726-1813)

Only fragments of his five-volume *Exposition of the Lord's Oracles* survive, and these through quotations by Eusebius the Church historian. Little of his life story is known, but Irenaeus says he was a friend of Polycarp (who knew St. John). Fragments of his writings give us traditions about the origins of Matthew and Mark.

Papias (birth and death dates unknown; presumably second century A.D.)

Pascal proved himself theologian, mathematician, and philosopher, and among his inventions was the barometer. Following his conversion in 1654, his theology centered on both the person of Jesus Christ and his own relationship with Him. A forerunner of much contemporary theology, Pascal's thoughts were deeply influenced by his interest in experimental knowledge with the result that he refused to rely on rational proofs alone. He said, "The heart has its reason that reason itself does not know," and he believed that the heart was the real means of discovering God. His *Pensées* (Thoughts) has been widely read in our time.

Pascal, Blaise (1623-1662)

He received a vision to evangelize Ireland and in 431 went to Ireland and was consecrated Bishop (432). He founded the Cathedral Church of Armagh which soon became the educational and administrative center of the Irish Church. In Ireland he organized the scattered Christian communities which he found in the north, did much to convert the pagan west, and brought the country into closer relations with the rest of the Western Church.

Patrick (c.389-c.461)

His *Confessions* and *Letter to Coroticus* are the chief sources of information on his life.

**Penn, William
(1644-1718)**
An apostle of religious freedom in America, William Penn was born in London. He became a Quaker and was in and out of jail many times for his stand. The persecution of the Quakers led him to turn his eyes toward America as a refuge. He acquired land—Delaware and Pennsylvania—and set up a government. All modes of religious worship compatible with Christian doctrine and practice were tolerated. When James II became King of England, Penn procured a pardon from him for all who were in prison "for conscience sake," which action freed 1200 Quakers. His first publication was a tract, *Truth Exalted* (1668). Others followed including *No Cross, No Crown,* and *Innocency with Her Open Face.*

**Philo of
Alexandria
(c.20 B.C.-
c.50 A.D.)**
Philo, a Greek-speaking Jew of Alexandria, Egypt, attempted to unite the religion of Moses with Plato's philosophy by means of an allegorical interpretation of the Old Testament. This was his method of arguing for the faith, for he tried to show that the truth of Greek thought had its origin in the teachings of Moses. In time, his method of interpretation became to the Christian Church a popular if misleading form of Biblical interpretation. (Allegorical interpretation is the figurative or symbolic treatment of one topic or event under the guise of another.)

**Polycarp
(c.69-c.155)**
Polycarp was one of the "Apostolic Fathers" and helped save the Church from the rising tide of paganism in the second century. He was an unwavering foe of heresy and remarkably successful in winning heretics back to Christ. He was Bishop of Smyrna and wrote many epistles of which only one has survived, the *Epistle to Philippi*. In this epistle he stressed the Christian walk and reliance on the New Testament. His main scriptural emphasis was on I Peter. Polycarp knew the Apostle John and was burned at the stake in Smyrna.

**Raikes, Robert
(1735-1811)**
Robert Raikes was born in Gloucester, England. Though not the first to have a Sunday School, he did so much to establish the idea that he has been called the "Father of the Sunday School movement." His interest was drawn to educating neglected children, especially on Sundays. Raikes, hearing about William King's Sunday School work in Dursley, soon started his first one with the aid of Thomas Stock. In 1783 he wrote an article about Sunday Schools in the newspaper he published; this article was the main starting point of one of the largest movements in England and the Western world. By 1786 over 200,000 English children were attending Sunday Schools. Knowledge of the Scriptures was strengthened by the teaching of reading and other elementary subjects.

Benjamin Titus Roberts was the founder of the Free Methodist Church of North America. He, with others, was expelled from the Genesee Conference of the Methodist Episcopal Church because of criticisms of conditions in the Methodist Church and insistence upon the doctrines of justification and sanctification. In 1860 he assumed leadership of a growing body which wished freedom of worship, emphasis upon Wesley's doctrine and experience, and a strict pattern of piety. The new Church was begun at Pekin, New York. Slavery, pew rent, and secret societies figured in the schism. Today Roberts' Church has a strong program of higher education and missionary outreach.

Roberts, B. T. (1823-1893)

A New Testament professor at Southern Baptist Theological Seminary, Louisville, Kentucky, he is especially well known for his *Harmony of the Gospels* (1893) and his *Syllabus of New Testament Greek Syntax* (1900). He was the author of many other works and took an active interest in modern Bible translation (he was on the R.S.V. committee until his death). His biography has been written by Everett Gill under the title *A. T. Robertson, A Biography (1863-1934)*.

Robertson, Archibald T. (1863-1934)

Robinson was an English clergyman who became the pastor of the Pilgrim Fathers. His early career is obscure, but it is believed that he was educated at Cambridge. He was the religious director of a group of Norwich worshippers, and some of them were excommunicated for following his teaching. In 1608 he went to Amsterdam with several members of the Church at Scrooby; in 1609 he went on to Leyden where he was ordained pastor. He worked with a project for emigration to America, and a number of people left Leyden, but he remained. He separated from the established Church of England, but he was not intolerant. His writings show good sense, ease and simplicity. Two of his better known works are *A Justification of Separation from the Church of England* and *Of Religious Communion;* also *Essays or Observations Divine and Moral.*

Robinson, John (1576-1625)

An American evangelist and hymn writer, he met Dwight L. Moody in 1870 and the two joined forces in revival work. Sankey served as organist, soloist, and song leader for the services, and he is particularly well known as the author of such hymns as "The Ninety and Nine" and "When the Mists Have Rolled Away."

Sankey, Ira D. (1840-1908)

Born in Italy, Savonarola is remembered as a reformer. A fiery preacher, he nevertheless failed in Florence in 1482 where he violently opposed its paganism. After preaching in other cities he returned to Florence where he now reformed the monastery and turned the city to repentance. His criticism of Rome brought him into conflict with Pope Alexander VI who forbade him to preach

Savonarola, Girolamo (1452-1498)

and ultimately dismissed him from the Church. Contending that the Pope had been illegally elected, Savonarola tried to organize a council to oppose him. Savonarola was hanged in Florence May 3, 1498.

Schlatter, Michael (1716-1790)

Organizer of the German Reformed Church in America, Michael Schlatter was born in Switzerland and sent to this country by the Dutch. He helped bring order into the American congregations, persuaded ministers to come from Europe to help spread the Gospel in the New World, and is marked as one of the great figures in missionary work among the German-speaking Americans. From 1869 to 1934 his denomination was known as the Reformed Church in the United States. In 1934 it merged with the Evangelical Synod of North America to form the Evangelical and Reformed Church which in turn has merged with the Congregational Christian Church to form the United Church of Christ.

Scofield, C. I. (1843-1921)

Born in the state of Michigan, he was admitted to the Bar at the age of twenty-six and subsequently elected to the Kansas State Legislature. Later he was U.S. Attorney for the District of Kansas. Converted to Christ, Scofield was guided in Bible study by James H. Brooks. He became a pastor and in 1902 began his reference Bible. In 1907 the *Scofield Reference Bible* was completed. Charles G. Trumbell has written the life story of C. I. Scofield (Oxford University Press, 1920).

Servetus, Michael (1511-1553)

A native of Spain, Michael Servetus is known as a physician and as a heretic. He was anti-Trinitarian in theology and denied the full divinity of Christ. His principal work, *Christian Restitution,* explains his doctrines in full. He was rigorously opposed by John Calvin and was burned as a heretic at Champel October 27, 1553.

Simons, Menno (1496-1561)

Born in Holland, Menno Simons left the priesthood of the Roman Catholic Church after twenty years of service and became an Anabaptist ("re-baptize") leader. He gave some organization and direction to this movement and the group known as Mennonites takes their name from him. He put stress on the New Testament, rejected infant baptism and the taking of oaths. He was a pacifist and rejected a state church. His most important work, *The Foundation of Christian Doctrine,* was published in 1681. Mennonites continue in America, some of them practicing foot washing.

Simpson, Albert B. (1844-1919)

A. B. Simpson is known today as the founder of the Christian and Missionary Alliance. A native of Prince Edward Island, Canada, he received his training at Knox College, Toronto, and pastored several churches. He also served as magazine editor and author of a number of books including a work on the Holy Spirit. The Christian and Missionary Alliance is especially known for its program of overseas missions.

A British evangelist and the son of a gipsy, he began his work with General Booth in London. About 1883 his evangelistic efforts were extended and eventually he was preaching in Scotland, England, America, Australia, and other parts of the world. He was a Methodist and wrote a number of books. His writing and preaching were always aimed at reaching the lost.

Smith, Gipsy Rodney

A Presbyterian layman, he was active in the Student Volunteer Movement, and along with John R. Mott influenced many young people to give their lives in foreign missionary service. He was a voluminous writer and an extremely active man. He was moderator of the Presbyterian Church in 1927. His biography has been written by W. R. Wheeler under the title, *A Man Sent From God*.

Speer, Robert E. (1867-1947)

Spener, founder of German Pietism, was born of devout Protestant parents in Alsace. He felt a call to revive the Luthern Church with evangelical fervor. The "Collegia Pietatis," which he started, was a group which gathered twice a week in his house for devotional meetings. This was one of the early steps in the movement of Pietism ("heart religion") which was to influence Moravianism and Methodism. His independent outlook, plus his endeavor to give the laity a real part in church life, offended many clergy. In 1694 the University of Halle was founded, largely under his influence. His best known work is the *Pia Desideria* (1675).

Spener, Philipp Jakob (1635-1705)

A Baptist preacher, Charles H. Spurgeon was born in England. He became famous as pastor of the Metropolitan Tabernacle, London, and during the course of his lifetime preached to many thousands of people. A strong evangelical, he opposed liberal forces. He was an orator and held people spellbound when he preached. Spurgeon wrote many books, including sermons and *The Treasury of David* (on the Psalms), and founded a pastor's college. He was witty and always preached with many illustrations.

Spurgeon, Charles Haddon (1834-1892)

A fiery Presbyterian evangelist, Billy Sunday was born in Ames, Iowa, and was a professional baseball player for a time. He began his evangelistic efforts in 1896 and saw thousands of converts during his years of preaching. His popularity reached its peak during World War I.

Sunday, William Ashley ("Billy") (1862-1935)

Serving as Archbishop of York from 1929 to 1942, William Temple became prominent in the national life of England through his interest in social work, economics, politics, and theology. He was appointed Archbishop of Canterbury in 1942 and was influ-

Temple, William (1881-1944)

323

ential in public speeches and broadcasts, and in the development of a statement of principles to guide a post-war settlement. He was a leader in the ecumenical movement. A theologian, he did *Nature, Man and God* and a devotional work on John's Gospel.

Tertullian, Quintus Septimius Florens (c. 150-55–c. 222-25)

Tertullian was the first major theologian to write in Latin and as such is known as the Father of Latin theology. He created much of the language of Western theology (he invented the term "Trinity"). He remained orthodox in most respects, and made contributions to the literature on the Trinity and Incarnation.

Thomas Aquinas (1225-1274)

The great systematic theologian of the Middle Ages, he is still the chief authority on theology for the Roman Catholic Church. It is said of his master work, *Summa Theologiae,* that it is "one of the grandest attempts at a complete science of theology ever planned by human intellect." The *Summa* records the classical "Thomistic" proofs for God's existence and shows Thomas' attempt to harmonize Aristotle and Christianity (Scholasticism). Other works include commentaries on Aristotle and commentaries on major books of the Bible.

Thomas à Kempis (1380-1471)

Thomas à Kempis was a German priest, educator, and the reputed author of *The Imitation of Christ.* The name by which he is known is a Latin school title derived from the German town of Kempen. He was educated in Holland at a school of the Brothers of the Common Life, an association newly founded by Gerhard Groote the mystic. At the age of twenty he entered a neighboring monastery and except for short intervals spent the remainder of his life there. Thomas à Kempis believed that in order to lead a useful spiritual life we must "imitate Christ" and have contempt for all the vanities of the world.

Tyndale, William (1494-1536)

William Tyndale was born in England. Having openly expressed his attachment to the doctrines of the Reformation, he came into collision with Roman Catholic officials and was suspected of heresy. Desiring to translate the Scriptures into the vernacular, he was forced to flee to the Continent where he worked on the New Testament (he translated Jonah and the Pentateuch too). He was constantly hounded by his opposers who sought his arrest. After many years of flight and yet prodigious literary activity, he was betrayed, imprisoned at Vilvorde (in Belgium), tried for heresy, condemned, strangled, and burned. William Tyndale is considered one of the greatest forces in the development of the English Reformation. He also was influential in shaping the thought of the Puritan party in England. He believed the Scriptures should be available to all and that they are authoritative. (See Chapter III.)

The Waldenses get their name from him. They were Protestants before Luther because they emphasized Scripture, rejected such things as indulgences, purgatory, masses for the dead. They still exist as a denomination quite separate from Roman Catholicism. Waldo was French and in his own day his followers were known as the Poor Men of Lyon, so-called because they gave up luxuries and cried out against the lust and greed of the clergy. They existed at an early date in Italy and today have a theological seminary in Rome.

Waldo, Peter (c.1140-1217)

The hymn writer of the Evangelical Revival in England, he wrote over 6,000 hymns. He traveled and worked with his brother John. He and Isaac Watts did more than any others to establish hymn singing (only Psalms were sung before Watts), and Charles and John used the hymn as a device to drive home the Gospel truths.

Wesley, Charles (1707-1788)

The founder of Methodism, he gathered around him a group who became known as the "Holy Club," "Bible Moths," or "Methodists" (after "methodical"). In 1735 he went to Georgia as a missionary and was unsuccessful. Wesley's heart was "strangely warmed" May 24, 1738, while hearing words from Luther's preface to his commentary on Romans at a meeting in Aldersgate Street, London. Wesley spent the rest of his life in evangelistic work. When the churches closed to him he began field preaching. Before his death his work covered all of the British Isles and was established in America. He taught two definite works of grace, conversion and sanctification, the former for forgiveness, the latter for cleansing and power. He is well known for his work, *The Plain Account of Christian Perfection,* and for hymns which he wrote, edited, and translated. He also edited fifty volumes of the *Christian Library* and a magazine for Methodists.

Wesley, John (1703-1791)

One of the great preacher-orators of all time, he, with Wesley and others, played an important role in founding the Evangelical Revival in both England and America. Eventually he broke with Wesley over Calvinism. He introduced Wesley to out-of-doors preaching. Seven times he went to America for preaching tours and on the last died and is buried in our own country.

Whitefield, George (1714-1770)

An Englishman, he was the founder of the Young Men's Christian Association which was born out of a burdened heart for the neglected youth of London's shops and churches. The miserable housing and working conditions preyed upon Williams, and he gathered eleven young men to meet more or less regularly for prayer; this was the beginning of his organization. His aim in starting the Y.M.C.A. was to "bring religion into the sphere

Williams, George (1821-1905)

of the daily occupation." He was knighted for his achievements (by then the Y.M.C.A. had spread around the world) and was buried in St. Paul's Cathedral, London.

Williams, Roger (c.1604-1683) Roger Williams started the first Baptist Church in America. While still in England he developed Separatist views, and went to Boston in the hope of complete freedom. His views, however, brought him into conflict with Massachusetts' leadership and he was banished. He then obtained a charter to make Rhode Island an independent colony which he dedicated to "liberty of conscience." He believed in experimental religion.

Woolman, John (1720-1772) John Woolman, the famous Quaker, was born in Mount Holly, New Jersey. He spoke and wrote much against slavery (he was one of the strongest anti-slavery voices in American history), labored with the Indians and poor whites. He was greatly concerned with the sale of rum to the Indians. He saw world peace if people would take their eyes off money and material things. He held that the Quaker Faith was a genuine means to this end. His best known work is his *Journal*.

Wyclif, John (1324-1384) A forerunner of the Reformation, he did a translation of the Bible (see the chapter on "English Translations"). He criticized papal abuses and was tried for heresy; unconvicted, he died a natural death. The Council of Constance condemned his doctrines in 1415 and his body was unearthed and burned. He believed in predestination, and advanced reformed ideas in social, political, and religious realms which were based upon the Bible. Among his writings are over two hundred tracts, largely unpublished.

Ximenez De Cisneros, Francisco (1436-1517) Born in Spain, Ximenez did the *Complutension Polyglot,* an edition of the Bible containing the Old Testament in Hebrew, Greek and Latin, and the New Testament in Greek and Latin. He also founded the University of Alcala and served his Church in various capacities.

Zinzendorf, Count (1700-1760) Zinzendorf was the founder of the Moravian Church, and he helped establish the town of Bethlehem, Pennsylvania, American headquarters of the denomination. In the early 1720's he started a Christian community on his estate in Germany (called Hernhutt) and invited Moravian Christians to live there. From there missionaries were sent out and he himself started work among German poor people in Holland, Estonia, the West Indies, and America. His communities broke with the mother Lutheran Church to form the Moravian Church. The closing years of Zinzendorf's life were spent traveling and writing as a representative of the new Church. Zinzendorf's one compelling idea was the concept of a "heart-religion." John Wesley was strongly influenced by his disciples and experienced "the strangely warmed heart." Moravians were pioneers in the modern missionary movement.

The beginning of the Reformation in Switzerland was in 1519 when Zwingli lectured on the New Testament and attacked purgatory, prayer through saints, and monasticism. Zwingli claimed the Gospel as the only basis of truth and rejected the authority of the Pope, the mass, and the rule that priests could not marry. Steps were taken to abolish the mass and remove images and pictures from the churches. The Lord's Supper was purely symbolic, a view which led to a conflict with Luther. The Reformation spread from Zürich to other parts of Switzerland; however, the Cantons of Lucerne, Zug, Schwyz, Uri and Unterwalden opposed it and in October 1531 their forces descended upon Zürich in war. Zwingli, one of the chaplains in the defense army, was killed in the battle.

Zwingli, Ulrich (1484-1531)

APPENDIX II

TOOLS FOR THE BIBLE STUDENT
(BIBLIOGRAPHY)

Study Bibles

The American Standard Version of the Bible. New York: Thomas
Nelson and Sons, 1901.

The Harper Study Bible. Revised Standard Version. Notes by Harold
M. Lindsell. Grand Rapids: Zondervan.

The New Indexed Bible. Chicago: John A. Dickson Publishing Company, 1941.

The Living New Testament (King James Version). New York:
American Bible Society. (With many pictures.)

The Westminster Study Edition of the Holy Bible. Philadelphia:
Westminster Press, 1948.

The Oxford Annotated Bible (Revised Standard Version). New York:
Oxford University Press, 1962.

Holman Study Bible (Revised Standard Version). Philadelphia: A. J.
Holman, 1962.

Concordances

Three exhaustive concordances for the English Bible student are
as follows:

Ellison, J. W. *Nelson's Complete Concordance to the Revised Standard
Version Bible.* New York: Thomas Nelson and Sons, 1957.
(Abridged edition also available.)

Strong, James. *The Exhaustive Concordance of the Bible.* New York:
Eaton and Mains, 1894. Now published by the Abingdon Press.

Young, Robert. *Analytical Concordance to the Bible.* Grand Rapids:
William B. Eerdmans, 1936.

A topical concordance is:

Joy, Charles R. *Harper's Topical Concordance* (Revised and Enlarged Edition). New York: Harper, 1961.

A handy desk size concordance, though not exhaustive, is:

Cruden, Alexander. *Complete Concordance to the Old and New Testaments* (edited by A. D. Adams). Grand Rapids: Zondervan, 1955. It has also been published by Baker, Revell, and others.

Another concise concordance is:

Metzger, Bruce M. and Isobel M., compilers. *The Oxford Concise Concordance to the Revised Standard Version of the Holy Bible.* New York: Oxford University Press, 1962.

A concordance to a modern language version is:

Gant, W. J. *The Moffat Bible Concordance.* New York: Harper, 1950.

Bible Dictionaries and Encyclopedias

Buttrick, George A. (ed.) *Interpreter's Dictionary of the Bible.* 4 vols. New York: Abingdon Press, 1962.

Corswant, W. *A. Dictionary of Life in Bible Times.* New York: Oxford, 1960.

Davis, John D. *A Dictionary of the Bible.* 4th Revised Edition. Grand Rapids: Baker Book House, 1945 (reprint).

Davis, John S. *Westminster Dictionary of the Bible.* Revised by Henry S. Gehman. Philadelphia: Westminster Press, 1944.

Douglas, J. D. (ed.) *The New Bible Dictionary.* Grand Rapids: William B. Eerdmans, 1962.

Hastings, James (ed.) *The Dictionary of the Apostolic Church.* 2 vols. New York: Charles Scribner's Sons, 1916.

Hastings, James (ed.) *Dictionary of the Bible.* Revised by F. C. Grant and H. H. Rowley, New York: Harper, 1963.

Hastings, James (ed.) *Dictionary of Christ and the Gospels.* 2 vols. New York: Charles Scribner's Sons, 1906.

Hastings, James (ed.) *Encyclopedia of Religion and Ethics.* 12 vols. New York: Charles Scribner's Sons, 1908–26.

Miller, M. S. & J. Lane Miller. *Encyclopedia of Bible Life.* New York: Harper, 1944.

Miller, M. S. and J. L. Miller. *Harper's Bible Dictionary.* New York: Harper, 1952.

Orr, James (ed.) *The International Standard Bible Encyclopedia.* 5 vols. (Now undergoing revision.) Grand Rapids: William B. Eerdmans, 1939.

Macauley, Samuel (ed.) *The New Schaff-Herzog Encyclopedia of Religious Knowledge.* 12 vols. Reprinted with two new volumes. Grand Rapids: Baker Book House, 1955.

Tenney, Merrill C. *The Zondervan Pictorial Bible Dictionary.* A thorough, extensively illustrated reference work. Grand Rapids: Zondervan Publishing House, 1963.

Blaiklock, E. M. *The Zondervan Bible Atlas*. Grand Rapids: Zondervan Publishing House, 1969.

Bouquet, A. C. *Everyday Life in New Testament Times*. New York: Scribners, 1955.

Grollenberg, Lucas H. *Atlas of the Bible*. New York: Thomas Nelson and Sons, 1956.

Heaton, E. W. *Everyday Life in Old Testament Times*. New York: Scribners, 1956.

Kraeling, Emil G. *Bible Atlas*. New York: Rand McNally and Company, 1956.

Kraeling, Emil G. (ed.) *Historical Atlas of the Holy Land*. New York: Rand McNally and Company, 1959. (Small paperback.)

May, Herbert G. (ed.) *Oxford Bible Atlas*. New York: Oxford University Press, 1962.

Pfeiffer, Charles F. *Baker's Bible Atlas*. Grand Rapids: Baker Book House, 1961.

Rowley, H. H. *The Modern Reader's Bible Atlas*. New York: Association Press, 1961. (Pocket size.)

Shepherd, William R. *Historical Atlas*. Pikesville, Maryland: Colonial Offset Co., 1956. 8th Edition.

Smith, George Adam. *Historical Geography of the Holy Land*. New York: Harper, 1931. 25th Edition.

Stirling, John. *An Atlas Illustrating the Acts of the Apostles and the Epistles*. London: George Philip and Son, Limited, 1954. (Small paperback.)

Stirling, John. *An Atlas of the Life of Christ*. London: George Philip and Son, Limited, 1954. (Small paperback.)

Van Der Meer, Frederick. *Atlas of the Early Christian World*. New York: Nelson, 1958.

Wright, G. Ernest and Floyd V. Filson. (eds.) *The Westminster Atlas of the Bible*. Philadelphia: The Westminster Press, 1956. Revised edition.

Youngman, Bernard R. *The Lands and Peoples of the Living Bible*. New York: Hawthorn Books, Inc., 1959.

❧ MAPS ❧

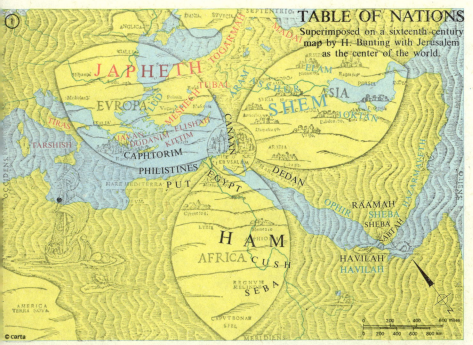

TABLE OF NATIONS

Superimposed on a sixteenth-century map by H. Bunting with Jerusalem as the center of the world.

SEPTENTRIO

DANIA   SVVECIA

ANGLICA   MADAI

JAPHETH   TOGARMAH

ELAM

ASHUR

EVROPA   SHEM   ASIA

MESHECH   TUBAL   PERSIA

TIRAS   JAVAN   DODANIM   ELISHAH   KITTIM   JOKTAN

TARSHISH   CANAAN

CAPHTORIM   JERUSALEM

PHILISTINES   DEDAN

MARE MEDITERRA   PUT   EGYPT   OPHIR   RAAMAH
SHEBA
SHEBA

HAM

AFRICA   CUSH   HAVILAH
HAVILAH

SEBA

AMERICA
TERRA NOVA

CAPVT BONAE
SPEI

MERIDIES

© carta

	200	400	600 miles
0 200	400	600	800 km

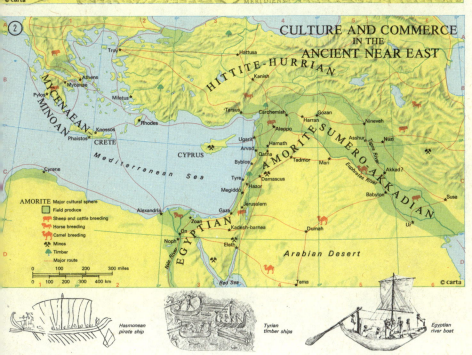

CULTURE AND COMMERCE
IN THE
ANCIENT NEAR EAST

Troy   Hattusa

HITTITE-HURRIAN

Kanish

Athens   Mycenae

MYCENAEAN

Pylos   Miletus   Tarsus   Carchemish   Gozan   Nineveh

MINOAN   Aleppo   Harran   Nuzi   Asshur

Rhodes   Ugarit   SUMERO-AKKADIAN   Tigris River

Knossos   Hamath   AMORITE

Phaistos   CRETE   Arvad   Qatna   Tadmor   Mari   Akkad?

CYPRUS   Byblos   Euphrates River

Mediterranean   Sea   Tyre   Damascus

Cyrene   Megiddo   Hazor   Babylon   Susa

AMORITE Major cultural sphere
- □ Field produce
- Sheep and cattle breeding
- Horse breeding
- Camel breeding
- ⚒ Mines
- Timber
- Major route

Alexandria   Gaza   Jerusalem   Ur

Zoan   Dumah

EGYPTIAN   On   Kadesh-barnea

Noph   Elath   Arabian Desert

Nile River   Tema

	100	200	300 miles
0 100	200 300	400 km	

Red Sea   © carta

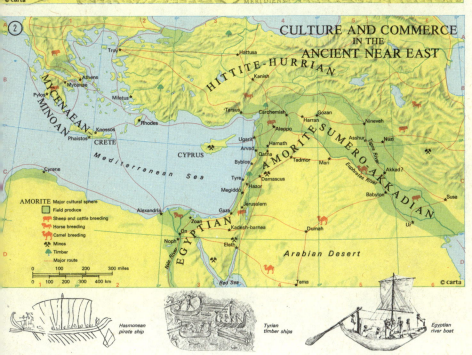

Hasmonean
pirate ship

Tyrian
timber ships

Egyptian
river boat

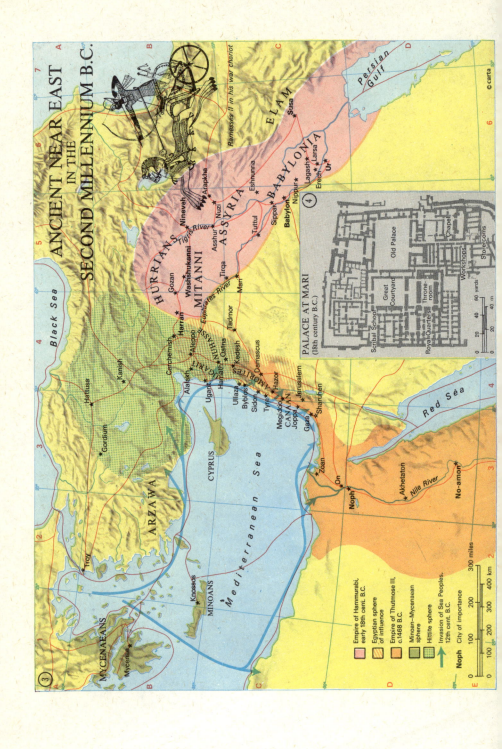

ANCIENT NEAR EAST
IN THE
SECOND MILLENNIUM B.C.

Ramesses II in his war chariot

Black Sea

Persian Gulf

Red Sea

Mediterranean Sea

ELAM

HURRIANS

ASSYRIA

BABYLONIA

MITANNI

Washshukanni

Tigris River

Euphrates River

Nile River

CANAAN

AMORITES

NUHASSE

UGARIT

ARZAWA

CYPRUS

MINOANS

MYCENAEANS

Susa
Atapkha
Nineveh
Asshur
Nuzi
Eshnunna
Gozan
Tirqa
Mari
Sippar
Babylon
Nippur
Lagash
Larsa
Erech
Ur
Tuttul
Harran
Carchemish
Aleppo
Alalakh
Tadmor
Qatna
Kedesh
Damascus
Hamath
Ullaza
Ugarit
Byblos
Sidon
Tyre
Hazor
Megiddo
Jerusalem
Joppa
Gaza
Sharuhen
Zoan
On
Noph
Akhetaton
No-amon
Hattusa
Kanish
Gordium
Troy
Mycenae
Knossos

PALACE AT MARI
(18th century B.C.)

Scribal School
Great Courtyard
Old Palace
Throne-room
Chapel
Workshops
Storerooms
Royal Quarters

60 yards
40 m

④

© carta

A   B   C   D

7   6   5   4   3   2

Noph City of importance

Empire of Hammurabi, early 18th cent. B.C.
Egyptian sphere of influence
Empire of Thutmose III, c.1468 B.C.
Minoan–Mycenaean sphere
Hittite sphere
Invasion of Sea Peoples, 12th cent. B.C.

0   100   200   300 miles
0   100   200   300   400 km

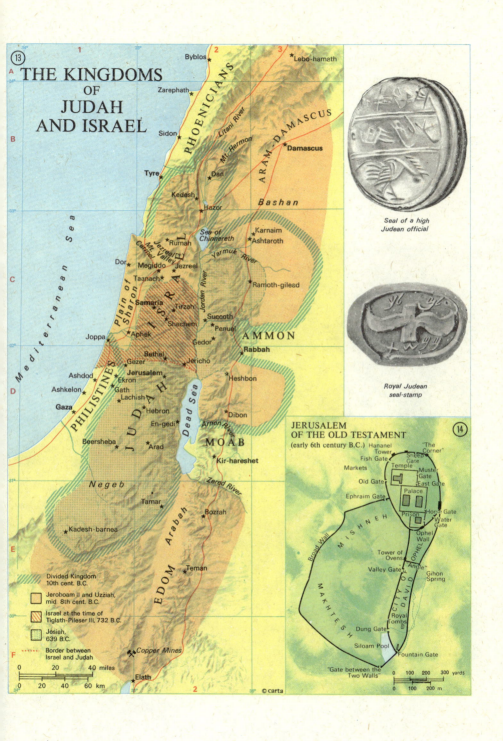

THE KINGDOMS OF JUDAH AND ISRAEL

13

A

B

C

D

E

F

1   2   3

Byblos

Lebo-hamath

Zarephath

PHOENICIANS

Litani River

Sidon

Mt. Hermon

ARAM-DAMASCUS

Damascus

Tyre

Dan

Kedesh

Hazor

Bashan

Mediterranean Sea

Karnaim
Ashtaroth

Sea of Chinnereth

Rumah

Jezreel Valley

Mt. Gilboa

Yarmuk River

Dor

Megiddo

Jezreel

Taanach

Ramoth-gilead

ISRAEL

Samaria

Tirzah

Jordan River

Plain of Sharon

Shechem

Succoth
Penuel

AMMON

Joppa

Aphek

Gedor

Rabbah

Bethel

Jericho

Ashdod

Jerusalem

Heshbon

Ekron

Gath

Lachish

PHILISTINES

Gaza

Hebron

JUDAH

Dead Sea

Dibon

En-gedi

Arnon River

Beersheba

Arad

MOAB

Kir-hareset

Negeb

Zered River

Tamar

Bozrah

Kadesh-barnea

EDOM

Arabah

Teman

Legend

Divided Kingdom 10th cent. B.C.

Jeroboam II and Uzziah, mid 8th cent. B.C.

Israel at the time of Tiglath-Pileser III, 732 B.C.

Josiah, 639 B.C.

Border between Israel and Judah

Copper Mines

Elath

0   20   40 miles
0   20   40   60 km

© carta

*Seal of a high
Judean official*

*Royal Judean
seal-stamp*

JERUSALEM OF THE OLD TESTAMENT
(early 6th century B.C.)

14

Hananel Tower

"The Corner"

Sheep Gate

Fish Gate

Temple

Muster Gate

Markets

Old Gate

East Gate

Ephraim Gate

Palace

Horse Gate

Prison

Water Gate

MISHNEH

Ophel Wall

Broad Wall

OPHEL

Tower of Ovens

CITY OF DAVID

Valley Gate

"Angle"

Gihon Spring

MAKHTESH

Royal Tombs

Dung Gate

Siloam Pool

Fountain Gate

"Gate between the Two Walls"

0   100   200   300 yards
0   100   200 m

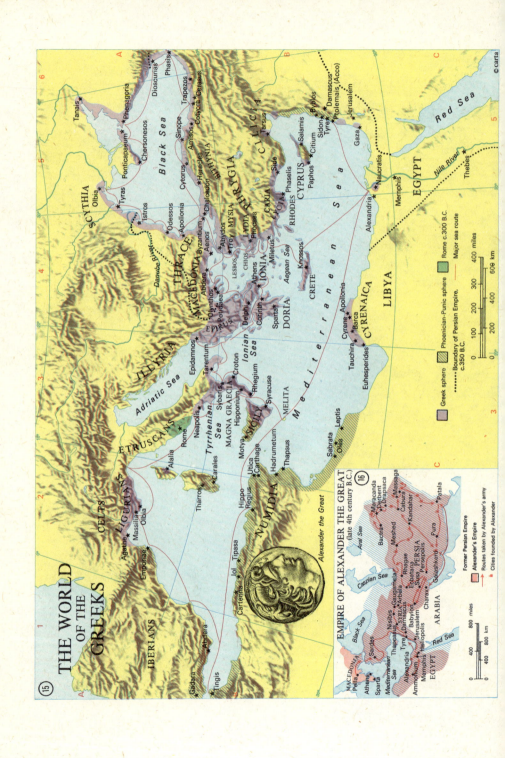

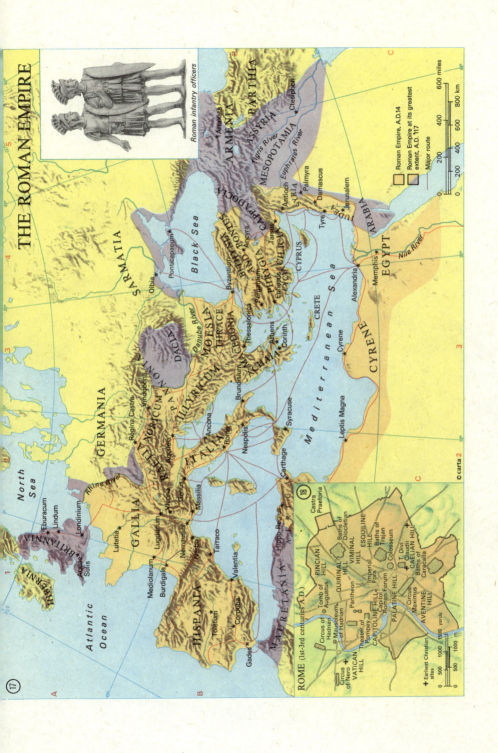

THE ROMAN EMPIRE

Roman infantry officers

Roman Empire, A.D.14

Roman Empire at its greatest
extent, A.D. 117

Major route

0   200   400   600 miles
0   200   400   600   800 km

© carta

Map labels

North Sea
Atlantic Ocean
HIBERNIA
BRITANNIA
Eburacum
Lindum
Londinium
Aquae Sulis
GERMANIA
GALLIA
Lutetia
Lugdunum
Mediolanum
Burdigala
Narbo
Tarraco
Valentia
HISPANIA
Toletum
Corduba
Gades
MAURETANIA
Regina Castra
Vindobona
Aquileia
Verona
Genua
Massilia
Mediolanum
ITALIA
Rome
Ancona
Neapolis
Brundisium
Carthage
Hippo Regius
SARMATIA
Rhine River
Danube River
NORICUM
PANNONIA
RAETIA
ILLYRICUM
DACIA
MOESIA
THRACE
MACEDONIA
ACHAIA
Thessalonica
Athens
Corinth
Syracuse
Leptis Magna
Black Sea
Olbia
Ponticapaeum
Byzantium
Pergamum
PHRYGIA
Ephesus
BITHYNIA AND PONTUS
GALATIA
Ancyra
CAPPADOCIA
LYCIA
CILICIA
Tarsus
CRETE
Cyrene
CYRENE
Mediterranean Sea
Alexandria
Memphis
EGYPT
Nile River
CYPRUS
SYRIA
Antioch
Palmyra
Damascus
Tyre
JUDEA
Jerusalem
ARABIA
ARMENIA
Artaxata
ASSYRIA
MESOPOTAMIA
Tigris River
Euphrates River
Ctesiphon
PARTHIA

Inset map

ROME (1st-3rd centuries A.D.)

18

Castra Praetoria
Circus of Nero
VATICAN HILL
Circus of Nero
Mausoleum of Hadrian
Tomb of Augustus
PINCIAN HILL
QUIRINAL HILL
VIMINAL HILL
ESQUILINE HILL
Baths of Diocletian
Baths of Trajan
Colosseum
T. Divi Claudii
CAELIAN HILL
Baths of Caracalla
Pantheon
Theater of Pompey
CAPITOLINE HILL
Capitol
Imperial Fora
Roman Forum
PALATINE HILL
Circus Maximus
AVENTINE HILL

+ Earliest Christian sites

0   500   1000   1500 yards
0   500   1000   1500 m

17

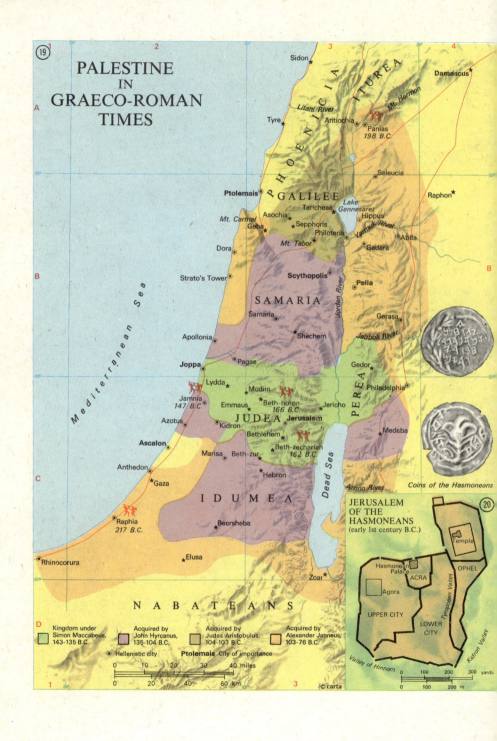

PALESTINE
IN
GRAECO-ROMAN
TIMES

Sidon

Damascus

Litani River

Tyre

Antiochia

Panias
198 B.C.

Mt. Hermon

Seleucia

Raphon★

Ptolemais

GALILEE

Lake
Gennesaret

Hippus

Mt. Carmel

Asochis

Taricheae

Geba

Sepphoris

Philoteria

Yarmuk River

Abila

Dora

Mt. Tabor

Gadara

Strato's Tower

Scythopolis

Pella

Jordan River

SAMARIA

Samaria

Gerasa

Shechem

Jabbok River

Apollonia

Pegae

Gedor

Joppa

Philadelphia

Lydda

Modiin

PEREA

Jamnia
147 B.C.

Emmaus

Beth-horon
166 B.C.

Jericho

Azotus

JUDEA

Jerusalem

Kidron

Bethlehem

Medeba

Ascalon

Beth-zechariah
162 B.C.

Marisa

Beth-zur

Dead Sea

Anthedon

Hebron

Arnon River

Gaza

IDUMEA

Mediterranean Sea

Raphia
217 B.C.

Beersheba

Rhinocorura

Elusa

Zoar

NABATEANS

Coins of the Hasmoneans

JERUSALEM
OF THE
HASMONEANS
(early 1st century B.C.)

Temple

Hasmonean
Palace

ACRA

OPHEL

Tyropoeon Valley

Agora

UPPER CITY

LOWER
CITY

Kidron Valley

Valley of Hinnom

0   100   200   300 yards

0   100   200 m

JESUS IN HIS LAND

(21)

Sidon

Damascus ★

Litani River

Tyre ★

★ **Caesarea Philippi**

TETRARCHY

GALILEE **OF PHILIP**

★ Chorazin

Capernaum ☆ ★ Bethsaida

Heptapegon ★ Gergesa

Cana ★ *Sea of Galilee*

Ptolemais ★ ★ Hippus

Sepphoris ★ Tiberias

Nazareth ☆ Dium ★

☆ **Mt. Tabor** *Yarmuk River*

Nain ★ Gadara Abila ★

Caesarea ★

Scythopolis ★ **D E C A P O L I S**

★ Pella

S A M A R I A

Samaria ★ *Jordan River*

★ Sychar Gerasa ★

Antipatris ☆ *Jabbok River*

Joppa ★

Lydda ★ Gadora ★

Mt. of Temptation Philadelphia ★

Jamnia ★ **P E R E A**

Emmaus ★ Jericho ★

Azotus ★ **Jerusalem** ☆ Site of Baptism ☆

En-kerem ☆ ☆ Bethany ★ Qumran

Bethlehem ★

Ascalon ★ **J U D E A**

Gaza ★ *Dead Sea*

Hebron ★ Macherus ★

Arnon River

Masada ★

Beersheba ★

Mediterranean Sea

Zered River

Legend:
→ Flight to Egypt and return to Nazareth
→ Baptism and sojourn in the desert
→ Galilean journeys and to Caesarea Philippi
→ Journey to Tyre and Sidon
→ Journey to and from Jerusalem
☆ Christian holy site

0 10 20 30 40 miles
0 20 40 60 km

© carta

Inscription of Pontius Pilate

JERUSALEM OF THE NEW TESTAMENT
(1st century A.D.)

(22)

Bethesda

Golgotha ★ Antonia Fortress

Temple

Herod Antipas' palace

Gethsemane

Herod's palace Royal portico

House of Caiaphas **U P P E R C I T Y**

L O W E R C I T Y

Tyropoeon Valley

Kidron Valley

Hinnom Valley

0 100 200 300 yards
0 100 200 m

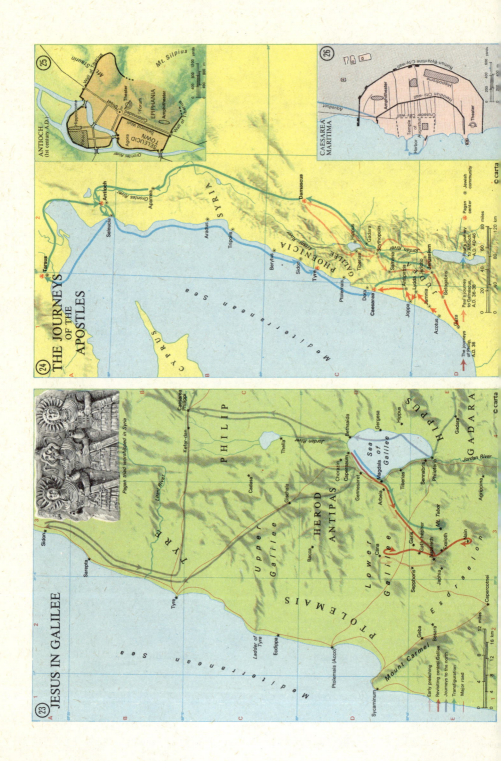

㉕ ANTIOCH
(1st century A.D.)

EPIPHANIA

SELEUCID TOWN

Mt. Silpius

㉖ CAESAREA MARITIMA

㉔ THE JOURNEYS OF THE APOSTLES

Mediterranean Sea

CYPRUS

SYRIA

PHOENICIA

GALILEE

JUDEA

Antioch
Seleucia
Tarsus
Aradus
Tripolis
Berytus
Sidon
Tyre
Ptolemais
Dora
Caesarea
Samaria
Joppa
Lydda
Jamnia
Jerusalem
Jericho
Azotus
Gaza
Bethgubrin
Damascus
Hippus
Gadara
Scythopolis
Tiberias

The journeys of Philip, A.D. 36
Paul's journey to Damascus, A.D. 35–38
Paul's journey in Judea, A.D. 40–45
Pagan center
Jewish community

© carta

㉓ JESUS IN GALILEE

Mediterranean Sea

PHILIP

HEROD ANTIPAS

TYRE

PTOLEMAIS

HIPPUS

GADARA

Upper Galilee
Lower Galilee
Sea of Galilee
Esdraelon
Mount Carmel

Sidon
Sarepta
Ecdippa
Tyre
Ptolemais (Acco)
Sycaminum
Caparcotnei
Geba
Besara
Sepphoris
Japhia
Nazareth
Cana
Gath-hepher
Garis
Mt. Tabor
Exaloth
Nain
Arbela
Gennesaret
Magdala
Capernaum
Chorazin
Bethsaida
Tiberias
Sennabris
Philoteria
Agrippina
Hippus
Gadara
Gergesa
Thella
Kefar-dan
Caddasa
Gischala
Baca
Caesarea Philippi

Pagan triad worshiped in Syria
Jordan River
Litani River

Ladder of Tyre

Early preaching
Revisiting central Galilee
Journeys to the north
Transfiguration
Major road

© carta

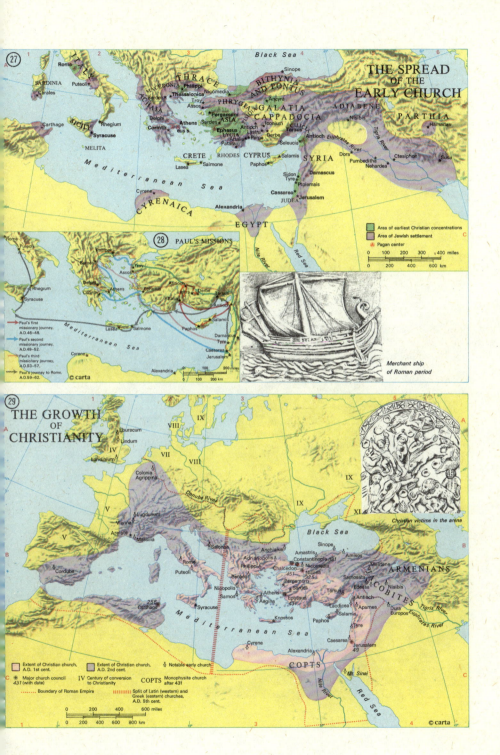

PALESTINE
IN THE TIME
OF THE
OLD TESTAMENT

Damascus

Zarephath
Litani River
Ijon
Tyre
Abel-beth-maacha
Mt. Hermon
Kanah
Beth-anath
Dan

Achziv
Abdon
Yiron
Kedesh
Janoah
Merom
Hazor

Acco
Beth-emek
Cabul
Hukok
Chinnereth
Sea of Chinnereth
Naveh
Kishon River
Aphek
Hannathon
Rimmon
Karnaim
Ashtaroth
Libnath
Achshaph
Adamah
Golan
Mt. Carmel
Beth-lehem
Beth-shemesh
Geba
Shimron
Aznoth-tabor
Anaharath
Yarmuk River
Joknean
Shunem
En-dor
Jarmuth
Edrei
Dor
Megiddo
Jezreel
Kamon
Beth-arbel
Tob
Taanach
Lo-debar
Bezer
Iron
Beth-shean
Ham
Mt. Gilboa
Pehel
Ramoth-gilead
Hepher
Gath
Dothan
Bezek
Jabesh-gilead
Socoh
Geba
Abel-meholah
Shiphthan
Tirzah
Zaphon
Samaria
Mahanaim
Jabbok River
Shechem
Succoth
Penuel
Arumah
Janoah
Zarethan
Tappuah
Lebonah
Adam
Geth-rimmon
Yarkon River
Aphek
Shiloh
Jogbehah
Joppa
Yehud
Zeredah
Geba
Betonim
Beth-dagon
Ono
Ophrah
Lod
Nebellat
Jazer
Rabbah
Jabneel
Gittaim
Beth-horon
Bethel
Ai
Gilgal
Beth-nimrah
Eltekeh
Gezer
Ramah
Jericho
Abel-keramim
Gibbethon
Shaalbim
Gibeon
Geba
Beth-hogla
Heshbon
Timnah
Zorah
Aijalon
Gibeah
Ekron
Kiriath-jearim
Jerusalem
Beth-jeshimoth
Ashdod
Chesalon
Medeba
Gath
Beth-shemesh
Bethlehem
Baal-maon
Azekah
Socoh
Etam
Ashkelon
Libnah
Keilah
Gedor
Tekoa
Mareshah
Lachish
Beth-zur
Zereth-shahar
Eglon
Beth-tappuah
Hebron
Jahzah
Gaza
Carmel
En-gedi
Dibon
Aroer
Yurza
Ziklag
Debir
Maon
Yattir
Eshtemoa
Sharuhen
Moladah
Arad
Beersheba
Kabzeel
Aroer
Kir-moab

Mediterranean Sea

Jordan River

Dead Sea

Arnon River

Zoar
Zered River

Tamar
Zalmonah
Sela
Bozrah
Punon

Rekem

feet / m scale

feet	m
8202	2500
6561	2000
4921	1500
3280	1000
1640	500
820	250
0	0

Below sea level

0 10 20 30 40 miles
0 20 40 60 km

© carta

Column from Isaiah scroll
from Dead Sea Caves

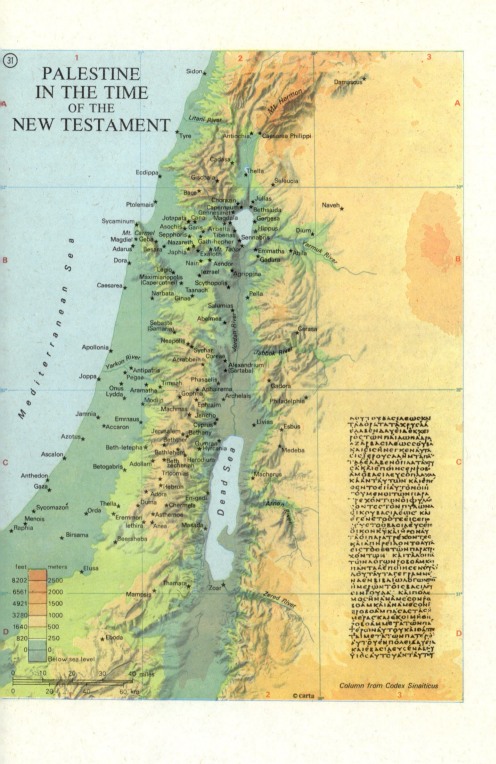

PALESTINE
IN THE TIME
OF THE
NEW TESTAMENT

31

Mediterranean Sea

Dead Sea

Jordan River

Yarmuk River

Jabbok River

Arnon River

Zered River

Yarkon River

Litani River

Mt. Hermon

Mt. Carmel

Mt. Tabor

Sidon
Damascus
Tyre
Antiochia
Caesarea Philippi
Cadasa
Ecdippa
Gischala
Thella
Seleucia
Baca
Chorazin
Julias
Naveh
Ptolemais
Capernaum
Bethsaida
Gennesaret
Magdala
Gergesa
Jotapata
Cana
Sycaminum
Asochis
Garis
Arbella
Hippus
Dium
Sepphoris
Tiberias
Magdiel
Geba
Nazareth
Gath-hepher
Sennabris
Adarus
Besara
Japhia
Exaloth
Emmatha
Abila
Dora
Nain
Mt. Tabor
Gadara
Legio
Aendor
Agrippina
Maximianopolis
(Capercotnei)
Iezrael
Scythopolis
Caesarea
Taanach
Pella
Narbata
Ginae
Salumias
Abelmea
Gerasa
Sebaste
(Samaria)
Neapolis
Sychar
Coreae
Apollonia
Acrabbein
Alexandrium
(Sartaba)
Yarkon River
Antipatris
Jabbok River
Joppa
Pegae
Phasaelis
Gadora
Onus
Timnah
Aphairema
Philadelphia
Lydda
Aramatha
Gophna
Archelais
Jamnia
Modin
Ephraim
Machmas
Jericho
Livias
Emmaus
Cyprus
Esbus
Accaron
Azotus
Jerusalem
Bethany
Medeba
Ascalon
Bethther
Qumran
Hyrcania
Anthedon
Beth-letepha
Herodium
Bethlehem
Macherus
Gaza
Betogabris
Beth
zechariah
Adollam
Tricomias
Sycomazon
Hebron
Menois
Adora
En-gedi
Raphia
Thella
Duma
Chermela
Orda
Birsama
Eremmon
Asthemoe
Beersheba
Iethira
Anea
Masada
Elusa
Thamara
Zoar
Mampsis
Eboda

feet meters
8202 2500
6561 2000
4921 1500
3280 1000
1640 500
820 250
0 0
Below sea level

0 10 20 30 40 miles
0 20 40 60 km

© carta

Column from Codex Sinaiticus

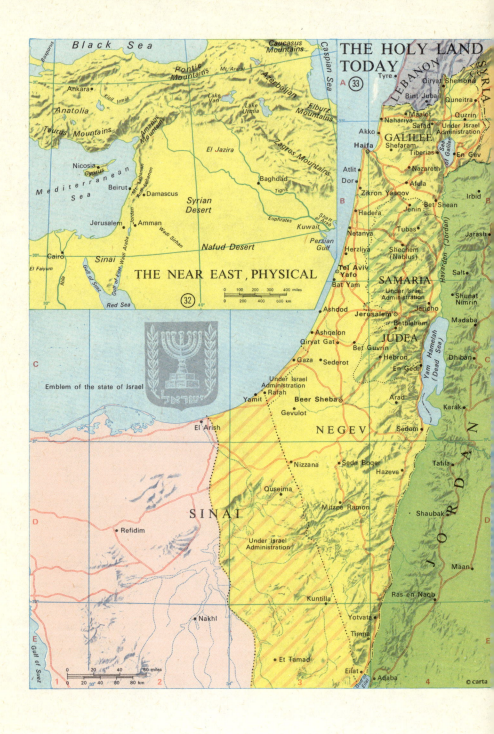

THE HOLY LAND TODAY

A ③③

THE NEAR EAST, PHYSICAL

③②

Black Sea

Caucasus Mountains

Caspian Sea

Pontic Mountains

Mt. Ararat

Ankara

Kizil Irmak

Lake Van

Lake Urmia

Elburz Mountains

Anatolia

Taurus Mountains

Amanus Mountains

El Jazira

Zagros Mountains

Nicosia

Cyprus

Mediterranean Sea

Beirut

Mt. Lebanon

Anti Lebanon

Damascus

Baghdad

Tigris

Syrian Desert

Jerusalem

Amman

Wadi Sirhan

Euphrates

Shatt al Arab

Kuwait

Nafud Desert

Persian Gulf

Cairo

El Faiyum

Nile

Sinai

Gulf of Suez

Gulf of Eilat, Wadi Araba

Jordan

Red Sea

0 100 200 300 400 miles
0 200 400 600 km

Emblem of the state of Israel

ישראל

LEBANON

SYRIA

Tyre

Qiryat Shemona

Bint Jubail

Quneitra

Maalot

Nahariya

Safad

Quzrin

Akko

Under Israel Administration

Haifa

GALILEE

Shefaram

Tiberias

Sea of Galilee

En Gev

Atlit

Nazareth

Dor

Afula

Irbid

Zikron Yaaqov

Jenin

Bet Shean

Hadera

Tubas

Jarash

Netanya

Shechem (Nablus)

Herzliya

Hayarden (Jordan)

Salt

Tel Aviv Yafo

SAMARIA

Bat Yam

Under Israel Administration

Shunat Nimrin

Ashdod

Jerusalem

Jericho

Bethlehem

Madaba

Ashqelon

JUDEA

Qiryat Gat

Bet Guvrin

Hebron

Dhiban

Gaza

Sederot

En Gedi

Yam Hamelah (Dead Sea)

Under Israel Administration

Arad

Karak

Rafah

Yamit

Beer Sheba

Gevulot

Sedom

El Arish

NEGEV

Nizzana

Seda Boqer

Hazeva

Tafila

Quseima

Mitzpe Ramon

Shaubak

SINAI

Refidim

Under Israel Administration

JORDAN

Maan

Nakhl

Kuntilla

Ras en Naqb

Yotvata

Timna

Et Tamad

Eilat

Aqaba

Gulf of Suez

Gulf of Eilat

0 20 40 60 miles
0 20 40 60 80 km

© carta

INDEX TO PERSONS, PLACES, THINGS

A

Aaron, 68, 70, 121, 122, 187
Aaron ben Asher, 30
Abdon, 76
Abednago, 108, 123, 213
Abel, 65, 188
Abelard, 300
Abihu, 121
Abijah, 82, 124
Abijam, 124
Abimelech, 75
Abisha Scroll, 37
Abner, 80
Abraham, 6, 63, 65, 187, 188, 198, 200, 207, 219, 235
Absalom, 80
Acacia, 264
Accuracy of the Bible, 29
Achaia, 190
Achan, 74
Acts, 141, 151, 153, 154
Adam, 65, 188, 196
Adonijah, 213
Aelfric, 45
Agrapha, 41
Agrippa I, II, 188, 197
Agur, 96, 97
Ahab, 82, 83, 124, 194

Ahasuerus, 91, 188, 196
Ahaz, 85, 100, 109, 114, 123, 124, 199
Ahaziah, 122, 124
Ai, 74
á Kempis, Thomas, 300
Aland, Prof. Kurt, 35
Albright, Jacob, 300
Alexander of Macedon, 26
Alexander the Great, 127, 128
Alexandria, 16, 36, 138
Alexandrian Canon, 18
Alfred, King, 45
Algum, 264
Almond, 39, 265
Almug, 40, 265
Alphaeus, 210
Alve, 265
Amalek, 219
Amalekites, 78, 206
Amasa, 80
Amaziah, 85, 124, 189
Ambrose, 300
American Standard Version, 51
American Translation, 55
Amittai, 113, 205
Amman, Jacob, 300
Ammon, 79, 207
Amon, 85, 125
Amorites, 74

Amos, 100, 109, 111, 188
Amoz, 111, 200
Amplified N.T., 57
Amram, 187, 211
Ananias, 189, 218
Ananias the Disciple, 189
Anathoth, 203
Ancient Versions, 42
Andrew, 25, 189, 190
Andrewes, Lancelot, 300
Anemone, 265
Animals of the Bible, 278
Anselm, 301
Ant, 278
Antioch, 141, 154, 163, 229
Antiochus, 128
Antiochus Epiphanes, 257
Antipas, 199
Aphek, 122
Apocalypse, 131
Apocrypha, 18, 19, 21, 36, 56, 127, 128
Apocryphal, 127
Apollos, 161, 190, 217
Appian Way, 157
Apple, 266
Aquila, 190, 217
Arabic Version, 42
Aramaic, 25, 26, 37
Archelaus, 129, 184
Areopagus, 152
Aretas IV, 199
Aristobulus, 128
Arius, 301
Armenian Version, 42
Arminius Jacobus, 301
Arrangement of New Testament, 8
Arrangement of Old Testament, 6
Arrangement of Paul's letters, 152, 153
Artaxerxes, 188, 190, 213
Asa, 82, 85
Asaph, 95, 199, 213
Asbury, Francis, 301
Asher, 207
Asp, 278
Ass, 278
Assassins (Sicarri), 263
Assyria, 84, 85, 113, 116, 240
Assyrians, 12
Athaliah, 85, 124
Athanasius, 18, 21, 301
Atonement, 68, 257
Augustine, 17, 21
Augustine of Hippo, 302

B

Baal, 83, 84, 85, 194
Baasha, 82, 124
Babylon, 84, 89, 127
Babylonia, 30
Babylonians, 107
Babylonian captivity, 103, 118
Balaam, 70, 190
Balm, 266
Barker, Robert, 49
Barley, 266
Barnabas, 137, 138, 190, 191, 201
Bartholomew, 191
Baruch, 103, 127
Basil of Caesarea, 302
Bat, 278
Bath, 294
Bathsheba, 80, 213, 221
Baxter, Richard, 302
Bear, 278
Beatty, Chester: Papyri, 33
Bede, the Venerable, 45, 303
Bee, 279
Beecher, Henry Ward, 303
Beeri, 109, 199
Bells, 253
Beersheba, 78, 200
Belshazzar, 104, 191, 193
Benedict of Nursia, 303
Benhadad, 83, 84
Benjamin, 217, 220
Beor, 190
Berechiab, 119
Berkeley Version 7, 56
Bernard of Clairvaux, 303
Bethany, 207
Bethel, 203
Bethlehem, 115, 230
Bethesda, 228
Bethsaida, 189
Beth-shemesh, 122
Bethuel, 217
Beza, Theodore, 303
Bible, 5
Bible Dictionaries and Encyclopedias, 330
Bible Geographies, Atlases, Customs, 331
Bible Interpretation and The Holy Spirit, 16
Bible in Basic English, 56
Bible Union Version, 52

Bildad, 93, 94
Bird's-Eye View of Palestine, 227
Birds of the Bible, 287
Bishop's Bible, 49
Boar, 279
Boaz, 76, 77, 218
Bodmer Papyri, 32, 40
Bohairic, 40
Boniface, Winfred, 303
Book of Jasher, 72
Booth, William, 304
Borah, 193
Box, 266
Breeches Bible, 48
Brewster, William, 304
Brooks, Phillips, 304
Broom, 266
Brother Lawrence, 304
Browne, Robert, 304
Bruce, Professor, 29, 57
Bull, 279
Bulrush, 266
Bunyan, John, 305
Buzi, 106
Byblos, 5, 229

C

Caedmon, 45
Caesar, 166, 199
Caesar, Augustus, 191
Caesar, Claudius, 191
Caesar, Julius, 191
Caesarea, 124, 166, 232
Caiaphas, 191, 263
Cain, 188
Caleb, 74, 191, 192, 206
Calendar of Jewish Feasts and Festivals, 260
Calf, 279
Calvin, 19, 147, 305
Camel, 279
Campbell, Alexander, 305
Cana, 145, 232
Canaan, 70, 186, 192, 206, 207
Canaanites, 233
Canaanites and Archeology, 234, 235
Canon Fixed, 21
Caper, 267
Capernaum, 209
Carey, William, 305

Carmel, Mt., 84
Carob, 267
Cartwright, Peter, 306
Cartwright, Thomas, 306
Cassia, 267
Castanets, 253
Cedar, 267
Centenary Translation, 54
Cephas, 161
Chadwick, Samuel, 11
Chained Bible, 48
Chaldean, 117, 198
Chalmers, Thomas, 306
Chapter Divisions, 22
Chenoboskion, 40
Cherith, 83, 122, 194
Chestnut, 268
Chilion, 212, 218
Chronicles, 85
Chronological Chart of Acts, 152
Chrysostom, John, 306
Church of the Nativity, 14
Cinnamon, 268
Citron, 268
Clark, Kenneth, 54
Clarke, Adam, 306
Clarke, Francis E., 307
Clement, 16, 138, 146, 144
Clement of Alexandria, 307
Clement of Rome, 307
Codex, 28
Codex Alexandrinius, 34, 35
Codex Bezae, 34
Codex Ephraemi, 34
Codex Sinaiticus, 33, 34, 35
Codex Vaticanus, 34, 36
Codex Washingtonianus, 34
Colet, John, 307
Colossae, 167
Colossians, 205
Columba, 307
Concordances, 329
Confraternity Edition, 56
Constantine, 307
Coptic Museum, 41
Coptic Versions, 40
Copy Errors, 29
Cor, 294
Coriander, 268
Corinth, 157, 160, 161
Corinthian Church, 163, 190
Corinthians I, 160
Corinthians II, 162

Cornelius, 192
Council of Constance, 46
Council of Trent, 19, 38
Coverdale, Miles, 47, 48, 308
Cowman, Charles E., and Lettie, 308
Crammer, Thomas, 308
Crete, 172
Cromwell, Oliver, 309
Cromwell, Thomas, 48
Cubit, 293
Cummin, 268
Curetonian Syriac, 39
Cutler, Ethel, 54
Cymbals, 254
Cypress, 268
Cyprian, 309
Cyprus, 191
Cyril, 42
Cyrric, 89
Cyrus, 107, 192, 196, 198, 241

D

Dagon, 122
Damascus, 155, 215, 229
Damasus, Bishop of Rome, 38
Dan, 203
Daniel, 106, 107, 123, 131, 191, 192–
  93, 213
Darby, John, 309
Darius, 107, 118, 241
Darius Hysapis, 188
Darius the Mede, 188
David, 76, 79, 82, 87, 95, 123, 193, 199,
  205–06, 212, 213
Day, 291
Dead Sea, 71, 228, 230
Dead Sea Scrolls, 19, 27, 31, 37, 91, 260
Deborah, 75, 193
Dedication, 257
Deissman, Gustav, 309
Deliberate change in text, 30
Delilah, 218
Demetrius, 180
Denarius, 296
Denny, James, 309
Deuteronomy, 70
Didrachmon, 296
Dinah, 207, 220
Diocletian, Emperor, 28
Diotrephes, 180

Divided Monarchy, 239–40
Dodd, C. H., 52
Dog, 280
Donkey, 280
Dorcas, 193–94
Doric, 296
Douai Version, 49
Drachme, 296
Dram, 296
Dromedary, 280
Drum, 254
Drummond, Henry, 310
Dulcimer, 254

E

Eagle, 88
Eckhart, Meister, 310
Ecclesiastes, 97
Eden, 188
Edessa, 38
Edom, 112, 113
Edomites, 112, 201, 234
Edwards, Jonathan, 310
Egypt, 14, 66, 67, 188
Ehud, 75
Elah, 82, 124
Elders, 263
Eleazer, 187
Eli, 78, 219
Elijah, 82, 83, 84, 122, 194, 204
Elimelech, 212, 218
Eliphaz, 93, 94, 194
Elisabeth, 194, 198, 204, 210
Elisha, 84, 122, 123, 194, 212
Elkanah, 198, 218
Elkosh, 116
Elkoshite, 212
Elon, 76
Emperor Claudius, 190
Emperor of Rome, 183
Enoch, 20, 194, 195, 211
Epaphras, 166, 195, 198, 218
Epaphroditus, 166, 195
Ephah, 294
Ephesians, 164
Ephesus, 145, 160, 164, 165, 166, 178,
  190, 321
Ephraim, 206
Epiphanes, 128
Epistle of Barnabas, 34

Erasmus, 311
Erechtheum, 156
Esau, 99, 112, 200, 201, 217
Eschatology, 168
Essenes, 168, 260
Esther, 90, 188, 195–96, 258
Ethan, 95
Ethiopian Version, 42
Eunice, 222
Eunuch, 215
Eusebius of Caesarea, 138, 311
Eusheba, 187
Evangelical prophet, 100
Eve, 65, 196
Evening, 291
Exilic and Post Exilic periods, 241–42
Exodus, 65
Ezekiel, 106, 196
Ezra, 84, 89, 90, 196, 208, 213, 263

F

Farthing, 296
Fathers of Israel, 235
Fathom, 294
Felix, 192
Felix, Aontonius, 196, 197
Festus, Parcius, 197
Fifth month, 257
Fig, 268
Fingerbreadth, 293
Finney, Charles G., 311
Fir, 269
First Complete English Bible, 47
First Fruits, 257
First Printed English
    New Testament, 47
Fish, 280
Flax, 269
Flea, 280
Fletcher, John, 311
Flute, 254
Fly, 280
Fourth Gospel, 146
Fourth Month, 257
Fox, George, 281, 311
Francis of Assisi, 312
Frankincense, 269
Frog, 281
Furlong, 294

G

Gad, 74, 77, 207
Gaius, 157, 180
Gall, 270
Galatia, 163
Galatians, 163
Gallio, 197
Gamaliel, 197
Garden of Gethsemane, 25, 206, 227
Garlic, 270
Gath, 114
Gath-hepher, 113
Gate Beautiful, 134
Gaul, 129
Gaza, 218
Gazelle, 281
Gebal, 5
Gehazi, 122
Genesis, 65
Geneva Bible, 48, 49
Georgian Version, 42
Gerizim, Mt., 37
Gibeab, 76
Gibson, Mrs., 39
Gideon, 74, 75, 197, 256
Gideons International, 22
Gilbey, 48
Gilboa, 206
Gnostic, 41
Gnosticism, 167
Goat, 281
Golgotha, 221, 243
Goliath, 79, 193
Gomer, 109, 200
Gomorrah, 121
Good Samaritan Inn, 233
Goodspeed, Edgar J., 54, 55
Goodspeed's New Testament, 54
Gordon, A. R., 55
Gospel, 132
Gospel of Thomas, 40
Gothic Version, 42
Gourd, 270
Graham, Billy, 58
Grape, 270
Grasshopper, 281
Greek, 25
Gregory, Caspar Rene, 35
Gregory I, 312
Gull, 288
Gutenberg, Johan, 46, 312

H

Habakkuk, 116, 197, 198
Hacaliah, 213
Hadrian, Emperor, 257
Hagar-, 188, 198, 200, 219
Haggai, 89, 95, 118, 198
Ham, 213
Haman-, 91, 95, 196, 258
Hampden-Cook, Ernest, 53
Handbreadth, 293
Hannah, 78, 198, 218, 219
Hanukkah, 257
Haran, 201, 207
Harclean, 39
Hare, 281
Harp, 255
Harris, F., 54
Harrison, R. K., 58
Hart, 281
Hasmoneans, 128
Hawk, 288
Hazael, 84, 194
Hebrew, 25
Hebrews, 174, 175
Heifer, 282
Hemlock, 270
Hen, 288
Henna, 270
Henry VIII, 312
Heratlea, Thomas of, 39
Herod, 242
Herod Agrippa I, 184, 199, 202, 242
Herod Antipas, 129, 198, 199, 205, 242
Herodians, 260
Herodias, 198, 199, 205
Herod's Temple, 250, 251
Herod the Great, 129, 198, 199, 242
Hezekiah, 82, 85, 96, 97, 100, 109, 114, 117, 125, 199, 225, 240
Higgs, Mrs. Mary, 53
Hildebrand (Gregory VII), 313
Hillel, 197
Hin, 294
Hittites, 233
Holiness, 68
Holy Scriptures according to Massoretic Text, 54
Homer, 294
Hooke, S. H., 56
Hooker, Richard, 10, 313
Hoopoe, 288
Horeb, 72

Horites, 233
Horn, 255
Hornet, 282
Horse, 282
Hosea, 109, 124, 199, 200
Hour, 291
Hugo, Cardinal, 22
Hunter, A. M., 143
Huss, John, 313
Hyena, 282
Hyreannus, 129
Hyssop, 270

I

Ibzan, 76
Iddo, 119
Ignatus of Antioch, 313
Ignatius Loyola, 313
Imperial library of St. Petersway, 34
Innocent III, 314
Interpretation of revealed word, 13–15
Invention of printing, 46
Irenaeus, 133, 144, 151, 314
Isaac, 17, 63, 121, 188, 200, 217, 219, 220
Isaiah, 12, 20, 100, 101, 109, 200
Ishbosheth, 80
Ishmael, 188, 198, 200, 219
Israel, 67, 68, 69, 76, 227
Israelites, 66
Issachar, 207

J

Jackel, 283
Jacob, 63, 112, 200, 201, 206, 207, 217, 220
Jair, 75
Jairus, 204
James, 176, 188, 189, 190
James, Son of Alpheus, 176
James, Son of Zebedee, 176, 202
James, the Just, 201, 202
James the Less, 176, 202
Jamnia, Council of, 21
Jannaeus, Alexander, 128
Japeth, 214
Jared, 195

Jehoahaz, 85, 124, 125, 202
Jehoash, 124
Jehoiachin, 85, 106, 125, 202
Jehoiakim, 85, 125, 202
Jehoram, 124
Jehoshaphat, 82, 122, 124
Jehu, 84, 85, 124
Jephthah, 76
Jeremiah, 81, 103, 104, 116, 127, 225
Jeroboam, 82, 85, 203, 239
Jeroboam II, 109, 111, 124, 189
Jericho, 74, 122, 206, 228, 229
Jericho Road, 142
Jerome, 17, 19, 38, 314
Jerusalem, 38, 89, 90, 125, 137, 142, 228, 257
Jerusalem Council, 164
Jerusalem Temple Area, 81
Jesse, 193, 218
Jesus, 21, 131, 136, 139, 143, 144, 146, 148, 210, 218
Jethro, 67, 202, 203
Jezebel, 83, 84, 194
Joab, 80
Joash, 85
Job, 92, 93, 94, 194, 204
Jochebed, 187, 211
Joel, 110, 204
John the Apostle, 133, 138, 144, 145, 146, 147, 178, 179, 189, 191, 202, 204–05, 210, 221
John the Baptist, 121, 179, 189, 194, 199, 204, 224
John, Bishop of Seville, 42
John, Father of Simon Peter, 179
John Mark, 147, 190, 205
John Wesley's New Testament, 50
John I, 178
John II, 179
John III, 180
Jonah, 113, 116, 123, 205, 215
Jonathan, 79, 193, 205, 206
Joppa, 193
Jordan, 70, 71, 122, 207
Jordan River, 73, 230
Jordan Valley, 228–229
Josiah, 82, 85, 103, 117, 128, 198, 202, 203
Joseph, 17, 21, 63, 65, 202, 206, 210, 220, 236, 239
Josephus, 29, 204
Joseph Barsabbas, 210
Joseph of Arimathaea, 263

Joshua, 17, 70, 72, 75, 118, 119, 192
Jotham, 85, 100, 109, 114, 123
Jowett, John, 314
Jubilee, 257
Judah, 74, 85, 89, 90, 104, 207, 240
Judas Iscariot, 206
Jude, 177, 180, 207
Judges, 75
Jung Codex, 41
Juniper, 271
Justin Martyr, 38, 181, 314

K

Kab, 294
Kadesh-Barnea, 70, 193
Kent, Charles F., 54
Kenyon, Sir Frederic, 30, 33, 312
Kid, 283
Kierkegaard, Soren, 315
King James Version, 49
I Kings, 81
Kinsman-Redeemer, 77
Kish, 220
Kite, 288
Knox, John, 315
Knox, Ronald A., 56, 315
Knox's Translation, 56
Korah, 70, 95, 122
Kuyper, Abraham, 315

L

Laban, 201, 207, 217
Lake of Galilee, 230
Lamb, 283
Lamech, 211
Lamentations, 105
Language of revealed word, 13
Language of the Testaments, 10
Lamsa, George, 55
Lamsa's Translation, 55
Last Supper, 137
Latin Versions, 38
Law, Wm., 315
Lazarus, 145, 207, 208, 209
Leah, 207, 220
Lebanon, 229, 230
Lebbeus, 207, 222

Leech, 283
Leeks, 271
Lehi, 122
Lemuel, 96, 97
Lentils, 271
Leo the Great, 315
Leopard, 283
Lepton, 206
Levi, 68, 207
Leviathan, 284
Levite, 118, 211
Leviticus, 68
Lewis, C. S., 58
Lewis, Mrs., 39
Lights, 258
Line, 294
Lion, 284
Living Letters, 58
Livingstone, David, 312
Lizard, 284
Lochman Foundation, 51, 57
Locust, 284
Lois, 222
Longinus, 21
Lord's Supper, 67
Lot, 188, 207
Lot's Wife, 2, 121
Loz, 294
Lucian, 189
Luke, 131, 132, 133, 138, 141, 145, 153, 154, 208
Luther, Martin, 19, 316
Lydia, 166, 208
Lyre, 255
Lysias, Claudius, 192
Lystra, 170

M

Maccabees, 127
Maccabeus Judas, 128
Macedonia, 162, 170, 208
Machen, J. Gresham, 316
Machpelah, 207, 220
Magdala, 209
Magna Carta of Christian liberty, 164
Magnus, Simon, 216
Mahlon, 212, 218
Makemie, Francis, 316
Malachi, 120, 208
Malan, E., 53

Manna, 121
Manasseh, 85, 125, 200
Manes, 316
Mara, 212
Marah, 121
Marbeck, 48
Margolis, Max L., 54
Mariamme, 129
Mark, 132, 133, 137, 141, 142, 145
Martha, 142, 207, 208
Mar Thoma, 222
Martin of Tours, 316
Mary, 137, 138, 142, 194, 198, 202, 204, 205, 209, 210, 217, 220
Mary Magdalene, 209, 275
Massoretes, 25, 27, 30, 31, 38
Matthew, 132, 133, 135, 136, 138, 141, 142, 145, 210
Matthew's Bible, 48
Matthias, 210, 211
Mazarin Bible, 46
Measures, 293
Mee, Mrs. Sarah, 53
Meek, T. J., 55
Melanchthon, Philip, 317
Melchite Church, 40
Melchizedek, 211
Melville, Andrew, 317
Menahem, 85, 124
Mephibosheth, 30, 206
Meribah, 122
Merom, 74
Meshack, 108, 123, 213
Mesopotamia, 38
Mesrop, 42
Messiah, 224
Methodius, 42
Methuselah, 195, 211
Micah, 76, 109, 115, 193, 211
Micaiah, 123
Michmash, 205
Midian, 203, 211
Midianites, 190, 197
Midrash, 207
Mile, 294
Mina, 295
Mint, 271
Miracles in the Gospels, 150
Miriam, 187
Mite, 296
Moab, 71, 84, 207, 212, 228
Moabites, 234
Moffatt, James, 52, 54, 317

Moffatt's Translation, 54
Monarchy, 237, 238
Money, 295
Montgomery, Helen B., 54
Month, 292
Months of the year, 292
Moody, Dwight, 317
Mordecai, 91, 195, 258
Morgan, G. Campbell, 13, 15
Moses, 6, 17, 20, 63, 66, 67, 70, 71, 72,
    187, 192, 203, 206, 211, 212, 236–
    37, 257, 263
Mosque of Omar, 81
Mosquito, 284
Moth, 284
Mott, John R., 317
Mouse, 285
Mt. Aararat, 213
Mt. Carmel, 194, 232
Mt. Hermon, 230
Mt. Horeb, 194
Mt. Nebo, 228
Mt. of Olives, 227, 228
Mt. of Temptation, 228
Mt. Sinai, 6, 33, 34, 39, 67, 87, 206
Muhlenberg, Henry, 318
Mulberry, 272
Mule, 285
Muller, George, 318
Multitude of Manuscript Witnesses, 36
Muratorian Fragment, 181
Mustard, 272
Myrrh, 272
Myrtle, 272

N

Naaman, 84, 122, 195, 212
Naboth, 83
Nadab, 121, 124
Nag Hammadi, 41
Nahab, 82
Nahum, 116, 188, 212
Nain, 232
Naomi, 76, 77, 212, 218
Napoleon, 34
Nathan, 77, 80, 123, 210, 213
Nathanael, 191
Nazareth, 135, 232
Nazarite, 218
Nebat, 203

Nebo, 212
Nebuchadnezzar, 85, 89, 105, 107, 112,
    188, 193, 196, 202, 213, 225, 240,
    256, 257
Negeb, 228
Nehemiah, 113, 116, 205, 212
Nero, 197
New English Bible, 52
New Moon, 258
New Testament Era, 242
New Testament Revised Standard Ver-
    sion, 51
New Testament Rulers, 183
Newton, John, 318
New World, 57
New Year, 258
Nicodemos, 145, 213, 214
Nicholas of Hereford, 45
Night Watch, 292
Nile River, 26, 67
Ninevah, 113, 116, 205, 212
Noah, 65, 211, 214
Norlie, Olaf, 58
Norlie's Simplified New Testament, 58
Nubian Version, 42
Number of Chapters, verses and words,
    22
Numbers, 69

O

Oak, 272
Obadiah, 112, 214
Obed, 76, 218
Oboe, 255
Ogden, Charles K., 56
Old Syriac, 39
Old Testament and New Testament
    Together, 9
Olive, 272
Omri, 82, 124
One Central Message of Bible, 11
Onesimus, 173, 214, 216
Onkelos, 37
Organ, 255
Origen, 16, 138, 174, 318
Originals Greek and Hebrew, 28
Orlinsky, Harry M., 54
Orpha, 212, 218
Orphan Psalms, 95
Osprey, 289

Ostrich, 289
Othniel, 75
Otterbein, Philip W., 319
Outline of Acts, 156, 157
Outline of Romans, 159, 160
Outline of I Corinthians, 161, 162
Owl, 289
Oxyrhynchus, 41

P

Palestine, 227
Palestinian Syriac, 39
Palimpsest, 34
Palm, 273
Papias, 138, 319
Papyri, Uncials, Minuscules, Lectionaries, 35
Papyrus, 273
Papyrus and Parchment Manuscripts, 26
Parables, 148, 149
Paran, 200
Parker, Archbishop Matthew, 49
Partridge, 289
Pascal, Blaise, 319
Passover, 67, 206, 258
Pastorals, 170
Patmos, 181, 204
Patrick, 319
Paul, 21, 25, 27, 131, 132, 133, 138, 152, 155, 160, 162, 163, 164, 165, 166, 167, 170, 171, 172, 173, 174, 188, 190, 191, 192, 195, 197, 201, 205, 208, 214, 215, 222, 223
Peacock, 289
Pekah, 85, 124
Pekahiah, 124, 85
Pelican, 289
Peninnah, 198
Penn, Wm., 320
Pentecost, 137, 158, 189, 209, 258
Pentateuch, 36, 64, 66, 72, 96
People of Palestine, 233
Perga, 138
Pergamum, 27
Period of Conquest, 237
Period of Moses, 236
Persia, 92
Peshitta Syriac, 39

Peter, 131, 133, 138, 152, 155, 177, 178, 189, 192, 193, 205, 209, 215, 216, 219, 221
I Peter, 177
II Peter, 177
Pethor, 190
Pethuel, 110, 204
Pharisees, 128, 262, 263
Pharoah, 67, 211
Pharoah-necho, 202
Philadelphus, 127
Philemon, 173, 195, 214, 216
Philip, 129, 191, 221, 215, 216
Philippi, 207
Philippians, 166
Philistines, 122, 218, 234
Phillips, J. B., 58, 139, 172
Phillips' Translation, 58, 215
Philo, 16, 320, 260
Philoxenian Version, 39
Phinehas, 37
Pig, 285
Pine, 273
Pipe, 255
Pistachio, 273
Plane, 274
Planta of the Bible, 264
Polycarp, 320
Pomegranaate, 274
Pontius Pilate, 129, 191, 216, 217
Poplar, 274
Pound, 295
Priscilla, 190, 217
Procurator of Judea, 184
Procurator of Palestine, 184
Promised Land, 66, 71, 212, 228, 259
Prophecy, 99
Proverbs, 96
Psalms, 95
Psaltery, 256
Pseudepigrapha, 20
Purim, 91, 258
Purposes of the Gospels, 133
Purvey, John, 45

Q

Quadrans, 296
Quail, 290
Quelle, 133

Queen of Sheba, 82
Qumran, 31, 37, 260

R

Rabbula, 39
Rachel, 206, 207, 217
Rahab, 74
Raikes, Robt., 320
Ram, 285
Rat, 285
Raven, 290
Raw materials of Textual Critics, 50
Rebekah, 200, 201, 217, 218
Red Sea, 121
Reed, 274
Reformation, 19
Rehoboam, 82, 96, 203, 218, 222
Renan, 141
Repidim, 121
Reuben, 74, 207
Reul, 204
Revealed word and its authority, 13
Revelation, 181
Revelation of the Bible, 12
Revelation and Inspiration, 12
Revelation and Response, 12
Revised Standard Version, 51
Reynolds, John, 50
Rhoda, 274
Rieu; E. V., 57
Rieu's Gospels, 57
Riverside New Testament, 54
Roberts, B. T., 321
Roberts, E. H., 32
Robertson, A. T., 321
Robertson, J. A., 53
Robinson, John, 321
Rogers, John-, 48, 49
Roman Catholic Bible, 49
Romans, 157
Rome, 138, 157, 166, 205
Rose, 274
Rosh-Hashanah, 259
Rotherham's Emphasized Version, 52
Rotherham, Joseph Brant, 52
Rue, 274, 275
Ruler of Herod Line, 185
Rush, 275
Ruth, 76, 77, 212, 218
Rylands Fragment, 32

S

Sabbath, 259
Sabbath Day's Journey, 295
Sackbut, 256
Sadduces, 128, 262
Sahak, 42
Sahidic, 40, 41
Salome, 129, 199, 202, 204
Salonika, 168
Samaria, 84, 124, 232
Samaritan Pentateuch, 3
Sampson, 48
Samson, 76, 122, 218
Samuel, 75, 77, 78, 193, 198, 218, 219, 220, 237
I Samuel, 77
II Samuel, 79
Sandalwood, 275
Sanhedrin, 263
Sankey, Ira D., 321
Sapphira, 189, 219
Sarah, 187, 198, 200
Saul, 78, 79, 124, 205, 220, 238
Saul of Tarsus, 189, 193
Savonarola, G., 321
Scarlet, 275
Schlatter, Michael, 321
Schoeffer, Peter, 47
Schonfield, Hugh J., 57
Schools of Bible Interpretation, 16, 17
Scofield, C. I., 322
Scorpion, 285
Scotland, 48
Scribes, 262
Scripture, 5
Sea of Tiberias, 230
Seah, 295
Seasons, 292
Second Coming, 169, 278
Selah, 96
Selericids, 128
Seneca, 197
Sennacherib, 85, 123, 240
Septuagint, 18, 36, 38, 40, 66, 81, 127
Serpent, 286
Servetus, Michael, 322
Seth, 88, 214
Shadrach, 108, 123, 213
Shallum, 85, 124
Shamgar, 75
Shaphat, 194
Sheba, 80

Shechem(Nablus), 37
Sheep, 286
Shekel, 295, 296
Shem, 214
Shepard, Hermas, 34
Sherman, H. A., 54
Shorter Bible, 54
Shulamite, 99
Shunammite, 84, 122
Siewert, Frances E., 58
Silas, 220
Silvanus, 220
Silver Codex, 42
Simeon, 207, 220
Simon, 221
Simons, Menno, 322
Simpson, A. B., 322, 33
Sinai, 70
Sinai Desert, 66
Sinaitic Syriac, 39
Sisera, 193
Sistrum, 256
Slavic Version, 42
Smith, Gipsy, R., 323
Smith, John Merlin P., 55
Smyrna, 182
Sodom, 121, 188
Sogdian, 42
Solomon, 79, 32, 87, 92, 95, 96, 97, 99,
    124, 217, 199, 203, 213, 218, 221–22,
    238
Solomon's Temple, 247–49
Soncino Press, 46
Sources of Synoptics, 132
Span, 293
Span of writing of Testaments, 10
Sparrow, 290
Spener, Philip, 323
Speer, Robert E., 323
Spider, 286
Spikenard, 275
Spurgeon, C. H., 323
St. Peter's Cathedral, 159
Stater, 297
Stead, W. T., 53
Stephen, 214, 222
Stephens, Robert, 22
Stork, 290
Study Bibles, 329
Sunday, William A., 323
Sundial, 292

Swallow, 290
Sycamine, 275
Sycamore, 110, 276
Synagogue, 251–52
Synoptics, 132, 141, 145, 146
Syria, 84
Syriac Versions, 38
Syrian, 122

T

Tabernacle, 68, 247
Tabernacles, 259
Tabitha, 193
Tabor, 232
Tabret, 256
Talent, 295, 297
Talmai, 191
Tamarish, 276
Tambourine, 256
Tares, 276
Targums, 37
Tarshish, 205
Tarsus, 214
Tatran's Diatessaron, 38
Taverner's, 48
Taylor, K., 58
Tehillim, 95
Tekoa, 111, 189
Tekoa, Widow of, 123
Temple, 244, 247
Temple, Wm., 323
Terah, 187
Terebinth, 277
Tertius, 157
Tertullian, Q., 6, 324
Testament, 6
Theophilus, 141
Thessalonians, 168
Thistles, 277
Thomas, 222
Thomas à Kempis, 324
Thomas Aquinas, 324
Thorns, 277
Thumbnail sketches of Personalities in
    Church History, 299ff.
Thyatira, 208
Thyine, 277
Tiberias, 30

Timbrel, 254
Time, 291, 293
Timnathserah, 206
Timothy, 170, 222–23
I Timothy, 170
II Timothy, 171
Tischendorf, Constantine van, 33
Titus, 162, 172, 223, 257
Tobit, 188
Tola, 75
Tools for the Bible Student, 329
Torah, 27, 63, 72, 129
Torrey, C. C., 54
Troas, 127, 207
Trumpet, 256, 259
Twentieth Century New Testament, 53
Tychicus, 166
Tyndale, 38, 46, 48, 324

U

Ulfilas, 42
Unleavened bread, 259
Uppsala, University of, 42
Ur, 187
Uriah, 80
Uz, 204
Uzziah, 100, 109, 111, 123, 189, 223, 122, 124

V

Valley of Esdraelon, 232
Variations inconsequential, 30
Variety in Testaments, 10
Vatican Library, 37
Velasquez, Isaak, 42
Velvorde, 47
Venus, 161
Verkuyl, Dr. Garit, 56
Veronica, 21
Verse Division, 22
Via Dolorosa, 227
Vine (Grape), 277
Viper, 286
Vitellus, 217
Vulgate, 19, 45, 56
Vulture, 290

W

Wade, G. W., 55
Wade's Translation, 55
Waldo, Peter, 325
Walnut, 278
Wand, J. W. C., 56
Wand's N. T. Letters, 56
Waterman, Leroy, 55
Way, Arthur S., 53
Way Translation, 53
Weeks, 259, 293
Weights, 295
Weigle, Luther A., 52
Wesley, Charles, 325
Wesley, John, 325
Westminster Confession, 13
Weymouth Translation, 53
Weymouth, Richard F., 53
Wheat, 278
Whitefield, George, 325
Whittingham, 48
Wilderness, 69
Williams, Chas. B., 55
Williams, Chas. K., 57
Williams, George, 325
Williams, R., 326
Willow, 278
Witch of Endor, 79, 220
Wood carrying, 260
Wolf, 286
Woolnan, John, 326
Worm, 286
Worms, 47
Wormwood, 278
Wuest, K., 57
Wyclif, 45, 46, 326

X

Xerxes, 223
Ximenez de Cisneros Francisco, 326

Y

Year, 293
Yoke, 295
Young, R., 52
Young's Translation, 52

Z

Zaccheaeus, 223–24
Zacharias, 194, 204, 224
Zealots, 262
Zebedee, 202, 204
Zebulu, 207
Zechariah, 85, 95, 198, 224, 124
Zelah, 206
Zephaneah, 117, 119, 225

Zereda, 203
Zerubbabel, 89, 118, 119, 225, 241, 250
Zeus Olympius, 128
Zimri, 82, 124
Zinzendorf, Count, 326
Zipporah, 203, 211
Zither, 257
Zorphar, 93, 94
Zwingli, Ulrich, 327

INDEX TO
SCRIPTURE
REFERENCES

GENESIS

VERSE	page	VERSE	page	VERSE	page
1:1	17	12:6	277	27:9	283
2:17	188	12:6-7	236	28:12-15	201
3:7	269	12:8	236	29:6	217
3:18	277	12:16	279	30:37	274
3:20	196	13:3-11	236	35:4	272
4:1	196	13:18	236	37:25	266, 272
4:21	253, 255	14:18	211	37:28	206
5:18, 21	195	16:3	198	37:31	283
5:24	194, 195	18:6	294	40:10-11	277
5:27	211	18:7	279	41:1-7	278
6:5	195	19:36	207	41:43	282
6:18	6	19:27-28	207	43:11	265, 272,
8:7	290	21:25-34	236		273
8:11	273	21:33	274	47:17	282
11:29-31	188	24:30	279	49:5-7	220
12:1-2	188	25:33	201	49:9	284
12:1-3	64	25:34	271	49:21	282

EXODUS

2:1-10	266	13:13	280	25:5, 10	264
2:10-15	211	15:20	254	26:1	269
2:15	211	16:13	290	26:26	264
3:8	65	16:31	268	28:6	269
4:31		17:8-16	206	28:16	293
7:9	286	18:19-23	204	28:31, 33-34	274
7:12	187	20:1-17	212	28:33-35	253
8:1-15	281	20:8-11	259	29:9	187
8:16-19	284	20:17	280	29:40	294
8:21	281	21:33	280	30:10	257
9:31	266, 269	22:29	258	30:23	268
9:32	274	23:16	258, 259	30:23, 33	272
11:7	280	23:19	258	30:24	267
12:15-20	259	23:28	282	32:19	257
12:22	270	24:3-8	6	34:22	259
13:1-10	258	24-4	63	40:2, 17	258

LEVITICUS

1:10	281	14:4	271	23:34-36,	
5:15	285	14:10	294	39-44	259
11:4	229	14:54	275	23:40	268
11:6	281	20:26	68	25:2-5	259
11:13-19	289	23:13	259	25:8-55	258
11:16	288	23:5-14	258	25:9	285
11:17	287	23:10-21	258	25:11	258
11:19	278, 288, 290	23:24-25	259	25:25,	
		23:27-32	257	47-49	77
11:29, 30	284, 285			27:17-24	258

NUMBERS

1:2-3	69	13:23	274	28:11-14	258
7:3	279	14:6, 38	206	28:26-31	258
7:17, 23	281	14:19	69	29:1-6	259
9:2-14	258	14:24	192	29:7-11	257
10:1-10	257	14:29-31	257	29:12-40	259
10:10	258	15:4	294	31:8	190
11:5	270, 271	17:8	265	31:23	282
11:6-9	268	19:2-22	282	33:9	273
11:16-24	263	22:23-30	190	33:38-39	187
11:31-33	290	23:10	266		
13:6, 8	206	24:14	64		

DEUTERONOMY

1:44	279	14:13	288	25:4	279
4:12	29	14:15	288, 289	25:5-10	218
5:6-21	212	14:17	287	27:4	37
7:20	282	14:18	278, 288	28:38	284
8:8	274	16:3-8	259	29:18	270, 278
8:15	286	16:9-12	288	31:9, 24-26	63
10:12-13	71	16:13-15	259	31:10-13	259
12:15, 22	281	21:3	282	32:14	286
14:5	282	22:10	279	32:33	278
14:7	281	22:11	269	34:1	218
14:12-18	289, 290	24:20	273		

JOSHUA

1:2-3	73	6:4	285	18:3	74
1:7-8	63	6:4, 6, 8, 13	255	24:1-26	72
2:6	269	17:13	74	24:12	282

JUDGES

2:16-17	75	6:34	75	14:18	282
2:19	75	7:16-23	256	15:16	218
3:11	293	7:19	292	16:3	218
3:31	75	9:7	268	16:29-30	218
4:3	293	11:34	254	17:1, 4	114
4:5	193	14:5, 6	284	17:6	75
5:16	254	14:8, 9, 18	279		

RUTH

1:16	212	1:22	266	3:2, 15	266
1:16-17	76	2:17, 23	266	4:5-6, 17	76

I SAMUEL

1:20	218	13:14	205	24:14	280
5:6	285	13:18	283	25:18	277, 286, 294
6:7	279	16:16	255	26:20	280, 289
8:19-20	77	16:23	255	28:24	279
10:5	256	17:34	284	31:1-3	206
10:25	77	17:34, 36, 37	278	31:13	276
11:11	292	22:6	276		

II SAMUEL

5:5	79	12:1-10	213	18:9-10	277
5:23-23	272	14:26	297	22:34	282
6:5	253, 254	16:9	280	23:6	277
	256	17:28	271	23:11	271
7:12-16	82	18:9	285		
8:17	262				

I KINGS

1:9	279	9:11	267	16:4	280
2:1	82	9:26-28	239	17:1	194
2:3	63	10:2	279	17:5-6	194
2:11	79	10:11-12	265	17:10-16	194
4:22	294	10:17	296	18:5	285
5:6	267	10:22	239, 289	18:20-39	194
5:10	269	10:27	276	18:26	194
6:4	248	12:25	239	19:4	266
6:7	267	12:26-30	203	19:15-17	194
6:15-35	268	12:28	279	19:16	194
6:23-28	249	14:11	280	19:19	194, 279
7:21	248	14:19	81	21:19, 23	280
8:10	249	14:29	81		
8:25	81	15:18	194		

II KINGS

1:8	194	5:15	194	17:19-20	83
2:11	282	6:1-7	195	18:4	286
2:19-22	11	6:25	294	18:26	25
4:1-7	194	7:1, 16, 18	266	19:35	285
4:9	194	8:9	279	20:11	292
4:24-44	195	10:29	279	21:4	11
4:38-41	195	11:41	81	23:1-12	11
4:39	270	14:25	113	24:17-25:7	225
5:1-14	195	16:8	11	24:18	81
5:10	212	16:17	11		

I CHRONICLES

13:8	256	15:19	254	28:9-10	86
15:16-24	253	27:28	276	29:29	77

II CHRONICLES

2:8	264	5:12	256	34:14	63, 87
3:3	294	9:21	289	36:8	202
3:15-17	248	26:19-21	223	36:14	87
5:1	87	28:15	273	36:22	192

EZRA

1:3-7	192	3:10	254	7:12-26	10, 25
2:1	89	4:6	188	7:22	278
2:1-4	89	4:8-6:18	10, 25	8:22	296
2:66	285	5:1	118	9:1-3	196
2:69	296	6:14	118	10:17	196
		7:11	262		

NEHEMIAH

1:7-8	213	4:6	90	12:16	119
1:10	213	8:15	260	13:31	260
4:3	281	10:34	260		

ESTHER

1:1	188	4:14	91	9:26, 31	258
2:7	272	9:17-10:3	196		

JOB

1:21-22	92	15:22	194	30:27	290
2:11	194	19:25	204	30:29	289
4:1-5, 27	194	20:14	278	31:40	276
4:19	284	21:12	255	39:26	288
8:11	274	28:7	288	42:12	204
8:14	286	30:1	280		

PSALMS

1:1-2	95	14:1	15	33:2	257
1:4	96	16:6	294	39:11	284
8:12	256	32:9	285	42	282

PSALMS—*Continued*

44:19	*283*	74:8	*252*	104:17	*290*
45:8	*265*	74:14	*284*	104:26	*284*
51:7	*271*	78:	*281*	105	*281*
55:21	*273*	80:13	*279*	105:31	*284*
58:4	*278*	78:47	*276*	110:4	*211*
58:9	*277*	81:3	*258*	114:4, 6	*283*
59:14-15	*280*	81:16	*278*	118:12	*279*
63:6	*292*	84:3	*290*	137:1-5	*278*
68:25	*254*	91:13	*278*	144:9	*257*
69:21	*270*	98:6	*254*	150:4	*255*
71:22	*256*	102:6	*289*	150:5	*252, 254*

PROVERBS

1:1	*96*	7:17	*265, 268*	27:26	*286*
3:5-6	*96*	10:1	*96*	30:15	*293*
5:3	*273*	25:1	*96*	30:24	*273*
5:19	*281, 282*	25:11	*266*	30:28	*284, 286*
6:6-8	*273*	26:2	*290*	31:13	*269*

ECCLESIASTES

1:12	*97*	11:9	*97*	12:13-14	*97*
2:11, 13	*97*	12:5	*265, 267*		
10:1	*280*	12:12	*97*		

SONG OF SOLOMON

1:12	*275*	2:13, 15	*277*	6:11	*273*
1:14	*270*	4:13	*270*	7:8	*266*
2:1	*274*	4:14	*266, 268,*	7:12	*273*
2:3, 5	*266*		*275*	8:5	*266*
2:9, 17	*281*	5:13	*271*	8:6-7	*99*

JEREMIAH

1:5	*103*	8:22	*266*	13:23	*283*
8:7	*287, 290*	10:11	*27*	17:6	*271*
8:13	*277*	12:9	*283*	17:11	*289*

22:7	267	31:31-34	6	46:20	282
23:15	278	33:16	103	50:39	289
26:2	29	36:1-8	103		
27:17-19	114	36:18	27		

LAMENTATIONS

| 1:1 | 105 | 3:10 | 279 |
| 2:19 | 292 | 5:18 | 281 |

ISAIAH

1:3	280	17:6	273	38:21	268
2:13	272	18:2	274	40:12	293
2:20	278	24:13	273	41:19	226, 272
3:16-18	253	27:1	284	42:3	274
5:2-7	277	28:1	277	44:28	192
6:13	277	28:25	274	53:7	283
7:14	100, 200	28:27	268	55:13	268, 272
7:18	279, 280	30:6	279	56:10	280
7:21	286	30:24	280	59:5	286
11:6	283, 286	34:11	287, 289	59:11	279
11:7	278	35:1	274	60:13	268, 269
11:8	278	35:6	282	61:1-3	100
11:53	200	37:24	269	65:25	286
13:21	289	37:26	285	66:17	285
13:22	282	38:8	292		
14:23	287	38:14	287, 290		

EZEKIEL

1:1	106	17:22-24	267	31:8	274
1:10	284, 288	24:1	106	34:17	281
2:6	286	28:3	106	36:24-28	106
3:17	196	24:16-18	106	36:25-27	106
4:9	271, 274	27:6	266, 272	40:3	274
4:11	294	27:19	266, 267	25:12	297
13:4	281	28:24	277		
14:14, 20	106	29:17	106		

DANIEL

1:8	*193*	4:19, 33	*291*	7:6	*283*
1:21	*192*	5:5	*291*	7:13-14	*108*
2:4b-7:28	*10*	5:5-30	*191*	8:3-4, 20	*285*
3:5, 7, 10,		6:10-24	*193*	8:5	*281*
15	*254, 256*	6:28	*192*	9:1	*188*
3:6, 15	*291*	7:4	*284*		
3:28, 30	*213*	7:5	*278*		

HOSEA

2:6	*277*	5:12	*284*	10:11	*282*
3:1	*109, 277*	5:14	*284*	14:6	*273*
4:11	*277*	10:1	*277*	14:8	*268*
4:13	*274, 277*	10:8	*277*		

JOEL

1:12	*266*	2:19	*278*
2:1	*284*	2:28-29	*110*

AMOS

1:1	*111, 189*	5:14, 15	*111*	7:10-17	*189*
2:6-8	*111*	5:10	*279*	7:14	*111, 276*
2:9	*272*	5:21-24	*111*	7:15	*111, 189*
3:12	*284*	6:4	*286*	8:5	*258*
4:11-12	*111*	6:6	*111*	9:1-8	*111*
5:12	*111*	7:4	*189*		

OBADIAH

15	*112*

JONAH

1:1-2	*205*	2:10	*205*	4:6-10	*270*
1:12	*113*	3:5	*113*	4:11	*113*

MICAH

1:1	114	4:3	114	6:8	114, 211		
1:8	289	5:2	115, 211	7:18	115		

NAHUM

1:1	116	3:7	116

HABAKKUK

1:1	197	1:13	117	2:6-19	117
1:2-4	117	2:1	117	3:17-19	117
1:5-6	117	2:4	117, 158, 198	3:19	197
1:8	283				

ZEPHANIAH

1:1	117	2:14	287, 289	7:5	119
1:2, 3	119	3:8	119	9:9-10	119
1:4	117	4:6	119		

HAGGAI

1:1	118	2:2	118
1:14	118	2:21	118

ZECHARIAH

1:8	282	11:2	272	13:7	224
4:6	224	11:12-13	224	14:2	224
5:9	290	12:10	224	14:4	224
9:9-10	224	13:1	224	14:15	285
		13:6	224		

MALACHI

1:3, 4	120	2:1	120
1:6	120	3:9	120

MATTHEW

1:18-21	210	12:13	21	24:28	290
2:1	199	12:34	286	24:31	257
2:11	269, 272	12:40	205	25:31-46	281
3:4	279	12:40-41	114	26:6	275
3:16	288	13:24-30,	276	26:15	206
5:17	6	36-43		26:17	259
5:22	263	13:31-32	272	26:28	6
5:26	297	13:55	180	26:34, 74-	
6:19-20	285	14:1-12	265	75	287
6:27	294	14:19	280	26:47-50	206
6:28	265, 271	16:18	11, 135	26:57	263
7:6	285	17:20	272	26:59	263
7:10	280	17:24	296	26:61	191
7:15	286, 287	17:27	297	26:64	191
7:16	269, 277	18:17	135	26:73-75	215
8:11	77	20:2	296	27:2	217
8:20	281	21:42	5	27:3-5	206
8:30	285	22:7	134	27:32	221
9:9	210	22:15-22	262	27:34	270
10:2-4	201	22-19	296	27:46	25
10:3	134, 191,	23:7	262	27:51	251
	202, 222	23:23	266, 271,	27:56	202, 209
10:16	286, 287		286	27:61	209
10:29	296	23:37	287	28:18-20	136
10:29, 31	290	23:37-39	135		

MARK

1:1, 11	139	3:18	134, 191,	7:34	25
1:10	288		221, 222,	9:7	139
1:21	253		263	10:25	279
2:14	134, 202,	5:1-11	143, 285	10:45	139
	210	5:7	139	11:2	280
3:2	204	5:41	25	11:13	268
3:6	262	6:3	201	12:10	5
3:9	206	7:1-13	262	12:13-17	262
3:17	202, 204	7:11-16	143	12:18-27	262

12:28	262	14:12	259	15:25	291
12:42	296	14:33	204	15:34	25
13:1	250	14:51	137	15:39	139
13:3	189	14:55	263	16:1	209
13:10-17	143	14:61-62	139	16:9	209
13:35	287, 292	15:1	217	16:16	215
14:1	258, 259	15:8	251	17:11-19	143
14:1-6	143	15:21	221	22:49-51	143
14:3-6	275	15:23	270, 272		

LUKE

1:2	208	6:14	191	13:34	287
1:5	194, 199	6:15	134, 221	14:1-6	262
1:5-25	204	7:37	209	15:8-9	296
1:43	194	8:2	209	15:15	285
1:57-63	194	8:32	285	15:16	267
1:57-80	204	9:58	281	16:29	6
2:1	191	10:3	286	17:6	275
2:6, 7	210	10:19	286	17:28-32	208
2:24	287	10:25	262	19:1-4	276
2:33-35	220	10:30	142	19:8	224
2:41	258	10:35	296	19:10	141
3:18	32	11:1-46	207	20:39	262
3:22	288	11:12	286, 287	22:1, 7	259
3:25	189	11:42	271, 275	22:66	263
3:37	195	12:6, 7	290, 296	23:1	217
4:20	253	12:24	290	23:26	221
4:21	5	12:25	294	24:1, 2	293
5:10	204	12:27	265	24:27	64
5:17	262	12:33	285	24:32	5
5:27-28	210	13:32	281	24:44	6

JOHN

1:32	288	6:5-14	145	10:22	257
1:45	64, 191	6:8	189	11:1	208
1:48-49	191	6:19	294	11:9	291
2:1-11	210	6:19-21	145	11:16	222
2:20	250	7:2	259	11:20-27	208
3:5-8	214	7:5	180, 201	11:21, 32	209
3:16	145, 146	7:50-52	214	11:47	263
6:1-13	266	10:12	286	12:3	294

JOHN—*Continued*

12:13	273	18:31-33,		20:11-18	209
12:20-22	189	37-38	32	20:28	222
13:23	144	19:14	258	21:2	191
14:22	222	19:25-27	210	21:7, 24	144
14:26	16	19:26	144	21:8	294
15:1-8	278	19:29	214, 270,	21:9	280
15:8	32		294	21:19	144
18:28-29	217	19:39-40	272	21:25	28

ACTS

1:8	154	10:30	291	19:29	197
1:12	295	10:44	192	20:3	157
1:13	190, 191,	11:28	191	20:6	259
	202, 221	12:1-17	215	20:16	258
1:14	188, 210	12:2	202	20:29	286
1:15	134	12:3	259	21:8	201
1:15-20	206	12:12	137, 215,	21:28	264
1:15-26	210		209	21:31	192
1:19	25	12:13	209, 274	21:38	263
2:10	158	12:23	287	22:3	194, 214
2:16	110	13:5	253	22:5-16	215
3:2	134	13:13	138, 205	22:19	253
4:6	178	15:22-40	220	22:24	192
4:7	178	15:36-39	138, 190	22:30	263
4:15	263	15:37-39	205	23:1	263
4:32-37	260	16:1	170, 222	23:2	263
4:36	191	16:3	223	23:6	262
5:1-11	189	16:10	208	23:6, 8	262
5:7-10	219	16:13	252	23:24	197
5:21	263	16:15	166, 208	23:26-30	192
5:34	197	16:22	157	24:20	263
6:12	263	16:23	157	24:27	197
7:58-8:1	214	16:25	166	25:31	188
8:9-24	221	17:1-10	168	26:5	262
8:23	270	17:7	191	26:12-18	215
9:1-19	215	18:2	191	27:28	294
9:2	263	18:2-3	190	28:3-6	286
9:10-19	189	18:2, 18,		28:23	64
9:25	155	26	217	28:30	166
9:36	281	18:12-16	197		
9:36-43	193	18:24	5, 190		

ROMANS

3:21	*10	8:15	*25*	16:3-4	*190*
6:23	*197*	16:3	*217*	16:5	*190*

I CORINTHIANS

1:10	*190*	9:5	*201*	15:7	*201*
1:14	*197*	11:25	*6, 278*	15:52	*257*
4:17	*223*	13	*215, 254*	16:8	*258*
5:9	*163*	13:1	*160*	16:19	*190, 217*
5:22	*188*	14:33	*160*		

II CORINTHIANS

1:19	*220*	4:5	*163*	11:3	*196*
2:13	*162*	5:20-21	*163*	11:33	*155*
3:6	*6*	6:14	*163*		
3:14	*6*	7:1	*163*		

GALATIANS

1:2	*163*	2:3	*223*	5:1	*201*
1:17	*215*	2:9	*201*		
2:1	*223*	4:6	*25*		

EPHESIANS

1:1	*164*	2:18-20	*165*	4:4-6	*165*
1:3	*165*	3:1	*164*	4:16	*165*
1:5, 12, 13	*165*	3:14, 16,		5:23-32	*165*
1:13, 14	*165*	17, 19	*165*	6:20	*164*
1:15-23	*165*	4:1	*164*		
1:23	*165*	4:1-16	*165*		

PHILIPPIANS

1:7, 13,		2:25	*195*	4:4	*166*
14, 16	*166*	2:25-29	*166*	4:18	*166*
2:2	*166*	3:5	*262*		
2:5-11	*166*	4:1-14	*166*		

COLOSSIANS

1:7	167, 195	2:16, 20,		4:12	167
1:9-20	168	23	167	4:12-13	195
1:18-20	167	3:1-17	168	4:14	141, 208
2:6-7	168	4:7-8	167		
2:9-15	168	4:10	137, 138,		
2:10	167		190, 205,		
2:16	258		209		
2:16-18	167	4:10-17	173		

I THESSALONIANS

| 1:1 | 220 | 2:3-6 | 168 | 4:13-18 | 168 |
| 1:9-10 | 168 | 4:6 | 257 | | |

II THESSALONIANS

1:1	220	2:1-12	169	2:15	169
1:3-4	169	2:2	169	3:6-15	169
1:5-10	169	2:3-8	169		

I TIMOTHY

| 1:3 | 223 | 3:15 | 170 |
| 2:13 | 196 | 4:12 | 170 |

II TIMOTHY

1:5	170, 222	4:1-5	171	4:11	138, 141,
3:14-17	171	4:6	171		208
3:15, 16	5, 10	4:10	223	4:19	217

TITUS

| 1:5 | 223 | 2:11-15 | 173 |
| 2:11-14 | 172 | 3:10 | 190 |

PHILEMON

2	173	24	141, 173,
17-19	173		205, 208
23	195		

HEBREWS

1:1-2	9	11:5	195	11:37	100
4:14	175	11:8-13	188	13:8	175
8:13	6	11:31	74	13:23	223

JAMES

1:1	176	2:1	176	2:20	176
1:18, 21	176	2:7	176	3:3	282
1:27	176	2:8	5	5:2	285

I PETER

1:1	177	5:8	284	5:13	138
4:12-13	177	5:12	220		

II PETER

1:2-7	178	2:1-8	178	2:9	178
2:1	178	2:7	208	3:16	5

I JOHN

5:11-12	179

II JOHN

1	179	9-10	159
7	179	12	27

III JOHN

11	180	13	27

JUDE

1	207	4-16	180
3	180	7	180

REVELATION

1:1	181	8:10-11	278	18:12	277
1:4, 9	181	8:13	257	19:11-16	282
1:5, 6	181	9:3, 5, 10	286	19:11-21	182
1:11	182	9:7	282	21:17	294
4:7	284, 288	9:16-19	282	22:8	181
5:5	284	13:2	278, 283	22:21	16
6:2-8	282	14:20	294		
8:2	257	16:13	281